The Early Prose Writings of
WILLIAM DEAN HOWELLS

William Dean Howells in Columbus, 1861

The Early Prose Writings
of
WILLIAM DEAN HOWELLS
1853–1861

·

Edited by

THOMAS WORTHAM

OHIO UNIVERSITY PRESS

Athens

Copyright © 1990 by Ohio University Press
Printed in the United States of America
All rights reserved
Ohio University Press books are printed on acid-free paper ∞

Library of Congress Cataloging-in-Publication Data
Howells, William Dean, 1837–1920.
The early prose writings of William Dean Howells,
1853–1861 / edited by Thomas Wortham.
   p. cm.
   ISBN 0–8214–0960–3
   I. Wortham, Thomas, 1943– . II. Title.
PS2028.E27   1990
818'.409—dc20   89-26536
                                          CIP

Contents

Acknowledgments

To WILLIAM WHITE HOWELLS and the heirs of William Dean Howells for granting me permission to print previously unpublished writings by their ancestor (this material may not be reprinted without first obtaining their permission through the Howells Committee, in care of the Houghton Library, Harvard University, Cambridge, Massachusetts);

To the librarians and staffs of the Houghton and Widener Libraries of Harvard University; the Ohio State Historical Society, Columbus; the Western Reserve Historical Society, Cleveland; the Walter Havighurst Special Collections, Miami University Libraries, Oxford, Ohio; Alfred University Library, Alfred, New York; the Kansas State Historical Society, Topeka; the Minnesota Historical Society, St. Paul; the Henry E. Huntington Library, San Marino, California; the Bancroft Library of the University of California, Berkeley; and the Research Library of the University of California, Los Angeles, for facilitating my work in their collections;

To Gary J. Arnold, Ohio State Historical Society; Mary E. Cowles, Oberlin College Library, Oberlin, Ohio; Norma Higgins, Alfred University Library; the Reverend Alphonse Hoernig, St. Vincent's College, Cape Girardeau, Missouri; Joseph Krise and Ursula Roth, Heinrich-Heine-Institut, Düsseldorf, West Germany; Margaret Lowe, the Public Library of Coshocton, Ohio; Helen Lundwall, the Public Library of Silver City, New Mexico; Susan Masirovits, Henderson Memorial Public Library, Jefferson, Ohio; Hildegard Schnuttgen, Youngstown State University Library, Youngstown, Ohio; Anthony W. Shipps, Indiana University Library, Bloomington; and Paula Ware, the Public Library of Oskaloosa, Kansas, for taking time from their busy schedules to help me solve particular problems;

To William D. Baker, Wright State University, Dayton, Ohio; David C. Frazier, Miami University, Oxford, Ohio; Howard Kerr, University of Illinois, Chicago; Lawrence J. McCaffrey, Loyola University,

Chicago; and R. Lawrence Moore, Cornell University, for sharing with me their expertise;

To my colleagues and the staff in the department of English, University of California, Los Angeles, in particular, my friend and fellow editor of *Nineteenth-Century Literature*, G. B. Tennyson, for giving meaning to the idea of academic community;

To the American Council of Learned Societies, the National Endowment for the Humanities, the American Philosophical Society, and the Research Committee of the University of California, Los Angeles, for their generous support of my work;

To my fellow Howellsians, George Arms, John W. Crowley, and David J. Nordloh, for their encouragement and criticism;

To Julie Dock for her interest in this work in its early stages;

To George Chavez for his valuable assistance and support;

And to Edwin and Norma Cady for their teaching, example, and friendship, the editor extends his thanks.

Whittier, California, 1 October 1988

A Buckeye View

WHEN WILLIAM DEAN HOWELLS came to write his life, he found that he could not remember how the notion of authorship first entered his mind. His earliest ventures in literature—verses, plays in rhyme, prose meditations—had been merely the imitative acts of a child exploring the ways in which the world of words worked, essentially private exercises not meant to be shared with others. The first of these compositions, so he remembered, was an "essay on the vain and disappointing nature of human life" which, in his sixth or seventh year, he had set up and printed off in the office of the Hamilton *Intelligencer*, the Whig newspaper his father edited during the formative years of his boy's youth. Afterwards, Howells was fond of saying that this print shop was his familiar schoolroom, the place of his first literary victories and defeats, and to the end of his days, the smell of the ink, the dusty type, and the dampened paper brought back the bittersweet memories of youth, "that tender swelling of the heart which so fondly responds to any memory-bearing perfume" (*A Boy's Town*, p. 239).

Though he spoke of them more guardedly, there were other memories too, harsher, even—in some of the events they registered—life denying. The drudgery and sheer physical labor that was frequently the country printer's lot in the Middle West during the decades before the Civil War defeated most, and it is a wonder that the family of William Cooper Howells fared as well as it did, eventually finding a reasonably safe haven in Jefferson, the seat of Ashtabula County in the Western Reserve of Ohio. Shortly before the family's arrival there, however, during those dreadful months they labored so unsuccessfully in Dayton, there appeared a curious item on the first page of the 15 June 1850 number of the Dayton *Transcript*, the paper William Cooper Howells edited after his fall from political grace in Hamilton, Ohio:

FAIR TYPESETTING

William D. Howells, son of the editor, thirteen years old, who has set type occasionally in the last two years, began setting type yesterday on bourgeois, at six o'clock in the morning, and by six in the evening he had set up nine thousand and five hundred ems, or four columns of this day's paper. He carried his route of papers in the morning before he began.

Was this simply the manifestation of a father's pride in a son's work well done? Or was it, in part, even unconsciously, a public confession of the extremes parents must at times resort to in order to insure their loved ones' survival? William Cooper Howells was a kind man, and, after his fashion, a good parent; still, his son carried to his death a resentment toward his sire's unworldly lack of concern for the physical comforts and necessities of his wife and children. But this was the judgment of age, and it is doubtful that the thirteen-year-old boy himself was able to measure the harsh conditions of his situation. Fortunately for youth, events largely appear to occur in the very nature of things; and fortunately for Howells, the hardships of the Dayton episode of his life were fairly short-lived.

Following the family's removal to Jefferson in 1853, Howells's literary life began in earnest. After the measure of work was done in the *Sentinel* office which the father and son had agreed upon to be fair to the both of them, the boy would retreat to his studyhole under the stairs of the family home and there pass the hours with his books and manuscripts. In comparison to life in the southern regions of the state, the literary atmosphere of the Western Reserve, that outpost of New England radicalism and westering spirit, was tonic to the boy, and he found himself at home among this new breed of Buckeyes:

> Old and young they read and talked about books, and better books than people read and talk about now, as it seems to me . . . ; the English serials pirated into our magazines were followed and discussed, and any American author who made an effect in the East became promptly known in that small village of the Western Reserve. . . . Literature was so commonly accepted as a real interest, that I do not think I was accounted altogether queer in my devotion to it. (*YMY*, p. 92)

But he was a queer child, as young genius always is. Howells's dedication to his craft was extraordinary. For seventy years he practiced his art, the result being an array of books so vast that he was humorously tempted to claim they could not have been written by one man, but a committee named W. D. Howells. Over thirty novels, a dozen books of travel, critical studies, collections of poems, biographies and autobiographies, altogether some two hundred books wholly or in part by him, as well as fourteen hundred periodical articles, many of them never gathered between hard covers: Howells's literary life is not wanting in sufficient documentation, though his critics have frequently been wanting in adequate preparation to discuss that life. Still, his apprentice work, that long foreground which has in his instance been too largely represented by a handful of mediocre poems, has been lost in old files of newspapers, obscure journals, and manuscripts. This volume has been compiled in order to redress that situation. Collected here are many of those original writings in prose which can be ascribed to Howells with a high degree of certainty and which were published or completed before he sailed for Venice in 1861. Excluded are his poems (except in a few instances when they provide a useful gloss on his work in prose) and his early translations (none of which have been ascribed to him with certainty). Also it has not seemed necessary to reprint the newspaper letters Howells sent back to Ohio during his eastern pilgrimage in the summer of 1860 as these have been superbly edited by Robert Price ("The Road to Boston: 1860 Travel Correspondence of William Dean Howells" in *Ohio History*, vol. 80, Spring 1971). The absence of those reports that Howells wrote for the *Ashtabula Sentinel*, the Cincinnati *Gazette*, and the Cleveland *Herald* during the 1857 and 1858 sessions of the Ohio legislature is regrettable. These letters are important literary documents in the study of Howells's growth as an author, but their political and topical character requires an editorial handling uncongenial to the other pieces in this collection (in addition to adding greatly to the volume's size), and the editor has decided that they are better published separately.

The arrangement of the volume is primarily chronological, beginning with Howells's first prose compositions to appear in print and ending with his reports concerning Ohio's mobilization following the outbreak of sectional hostilities in April 1861. Within this general chronological scheme, however, there is arrangement on generic lines. Because there is some overlapping of dates between the various chapters or gatherings of texts, it may prove useful to give here an overview of the volume's contents.

The first chapter is made up of Howells's earliest prose writings, those apprentice pieces that were published before his eighteenth birthday: these include his original prose pieces that appeared in the *Ashtabula Sentinel*, the Kingsville Academy *Casket*, and the *Ohio Farmer* (most of them previously unidentified), as well as the complete text of "The Independent Candidate," his first attempt in print at an extended work of fiction. Chapter 2, "Pictures of River Travel," reprints the important letters he sent home for publication in the *Sentinel* in the early summer of 1858 during a voyage he made with one of his riverboat uncles on the Ohio and Mississippi rivers. The third chapter offers a fairly full sampling of

Howells's work as a practical journalist on the staff of the *Ohio State Journal* from 1858 to 1861; included are selections from his column "News and Humors of the Mail," especially those items which best reveal his own manner and interests; selections from another column he conducted, "Literary Gossip"; and the complete texts of most of the editorial and occasional pieces in the *Ohio State Journal* which through Howells's letters and other documents can be identified as his.

Much of Howells's writing for the *Ohio State Journal* was in the nature of literary essays and reviews, and these pieces are collected in the fourth chapter, "Western Poetics and Literary Prejudices," providing us with a remarkably complete view of young Howells's position on the important literary issues during this crucial period in our literary history which saw the decline of Romanticism and the emergence of that Realistic sensibility with which Howells would later be so closely identified. Chapter 5, "Town and Country Sketches," gathers those compositions which were of a decidedly more literary bent than Howells's usual journalistic work; intended for entertainment, such pieces as these were a literary staple of both newspapers and magazines during the 1850s. The sixth chapter, "The Matter of Dulldale," brings together the sketches and stories of village characters and Midwestern life in which one finds Howells returning, tentatively and not altogether successfully, to the publication of fiction, five long years (for one so young) after his embarrassing failure with "The Independent Candidate." Included in this chapter is the text of Howells's novella, "Geoffrey: A Study of American Life" (also called by some of his biographers "Geoffrey Winter"), which he completed in 1861 but failed ever to publish. The final chapter, "War Movements in Ohio," reprints Howells's letters to the New York *World* in which he recorded his impressions and experiences relating to Ohio's early responses to the declaration of Civil War.

These early writings of Howells vary greatly in purpose and success, but together they are a testimony to an enormously productive youth. Viewed in terms of the context provided by these many pages, the emergence of Howells as a finished writer of prose with the publication of *Venetian Life* in 1866 is not so remarkable as it might otherwise seem. By then he had published probably well in excess of a half-million words— essays, stories, travel letters, legislative reports (which more often than not read like political satire), translations, and the more familiar poems. And though only rarely did Howells's audience extend beyond the neighborhood in which he was then living, the young writer enjoyed all the benefits and pitfalls of being a published author, accountable to his readers to persuade and amuse. It was an extraordinary education for a boy with a decided literary bent, an education of which the man proved himself greatly the beneficiary.

CHAPTER ONE

The Poor Boy's College

[Anecdote credits Abe Lincoln with having called the print shop the "poor-boy's college." The truth of that observation, whether Lincoln's or not, is profound, particularly in the middle-western region of the United States during the years before the Civil War. The newspaper office served not only as the village's political and intellectual center, effectively usurping the authority tradition had bestowed upon the pulpit in matters relating to citizens' understanding of their world; but it also cultivated the tastes and satisfied the grosser appetites of a people who were extending the meanings and consequences of modern civilization as fast as railroad lines and telegraph wires would let them. It was a schoolroom that did not ameliorate experience; its rules were those of the marketplace and fickle human nature.

The record suggests that William Dean Howells was less vain even than most decent men; still, in later years he showed much of the autodidact's defensive pride in the peculiar course of his education. As a printer's boy, he met the world of affairs and ideas at a compositor's bench, and he was fond of recounting that while he could remember when he had first learned to read letters, he could not recall the time he had started setting type. Altogether little more than two years of his youth appear to have been spent in conventional schoolrooms, and those haphazardly and with little lasting impression. His learning place was instead the printing office, and there, like countless American boys before him, he came to terms with life's realities. It was a costly education, no doubt, especially in its frequent demands that a boy find his way through the mysteries of things alone, unguided and uncertain of his achievement, and in maturity Howells came to regret all he had not known to learn and the lack of that discipline which he was convinced systematic education alone can instill in a boy's carefree nature. But the benefits could be just as real, particularly if judged against the limits of provincial instruction in the 1840s and the 1850s. And if the boy had a caring and knowledgeable companion such as William Cooper Howells, the end

5

would likely prove a magnificent measure of the means. Nor did Howells's private success in the matter of education go unnoticed by his peers;
in time he was offered professorships at several distinguished American
universities and decreed an honorary doctor of letters both at home and
abroad. In the calmness of retrospect he considered these tributes proper
and just.

William Cooper Howells was wise enough to value his second son's
insisting, intellectual self-reliance, not only because of its worth as a com-
modity in the family's newspaper office, but also because it sometimes
allowed the two to meet on grounds generally forbidden the generations.
During their frequent walks in the sheltering woods that were never far
distant and in the sanctity of the family circle, they talked out ideas,
whether of literature and poetry, of politics, or of human spiritual needs
and hopes. They were of "a reading race," the son liked to say, and the
family was never so poor but a few cents could be spared on the rare
occasion a book peddler passed their way. In the bookcase at home were
kept the father's favorite poets alongside his Swedenborgian tracts and
scriptures, and soon the boy was acquiring a library of his own cherished
authors. William Cooper Howells taught his children by encouragement
and example, and young Will was a ready pupil. By and by, his literary
skills were put to good use on the *Ashtabula Sentinel*, and in a short time
his intellectual promise was a matter of local interest. Once it was proposed by some neighbors that he be fitted up at their expense for Harvard,
but without the encouragement of the proudly shy boy nothing ever came
of it. At another time Howells suggested to his father and elder brother
that he be spared from the printing office in order to attend the Grand
River Institute in neighboring Austinburg, but it was decided that neither
the money for fees nor Will's absence from the *Sentinel* could be afforded.
Characteristically, he did not much lament his hardship but made the
best he could of limits and necessities.

In the time since their disappearance from the American scene, there
has been a tendency on the part of local antiquarians to exaggerate the
quality and substance of country newspapers that flourished during the
middle years of the last century. Partly this is owing to the lack of any
meaningful object of comparison in our own times, and partly to that
ignorance which is generally the occasion of modern nostalgia. Howells
himself contributed to this myth of "The Country Printer" in an 1893
essay written for a series on "Men's Occupations" in *Scribner's Magazine*,
an idealized portrait held up in measure against those plutocratic trends
in sensational journalism that he had come so to abhor. But, by and large,
the *Ashtabula Sentinel* did live up to the recollections of the older man,
and in the annals of Ohio journalism the Howells's newspaper held a

distinguished place for nearly a half-century. It was a victory of hard work, literary taste, and the historical justification of the politics its editor espoused. The weekly issues made for good and interesting reading which time has done surprisingly little to diminish. In editorial makeup it followed the prevailing models, and even in the nature of that "news" it thought worthy of print, it did not differ much from other country journals. The only difference is that generally it did these things better. The description Howells gave in his essay on "The Country Printer" is fairly typical of those issues of the family newspaper published during his years in the *Sentinel* office:

On the first page was a poem, which I suppose I must have selected, and then a story, filling all the rest of the page, which my brother more probably chose; for he had a decided fancy in fiction, and had a scrap-book of inexhaustible riches, which he could draw upon indefinitely for old personal or family favorites. The next page was filled with selections of various kinds, and with original matter interesting to farmers. Then came a page of advertisements, and then the editorial page, where my father had given his opinions of the political questions which interested him, and which he thought it the duty of the country press to discuss, with sometimes essays in the field of religion and morals. There was a letter of two columns from Washington, contributed every week by the congressman who represented our district; and there was a letter from New York, written by a young lady of the county who was studying art under a master of portraiture then flourishing in the metropolis—if that is not stating it too largely for the renown of Thomas Hicks, as we see it in a vanishing perspective. The rest of this page, as well as the greater part of the next, was filled with general news clipped from the daily papers and partly condensed from them. There was also such local intelligence as offered itself, and communications on the affairs of village and county; but the editor did not welcome tidings of new barns and abnormal vegetation, or flatter hens to lay eggs of unusual size or with unusual frequency by undue public notice. All that order of minute neighborhood gossip which now makes the country paper a sort of open letter was then unknown. He published marriages and deaths, and such obituary notices as the sorrowing fondness of friends prompted them to send him; and he introduced the custom of publishing births, after the English fashion, which the people took to kindly.

The move in 1853 from Ashtabula to Jefferson, the county seat, was propitious, and in time both the newspaper and the family's outlook flourished. Not that their enterprise ever brought any of them great fortune, but the social acceptance and political sympathy the family found in the

Western Reserve were of enormous satisfaction after the years of rejection and apparent failure in the communities where they had earlier struggled. In time, the printing office moved from the sash-and-blind factory where it had first been established to a comfortable wooden business block newly constructed nearer the village's center. The editor and his crew welcomed interruption, and the neighboring farmers and townspeople felt free to come and go as their opinions dictated, making the office the center of civic and social interest. Howells found his memory of the gaiety manifest on publication days something incredulous in retrospect, and the scene he recounts does present the village life in happier light than was his usual custom.

> The place was as bare and rude as a printing-office seems always to be: the walls were splotched with ink and the floor littered with refuse newspapers; but lured by the novelty of the affair, and per-haps attracted by a natural curiosity to see what manner of strange men the printers were, the school-girls and young ladies of the village flocked in and made it like a scene of comic opera, with their pretty dresses and faces, their eager chatter and lively energy in folding the papers and addressing them to the subscribers, while our fellow-citizens of the place, like the bassos and barytones and tenors of the chorus, stood about and looked on with faintly sarcastic faces. It would not do to think now of what sorrow life and death have since wrought for all those happy young creatures, but I may recall without too much pathos the sensation when some citizen volunteer relaxed from his gravity far enough to relieve the regular mercenary at the crank of our huge power-press wheel, amid the applause of the whole company. ("The Country Printer," p. 10)

It was not only common but frequently a financial necessity for estab-lishments like the *Ashtabula Sentinel* to do job work in addition to the publication of their weekly newspapers. Ballots for elections, advertising bills, circulars, and professional letterheads—all the printing needs of the community were provided for by a village printing office. Sometimes an enterprising bookseller would venture a reprint of a book then in fashion and unprotected by copyright, and desperate authors, then as now, were willing if able to subvert the publication of their own effusions, almost always in verse. Not much work of this larger sort appears to have come the *Sentinel's* way during these early years, though it did print a few issues of a literary magazine titled, not very originally, the *Casket*, and published by the academy in nearby Kingsville.

Founded in 1834, the school enjoyed a high degree of prosperity during the 1850s, its enrollment always in excess of one hundred and fifty stu-dents. The attractive monthly enhanced its prestige as well as that of its community, though its influence and interests were purely local. The editor apparently was not limited for his copy to the academy's enrollment, and in August 1853 he found room for a sketch of "Don Pedro II, Emperor of Brazil," translated from the Spanish by a self-taught student of that language "only about sixteen years old." The piece is signed by the initial "W.," and while there is no reference in Howells's writings or extant letters to his contributions to the *Casket*, Edwin Cady is unquestionably correct in identifying this and several other similarly signed pieces as Howells's. "Beauties of Mythology," an "original composition," appeared in the *Casket* for September, and later in the year a Christmas poem was "written expressly" for the monthly. Soon afterward, the magazine ceased publication, neither Howells nor the literary fortunes of the Western Reserve much the worse off for its demise.

Howells's essay on mythology reflects his earliest literary passion, the stories and fables of the ancient world which he had picked up in popular editions in his father's library of Pope's translations of Homer, particularly the *Odyssey*, Dryden's Virgil, Goldsmith's histories of Greece and Rome, the allegories and tales of the *Gesta Romanorum*, as well as a small volume of Greek and Roman mythology of whose title and author Howells left no record. Goldsmith's histories, which Howells valued above all his "classical" reading, inspired him to compose "a rhymed tragedy . . . in octosyllabic verse" (*MLP*, p. 12), a drama about the Romans which he intended for his schoolmates to act. Nothing apparently came of the venture, and even the manuscript was lost in the shuffle of years. But a mock-heroic account of the battle between two alley cats has survived, and one must suppose it was only the boy's reticence that kept his father from seeing the verses into print, for the elder Howells was greatly proud of his son's masterful burlesque. Will Howells had found Thomas Parnell's translation of the timeless "Battle of the Frogs and Mice" printed in the back of James Crissey's Philadelphia edition of Pope's *Odyssey of Homer*, and, in his own words, "it took me so much that I paid it the tribute of a bald imitation in a mock-heroic epic of a cat fight, studied from the cat fights in our back yard, with the wonted invocation to the Muse, and the machinery of partisan gods and goddesses. It was in some hundreds of verses, which I did my best to balance as Pope did, with a cæsura falling in the middle of the line, and a neat antithesis at the end" (*MLP*, p. 39). Far more reverential and even more indebted to his reading of Pope and Goldsmith for its inspiration and familiar epithets is "Beauties of Mythology" that had appeared in the Kingsville *Casket*. The essay is heavy in learning, serious in purpose, and true to the needs and desires of its first audience. Its limitations are not entirely Howells's fault; they are in some part a reflection of serious culture in the 1850s, or, for that matter,

9

serious and pompous culture throughout human history. It was such an attitude, after all, that led to the happy invention of burlesque sometime back in the first light of the civilized beginnings of mankind. Either one of these two exercises would, of course, by itself augur well for the education of any boy, though one is apt, like William Cooper Howells, to prefer the mock epic; together they reveal an imagination deeply engaged in the meaning and value of literary culture. There is no doubt that young Howells was managing his education quite well.]

THE BATTLE OF THE CATS

Again oh Muse, attune my listless lyre
Celestial fervor let my song inspire
Of warlike enemies once more I write,
Who seek for vengeance in the chance of fight.
Let Pallas,* dreadful, with her hissing shield,
And godlike wisdom guide th' ensanguin'd field;
And let Stern Fates† with irrevocable decree,
Point who shall victor and who vanquish'd be;
Then let dread Mars‡ close wheeling in the war,
All his red vengeance on the victor pour.
To the fair Nine§ all things of rhyme belong
And thus the Muse records the warlike song.—
Long ere the mice in battle's fierce career
Twirl'd the long lance and winged the shining spear,
And long ere crabs with fearful slaughter drove
These mice, on whom dire fell the wrath of Jove—
At night (o'erheated by the recent day)
Stretched on a lawn, a weary tom-cat lay.
As calm he slept, a cat of haggard mein,
Advancing near, outstretched him on the green.
Fatigued and worn the cat too heavy fell
The plain resounds and loud the echoes swell.
The dire concussion harsh the sleeper shakes—
He turns around and stretches, yawns and wakes.
He sees the other—anger filled his breast
Glistens his eye and heaves his massy chest
He loud demanded (as upright he sate)
In tones sonorous with his rising hate,
"Discourteous cat why dost thou intrude
To fright my sleep and break my solitude?

*A name for Minerva, the goddess of wisdom, daughter of Jupiter
†Three goddesses, who controlled the fortunes, fates, etc.
‡God of War.
§There were nine muses, goddesses of poetry, music, etc.

If you would not arouse my virtuous ire,
Hence from my lawn oh foolish cat retire."
He ceased and then reclined upon his side,
While calm and cool the other thus replied—
"Worn by the heat I sought this cool retreat,
Nor even tho't another cat to meet
But I'll not leave it till the dawn of day,
Or you stand victor o'er my lifeless clay!"
He paused—looked on the other with unflinching gaze,
Who thus replied with eyes that fiery blazed,
"Oh moth that flutters in the tapers flame,
Dost know oh cat Grimalkin is my name.
Before bright luna's cooling beams grow dim
In deadly fight I'd rend thee limb from limb
Retire retire before it is too late
Rouse not the sleeping embers of my hate."
"I've given my word (twas thus the other said
While o'er the green with furious pace he leaped)
When fair Aurora, goddess of the dawn
Opens the east then I will leave your lawn.
Peaceful I came, but now I thirst for fight,
Here is the place, and the time is to-night
And if you shrink not from the coming fray
Let heaven nor earth no longer us delay.
You gave your name, for it my thanks receive
But know thy enemy has none to give

Thus saying, each as if by mutual thought
Their mutual places for the combat sought
Grimalkin cautious chose a rising ground,
Whence on his foe, resistless he could bound,
But Nameless, scornful, gazed upon his foe
And chose the plain that outstretched just below.

As low the thunder from Olympus rolls
And louder grows as thro' th' expanse it bowls,
So roll the thunders from these deadly foes
As claw to claw, and tooth to tooth they close.
Each was an army.—In his own broad breast,
Each felt the fate of future cat-fights rest.
And now the hating two—the embattled twain
Roll down the hill and tumble on the plain
Now leaping, springing, bounding high in air
As each descend, so each a clawful tear,
Of gory fur and full a span of skin.

11

Yet louder, louder grows the battle din.
Grimalkin saw his foe's defenceless part
As lightning swift his sharpened talons dart,
Where spinal joints in lengthened numbers trail
And form the limb that mortals call a tail
He braced himself and tugged with vigorous strain
And wrenched and pulled and tugged and pulled again.
The skin gives way the fickle sinews crack
And Nameless tail is severed from his back.

Nameless sat upright and gazed upon his tail
The tears well up but rage o'er tears prevails
From out his nostrils flies the scorching breath
Floats on the gale and bodes impending death.
With vigorous paw Grimalkin back he pressed
And placed the other on his tabby vest.
Deep in the flesh the poisoned talons bore
Then thrust apart a gaping wound they tore
On either side the loosened pieces lay
On the raw flesh the cold night breezes play
They back retreat again together rush
(Again they roll and all the verdure crush)
Till both fatigued they mutual turn to slake
Their burning thirst within a placid lake
With eager tongues the cooling draught they drink
Lap yet again and linger o'er the brink
Till Nameless starting dares his foe to come
And combats start that soon must seal their doom.
Grimalkin soon with ready vision saw
Where heedless lay his foeman's velvet paw.
He sprang upon his foe and brushed aside the hair
Tore the tough skin and laid the sinews bare.
Then Nameless starts and gets his foe beneath
And thro' his ear he meets his grinding teeth
Grimalkin springs upon his cruel foe
And to the plain he felled him with a blow
Awhile he lays as if he slept in death
And from his nostrils starts no warming breath
Grimalkin thotless deemed the victory won
And to the lake athirsting he has gone.
But crafty Nameless marked his foeman's track
And swift yet stealthy lingers at his back
Now while waves Grimalkin's whiskers break
The cat he left for dead quick thrusts him in the lake
With vigorous arm awhile he stemmed the tide
And for the land he thrusts the waves aside

But Nameless saw the Grimalkin near the land
And with great stones he drives him from the strand.
One stone of great proportions fell
Near the bare swimmer and raised a swell
For when it sunk elastic waters rise
And with the volume pierce the ambient skies
Then loud descending from a mighty wave
Beneath its weight Grimalkin found his grave
   To float in vain the anxious warrior tries ⎫
   He sinks below and quickly as he dies   ⎬
   In monstrous bubbles all his breathings rise ⎭
And by foul crime neer perished from the earth
A braver cat nor one of nobler birth.
Back to the plain the Nameless takes his way
Where stiff and cold his long dependant lay.
Arriving there the follower of Mars
Raises his voice to thank the gods of wars.

If all Cerebus' tongues had howling bayed the moon
Twere zephyrs breathing's to that direful tune
As loud below the answering echoes swell
Old Pluto hastes to close the gates of hell
Lest suffering souls who in his domains rove
Should think there was another hell above.
And Charon, eager, plies the bending oar
And quickly moors his restless bark to shore,
As on the beach his sooty form uprears
His toilworn fingers fill his bursting ears.
And now, oh muse, my wandring footsteps lead
From hell to heaven, oh swift Pegasus speed
Oh muse describe how gods in conclave sit
And how each god doth rack celestial wit,
To find some means to stop the direful song
They rack in vain and round great Jove they throng,
Great Mars demands and Pity supplicates with tears
Till all in vain the immortal has no *ears*.*
And then dread Mars to whom the thanks were said
Wrathful at length no more in heaven delayed.
Filled with dire rage the warlike god appears
Strides to his steeds to fix their shining gears
Their harnesses were made with silver thong
Wrapped o'er with steel to make it double strong;
And with each trace firm fastened with a star
Low stooping down he vaults into his car

*This was a sorry mistake with the Greeks to represent Jupiter without ears

At his right side his trusty falchion hung
While at his left a ponderous boot-jack swung,
Celestial trophy from the Titons won
And which at night Jove doffed his sandals on.
From his broad back his spear and javelin trail
Down to his feet, across his shirt of mail
He strikes his falchion on his brazen shield
His horses gallop, time and distance yield.
Jove saw the boot-jack for the god has eyes
The thunder rattles and the lightning flies.
In vain round Mars the writhing lightnings dance
Quick as themselves he impales them on his lance,
Stamped 'neath his feet their fiery wings he tore
And thus to Jove loud spake the god of war—
"Thou earless being blest of all the gods
Beneath whose will all things obedient nods
Thou gavest the sea to him who rules the main
And thou gavest hell to dreary Pluto's reign
But there's one thing to which I'll not agree
Thou gavest this jack which Hermes* filched for me
When it has pierced yon feline monster's brain
Then to thy hand I will restore it again."
Again he strikes his javelin on his shield
His good steeds gallop down the azure field
In a less time than takes my pen to write
He arrived upon the field of fight
He sternly paused and viewed with rising hate
The doomed tom-cat unconscious of his fate
His brawny arm he quickly then laid bare
And poised the direful bootjack high in air
Back his strong frame he bent with a full sway
Then fiercely sped the bootjack on its way.

Hissing with wrath—and with aim too true,
With dire intent the direful missile flew.
A dreadful scream a mighty yell of pain
And Nameless, lifeless stretched upon the plain.
See where the glorious god of combats glides
Oer the smooth lawn with huge devouring strides
And at length where Nameless bleeding lay
Low stooping down he raised the lifeless clay
Then where on his back his spear and javelin crossed
With both legs in one hand the cat he tossed
Then striding back his horses swiftly take

*A name for Mercury the god of thieves, trade &c.

(At his nod) their course toward the lake
Arriving there upon the grassy brink
His tired horses stoop their heads to drink.
He stands in car and bends his massy back
To speed the Nameless on his aerial track.
  As lightnings part the ethereal main above
Where speed from out the mighty hand of Jove
As speed on fiery wings thro out the sky
Yet swift tho' lifeless Nameless rose on high.
At length he pauses reverses in his course
And then descends with thrice redoubled force
Convulsed the waters part again close oer
He seeks the shades to rise on earth no more.

BEAUTIES OF MYTHOLOGY

When poets and men of imaginative minds embodied their better passions and aspirations, and gave a "local habitation and a name," and worshipped in another shape that good which was in their own hearts, they performed an act upon which we are prone to look without censure. And such, no doubt was the beginning of that beautiful idolatry which was once almost the only religion of the known world, and whose sublime and poetical myths commanded the admiration of men long, long after they had ceased to cherish them as a belief. Such, we say, was the beginning. But in time, men embodied and worshipped the vices and the darker passions of their nature. Undoubtedly all men were at first aware of the existence of, and adored the true God. They adored the true God, and they adored, also, symbols of goodness, of mercy, and of truth— his genuine attributes; but they gradually came to worship symbols of lust, of revenge, of war, and an infinity of other evils—the attributes of man.

The earlier Greeks endowed their artificial deities with their own passions, their desires, their goodness, and their wickedness, and their posterity, naturally enough, emulated the seeming example of their gods. The myths and traditions handed down from generation to generation, were as essentially a part of the religion, as the worship of the gods.

Whatever is beautiful in the mythology of the ancients, is exquisitely so. Its beauty breathes of fresh spring flowers, of echoing dells and verdant plains; of tinkling fountains, of feeding flocks, of harmless shepherds and of peaceful swains. These images seem to have gushed like springs of living water from the hearts of the poets, and flowing into the souls of men, awakened there delicate sentiment, and love for the genuinely beautiful.—All believed the leg-

15

ends and the tales of the poets, and when the cares of earth were thrown aside, they revelled in a world of imaginary beings. To them the hills, and valleys, and plains, were peopled with countless sprites and terrestrial deities. Laughing Naiads sported among the emerald waves of every stream. Beauteous Nymphs haunted the green sides of the valleys, and floated in mazy dances on the flowery plains. Dryads reposed amid the boughs of the verdant oaks. Echo, a formless nymph, answered their songs from the distant caves. The sunflower was to them the conscious nymph who pined away in love for the sun, and who still meekly followed his daily course. The pale yellow flower which bloomed earliest in spring, was the beautiful and selfish Narcissus. The red roses still blushed from the blood which the flying Venus dropped upon the first of their race, and the lily was pale because of the milk which fell from heaven.

The flowers, the fruits, the grain had their patron deities. It was the care of such to watch the tender green shoot bursting from the earth, to guard its infancy, to assist the toiling swain, and to bless with smiles and favor, the yellow-glowing fields at last. Pomona pruned the trees, cleansed the green orchards, freed them from insects and from worms, and dispensed her rosy-blushing apples, her luscious peaches, and her azure plums upon the thankful tiller of the soil. The vine's god, Bacchus, showered his purple grapes upon the vintagers, and they, in goblets "crowned with rosy wine," drank to the god of riot and of mirth. Ceres bound her yellow wheat in sheaves, and blessed the reaper's toil. The grotesque Pan surrounded by his dancing satyrs and his fauns, guarded the shepherd's timid flocks, discoursing sweetest music on his pipes the while.

On Morpheus' viewless wings, the soothing dreams at night were wafted to the sleeper's couch, charming his conscious gaze with heaven caught scenery and ravished his hearing with celestial songs.

A god was believed to preside at every meal, and libations were poured out to him before the repast was begun. Beneficent deities attended at every step and directed all efforts. And stern Lachesis measured out life's thread the while, and grim Atropos severed it at death.

That man who lived a virtuous and an upright life, was ever assisted by the powers above, or at least by those who represented good and truth. Ulysses was attended by Minerva through all his perils. She endowed him at times with celestial wisdom. She clothed him in immortal youth. She filled his muscles with gigantic strength. She shed over his person, at different times, a god-like grandeur, to awe and dazzle all beholders.—She shielded him from the wrath of ocean's angry lord, triumphed over Neptune in the synod of the gods, and returned her charge secure to "Ithaca the fair."

The love of home and of country was strong in the bosom of the Greek and Roman. It was of no distant land or people, therefore, that their poets sang. Their own countries were the scenes of the greatest actions of the gods, and the people loved their faith the more, because it breathed continually of home. The father of the gods had invented the Greek alphabet. The gods held their synods on the summit of Olympus. The Muses loved and haunted the verdant groves of Parnassus. The city of Athens was under the special patronage of Pallas.

Saturn, when deposed by Jupiter, wandered to Italy, where he taught the people the use of the plough, and instructed them in the peaceful arts of agriculture. Venus who was the mother of Æneas had guided him to the inviting shores of Italy. It was among Roman hills and forests that Pan held his sylvan court. It was in the Roman valleys that the nymphs loved to repose. It was on the blue waves of the Mediterranean that the Neriads floated in their "shelly skiffs." It was in the silvery streams of Italy that the Naiads bathed, and sported with celestial grace.

The Elysium of the ancients was the most beautiful picture of a future state of the good that was possible to conceive. There, released from the cares and troubles of life, the happy souls dwelt in blissful freedom and peace with each other; retaining their memories and identity for many ages, when they drank of Lethe's water, and returned to earth again.

And here, we find that a Greek heaven was but the likeness of Greece herself. A Greek could imagine no place fairer than his own country. Voluptuous and indolent, he desired to see her stripped of all disagreeable irregularities, but retaining everything that made her dear to him before. He transferred to Elysium her own green plains and verdant hills. He planted there the myrtle groves of his country, and adorned the valleys with familiar flowers, but he carried not with him the frowning rocks and craggy mountains of earth. Cliffton, an American poet, has celebrated the delights of Elysium in the following exquisite verses:

"There rage no storms; the sky diffuses there
His temper'd beams thro' skies forever fair.
There gentler airs thro' brakes of myrtle blow,
Hills greener rise and purer waters flow.
There bud the woodbine and the jes'mine pale,
With every bloom that scents the morning gale;
While thousand melting sounds the breezes bear
In silken dalliance to the dreaming ear;
And golden fruits 'mid shadowy blossoms shine,
In fields immortal and in groves divine."

[Signed "W.", *Casket*, September 1853]

[Probably we shall never recover nor even realize the extent of Howells's apprentice work. The testimony of his own memoirs indicates a far greater amount of published writings than that which circumstance has allowed us to identify with certainty. Speculation based on style and manner is difficult even when dealing with a mature, established author; with the youthful, imitative art of a boy, it is fairly impossible. Without some identifying initial or pseudonym, or some other concrete record of his authorship either in his letters and autobiographical recollections or in those of other contemporary witnesses, attribution will always be suspect. Even when they do exist, references in Howells's writings are more often vague than not. In *Years of My Youth*, for example, he tells of "doing sketches and studies and poems for our own paper, which I put into type without first writing them, and short stories imitated from some favorite author of the moment with an art which I imagined must conceal itself from the reader" (p. 83); and to a large extent these pieces indeed have remained concealed in the pages of the *Ashtabula Sentinel*.

We are more fortunate, however, in identifying Howells's early contributions to the *Ohio Farmer*, a Cleveland weekly edited by his father's friend, Thomas Brown. Though primarily a publication for the dissemination of agricultural news and information, the handsomely printed journal devoted the last page of each of its issues to original literature and items of home and family interest. Encouraged by William Cooper Howells's faith and persistence, young Will reluctantly allowed the proud parent to send one of the son's prose pieces to the paper in the autumn of 1853, "a sketch of an old log cabin which I had seen in ruins, and which I described with the utmost faithfulness." The memory of the family's year in a log cabin at Eureka Mills was still fresh in the young author's mind, and he drew upon this resource, he later recollected, to give his sketch "human interest by imagining the life that had passed in it and then passed out of it." Shortly after the piece's publication, the good-hearted editor paid a visit to his friend's home in Jefferson where he met the young contributor. Howells remembered Brown as "a very kindly man, and although I shunned his presence as much as possible, he encouraged me to write more and more for his paper" ("Young Contributors and Editors," p. 245). Howells afterwards doubted that he had needed much encouragement, but it certainly did not hurt, and for a while he became a fairly regular contributor to the *Ohio Farmer*. His contributions, both in prose and verse, appeared next to those by "Nellie," "Myra," "Ariel," "Jeune," "Ichabod Homebred"; it was in stark contrast to these sentimental and imaginative pen names that Howells chose as his identifying mark the amusing pseudonym "Will Narlie."]

THE LOG CABIN
A BEAUTIFUL SKETCH

By the side of a deserted highway, where the sound of your horse's hoof is broken by a thick growth of stunted grass, stands an old log cabin. It is one of those objects which sometimes meet your eye in the older parts of the country, and on which, for the sake of the past, you bestow a momentary thought. As you tie your horse to the gate-post, and tread the tangled pathway to the house, you pass the old well. Grass grows upon the curb, and almost hides it from you. The long sweep, with the grape vine rope, is broken in the middle, and lies athwart the curb, and

"The moss covered bucket that hung in the well,"

has long since fallen apart. You go up to the house. Every thing bears the marks of age and desolation. The little porch, where, many summer evenings, years ago, the old grandfather sat and smoked, the children played, and the farmer and his hale wife talked over the news, has swaged nearly to the ground. One post is gone, and the floor is rotten and worm-eaten. The mud built chimney, which once stood at the gable of the house, has fallen, and mingled its dust with the ruins of the porch. The roof of the cabin has sunken in, and the ragged edges of the clapboards project over the eaves.

In startling contrast with all this, is the luxuriant verdure which surrounds the old house on every side. Over all its front, a tangled sweet briar clings, and hangs its odorous blossoms from the corners of the logs and the projecting shingles of the little porch. Through the broken sash of the narrow window, a white rose has climbed, and now blooms upon the wall inside. Dark moss covers the door sill, and the rotten logs teem with unwholesome parasites. You enter. Every object is rich with melancholy.—Every corner has its pathetic story. The iron crane creaks rustily in the fire place. Pale, green weeds, which the sun never ripens, spring out from the battered jams.

How often the hardy old pioneer sat by this same hearth, with the baby on his knee, relating to his white headed grand-children long stories of Indian inroads upon the settlements, and recounting the perils of himself and his friends, till the young listeners cling closely to him, and picture with filial plainness to themselves, murderous hoards of savages, with blood-stained tomahawks, who loom darkly from the farther corners, and peep down through the small trap door of the loft.

By the side of the fire-place lies the old bullet-proof oaken door. A thick coat of dust has gathered on its surface, and the marks of the Indian tomahawks, which the children once viewed with superstitious awe, are almost hidden from sight. The walls of the room are stained and broken, and the floor is upturned and covered with rubbish. In the farther corner, now broken and dirt-begrimed, lies an old table.—How often the happy little circle gathered around it, in days gone by, with thankful hearts, while a blessing was asked by the old grandsire, whose thin hands trembled as he lifted them above the board. But now no more shall they gather together around the table, nor cluster at even around the blazing hearth. They are scattered and gone. It were a sad story to tell, how one bright summer evening, the little children found the old man dead in his rude arm chair; how one year the crops failed; how the cattle died; how the farmer saw with sorrow the growing barrenness of his land; how he sold the farm; how he determined to go west; and how one autumn morning they all started, the farmer taking the lead, with his rifle on his shoulder, and the family following in the stout covered wagon.

Poor old house! It is passing away. It will soon be leveled with the earth. A gaudily painted Swiss cottage will rise over its grave.— Foreign trees will flourish, and exotics will bloom where now grow the elm, and blossom the sweet briar and the honey-suckle. Prim gravel walks will be laid out. A careful gardener will project garden beds, and form borders with mathematical exactness, and the uncouth rail fence will be replaced by rows of white palings. It is for the best, perhaps; and yet as you linger about the old house you feel like shielding it from aggression.

[*Ohio Farmer*, 24 November 1853]

[The New Year A.D. 1854 provided the sixteen-year-old boy with an occasion not, as one might expect, for looking into the future, bright with the promise of youthful hopes and dreams, but for melancholy meditation, similar to that manifested in the sketch of "The Log Cabin." In part, this was again a reflection of those sentimental days, the fashions of taste which held up such as Ik Marvel and Alexander Smith as writers the young should emulate. But revealed here, too, as in so many of the pieces of Howells's youth, are the personal uncertainties, the debilitating fears and doubts that lead some young people to anticipate imaginatively the completion of life before they have won an opportunity truly to begin. And as Howells later realized, it is this universal, timeless condition of older youth that accounts for the passing popularities of particular talents like that of the author of *Reveries of a Bachelor: or a Book of the Heart* (1850) and *Dream Life: A Fable of the Seasons* (1851).

Though echoes of Lamb, Irving, and De Quincey, among others, are clearly heard in these *Ohio Farmer* pieces, Howells was correct in remembering the chief influence on his style and literary concerns at this period to have been Donald Grant Mitchell, who under the pseudonym of "Ik Marvel" charmed several generations of readers with his essays of reverie and dream life, those "fleecy cloud-drifts that float eternally, and eternally change shapes, upon the great over-arching sky of thought!" That tender pathos, that vital thrill, that rapid and dramatic shift of mood from hopeful expectation to melancholy regret which young people in every age take to be the full range of poetic sentiment are the hallmarks of Mitchell's popular works, nowhere more appropriately demonstrated than in this passage from "A Home Scene" in *Dream Life*, Howells's favorite of the two immensely popular books.

Little does the boy know, as the tide of years drifts by, floating him out insensibly from the harbor of his home, upon the great sea of life,—what joys, what opportunities, what affections, are slipping from him into the shades of that inexorable Past, where no man can go, save on the wings of his dreams. Little does he think—and God be praised, that the thought does not sink deep lines in his young forehead!—as he leans upon the lap of his mother, with his eye turned to her, in some earnest pleading for a fancied pleasure of the hour, or in some important story of his griefs, that such sharing of his sorrows, and such sympathy with his wishes, he will find no where again.

Little does he imagine, that the fond Nelly, ever thoughtful of his pleasure, ever smiling away his griefs—will soon be beyond the reach of either; and that the waves of the years which come rocking so gently under him, will soon toss her far away, upon the great swell of life.

But *now*, you are there. The fire-light glimmers upon the walls of your cherished home, like the Vestal fire of old upon the figures of adoring virgins, or like the flame of Hebrew sacrifice, whose incense bore hearts to Heaven. The big chair of your father is drawn to its wonted corner by the chimney side; his head, just touched with gray, lies back upon its oaken top. Little Nelly leans upon his knee, looking up for some reply to her girlish questionings. Opposite, sits your mother; her figure is thin, her look cheerful, yet subdued;—her arm perhaps resting on your shoulder, as she talks to you in tones of tender admonition, of the days that are to come.

The cat is purring on the hearth; the clock that ticked so plainly when Charlie died, is ticking on the mantel still. The great table in the middle of the room, with its books and work, waits only for the lighting of the evening lamp, to see a return to its stores of embroidery, and of story.

Upon a little stand under the mirror, which catches now and then a flicker of the fire-light, and makes its play, as if wanton, upon the ceiling, lies that big book, reverenced of your New England parents—the Family Bible. It is a ponderous square volume, with heavy silver clasps, that you have often pressed open for a look at its quaint old pictures, or for a study of those prettily bordered pages, which lie between the Testaments, and which hold the Family Record.

Ik Marvel's sentimental, tender phrases, rich with those emotional associations which some aestheticians then thought was the purpose of art and the imagination: this too was part of Howells's early literary passions, one which he afterwards confessed openly, albeit with a tenderness that protects from shame the honest miscalculations of youthful taste.]

A New Year's Glimpse of Memory Land

New Year's night, and the fire bright upon the hearth, and the old man alone in his room. It was ten o'clock by the city clock, which had just tongued the hour; ten by the clock on the mantelpiece; ten by the old man's watch.

He was a strange, quiet person—like a memory—not a rosy, joyful memory—but a dim, dark, shaded memory; a memory of something sorrowful; a relique of a woe. No one knew him, no one cared for the nasty old gentleman in black; yet he was a good, mild-looking man, not at all brusque or crabbed, but a little sad, may be.

Sitting by the hearth, with his hands upon his knees, peering into the blaze! Being with the present, living with the past!

Oh! the past! it is a great land, where our feet never tire, where our limbs never weary with straying. There are wide, sunny plains in it, where the heart-errant loves to wander; there are green vales in it, silver veined with streams of joy; there are in it dark valleys and cemeteries, where the twilight-evoked thought steals forth to weep on the tombs of dead hopes, and fears, and loves, and hates, and despairs. We love the past, and clasp to our breasts its phantom joys, and weave into garlands its ghostly flowers and withered hopes, and, mockeries though they be, wreathe our brows with them. The future is God's, the present the World's and Care's, but the past is all our own.

And the old man, whose memory land was wide and thickly peopled, and whose only hope-land now was Heaven, loved the past; and he gathered it about him, called up familiar faces and words, conjured up shadows of dear forms, and kissed their unreal lips, and strained their forms of nothingness in his arms.

He was a boy again. The memory-land was short, but the hope-land was wide and flowery before him. It was New Year's night at home. His mother was there, and his father near him, the brothers and the sisters that loved and knew him, were there. He told his mother in a low voice of his hopes (hopes that breathed once—ghosts now.) He would go into the world, and would carve himself a name among the proudest. Men should bow to the genius of one whom they now scorned. Still, he told his mother, in all his pride of station, he would remember those at home. It was not for himself alone that he wished for fame. It was because they would rise with him. And the mother smiled on the ambitious boy, and thanked God for the noble and good that was in him. His little sister climbed on his knee, and he stroked her hair. It was home, and it was New Years, and he was a boy again.

Still it was hope—sometimes storm, sometimes shine, was on his path—but the youth was as the boy, strong in the good, though fierce and proud in his ambition.

And now a warm presence was in the room beside the old man. Other arms than his sister's were on his neck, other lips than his mother's kissed him, and there was a new feeling in his soul. His breast was bashfully aglow with something he would not have there, and yet would.—His name was breathed by lips of music, and *his* tongue had learned a new name and a new language. Eyes—soft, dark eyes—were fixed on his, and seemed to be melting there. A cheek, hot and passionate, pressed his own, a warm and snowy hand lay in his.

And now he lingered in the by-paths of life, and plucked the flowers that lined his way, and wove garlands for her. The song of his heart was changed; it was once like the leap of a mountain stream—pure and ringing, yet cold and passionless. Now it was like the warm tinkle of a southern fount, laughing and carolling in the sunshine. It was a moonlight night, he well remembered, when he first breathed his love, and drew to his breast unstruggling, her to whom he had bared his heart. The moonlight, as he walked home after parting, seemed to have a richer glow in it, and the stars looked down like eyes of joy on him, and the great earth sleeping, wore a serene and quiet look of beauty. He had something now to toil for, and he worked with passionate ardor, yet with an ambition less stern, and soul attuned to beauty and melody.

Years rolled on. The hope-land was growing shorter and less bright, and the memory land was widening behind, and there was a grave in it.

Our past follies we laugh at, if they bear with them no present sting of remorse; the remembrance of our joys and pleasures are sweet to us, though we do not recall them often, but the ghosts of our woes and our griefs we fondle to our hearts. We love to turn them over like flower-leaves pressed between the pages of a book of poems; we place them to our lips and kiss them; and in more quiet hours, we unlock the silent chambers of our souls, where dwell the shades of griefs that once were, and hold melancholy talks with them—all in a God-thanking spirit that they are no longer real.

And the bright presence was gone from the old man's side, and the path through memory-land, that his soul was now tracing, was decked with flowers no longer, but willows drooped around, and swept him with their tomb-hallowed boughs. It was hard to believe that she could die. But, day by day, the dark eye sunk and faded; day by day, the rich lips grew thin and bloodless; day by day the color fled from her cheek; day by day the penciled veins grew bluer, and—so she died. The heavy black locks were shorn away, the white lids were closed over the glassy eyes, and the thin white lips were set in a quiet smile. Locks that had twined themselves through the subtlest fibers of his heart, eyes in whose passion-beams his soul had reeled in delightful drunkenness, lips that once had thrilled his whole being with joy unutterable! Maud was dead! Oh God! it was too much!

He was stunned, stupified. He went forth in the world like one in a dream. But the voice of an aged, grave-nearing mother was in his ears; the lips of a sister breathed comfort to him, and there was a book often in his hands, which turned his thoughts from earth, (where, indeed, he had little now to love as he once loved,) and drew them towards Him who said:—"I am the resurrection and the Life."

As yet none of the hopes of his boyhood and his youth had been realized. Be he thought little of fame now, and the scorn and the praise of the world were as one to him. His dreams were no longer of earth's magnificence and glory, but were turned to something higher. And the memory-land was each day becoming dearer and dearer to him, and his soul blessed the spirits that dwelt in it, and he smiled incredulously at the gay hope that pointed to the future with her changeless song of "Yet a little while.'"

The clock on the mantle struck eleven and startled the old man from his reverie. The fire on the hearth was dying slowly away, but he raked up the smouldering embers, and placed more wood on the fire-dogs, and wakened the blaze with his breath.

He was now, he thought, a stout hale man of forty. The convulsive flutters of his early anguish were past. Sorrow, like a resistless flood, had swept over him, and like the flood that beslimes the fair fields and valleys, and lodges drift and rubbish, where once smiled cottages and towns, it had torn away the old land-marks of his soul, and strewed the banks of the former channel of his hopes with the wrecks of half-blown aspirations and noble thoughts. His mother and his sisters, and all his kindred, were gone to their rest, and he was now quite alone.

And he was going back to the old place.

Sad memories were his, as he recalled, one by one, the faces of the dead; while he gazed on their tombs in the old village grave-yard. There was his father's grave, with its modest sand-stone monument, its quaint inscription and epitaph.—His sister's grave was there—by it her child's. Her husband stood over the grave with him, and, stifling his own heart's cry, he could say to the young man, "Poor George, Poor George." His mother's grave was near. The sod was thick upon it, and a willow of five years' growth bowed over it, violets were growing on its breast, and a new-leaved rose-tree, (for the spring had not yet glowed into summer,) twined its arms around the head-stone. It was a quiet, holy spot, hallowed, it seemed to him, by the sacred dust that slept there; and he wept long and with a feeling of relief—for his tears were like prayers, they drew his soul nearer to God!

His companion drew his arm kindly into his own, and pointed to a corner of the grave-yard, where a narrow shaft of white marble rose over a little mound. He dared not trust himself so far. "George, George," he said, "I must not go;" yet he went. It did not affect him as he thought. He was strangely calm. No tears came to him, no outburst of passionate grief swept over him, and save a slight quiver of his lips, he was wholly without emotion. He stood by her grave, he placed his hand upon the marble shaft, he read the inscription: "Maud—aged 16," and the simple epitaph,—"I loved her"—which he himself had written, and it was all new and strange to him.

But as he turned to go away, a little, stunted rose bush at the root of the oak that shadowed her grave, caught his eye. It was one that they had planted together, in the days when love went a-maying. He knelt down and kissed it, and as he rose, his smouldering grief burst into a flame, his dead hopes and aspirations came to him, and while the ghost of the old love rose from the grave he had digged for it in his heart, a sense of his utter desolation and oneness rushed upon him.

He was growing to be an old man. His cane was often in his hand. His brown hair here and there confessed a silvery brother, the wrinkles were gathering on his brow, the lines of age were deep in his cheek, his speech was slow and feeble, and his once stout frame was bent and frail.

He was living in a distant city alone. George had followed his wife, and slept peacefully in the little grave-yard.

The memory-land was the old man's greatest treasure, albeit its path had been a journey of grief to him. The hope-land was withdrawn beyond the confines of earth, and peace had taken the place of the gay charmer that once waved him on.

25

New Year's night, twelve o'clock, and the old man alone in his room. The fire had gone out, and the shades of darkness were gathered in the room, and they were like *him*, for the shades of woe brooded on his soul, and the ashes of desolation lay thick upon the hearth-stone of his heart!

[Signed "Will Narlie," *Ohio Farmer*, 5 January 1854]

[Young Howells turned instinctively to his surroundings for literary material and attempted to find in them the meaning and commonday mystery that was for the romantic age to which he was heir the matter of the literary imagination. Though he looked back upon his prose contributions to the *Ohio Farmer* as "minutely realistic sketches in which I had begun to practise such art as I have been able to carry farthest" (*YMY*, p. 83), his attitude at the time toward his subjects was quite other from that dictated by the creed of literary realism that he would develop during the following decades. The fireside, the village, the rural landscape, and the events and places of which it was then his fate to be a part must need be redeemed from their barren and mundane character whose bleak truth it would have been too terrible for the boy to have admitted. "A Sunny Day in Winter," printed in the *Ohio Farmer* in late January 1854, and the two "Letters from a Village" that followed in March and April are pleasant enough genre pieces: the world in miniature, or, as Howells would have it, "in epitome," and he the sentimental explorer. The hearth fire and the early spring warmth gave assurance that all was well or soon would be. Such tenderly humorous, "poetically" sublime panoramas of their days and hours could not help but have charmed his reader just as they did the management of the *Ohio Farmer*. In an editorial note attached to one of Howells's contributions in March 1854, Thomas Brown made a modest prediction that time and hard work eventually bore out: "'Will Narlie' is yet a mere lad; if riper years do not cheat the promise of his youth, he will make his mark among the Poetical and Prose writers of the nineteenth century."]

A SUNNY DAY IN WINTER

MORNING AND NOON

The pools of water which the melted snow had made, stood glassily in the meadows, and the little swollen springs sparkled down the sides of the valley, like rich leaps of child-laughter, and lost themselves among the grass, or gurgled into the sedgy run that skirted the foot of the hill. A thin, warm mist rose from the stubble fields around, and clothed in its light vapor the base of the neighboring wood, whose top, rising bold and darkly at first, gradually melted away into the blue horizon beyond. The sky was serene and clear, and save two or three soft and lucid flakes that dozed upon its breast, was cloudless, while the sun looked down with summer smile. A quiet south wind stole soothingly along whispering among the leafless spray as softly as a blithe zephyr of June, and wafting now and then a snatch of a fragrance from the moist limbs of the maples and hickories.

A few sheep in the field, gnawing the grass roots. Cattle wandering over the hills, browsing the juicy boughs of the low beeches, their bells dropping soft, dull notes at every toss of the head. A horse standing by the meadow fence, his head raised, his nostrils stretched wide, snuffing the air, the wind playing among the hairs of his mane, and lightly tossing them. The chickens from the barnyard, scattered over the fields, picking up stray grains of wheat and corn, and now and then their cackling noisily at the apparition of a floating leaf above their heads. A little huddle of quails, hiding among the old logs and piles of brush. The ground squirrels racing along the worm fences with sharp, birdlike chirps, and the grey squirrels in the woods dozing on the tops of the oaks, their broad, plumy tails dangling in the breeze, or chasing each other in spiral gambols around the trunks of the ashes and chestnuts, their harsh, guttural cries floating mystically across the fields.

The house dog lay in a sleepy coil on the bit of carpet that covered the doorstep, opening and shutting his eyes with quiet pleasure as the sunlight beat full upon him, and now and then half raising his head as a hardy young chicken tried to gain the forbidden threshold. The floor was cleanly swept, and the chairs were set in careful order. The hearth was dusted, the ashes brushed back into the fire-place, and beside either jam lay a little pile of sweepings—down, torn bits of paper, stray broom straws, partly consumed by fire. On the breast of the heap of ashes, smoked the remnants of last night's back-logs, breaking now and then into a lazy flicker and lending a faint glow to the polished tins that lined the other wall.

I like to trace all these little belongings of home. I like to jot down its thousand and one quaint, yet endearing features, which raised my wonder when a child. Through the wide hall, with its railed and banistered stairway, the garret with its mystery and darkness, the bed rooms with their many closets, the dining room with its cupboards and pantry, even the kitchen with its stove and tins, and the cellar with its great heaps of apples and stores of potatoes, its empty old barrels and boxes, and its barred window where the sun never looked in, memory ranges with infinite delight; and if from my own remembrances I draw a true picture of home, or a picture whose tints recall to the heart a glimpse of the home it knew and loved once, I shall have done a good work, and he who cons my picture will be bettered and strengthened.

The warm, rich sunshine pouring its flood of amber light along the floor, turning the particles of flying dust into silvery sparkles, gilding the backs of the grim old chairs, and flushing the face of the clock upon the mantle with its unseemly smiles; drifting through the half-curtained windows, and falling in mellow angles on the settee, and resting goldenly on the work-stand near by; painting on the carpet every bubble in the glass, the creaks that ran through it, and stretching there in soft brown colors the bars of the window sash, and tracing over the face of all its work, the vine-like boughs of the rose bush on the outside, gently moving to and fro in the wind.

Upon the wall hung the rifle, and the powder horn, with a strip of buckskin for a string, and the stout leathern pouch, with its broad band and buckles. A squirrel's tail drooping above them, and a wild turkey's wing—the trophies, may be, of some fond boy-hunter, who would fain have hung them in the "best room" for the delight of visitors.

From the mantel-piece came the quiet tick-tack of the clock. A quaint, odd piece of furniture, with its two carved mahogany columns at the sides, ending in two feet at the bottom, neatly sculptured to represent almost any wild animal's claws, its door opening by a bright brass button, with a little strip of veneering running across the middle, below which was painted a vase full of very bright flowers, with a clear space where the pendulum might be seen as it swung to and fro. A Yankee clock, a wooden one at that. Inside, near the bell on which the hammer struck its clear, ringing notes, and just back of a little wire which would make it strike anytime when pulled slightly, was a quiet label, giving the maker's name, and the name of the place where it was made, in full black letters— "Bristol, Conn." By the side of the clock a bunch of thread, the scissors and beeswax, a little bundle of sage, and at either end of the mantel, a Plaster Paris vase full of green and red tomatoes, very naturally done.

Indeed, it was not a richly furnished room—but it was a home room—like one that you have seen, perhaps, and known, ah! very well!

An old woman sitting near the fire-place, knitting, her spectacles resting on her cap, and her dim eyes fixed dreamily upon the hearth. A child playing at her feet with a kitten, drifting her yellow curls with a roguish quickness along the carpet, and the cat striking at them with her white paws, softly and carefully.

"How soon are father and mother coming home?"

The curls rippled from the carpet, and the child's flushed face was turned to her grandmother, while the kitten glided gravely out on to the porch.

28

"Not till afternoon. Why Clara, how red your face is! I declare you'll be sick if you put your head down so."

"O well, never mind. I aint going to do so any more. It's most twelve, now. I want to set the table—can't I? And then I'll be the mother and pour out the tea."

"Well, child, you may, if you think it's going to do you so much good. But I must help you out with the table."

The table was drawn out, and while the grandmother held up the leaves, the little girl darted busily about, and drew out the legs, and after bumping her curly head against the corner of the table on getting from under it, went out to cool herself, smoothing her hair from her forehead with her two fat hands as she went.

"Seems just like the day you tell about, grandmother, when uncle George, that I never seen yet, went away. It's most like spring. Such *beautiful* weather! O, hum!" (In an affected way, and with a great sigh.)

The plates were placed on the table with a noisy clatter, and the knives and forks were rattled a great deal, and the spoons jingled as much as possible, by the proud little housekeeper. And the two sat down at last, and the little girl chattered gaily on, about what mother was going to bring from town, how much she could tell mother about, how glad mother would be because she had got big enough to set the table and wash the dishes, as she meant always to do after this. And lost in dreamy thoughts, and deaf to the little charlatan at her elbow, musing about the "Uncle George," who went away on just such a day as this, many a weary year past, and feeling a sweet, sad longing to see her boy once more; a longing which was like a rich pant of heart music, wafted from the dells of long ago; so holy was it, the grand-mother sat and sipped her tea.

EVENING AND MORNING

Across the little pools in the meadow, a thin film of ice was spread, and the grassy sides of the rills were lined with frail links of cold, which were continually darting out into the current, and continually being broken off. The wind had changed, and now blew from the north, wrinkling the face of the brook, and vieing with the rocks in its channels to roughen its flow. The white clouds which had been lazily floating through the sky all morning, had drifted away to the east and now lurked darkly on the edge of the horizon. The sun had just gone down, and rich tints of his parting glow yet streamed redly up the sky, which elsewhere wore a *distant*, watery look. The ground-squirrels, hours since, had sought their leaf-lined beds, though here and there the dry leaves rustled to the hasty spring of a belated grey, as he leaped from the ground, whisked himself rattlingly up a tree, and crept into his hole; while on a 'rider' of the corn-field fence, his breast ebbing and flowing in feathery waves to his plaintive notes, a single quail piped querulously. The sheep stood huddled together in a corner of the fence. The cattle had passed down the lane, and in motionless groups were now gathered on the south of the barn. The horse in the meadow was keeping pace with a wagon on the outside, which rattled up the lane toward the house, and whinnering to a man inside, who answered with a familiar whistle.

"That's the house, George. Lordy, boy, mother'll be glad to see you. Twelve years, aint it? Gracious! you was a wild one them days, any how. But it's all forgot *now*. (O, there now, Molly, you needn't nudge me—George can take a little advice from his own brother.) Oh, well, never mind. Get up there, you Sal! That's my gal on the stoop there, George, Towse along with her. Towser wa'ant hardly a respectable pup when you left; was he?"

"Brother George, you must be very careful in meeting our mother—she's so very weak; don't take her too much by surprise."

"Ho, ho! Moll! your calling him *brother* George, reminds me that we wa'ant quite so near related a time back—hey Moll? Bo up here, Sal! Now I'll tell you what—you two git out here, and I'll drive Sal round to the barn."

Little Clara, who had waited on the porch nearly an hour, for the coming of her parents, at the sight of the stranger, mightily abashed, backed up close against the door, with the fingers of one hand in her mouth, and the other on the back of old Towse, whose eyes being rather weak, did not know George at first, and who began to growl suspiciously.

"Why bless you, old Towse, is that you? And this is my little niece. Got a kiss for Uncle George? There, there, Towse, have done licking my face, can't you? Where's your grandmother, little girl?"

"In here, brother George, in here!"

Not many such suppers as that, are ever eaten, I trow! The clean, white cloth, the shining plates, the snowy biscuits, exhaling a delicious odor; the moist teacups, sending up their several fantastic columns of fragrant steam, the china tea pot, rolling forth a prouder volume; the rich, yellow cream, the "best" preserves, in little dishes, each stationed near a large plate, like a planet and its satellites; and the lump of golden butter, beaming forth from the midst—Oh, it was very nice!

And when the supper was done, and the red blaze leaped in the chimney place, and the tins on the other wall blushed and glowed in the light, and the rifle sent back from its barrel a faint gleam, and the squirrel's tail and turkey's wings cast dark, plumy shadows on the wall, and the curtains were drawn, the chairs were wheeled round the hearth, and John and his wife sat at one corner, and

George and his mother at the other, while little Clara was again trailing her hair along the carpet for the kitten's amusement, and flushing her face unreproved.

And while the fire laughed and sparkled, and the starry gleams flew up the chimney, and the logs began to part in the middle, and drop glowing coals, George sat and told long tales of peril by land and sea. Of his first leaving home to become a waif and a stray; of his hopes, of their death, of his longing for home, of his coming back. And his mother, his hand in her own, sat listening, no reproach in her eye, none on her lips. She knew he came back poor, spotted, perhaps, in his struggle with the world; but he came back rich in his love for her, and pure in his thoughts of home, and she was blest in that knowledge. And she sat, smoothing his hand, looking into his face, her grey hair showing from beneath her cap, above her face so furrowed and wrinkled with years.

And while she sat thus, the smile that beamed upon her face, was very like a Sunny Day in Winter.

[Signed "Will Narlie," *Ohio Farmer*, 26 January 1854]

LETTERS FROM A VILLAGE

LETTER I

The day has been one of that dreamy Indian-summer kind, when instead of the bare, gray forests, we should see the rich, many-tinted autumn woods showing through the ashen haze that smothers the brighter blue of the heavens. It is more like the delicious season of falling leaves, of ripening fruits, and yellow fields, than the earliest spring-time. But the air and hazy sky, alone remind us of spring. A ramble through the dreary, sloppy forest, is not fraught with the pensive pleasure of an autumn wood-stroll. We miss, too, the jolly look of plenty which the autumn forest wears. There are no bunches of grapes now, peeping purply from golden coverts of frosted leaves, to tempt break-neck venture with their mocking juiciness; no chesnuts sleeping in glossy trios within downy beds, dropping occasionally with a little rustle among the leaves below; no hickory-nuts which may be had in showers by a toss of a club; no walnuts dangling on their fat, waxen stems, from leafless boughs, or scattered richly about the base of the parent-tree; none of the luscious and countless varieties of the wild fruits and berries of the ripe season. The trees are all bare, and the barren vine clambers over their bony limbs, and drooping, seems to mourn its fall-time prodigality.—Only a few black nuts are to be found among the dark and soundless leaves; haply at the bottom of some old sky-sweeping chestnut, lie a few worm-eaten nuts, which the careful squirrel has weighed and found wanting, and thrust from his nest above.

31

Yet, for all their barrenness, I love those early spring days. Their open mildness, betokens at least an end of winter, and the soft air and sunshine tell of and promise lovelier seasons. The birds, too, are far more dear than later songsters. The blue-bird, with its short querulous note, and quick uneven flight; fluttering from tree to tree, and tapping the bark of dead old stumps, and picking up the worms which the sunshine has quickened. The meadow-lark who greets the morning from the loftiest trees, with flowing, mellow carol, which bursts anon into joyous twitters, as if his breast were so full of song that it must ease itself in crowded gushes of music, who loves the moist-grass of the wood-pastures, whence he rises in lifts of song, to sink again into the marsh, or alight upon some fence and plume his wing, and revel in the shine. And the dear, gentle, *home*-robin, whose lilting matin floats in upon you when you first awake, and whose vesper sinks and dies away with daylight, and yet rises far on some twilight tree and then echoless expires; who builds his nest in the cherry tree beneath your window, in touching trustful-ness of your love—who picks the crumbs from your door-step, and whose lively chirp eases your heart of sorrow-loads sometimes.

The meadows yet wear their weather-beaten robe of yellow, and stretching far away on either side, intersected with scrambly worm-fences, to which distance gives symmetry and regularity, show no sign of spring. But if you will look at the grass which clings nearest the roots of the trees in your door-yard, and that which borders the walk, you will see sundry little blades of green, peeping from the general mass of yellow. And thus they are sprinkled all through the dreary-looking meadows; and though as yet their hue and being are swallowed up almost by the dead and faded of their kind, like little seeds of good among the general mass of evil, they will at last pre-vail, and beautify and give color to the whole. You will find proof, too, of the coming spring in the swelling buds of the peach trees, and in those little cones which bead the cherry twigs; in the soft, unfrozen ground, and the often rising vapors. There is a depth of genuine pleasure in thus marking day by day the coy opening of the tender year, which many never fathom. It is like watching the recovery of one long ill. These warm sunny days resemble the first smiles that flit across the wasted face of the convalescent, bringing the old light into the eye and the almost forgotten expression to the lips. The thin form grows fuller, the blood wells freely up the blue veins once more, and distends them with a fresh life, as the birds already come, fill again the long empty places with their songs, and the young buds swell and quicken. The smile bursts often into a laugh, the health-tinge deepens in the cheek, and a rugged glow of health spreads throughout the frame; and the fields and trees grow green, flowers spring up, and bloom and music gladden all the earth.

While I have been gossiping to you about the weather, and almost anything but the village, the mists have parted from the face of the setting sun, and he is slowly sinking out of sight. Shadows, long and deepening, dwell on all the village, save the church-spire, whose tin-covered belfry is all a-glow; the silver tip of the lightning-rod, too, has caught a vagrant beam of day, and glitters like a heaven-kindled lamp to light the way of wretchedness to God—so bright, so still, so pure! The pines that plume the eastern hills are bathed in the last splendor that the mighty sheds before his end; a yellow wave of light dances along the distant meadow. A rich crimson tint glows far up the western sky. But, as we have seen the rose-leaf when it withers, first whiten round the edge, far up the zenith the crimson tint is paling. Shade by shade it yields to the stealthy grey of twilight. The lamp on the church-spire has gone out. The plumy pines loom dark and cheerless on their distant hills, the meadow's golden wave has ebbed away.—Decay is whitely eating to the rose-leaf's inmost light; and twilight, creeping down to the very edge of the horizon, shuts the sunset out.

If you are a dweller in the city, in your walks abroad you have enough to do to see that you do not jostle your neighbor, and are not jostled yourself. You partake, too, more or less, of the stolidity and indifference of the brick and mortar about you, and are scarcely more inclined to make minute inquisition into the affairs of your fellows, than the five-story building of your own business place, that all day long stares dumbly down upon the exciting scenes of life below, without so much as opening a window about it. [The last line of type—about eight or nine words—in the first column of the newspaper page has been damaged, and the text cannot be recovered] during the greater part of your life in a small country town—if you have taken your little seat in the corner when a child, and listened to the discourse of divers antique dames, who drop in to knit and discuss the neighborhood; if in later years you have learned to pick up little matters of news at school, and retell them to delighted tea-tables at home; if a natural disposition of curiosity in regard to the pursuits and belongings of those around you, has been properly fostered, by the time you attain your majority, you will have acquired a very useful habit of observation. Such a habit, it is true, might make you unpleasantly conspicuous in a city, where it would probably betray you into a perusal of the signs, and untoward admiration of show-windows, and remarks to passers by in regard to the artistic arrangement of articles therein. But here, where everybody is at home, one may indulge his peculiar bent without stint. And, indeed, what can be more delightful than to stroll out into this sweet twilight, and while the actors on the stage of real life pantomime it before one, to hold little gossipy soliloquies with myself?

33

Now is it that the village, having recovered itself from its five o'clock "tea," begins to walk out, and stand at door-steps and gates, and whittle sticks, and smoke cigars, and trade horses and jack-knives, and—recreate itself generally.

Among those passing along the side-walk then, several smartly dressed young bucks are observable. You might tell where any one of those fellows is going, by the nervousness of his walk; his pleased look of trepidation—nay, by the very twitch of his fingers. How miraculously bright are those boots, albeit, they are coarse ones!— With what careful ungracefulness the hat is placed upon the head! That black suit, too, sacred to Sundays, dance nights, and occasions like this, how genteelly is it brushed! And what a pompous, though half-frightened, demeanor the chap has altogether. I dare say, if the season were a little more advanced, the infatuated fellow would spend a dollar and take his sweetheart an airing in a buggy. As it is, however, he must otherwise content himself. There he is at the door at last, and knocking. Presently—what a long time it is to the young man, all the while scraping imaginary mud from his boots— some one comes and opens the door, and then a running fire of greetings takes place—a shaking of hands, perhaps, and, and—the door shuts. I am not omniscient, and I, of course, cannot divine what takes place behind the door.

There are other and graver characters abroad. A portly old gentleman and his wife are slowly sauntering down the path, to catch a breath of the delicious breeze which blows so freshly from the south, surrounded by a body-guard of noisy children. It is pleasant to see old age thus walking forth in its obesity and good humor, with its quiet face dimpling at the sight of youth tossing its ball and rolling its hoop with uproarious joy! The good lady smiles the smile of recognition as two young girls—thirteen years old—skip by her, twisting their bonnet strings upon their fingers. Nor is the old gentleman displeased to see his son John make an awkward boy-bow, over the way, in answer to the laughing good evening of the little maids, who presently stop before a half-open gate, and bestow a marvellous number of kisses upon another girl standing thereby. It is observable that three girls of the before-mentioned years can laugh more, talk louder and faster, and make more noise, than any trio which could well be got together, and the amount of laughter and conversation these three carry on as they pass up the walk to the house, is, to say the least, very remarkable.

A little further up the street, on the stoop of the tavern, a parcel of choice spirits and village loungers are talking and smoking their cigars, while in an ample arm-chair in one corner, sits an honest gentleman fast asleep. Here it is that most choice stories are to be heard; and that startling and numerous exploits of divers steeds are

listened to with profound attention; the which horses, if you would
believe the owners and chroniclers of their merits, were no less than
Bucephalauses—every one of them. Perhaps there is a lawyer or
two in the crowd, who spins delectable and long sketches of criminal
practice, interspersing the narrative with many jokes, not particularly witty but very laughable.

Lights are beginning to be seen in the windows, and the loungers
are beginning to desert the tavern stoop for the post office. A lonely
cow is stalking homeward, looking vague and ominous in the dusk.
Youth, almost as boisterous in its fear as its joy, sings and whistles
loudly as it scampers home. The young bucks are taking walks with
their sweethearts, and the two thirteen-year-olds cast the eyes of
envy at them as they pass. Portly old age is wheezing on its front
step, and vowing that it has caught a cold, and its wife is trying to
light a candle inside.

Large and soft the round moon rises in the east, and calmly
floating the sky, flings the thin skeleton shadows of the leafless trees
along the paths, spreads the broad black shades of the houses like
sackcloth on the front-yards, and relights the lamp upon the lightning-rod of the church; and that glows there, stiller, brighter, purer
than before, and points with its beamy finger to the tranquil stars—
above—above!

Letter II

The Village Post Office

It is a place where the easy saunterers through the vale of life
may at all times turn aside, and enjoy lazy talks with their kind. It
is a place where toil and care may forget the primal curse, and devote
the evening of each day to gossip and tobacco. Here are met the
village urchin just beginning to talk "horse," and the veteran of an
hundred "swaps;" the young sprig putting forth the first buds of
trickery and law, and the old stalk gray in many years of knavishness
and *chicane*; the little Machiavel taking his earliest insight in the
workings of human life, and the old Cynic (your village philosopher
is always a cynic) hating, and making bitter fun of his kind. Here
virtue, slip-shod and dressing-gowned, faces vice in its every-day
seeming; here are age and youth, fatness and leanness, goodness and
evil. The place is an epitome.

And who has not seen an hundred times the universe in which
this little world doth move and is? The long, low-roofed room, with
a counter on either side, loaded with broadcloths and loungers; the
shelves behind the counters rich in the most thrilling of calicoes and
silks; the candy-jars, and the sweetness within them; the blacking
boxes and tea-canisters, the hardware and soft-ware, the dry-goods

and groceries; the ceiling decked with pendant boots and shoes, twine, clothes-line, and pails, wooden and tin; the show-case, moreover, with its wealth of jewelry—pens, pencils, drops and rings, papers of pins, hooks and eyes, shoe-strings, shirt-buttons, and gorgeous and-so-forths; and the strings of onions, and barrels of beans, and meal! Every one has seen and marked all—that is, every one who does not go about the village with his eyes shut.

The honest postmaster, who, in truth, fills a dozen other small offices, and is owner of the store beside, is a man of no little weight in his domain. To say that he was not surpassed in tact and acuteness by Wouter Van Twiller himself, would, indeed, be but just; and I should be sadly lacking in respect for his person and offices, if I failed to say also that he fills his place with becoming dignity— ill-minded people say, indeed, that he has too much dignity. But, ever since the time of Justice Shallow, it has been the fashion to say hard things of county officials; and one had better judge of them for one's self. I am bold to say, however, that the knowledge the good man has of the "President's American," is such as to raise the wonder of the most enlightened. Even a certain character in "Much Ado About Nothing," did not show more scorn for the beggarly and unworthy principles of grammar.

While this worthy officer, then, with his clerk takes care of the letters and papers, and the selling of goods, it is worth while to pass from group to group and listen to the talk of each.

The evening is cool, and there is a good fire in the stove. Candles blaze on every hand, and their rays are flashed back from countless candy-jars and blacking boxes. Bright eyes are seen, and loud voices heard on dusky corners; white clouds of smoke rise from a dozen pipes.

The place is an epitome, as I said, and to pass from group to group and hear their talk, is but to visit, in a small way, different countries, and note their ways and life. A plump gentleman, with a thick voice, is laying down the parts of some great political question, in one corner, with his forefinger, to a numerous auditory; and this mode of enlightenment is rendered much more forcible by the gentleman now and then dodging his head forward, and spitting over the shoulders of his hearers. Another person—a great while ago member of the Legislature, I think—is telling how he once helped to get a troublesome bill out of the way. The more bitter among the village wits say the gentleman mentioned is greatfully given to telling this story; insomuch that to be the least pleasant with him, is to entail the hearing of it upon yourself. I hope, however, I may not be giving weight to such ill-sayings, when I state that the listeners always laugh and admire in the right places; for that, indeed, is a proof of quickness of mind in them, rather than their often hearing of the story. On the counter near the stove a young man is holding forth on women's rights, and arguing with some one in the group who seems to be dead against the thing, to judge from the number of times he uses the words "firesides," "household gods," "ministering angel, thou," etc. Across the store from the young man, a lawyer,

"Content to give his little Senate laws,
And sit attentive to his own applause,"

is telling the most delightful yarns. And, indeed, who can wonder at the bursts of laughter which follow his every sally? Who can wonder if a smile is seen to bloom, even on the sterile features of the Deacon, under the sunshine of Redtape's wit. Ah! what fellows lawyers are to tell stories!—who can garnish the dullest occurrence with the most attractive remarks and *puns*—who can give to every narrative the most exciting and brilliant *denouement*! And how happy among his gifted kind in this respect is Redtape! But the flash of his wit and the cream of his jokes were unpennable, as the lightning's glare is transient; and it is as well to wander at once from the delectable mountains into the valley and shadow of a trio of grave gentlemen talking about the price of flour.

Now is it, that Whipstalk engages to team it for farmer Cloverseed, who is here every Tuesday night to get the "*Try*-bune;" that Rebate, the carpenter, promises to build neighbor Stubbs his woodshed "*immejut;*" that Shirtcollar confides to his bosom friend in hoarse whispers the account of his last interview with his Sarah Jane; now is it, in fine, that everybody talks to everybody, and fills the little universe with an awful buzzing.

Macaulay, I believe, holds to be a truism that when popular excitement reaches a certain point, a terrible lassitude follows; and really, one would almost think Macaulay in the right for once to mark the feeble ebb and flow of conversation from the time when the stage drives up till the throwing open of the delivery-door, and compare that feebleness with the late vivacity on all sides. But when the postmaster has spelt the directions of all the letters, and the papers, and the door *is* thrown open at last, if one has nothing in the mail it is amusing to stand aside and look at those who have. It is pleasant to know that young Jenks has a letter, and the little inward doubt as to whether it is a love-letter or not, does not lessen that pleasure. Gazing at the pile of papers Stubbs carries off with him, it is pleasant to wonder how he can afford it. It is pleasant to see the large, legal-looking epistles which Redtape gets, and to think how many hard feelings, and future curses and troubles they contain. It is pleasant to observe the despair of Grubbins, who is going to break, everybody says—as he opens a letter with a bank protest in it. It is pleasant to mark the trepidation of little Johnny Green,

37

as he rushes out of the door with a letter from his father in California, that will gladden or sadden his poor mother's heart—which, as yet, God only knows.

But all pleasures must have an end. The crowd leave the post-office one by one, light and heavy-hearted; every lounger has departed; and a single tallow-dip winks its bland eye in the thick darkness; the clerk comes round to the stove to warm his fingers; Justice Shallow leaves the store. Solitary candle—solitary clerk—are ye left only!

[Signed "Will Narlie," *Ohio Farmer*, 30 March and 13 April 1854]

[The gothic motive is in its great varieties one of the oldest and most universal of literary impulses. Vicarious terror, or, as Edith Wharton aptly put it, "the fun of the shudder," has proven an effective response to the uncertainties of mankind's fragile existence, and tales of mystery and supernatural horror are as old as human society itself. In late-eighteenth-century England, terroristic literature was codified through the remarkable successes of Horace Walpole, William Beckford, "Monk" Lewis, and Ann Radcliffe; through the influence on Western imaginations of *The Arabian Nights,* following Antoine Galland's modern translation; and, of course, through the literary discovery of folk tales and legends. Among American writers, the evocation of mystery and terror was achieved most brilliantly first by Washington Irving and, soon after, by Edgar Allan Poe. Irving, in his phenomenally popular *Sketch Book* (1820) pieces, "Rip Van Winkle," "The Spectre Bridegroom," "The Legend of Sleepy Hollow"; in the sportive gothicism of his *Tales of a Traveller* (1824); and in the oriental tales he retold in *The Alhambra* (1832), was undoubtedly the chief authorial influence on Howells's perception of literary gothicism. But the example of Poe, too, proved important in the boy's literary education, and Howells later recounted with amusement his youthful attempt to "play the sedulous ape" to Poe's *Tales of the Grotesque and Arabesque* (1840). In a story he called the "Devil in the Smoke-Pipes" (that is, tobacco pipes), he followed Poe's "The Devil in the Belfry" as closely as his youthful art could manage. When he read his imitation to the family, he was chagrined that they should note so quickly the resemblance of his tale to Poe's, being satisfied in his own mind as to its originality and individual distinction.

Unfortunately, at least for our immediate concern, Howells's Poesque story did not survive his youth, but a ghost story of his that appeared in the *Ohio Farmer* in May 1854 has. The last of "Will Narlie's" prose contributions to the Cleveland weekly during this period of Howells's youth, "Dropped Dead: A Ghost Story" disappoints whatever expectations its title and matter create; little of that fear that the narrator claims on his part is transmitted to the reader, and in its invention and execution it is hackneyed and confused in its aim. Years later Howells would return in his short fiction to that dream world "between the dark and the daylight," but then it would be for the serious purposes of exploring elusive human psychology.]

DROPPED DEAD

A Ghost Story

"Who's it for, Mrs. Clathers? Tom you little scamp take that mud right off the walk—straight now, or I'll be out with a stick to you."

The bell was tolling, and Mrs. Smith was trying to learn who was dead, from her neighbor. As she opened the door to speak, she beheld her son Thomas building mud-pyramids on the walk, and the sight and sound together, so filled her with wonderment and anger, that she could not but let off the double-barreled little speech which I have given above.

Mrs. Clathers, knocking the dust from her broom against the door-step, made answer that it was "Glen;" while Cheops, changing his mind at his mother's words, began to play that he was the American army, and the mud-piles were a pack of cowardly Hessians, and kicked them from the walk with a fierceness and bravery, that shed the brightest glory on the "Continentals" and carried off half a toe-nail.

"Well, Mrs. Clathers, what was the matter of him?—he might as well-a-ben dead long ago."

"Don't know—disease of the heart—dropped dead! Mr. Clathers saw"—what it was that Mrs. Clathers was about to say, or what it was Mr. Clathers saw, is as wholly lost to the world now, as the six books of the "Fairy Queen;" or General Tattoo's "History of the Pig Run Scummage," which went out of print when the "Tattooville American Spread Eagle" was stopped for want of subscribers. What Mrs. Clathers was about to say is lost, for at the speaking of the last word, her baby awoke, and yielding to the besetting sin of its kind, set up a most piercing squall, which, of course, hurried its mother away from her gossip. Good Mrs. Smith, therefore, could do nothing but open her mouth and lift her hands, as she went back to her work; and all the forenoon, she thought of nothing but Glen's not dying before, and of his dropping dead when he did die.

It was some two years before, that Robert Glen, as he called himself, came into the village on a hot Saturday afternoon. His seeming, though a little wild was that of a gentleman and a man of the world, and his clothes though stained and travel-worn, were of fine stuff and well-made. I have this fact from Mrs. Clathers, who afterwards cut them into carpet-rags. He carried a small bundle on his arm, and one at his back; and looked, in fine, like a tramp who had "seen better days."

After washing his face and hands at the tavern pump, and wiping them on his handkerchief, he walked into the "Union Hotel," took boarding, and paid for the first month beforehand. He then asked to be shown to his room in such a way as to cause not a few glances of wonder among the loungers in the bar-room, who were already much stirred-up by the fact that he had paid the landlord all in gold. As he went up stairs he was heard to mutter something to himself, which was so low, however, that even the stable-boy, who was showing him to his room, could not make out a word of it; albeit Jack had the keenest of ears. I am nice about this fact, for these were nearly the only words he was heard to speak to himself or any one else in the long two years before his death.

Glen did not come down to supper, but had it taken to his room, which was not a little harrowing to those at the table, who came away a great deal fuller of wonderment than salt-rising bread and weak tea. In the cool of the evening, however, he walked out into the stoop in his barehead and slippers, looked around him at men and things, but said not a word. The landlord, after vainly trying to lead him into making known his thoughts upon the weather, went back to his desk, and looked the money over again in fear that his guest was a counterfeiter. And when two or three loungers failed in like trials, the good gentleman was allowed to hold his tongue at will.

And thus it went on from day to day, from month to month, from year to year—Glen never speaking so much as a word to any one when he could help it. Where he got his clothes or his money, no one knew, but it was slyly whispered about that the thing looked bad. He was very fond of children, winning their love with those little candies and kindnesses by which their young hearts are so easily overcome, and I believe that Tommy Smith felt truly sorry, when, after having thoroughly beaten the Hessians, he fell back in the house to have his toe tied up, he was told that old crazy Glen was dead. Of the ladies, however, this worthy madman was very rightly afraid. Indeed, he was known to rush away and hide himself, more than once, when he found himself in the neighborhood of one of these fair beings.

Thus it went on, I say, till one fine summer morning as he walked out to taste the fresh air, a dozen eyes following him as wont, he was seen to stop and shiver, and then fall upon his face; when they went to him he was dead.

And now, that the man was dead, were we to be balked of all

knowledge of him and his life? were we, who had watched this man from day to day for the last two years, to know nothing of his belongings, his thoughts, his hopes and his griefs? Such were the thoughts uppermost in the minds of not a few worthy villagers as they listened to the slow and even tolling of the bell, and knew that it was for Glen. When therefore he was buried and once out of the way, everybody deemed it right that the landlord should search his room and papers for whatever might throw light on a subject so dark. Among the pile of papers and old clothes in his carpet-bag nothing was found but a few gold coins, and a couple of papers. One ran:

"I love this loneliness—it is selfish—but then, I love it. I can sit here and say—go your way, old world, bearing with you light hearts and heavy souls, young and spotless, souls old and poc-marked with grief and woe and guilt—go your way, for I care not, I am a unit. I love to feel that no living creature can cause me sorrow or pain, that I can wrap myself in my oneness, and laugh to scorn those who praise and those who blame. There is a glorious independence in this being alone. * * * My heart has no vagabond tendrils, training themselves about outside objects. It is a pine, firm, rock-rooted. It loves solitude, and its clouds and everlasting winter."

That they were the ravings of a madman was plain. Still, through all its craziness, some there were, who thought they saw faint gleams of greatness shining. But these were few, and most of those who read the paper were with the landlord in saying that it was well he had not killed some one. The other paper was much blotted, and folded into a very narrow strip. I shall not try to picture the wonder of all, when the landlord in a stout voice spelt out—

"I know not, ask not, reck not if beyond
  The silent grave another world there is:—
I long for sleep, unbroken and profound,
  Where aching heart may quiet find and ease."

I will say, however, that all thought the stanza a very bad one, and that Glen was twice mad in being a poet.

As I said before, nothing more was found. The gold was given to the landlord, who suddenly called to mind the fact that his last month's rent was owing, and the papers, as worthless, were bestowed upon the schoolmaster.

Years rolled on, as years will in time, and the old tavern was forsaken, and said to be haunted by Glen's ghost. Old ladies spoke of it in whispers, and the little boys, as they passed it after night, shut their eyes and whistled. Nearly every one had a story to tell of the doings of the uneasy shade. Jones, the doctor, had seen a ball of fire hovering over Glen's grave in the burying ground, one damp, drizzly night. Grubbins, the blacksmith, as he was tottering home

41

from a midnight wassail at the new tavern, was met by the sprite, who hurled him into a ditch, where the poor man's wife found him the next morning. By the elder folks he was sometimes seen washing his hands at the tavern pump, as he had done when he first came into the village.

In fine, then, Tom Smith, whilom Cheops was the only being in the place, who did not feel squeamish about the old tavern. He, however, was a boy for whom every one said no good was in store, and, to gloss not, he was a graceless chap enough. He had a most untoward dislike to spelling books and geographies, and bestowed all his time and love upon Robinson Crusoe, Arabian Nights, and the like. He played truant, and passed hours in the woods dreaming of Sinbad, when he should have been cyphering, and in an old cavern near the village he dwelt—two or three summer afternoons— as the wretched castaway, Crusoe, at times, and again as the forty thieves. Nothing however, seemed to please him so much as wandering through the hollow-sounding rooms of the haunted tavern, and making them answer his wild songs. He would saunter along the hall and up the stairway for hours, and coming out would frighten more fearful urchins than himself by rushing among them with an old hat, which gossip-spell said once belonged to Glen. The seat, which he loved above all others in the old building, was the window-sill of the room where Glen was laid out, and here he was often seen, with his back against one side of the casing, and his heels against the other, seemingly lost in thought. It was this wont of his that made me to write the story, for had it not been for this, there would have been no need to fix on paper those floating bits of village old wife talk, which I have given above.

I say, then, as he was swaggering by the old tavern one night with a crowd of boys at his heels, a dare-devil thought came into his rattle-brain, who should follow him into the house and up to Glen's room. The moon was shining brightly and the old building loomed grimly upon the light. In truth, it was a sorry looking place—the window panes broken, and the sash battered in; the doors fallen, the shutters hanging loosely on the outer walls; the roof sunken, and rotten shingles scattered about—some on end and bearded with moss.

Not a boy would go with him. Even Sammy Clathers' stout heart failed him, and his knees knocked together at the thought. He could lick Tom, and was not afraid of any boy in the crowd, but he was not a going to meddle with ghosts. When words like these fell from the lips of the doughty Clathers, my hero had nothing to do but to go himself, and whooping and singing, he ran up the ricketty steps, and faded from sight in the dim old hall.

When I come to this part of my story, my hand shakes so that I can hardly write; for I call to mind the time when I first heard it, and shiver at the thought of my old child-fears. It was my dear old grandmother ten years dead, who told it me, and I see her now, as she lights her nine o'clock pipe with a long thin bit of paper, which she treads out with her foot. She too has left poor Tom in the tavern hall, and we children are so frightened that the sweat oozes through the dirt on our little palms. If Glen would stand before us in his bare-head and slippers, we could not feel much worse. "Boys," says my grandmother—"some of you go out and get a back log—George, go after a back-log." George has such a sore thumb that he cannot walk. "Well, you go, Willie." I am taken with a headache, and do not like to go out into the cold air. "Well, children," says my grandmother, "we must freeze then till your father comes home." And she goes on with her story. I will do as much.

When my hero was once fairly on the stairway, he felt half minded to go back. But there were the boys who would laugh, and there were the dreadful Clathers who would perhaps thrash him; altogether, he thought flesh and blood were more to be feared than shadow, and so he went up.—The moonlight leaking through the weather-boarding and broken windows lay in ghastly strips along the floor. Tom had trodden the boards an hundred times before, yet never had his boots creaked so loudly, never had the sounds died away so like pain-wrung groans, when he came to the door of Glen's room; however all his fear left him, and he walked boldly in. He went up to the window, with a mind to call to the boys outside; no one was to be seen, however, and so, thoughtlessly seating himself upon the window sill, he began to watch the moonlight as it played along the floor.

How long he had been sitting here he did not know, when, chancing to raise his eyes, he beheld the dreadful spirit bareheaded and slippered as of old. A wan sad smile was on its face, and its voice was like the strain of a wind-harp, as it bade the boy to follow it. I said that Tom cared less for shadow then flesh and blood, and there was something about this weird meeting which was greatly to his liking. He rose, therefore, and went after the flitting ghost. As they passed through the hall by an open window, Tom saw the moonlight shining through his airy fellow.—He thought it odd, too, that his boots should make no noise, and was not sure that he was not a ghost himself. His mind was soon put at ease on this point, however, for on biting his finger, he could hardly forbear crying out with pain. When they came to the pump, which had been dry for a year, the ghost stopped and began to wash his hands in the thick stream which suddenly flowed from the spout. And the frightened boy shuddered to see the water as it dripped from his hands turn to blood!

43

On they sped noiselessly. They skimmed along the air on unseen wings, till they stopped in the heart of a great city. They flitted up the marble steps of a grand old house. Servants in dark livery answered their call, and talked together in dumb show. Not a sound was heard save the wailing of a harp, as they passed through the dim hall. Grim portraits lined either wall, and lamps in gauze drooped from the ceiling; keeping time with the weird music they floated up the stairway. There seemed to be an hundred doors opening from that second hall into which they came, on each of which was painted the dreadful emblem of the pirate's flag, which Tom had often seen in the pictures, which deck the pages of that beautiful novel, "The Buccaneer's Revenge, or Don Matartododeloshombres, el Pirato del Mar de Sangre." Soon they paused before one of these, and as it opened to them, flitted through, and found themselves in a dingy cavern, lighted only by a diamond which sparkled in the forehead of a marble statue. The ceiling was carved and gilded, and hung with cloth of gold.

A spring of water leaked from the pave, and gleamed far adown the windings of the cave.—Quaint tools were scattered about, and the walls were scribbled full of mottoes in an unknown tongue. A crucible and a broken retort, a piece of limestone half turned to diamond, and a bar part gold and part lead, told of the dreams and toils of the alchymist. The ghost seized the bar and dashed it on the floor. "It is the knowledge of evil that makes men mad," he said. They floated through the cavern, out into an open balcony; and the boy saw written over the doorway—"The love of gold is madness."

And now a crowded street was below them. Carriages moved to and fro, and great masses swayed uneasily about. But all was still. There was one in the crowd whose fat body was rubbed against and bruised by a carriage, who opened his mouth as if making a great outcry, but no sound came from his lips. The boy began to weary of the everlasting stillness. He was tired of the ghost who seemed to be growing dimmer and fading slowly away. He was tired of the speechless crowd below. Even wonder and fright could not rouse him from the feeling of carelessness into which he was falling.

Suddenly there came a rushing noise, like the shifting of many wings—the houses were jumbled together, the people and the ghost went out of sight in a flash, and a dull, heavy jar shook the boy's frame.

Poor fellow, he was lying among the rubbish on the outside of the old tavern with his collar bone broken! He cried lustily for help, and Sammy Clathers, whose heart smote him for allowing Tom to go into the old house alone, was the first one on the ground, and helped carry him home. It was many a long and painful day before

Tom got about again; and it was still longer till he was brought to tell the story which I have here given. It gave rise to the only schism which ever distracted the village of X.—one party stoutly holding it to be a dream, and another that it was a true meeting with Glen's ghost, which was never seen after that night. The story has, nevertheless, been handed down by word of mouth from gossip to gossip, and kept whole without break or hurt.

I do not vouch for its truth, but I would not like to have the story thought lightly of, inasmuch as Mr. Smith married my grandfather's second cousin, and is near kin to the Narlies.

[Signed "Will Narlie," *Ohio Farmer*, 11 May 1854]

[Howells's early stories and sketches in the *Ashtabula Sentinel* are rarely so easy to identify as those of "Will Narlie's" in the *Ohio Farmer*, and though his bibliographers have identified a good number of pieces in the family newspaper between 1853 and 1855 as very likely to have been written by Howells, several of these attributions appear highly suspect and others even in error. Fortunately, the items that can be said with certainty to be by Howells are in their execution and literary interest superior to those that editorial and critical prudence should choose to discount. Of the sketches gathered here, only the first, "How I Lost a Wife," an "episode" which appeared in the *Sentinel* in May 1854, is attributed to Howells on evidence solely circumstantial. His antipathy towards dogs, indicated as early as his 1852 diary; his choice of an elderly persona similar to those chosen for other early sketches; and a general agreement by those who have considered the piece that in style and attitude it is wholly in keeping with Howells's writings for this early period are convincing reasons for its inclusion in this collection of Howells's apprentice work.]

HOW I LOST A WIFE

AN EPISODE IN THE LIFE OF A BACHELOR

I am 'down' on dogs! I have the greatest possible antipathy to dogs of all breeds.—Your 'noble Newfoundland,' as they are—inappropriately, I think—termed by their admirers; your faithful St. Bernard; your wiry-haired, active, rat-destroying Scotch terrier; your long legged, consumptive looking greyhound; your pug-tailed, pug-nosed, and very pugnacious bull-dog; your sickly looking and snarling poodle—all, individually and collectively, I abhor. In short, and most emphatically, too, I detest the whole canine race. It is an old antipathy, and as deeply rooted as an elm of a century's growth.

I am aware, however, that the bow-wow tribe is an extensively favored one, and therefore am almost certain that 'I am myself

45

alone,' figuratively speaking, in the opinion I entertain in regard to their respective merits.—Even now, I imagine I hear some nothing-else-to-do young lady, as she lovingly manipulates the soft and glossy curls of her long-eared and red-eyed lap-dog, exclaim, indignantly, 'Oh, the brute!' And a thousand other equally ungenerous and quite as complimentary epithets, I have not the slightest doubt, will be applied to me by the fanciers of the 'noble race,' in their indignation to my individual aversion to—dogs!

'But why this aversion?' some will doubtless, and quite naturally, ask. Ah! 'thereby hangs a tale.' Listen and I'll tell it to you.

The unhappy event occurred years ago, when I was about twenty-three. At that age I was as bashful as a girl who has never indulged in a flirtation, and as modest as a Quakeress. To look a female square in the face would have brought blushes enough to my countenance to make beautiful an ordinary looking girl. That I admired, loved, adored the dear creatures, was true; but always silently and unobserved. However, after a while, I overcame many little peculiarities that kept me aloof from the charming society of dear women. Through the example, aid, and encouragement of an old chum and room mate, Charley B., I became initiated, 'broke the ice,' and was 'going in' with a rush, when I was—unfortunately, I must acknowledge—suddenly checked by an event brought about by a confounded dog! an event that deprived me of a lovely wife, a half dozen lively babies, probably, and a life of blissful happiness. Think of that, ye admirers of the canine race, and pity me; no, don't pity me, but exterminate the race! wipe them all from existence! Husbands who have lovely and confiding wives; wives who have affectionate and faithful husbands; children who have the whole in expectancy—'think of what I am now, and what I might have been'—if it hadn't been for an 'accursed dog,' and raise your voices loud, in unison, in favor of the formation of a Dog-Exterminating Association. I'll invest my pile in it. But to my sad and never-to-be-forgotten story.

My friend Charley had any quantity of lovely sisters and cousins, to whom he introduced me, and with whom I fell in love—one of whom, I should have said—one of the sisters, Mary was her name. Sweet name! And angelic possessor of that sweet name! Could but those happy days be recalled—could I but once more gaze into those brilliantly black eyes; could I but once more press to my palpitating heart that classic form; could I—'Hold your horses!' What am I taking about? I never got quite as far as this; suffice it to say, however, that I was 'up to my neck' in love with Mary, and I flattered myself she smiled approvingly on me.

What a delicious sensation one experiences, at times, when he is in love, doesn't he? If ever a man gets an idea of Heaven, it is about that time. It's some years since I experienced its heavenly influences; still, however, time has not wholly effaced its delicious recollection from my memory. Even now, when I think of Mary, my rather aged blood seems to course more rapidly and warmly through my old veins, giving new life and animation to my somewhat 'shaky' frame.—And then old recollections crowd upon my brain, the angelic face of Mary is before my eyes, and then comes the horrid image of that dog to dispel the enchanting illusion. Get out! Avaunt, ye cursed brute!

Well, as I said before, I fell in love with Mary. Of course I did! How could I avoid doing so? And I flattered myself that the very particular attention I paid to her for a brief period—until the unlucky event (confound that dog) occurred which I have before alluded to—was not at all objectionable.—Oh! what happiness was mine then! What blissful anticipations I revelled in! What—what— never mind now; it's useless to recall those pleasant memories of the past—they only add to the miseries of my bachelor life, and render more heinous in my eyes, a—dog!

Distance alone prevented me from being as frequently in the society of Mary as was my desire. Her residence was in the country, about eight or nine miles from the city; and as money was a limited article with me at that time, and a 'team' rather expensive, my visits were quite necessarily only semi-occasional. About every two weeks, myself and my friend Charley used to pay a visit to the farm; he to see his relatives, and me to—of course the reader can imagine my object. And here again is an opportunity to episode a little. Oh, what—Bah! that infamous dog again! All pleasant recollections of Mary vanish from my mind when I think of that detestable dog.

Well, as I said before, we used to ride out to the farm once about every two weeks; and it was during one of those excursions that a confounded dog 'knocked into a cocked hat' all ideas of matrimony that I ever had, and, of course, lost me a wife.

*   *   *   *   *   *

It was in mid-summer that I paid my last visit to the rural residence of Mary. The weather was excessively hot, and of course an opportunity to enjoy the refreshing atmosphere of the country—the fragrance of clover-fields, the perfume of sweet-scented flowers, and other rural luxuries—and above all the society of one so dear to me as Mary—an opportunity to enjoy all other luxuries, I say, I eagerly embraced. Myself and my friend Charley secured a week's furlough from our employer, and with happy hearts and anticipations of a pleasant time, we left the city.—That afternoon we arrived at our destination. Charley's parents, sisters, and the rest, and Mary, particularly, I flattered myself, were delighted to see us. And, I never can forget how lovely the sweet creature looked on that afternoon.

47

'The very air seemed lighter from her eyes,
They were so soft and beautiful and rife
With all we can imagine from the skies.'

To add to the pleasantness of our visit, also, three or four female cousins had been invited to spend a few days at the farm. They were all beautiful girls too, but so enamored was I of Mary, that I paid but little attention to their many charms. Charley romped and flirted with them, while I confined myself exclusively to the society of his charming sister. How we picked berries, hunted bird's nests and four-leaf-clovers together; what delightful *tête-à-têtes* we indulged in beneath the shade of fruit trees; our moonlight rambles through the garden; of all these, and many other luxuries I shall not speak further; their remembrance only serves to make me feel gloomy, and increase my antipathy to—dogs!

But to the catastrophe I have so frequently alluded to. At a short distance from the dwelling, just at the turn of a road leading from it, ran a fine stream of clear, cool water. It was a charming stream to bathe in, and Charley and myself early in the morning, before the folks were up, used frequently to indulge in the aquatic luxury. One morning, however, he felt like sleeping a little longer and I was obliged to take my usual bath without his company. I arose very early, just as the day was breaking. It was a charming morning— the air cool and refreshing. The rose-bushes were drying their dewy tears, as if in gladness at the approach of day; birds were carolling their morning lay, and—I was thinking. I was thinking of a dream I had the night previous. I dreamed that I was in Paradise—saw angels in profusion, and most conspicuous among them all—was— Mary. The rest of my dream I will leave to the imagination of the reader. I wended my way slowly to the stream, thinking of my dream and various other things.—Divesting myself of my clothes, in I plunged—bathed, swam, splashed and floundered about, for half an hour, until day had fairly set in. The people about the farm were up and about, and then I thought it about time to dress. I went to the spot where I had deposited my clothing, but instead of finding every article there as I had left them, and as I had reason to expect, nothing but my hat, boots and coat remained. Heavens! Here was a dilemma. I looked all around, faithfully and diligently, but the missing articles could not be found: 'Where could they have gone to?' I asked myself. 'Surely there can't be any thieves about so early in the morning. Ha! ha!' I chuckled aloud, consoling myself with the thought that Charley was playing off a practical joke. At that instant I cast my eyes up the road in the direction of the house. Horrors! Right in the middle of the road, and but a short distance from the house, I discovered a huge Newfoundland dog—a gigantic, shaggy brute—the pet of Mary and the rest of the girls—sporting with what I recognized as my new black cassimere pants, and other portions of my apparel. The dog had followed me to the stream unobserved, and the result was as I have mentioned. Oh, how the thieving brute was enjoying himself, tossing high into the air my pants, shaking my shirt, and apparently making merry over the perplexing predicament his mischievousness had placed me in. What misery was I in! I feared to go into the road to recover my clothes, lest my rather immodest appearance might shock some of the female folks, who could not fail to see me, if I did so, from the windows of the house.

'Here, Ponto! Ponto!' I called out, but Ponto didn't come.

I whistled, coaxed, and made all sorts of gestures usually used in such cases, but Ponto was heedless of them all. As if in unbounded ecstasies at my very ludicrous predicament, and apparently exulting over the trick he had served me he went to work with increased liveliness, tossing my clothes high in the air. Taking my fine cassimeres in his jaws, he would run towards me, as if in obedience to my call, but before he got half way to where I stood, he would halt suddenly, snuff the earth, bark, and dart back again like lightning, carrying my pants in his jaws, tossing them high up in the air again, and catching them, shake them in a manner that appeared as if he really enjoyed the sport.—None but one in the same position that I was then placed, can properly appreciate my feelings at that time. What to do I could not possibly conceive. Every moment I expected to see Charley and some of his female cousins— and probably Mary too—issue from the house in search of me, as I had been absent long enough to excite surprise. Well, I finally came to the conclusion to put on what portion of my apparel the thieving dog had left me. This portion, as I said before, consisted of a coat, pair of boots and a hat; a scant supply certainly, for a modest man, as I was, to appear before a bevy of females, as I momentarily expected, for I was positive that my absence would soon be inquired into.

I first drew on my boots, and next my coat. It was a dress coat too, made in the height of fashion, with narrow tails, which, on the occasion, served only to hide a very small portion of my nudity. Thus ludicrously attired, I awaited patiently, but ingloriously the appearance of some person from the house, to whom I could make known my misfortune, and thus get relieved from my very unpleasant predicament. I waited and waited, and began to tire of waiting, and still nobody came. Voices I distinctly heard in the distance, merry voices and ringing laughter greeted me as I sat despondingly contemplating the probable *dénouement* of my contretemps. The sound of the voices gradually grew nearer and nearer; the laughter became more audible; I heard the sweet, musical voice of Mary;

then Charley's joyous and hearty laugh broke in interspersed with the more witching and dulcet laughter of females. How I longed to be with them. What fear and anxiety I suffered as nearer and nearer the voices came.—Again I looked in the direction of the house, with the hope that I might see some of the male members. But such was not my luck. I looked again, standing on tip-toe, and straining my eyes till they seemed to be fairly bursting from their sockets. Hope, this time, dawned in the distance. Charley, my friend Charley, I distinctly saw emerge from the garden into the road. I laughed aloud and danced with joy. I saw a speedy release from my awkward predicament, and blessed the fate that sent it. But disappointment, and such a disappointment! soon stared me in the face, for looking a second time, I saw half a dozen girls, Mary, her sisters and cousins, following like young fawns, in the wake of Charley's footsteps.

'An agile fleetness in their forms,
A tint of morning on their brows,
Their posture full of girlish whims.'

Down the road they bounded, like a drove of frightened deer, crying out, in shrill tones, my name.

'Where is the runaway!'

'Where *can* he be!'

'Frank! Frank!' rang out several sweet voices, among whom I recognized Mary's.—All of a sudden, however, these joyous shouts were changed to different ones.

'We-e-e-e! We-e-e-e! We-e-e-e!' screeched a half dozen feminines.

'He's drowned! He's drowned!' cried some, a conclusion they all seemed to arrive at when they discovered a portion of my clothes.

Two or three fainted, and one or two with stronger nerves, caressed Ponto, the dog, for what they deemed his sagacity in making my sad fate known.

The whole household were speedily alarmed, and all came rushing towards the stream and directly to the spot where I had partially secreted myself behind a small clump of trees. Here was another dilemma. My position was every moment becoming more critical. If I remained where I was, I was certain to become exposed.

I looked eagerly around for a place of concealment. Oh! I felt as if I would have given a kingdom, if I possessed one, for some friendly tree, wherein I might take shelter. I looked again, and, thank heaven! I discovered one. It was but a short distance from me, and unobserved, and with the agility of a squirrel, I mounted it; and just as I had fairly seated myself on an outstretching branch, in a manner that perfectly screened me, half a dozen girls, Mary among the number, arrived on the spot and halted directly under the tree.

'Can he be drowned?' sympathizingly asked Mary. And then I

thought I heard her sob. Delighted at this evidence as I took it, of an attachment to me on her part, my curiosity was excited, and anxious to catch every word spoken by her, I carefully and noiselessly stretched out my body forward on the limb on which I was reposing. Treacherous limb! Unlucky movement! Just as I did so, with a report like a pistol, the limb broke, and down I went, headlong, in the midst of my sympathetic female friends.

The sudden and unexpected catastrophe bewildered me for a moment, and it was some seconds before I fairly recovered from the shock. The first recollection I had was being surrounded by a group of astonished maidens, having each one the appearance of a marble statue. Mary was nearest to me,

'And half in wonder, half in fear,
She gazed with blushes warm.'

But she gazed for only a moment; then uttering a scream, equal in shrillness and loudness to a locomotive whistle, she darted off like lightning, followed by the rest of the astonished crowd. Such a fluttering of muslin, such a screeching, and such a general stampede, I never heard or witnessed. Away they went, like young colts with unlimited pasturage, and soon they were out of sight. I looked round to see if I had been entirely deserted and discovered, but a short distance from me, my friend Charley, rolling on the grass in a paroxysm of laughter. With him the thing was a capital joke, and he enjoyed it wonderfully. But it was far different with me. When I thought of my ludicrous costume, its scant amount—hat, boots and coat—and a narrow-tailed coat—too—when I thought of this, and reflected, that thus attired, I had been seen by Mary, her sister and cousins—but particularly Mary—none of the persuasions, coaxings, beseechings of my friend Charley, could induce me to make my appearance at the breakfast table that morning. No: I resolved instantly to take my departure for the city, and did so as soon as I obtained the requisite wardrobe. I never saw Mary afterwards. She was soon after married, and is now the happy mother of a happy and quite numerous family, and—I'm a bachelor.

Yes, I'm 'down' on dogs—the whole canine race. Don't you think my antipathy to the brutes is justly founded?

[*Ashtabula Sentinel*, 18 May 1854]

[While Howells appears never in public at least to have recalled his early sketch, "What I Saw at the Circus," his elder brother years later identified it as Will's. Joseph Howells was in part correct when he told a Cincinnati reporter in 1883 that his brother's "peculiarities of description" and the characteristic manner in which he treated incident were already here revealed and that he was essentially the same writer in 1854 that the greater world knew afterwards. Howells himself probably would have despaired at the comparison, remembering instead the sketch's precious literosity and the sentimental guise the adolescent chose as a persona. However, he might have been impressed by the boy's interest in the "smaller passions" of life, the "little side-shows of human nature" which it had been his care to record. Several of the phrases and incidents recorded in the sketch remained quick in his memory and recur forty years later in the chapter on "Circuses and Shows" in *A Boy's Town*. But even closer to the fact of the sketch is Howells's poem, "At the Circus," published in the *New York Saturday Press* on the last day of December in 1859.

> I smell the sawdust and smoking lamps,
>   And the ice-cold lemonade;
> And I hear the cries of the little scamps,
>   In their country-best arrayed.
>
> The boys that would like to be trampled to death
>   Under the horses' feet,
> And would think, I suppose, they sold their breath
>   Very dear, for a death so sweet.
>
> They think, God bless them! it's might fine,
>   They count it the highest joy;
> With the painted actress of forty-nine
>   They fall in love, to a boy!
>
> They think that the brass on her arms is gold,
>   And her spangles are silver-flakes—
> They believe she could fly, poor soul! if she would,
>   On the gauzy wings she shakes. . . .
>
> Ah well! I remember, we came together,
>   Playfellows, brothers and all,
> In the wagon; 'twas sweet September weather,
>   The earliest days of the Fall.
>
> And as we went back home through the night,
>   To my heavy, drowsy eyes,
> The stars were the circus-lamps so bright,
>   Swinging about in the skies!
>
> And the yelping of dogs along the road
>   Seemed to me, half-asleep,
> The cheers of the folks, when the poor clown crowed,
>   And mowed, at the smacking whip.

And I had a dream of a circus-world,
  Where the people all wore tights,—
Spangled and painted, and crimped and curled,
  Like the actors under the lights.

The sad-eyed clowns with their dreary hearts
  Made the spectator-world to laugh;
The actors performed their four-horse parts,
  Leaped through balloon, and over staff.

And the women, the wretched tawdry things,
  Made play with their hollow eyes—
Like shabby angels, with moulting wings,—
  Like devils, so evil-wise.

And I, unheeded of all the throng,
  In a very doleful tone,
Stood singing a sentimental song,
  To a dreadful air of my own.

Sometimes I think, when dyspepsia cramps
  My soul, that I live in that dream;
I smell forever the smoky lamps—
Around the ring the stiff piebald stamps,—
  The people applaud and scream!

The advantages that several years' apprentice work gave Howells and the tighter control that the verse form placed on his treatment of the subject favor the later composition, but in matters of observation and response, the two works are clearly one piece.]

WHAT I SAW AT THE CIRCUS

Old Smith's Experience

"E'en learned Athens to our art must stoop,
  Could she behold us tumbling thro' a hoop."

I am an old man, and the brown locks of earlier years are flecked with silvery hairs.—Time has not used me ill, and yet it is many a weary day since I stood, a hopeful boy, and gloated on the doings of the ring.

Long ago, I found that show-bills were deceitful, and the actors never did half the gaudy wood-cuts promised. Long ago, I saw that a grand chariot might be a very shabby wagon. Long ago, I learned that circus-dresses were blazoned with tinsel, and not, as I had fondly thought, with flakes of pure silver. Long ago, I ceased to believe in the newness of the clown's wit. Long ago, I discovered that the actors were often arrant vagabonds, and the actresses were often—ladies! Still, I love the circus, with all its shallowness, and poor succession of hacknied feats. I love to see the antics of Mr. Merryman, and smile at his time-honored jests. I love the parade of ambling steeds, the showy splendor of the ring-master, the flaunting ribbons, gay bannerols, and graceful riders. I love the very prestige that light and dressing lends the thin display; for there is something in the hollowest mockery of grandeur, that lifts the soul above every-day life. So, I took my cane and walking to the pavillion, soon made one of a motley throng of pleasure-seekers.

There were good people from the country, with their children, and the baby that was dandled without rest; there were smart young sprigs in black coats and patent gaiters, with fair girls upon their arms; there were stray little boys, plump and dirty-faced, who stared, with all their eyes, at the lights and empty ring; there were gray old fellows like myself, who gave me good evening as I passed; there were staid villagers with their families, and raw youth from the interior, with thick boots and brief trowsers. Precocity, tart and exacting, was seated side by side with years and sense; folly and wit were crowded together on the same plank; beauty and ugliness were cheek by jowl. I saw grave men and fops, beaus and bachelors, grandmothers and belles, all thrown together, higgledepiggledy. And as I squoze my way to a seat, I could not but liken the scene before me to the great world in which we live. I glanced over the row of faces, and fancied I could discern in their eager looks, an inkling of that strained life-principle that is always hoping and waiting for something. Vice and virtue were betrayed by their several seeming; and coarseness and refinement were relieved by contact; pretence and worth were to be seen in truthful contrast, and the smaller passions were brought into play, and accorded with the epitome in their very littleness.

A burst of a music, however, suddenly put these musings to flight, and lifting my eyes, I saw the arena filled with actors, habited as Roman soldiery. Then came, after a space, the tourneyment, and a knight-templar with a tin shield, hacked swords valiantly with another cavalier, and vanquishing him, received a muslin scarf from the queen of beauty, whose paste-board coronet glanced gayly in the light. All clapped their hands and cheered, the tourneyment broke up, and the knight-templar assisted in putting up a slack-rope! I remember that I witnessed a like scene at my first circus, and thought nothing of the translation of a knight-templar into a supe; but now, I felt a thrill of melancholy as I contemplated the fallen cavalier. He was but a type of a very numerous class; for how many a ball-room belle goes home to dish-water and cows after her gayest triumphs! How many an orator, with the glad shouts of the crowd still ringing in his ears, sits meekly down under the wrath of a scolding wife! How many an editor after writing a vaunting leader, subsides into the humiliation of an empty pocket! How shall I, when you have read my article, become again the rusty old fellow whom nobody knows!

It would be rank impertinence to attempt a description of the ensuing feats. One actor facetiously rolled his body into a lump, and hung by one leg from the ring; another twisted himself in and out of an odd swing; and the slack-rope man whirled ceaselessly, while a gentleman on a carpet below, stuck a feather in his eye, and bumped himself with a cannon ball.

But, if I despair in this, how shall I begin to do justice to the clown! Such "flashes of merriment," such brilliant repartee, such a genial flow of double-intenders! At every sally, a shout of laughter went up from the crowd; and if *I* had read much of the harlequin's wit in the newspapers, I had no right to sneer at those who now heard it the first time. I said, I loved the clown's humor, and so I do; but I found more food for laughter in the glee of those around me. I more enjoyed the delight of the honest countryman, who writhed in convulsive merriment, or the seeming of the urchin who watched the clown with envious laughter, than the brightest efforts of that marvellous creature himself. However, I am quite ready to throw my hat into the air and cry, "Live Dan Rice!"

Nor was I less diverted, with other little side-shows of human nature, which I witnessed on the benches, enacted as they were without previous rougeing and preparation. The mute appeals of the lemonade-boy, as he passed his wares among the crowd, the ruffianism that shewed through a shallow seeming of gentility, as a well-dressed man flung a vulgar epithet at him; the air of patronage that an old gentleman wore as he took a glass of the drink, and paid for it with a bad sixpence; the bumpkin's tender gallantry as he "treated" his inamorata—formed an array of selfnesses, that was pleasing to behold.

At length, however, the performance drew to a close; the ladies had ridden and leaped banners; Paul and Virginia had appeared in a new tableau, for I believe there is no scene in the child-romance, where Paul and Virginia stand on the backs of two rapid steeds with their arms clasping each other's necks; the actors had tumbled, and vaulted; and the clown had exhausted the fountain of his wit.

I confess, that I viewed the departure of the weary crowd with something akin to reluctance; but the demolition of the pavillion was already begun, and they were forced to go. I saw many an urchin who looked vain regrets at the now fading lights, and the silent ring, erewhile the scene of so much gayety. I saw the youth who had been playing gallant for the first night in his life, as he turned the eyes of wistfulness upon the bench where he had been seated so long beside *her*; brightening, at length, as I fancied, over the thoughts of the walk home, and haply, a tender parting. He was a quiet, red-faced boy, in a sultry cravat and black clothes.—I saw, too, the worthy country-gentleman, with his ever-dandled baby, and his wife with her body-guard of children. They were a little tired, I thought, and the children took walking naps on the way out. I saw the smart fellows as they chatted gayly to their companions. I saw the country youth jostled by rowdyism, pass it contemptuously by, and walk forth in sturdy good-humor.

And, as I saw all this, I forgot away some scores of years, and stood among the throng—proud, and happy, and young. I was once more a devout believer in the verity of spangled dresses. The sallies of harlequino, were once more fraught with all their zest and freshness, and I felt an urchin's passionate longing for flesh-colored tights. I was once more filled with the determination that I felt so many years ago, to become proficient in the art of somersaulting; and had a vivid foreshadowing of my first appearance on the sawdust, as ring-master.

It was an idle revery, conjured up by an idle scene; and it was as well, perhaps, that I was abruptly roused from it by stumbling against a candyman's table.

[*Ashtabula Sentinel*, 7 September 1854]

[Young Will no doubt reveled in the cordial and encouraging responses which these apprentice-pieces drew from his family and the readers of the *Ohio Farmer* and the *Sentinel*. But then with the appearance of his first long work of fiction, "The Independent Candidate" which was serialized in the *Sentinel* during the fall and early winter of 1854–55, the bottom dropped out. It was a nightmare from which his creative consciousness was long in freeing itself.

Sometime earlier he had written, or at least begun, an historical romance; but this had not been meant to be seen by others, and when he was found out and the first chapters were read to his amused family, he was justly resentful. That experience was happy, however, compared to the shame he felt when his ambitious romance about contemporary politics failed to develop as smoothly as the novels of others he had so attentively read in preparation. But "after a succession of several numbers," it "faltered and at last would not go on" (*YMY*, p. 83). The boy was in utter despair, and the man the boy became remembered the bitter taste of public shame.

It was all very well at the beginning, but I had not reckoned with the future sufficiently to have started with any clear ending in my mind, and as I went on I began to find myself more and more in doubt about it. My material gave out; incidents failed me; the characters wavered and threatened to perish on my hands. (*MLP*, pp. 66–67)

The only thing for him to do was "to force it to a tragic close" (*YMY*, p. 83), simplifying through death and marvelous disaster the wonderful complications into which the plot had innocently wandered. Before its ignoble finish, however, one old farmer came to the *Sentinel* office and berated the editor within the author's hearing for giving his readers such drivel in the name of fiction, and even William Cooper Howells, trying as best he could to comfort his son in this strange disaster, could find no word of praise for "The Independent Candidate."

Still the story has its merits and moments, and Howells afterward thought it neither badly conceived nor "attempted upon lines that were mistaken" (*MLP*, p. 67). If it had not been for the shame and anguish that he had suffered at the time, he should have liked, he believed, some time after mastering his art to have written a story on the same lines, and it is a pity he didn't. Certainly had he kept his focus on the political issues and situations and shunned the sentimental and the romantic, he would have made something worth his time and tears. Politics were the nation's pastime, its amusement and public ritual; the aggression and hostility they allowed were far more satisfying than that decorum which was becoming synonymous with polite, middle-class life in America. As Alexis de Tocqueville had noted a few years earlier: "The greatest concern and almost the only pleasure which an American knows is to take part in his government and to discuss its measures. . . . If an American were condemned to occupy himself only with his own affairs, he would be robbed of half his existence . . . and his wretchedness would be unbearable." But the forms of sentimental fiction that reigned in America during the 1850s were hardly compatible with the political realities of caucus meetings and public rallies, and besides, Howells, while ardent in his political beliefs, was not especially drawn to the intricacies of political machinery. That sentimental love interest and maudlin emotionality should finally triumph in "The Independent Candidate" is not in the least bit surprising; that they did, however tenuously and briefly, coexist with the commonplace realities and situations, the humor and generally truthful portrayal of village life, is what makes the story matter; and although it would take Howells fully twenty years to learn the lessons and rid himself of the debilitating fear "The Independent Candidate" represented for him, this too was a necessary part of his education, and his only regret should have been that it had taken place in the pages of the *Ashtabula Sentinel*, and not in his private study hole under the stairs at home.]

THE INDEPENDENT CANDIDATE

A STORY OF TO DAY

CHAPTER I—WAT'S LETTER

BEAUVILLE, July—.
Beauville, my dear George, would hardly be called a business place in its liveliest moments; and as I rode along its turfy streets this afternoon, the little village seemed to have fallen asleep. A couple of law-students were having a very listless game of checkers in the shade of some locust trees fronting the office, and a boy whose legs were scorched a mellow brown from exposure to the sun, was gravely wading up and down the gutter behind a shingle, which he had cheated himself into the belief was a ship. There was a single steed hitched to a post in front of J. Hasker's store; a very smart boy stood upon the threshold of that establishment, who twisted his brimless chip hat as I passed, and requested me to go it. My attention, moreover, was called to the fact that my horse's legs went up and down, and that I was a roarer. With the exception of this pleasing youth, the horse, the brown-legged boy and the law students, I saw no live thing in Beauville, till the ostler of the Napoleon Hotel came forth and took my horse. In justice to all, however, I must say that I had to call for some minutes before the varlet deigned to notice me. I walked into the bar-room. A beer-keg lay in one corner, and a party of blue-bottle flies were making merry over the vile stuff that oozed from the bung. The other corners were severally taken up by a dog, a saddle, and a gun. Upon a row of shelves against the eastern wall were set decanters of brandy, gin, wine, and so forth. A dingy phalanx of Boston crackers graced the outer edges of the shelves, and tumblers of cigar-lighters were stationed at intervals between the liqueur-jars. Over all drooped a branch of asparagus.

But I need hardly describe the inside of a country barroom. It is enough that in the centre of the floor, the worthy John Trooze was taking a cozy trip to the Land of Nod, in the only chair to be seen. He did not seem in any hurry to get back, and snored with the lustiness of a man who got some good of his sleep. I cannot say, my dear George, that my spirits rose at the sight of him either on your account or mine. You would not, I thought, be likely to find a very active champion in John Trooze; and I was in deadly fear of waking the dog in the corner, if I ventured to punch up his master.

58

By dint, however, of skillfully tickling the sleeper's nose with my whip-lash, I made out to route him.

He was all life in twinkling.

"Mr. Trooze?" I said, handing him your letter.

"Oom," and he opened the epistle and read through with many commendatory puffs and snorts. When he was done, he said it was blamed scaly, and wanted to know how I did: shaking hands with me at the same time till my arm tingled.

I was quite well, I thanked him, and not knowing what else to say, I begged to be enlightened as to the health of Mrs. Trooze, and family.

Mr. Trooze assured me they were alive and kicking, and then opening a door, he bade Sary Ann get something to eat.

"Blamed scaly!" said Mr. Trooze. "I could 'a' told 'em that old skunk of a Cuffins 'ud a run in, in spite of 'em, with that mealy-mouthed delegation from Vosentown. I saw how it was goin', the second ballot; and says I, 'you're a cocked hat. But we'll do what we kin for you, George,' says I, 'but he's agoin' ahead of you.' 'Cuss me, if he aint,' says George." And Trooze took a chew of tobacco.

Perhaps Mr. Trooze's report of your conversation was not *verbatim*. I was so shocked at the profanity attributed to you, that I could not but deem it an interpolation.

"And so," said Mr. Trooze, "George is goin' to cut under 'em."

"Mr. Berson," I replied, "has consented to the use of his name, as an independent candidate, feeling that Mr. Cuffins is unworthy to receive the votes of a free people. Believing that Mr. Cuffins has been put in nomination by a clique which has brooded like a—a— a night-mare over the councils of the people of Ecks County. Confident that if Mr. Cuffins were elected, anarchy and misrule would involve our now happy land, and the folds of the American flag would be tarnished forever. Therefore, Mr. Trooze, with a beautiful trust in the virtue of the freemen of Ecks, Mr. B. has consented to run as an independent candidate for our State Legislature. Aware of the flattering fact that the great body of his friends is to be found among the citizens of Beauville, he has so far honored me as request that I get up a public meeting this evening, in Beauville, and address the people in his behalf."

I was rather proud of my little speech; and Mr. Trooze told me I would pass, and gave me a very meaning look. "And now," added he, as Sary Ann rung a bell to let us know that she had got something to eat, "I'll g' round, an' see ef you can hev the school-house."

Sary Ann, whom I afterwards found was the spouse of John Trooze, conducted me into the dining room, and poured out my tea with an air of such coldness that I was afraid I must have given her some offence. Be that as it will, the kind lady melted almost into good humor, when I kissed her latest-born, and vowed rapturously that it was the very picture of its mother. Indeed, it did look like her, for it had a wide mouth, and a nose that pointed skyward with an ugliness wholly the landlady's. Young Trooze was seated on his mother's knee, and I must say that I never saw a pugger pair in my life.

"What's your name, bubby?" I ventured to ask, after the picture had shewn his liking for me by filching a bit of meat from my plate.

"Marquis de Lafayette Trooze," answered the picture, stoutly enough. Whereupon his mother put him through a series of tricks for my amusement.

Luckily for me, Mr. Trooze burst into the room, just as the picture was making-believe to drive the rocking chair down a very steep hill, and told me that several of your friends wished to see me in the barroom. I bowed to the landlady, parted lovingly with the picture, and followed John Trooze.

I hope, my dear George, I will not have to meet a *great* many more of your friends, for those whom I have seen already are a sorry pack of Yahoos. In the barroom I found some half dozen fellows, in costumes that varied between the fashions of the last century and those on Scott's plate for the year of grace 18—. Your friend Bokus, your legal friend Sliprie, your mercantile friend Hasker, your publican friend Trooze, and your wretched friend Larrie were all met. The chief business of this mighty conclave seemed to be the spitting of tobacco-juice upon every side. By dint of much explanation I was introduced to the crowd; and was informed by Sliprie, that the gentlemen before me were a committee of G. Berson's political admirers. They had consulted together as the propriety of my addressing the citizens of Beauville, and were agreed that it was best to postpone the intended meeting until next week. Of course, I could say nothing to this but that if they were so agreed, I would submit to their decision. So you see that I have done nothing as yet—thanks to your Beauville admirers. However, I shall stop here until next week, when I will lay myself out in your behalf.

Punch up the *Herald* man. He ought to come out savage. Remember me to *la cousine*, and believe that in Beauville and elsewhere, I am very affectionately yours,

Walter Larrie.

I dare say, that young Wat Larrie is no more given to romancing than other gentlemen of his age and disposition; and I would have my readers look kindly upon the fibs in the foregoing epistle. Above all would I have them forget away the wickedness of the little humbug which he makes use of when he says that he will stop at Beauville until next week.

CHAPTER II—MERLA

There is a witchery even in the name.—It seems to melt upon the tongue and leave a sweet taste in the mouth after it is spoken. Walter never can pronounce the word like other people. There is old Mr. Carmin who gives it a strong nasal twang; and there is Merla's widowed aunt, who has a voice as musical as a cracked cowbell, and throws all its melody into utterance of that fairy name. But that does not change the affair in the least; for when the soft young fellow ventures to speak it himself, the two laughing syllables bubble from his lips, and the dream-picture of a dear face smiles him into a very languor of bliss and vexation.

I am not rash enough to hazard the assertion that the fat gentleman who may give this a chance reading, was ever in love. Nor do I mean to say, either, that one of the "first men of our place," who had bartered this many-a-year the thoughts of bright eyes for the glitter of bright dollars, ever so much as winked when he used to hear somebody's name pronounced. If I do not venture anything of this, what folly would it be for me to hint that several grave heads of families whom you have all seen, once thrilled at the sound of a step that was all grace! or the sight of a form and a face that were a union of all the beautiful forms and faces in the world! Very long ago the grass grew green upon the graves which hide the faces and the forms; and the little worlds of hope and love that clothed them broke, and left life cold and real!

Nevertheless, Wat Larrie is hopelessly in love with Merla, and has been ever since the party given at the Cuffinses, which all the young folk of Errington remember so well.

"Miss Cuffins, Mr. Larrie," cried Wat's cousin Lizzy, who had been in a fever for more than two weeks, to bring them together. Indeed, Lizzy declared she would neither eat nor sleep till Wat had seen Merla. But she did both heartily, notwithstanding.

Merla and Walter sat down together, and Wat suddenly forgot what to do with his hands, and twisted his fingers together in a weak and foolish manner.

The talk was of a thousand and one silly things, and when Wat found himself at his uncle's house, after the party, he sat down and wrote a long epistle to a friend:

"P.S.—I had almost forgotten to say that I have been fool enough to fall in love. A beautiful piece of business for a youth who has been 'love's whipster'! Do not be very hard upon me for she is as fair as sunrise! I could not help it."

As for Merla, she was seized with a great desire to visit her dear Harry, the next morning, before breakfast was fairly over.

"Poor Harry is so sick, you know, aunt, and I think I ought to go and see her. Besides I've got so many new things to shew her,—and—and she'll want to hear all about the party."

So Merla went.

Harry was ill enough. Her cheek and eye were very bright; and her lips were hot and crisp. But she greeted Merla with a tender smile.

Merla shewed her "new things,"—her winter bonnet, and shawl and muff—asked Harry if they were not nice, dear—and then began to talk of the party.

"And O! Harry,—you ought to see my new beau. He is mine—because—wait I'll whisper it—because he didn't speak to hardly anybody else the whole evening."

"Well, is he handsome, Merla?" asked Harry, with true girlish curiosity in her friend's amour.

"As a picture!" cried Merla.

"And smart?"

"You'd better believe it!"

"Can't you think of anybody he looks like? What sort of a nose has he got?"

"Why—I don't—I couldn't say exactly. Only it's a very pretty one. And such eyes! O d-e-a-r!"

"Has he straight hair or curly?" Merla's questioner went on, lifting herself upon her elbow.

"O! it's a lovely black—and as curly as—as"—

"Dinah's, maybe," said Harry.

"Why H A R R Y!" cried Merla, prolonging her words with feminine emphasis. "What a little wretch you are!"

And then Merla pretended to be very angry, and made-believe to cry, and laughed, and declared that she was going to set her cap for Mr. Larrie, and found out that she ought to have been home hours ago—and so went.

I am afraid to follow up the friendship of Walter and Merla to the point where its platonic-ness deepened into something warmer, and gossip began to grow rife as to the likelihood of their making a match: I say I will not dwell upon these matters, lest the reader's patience give out. It is enough that the day following Wat's arrival in Beauville, saw his departure thence upon a long self-promised jaunt to see Merla.

The road to Errington runs through the richest bottom lands in Ecks. A silver stream keeps the turnpike company nearly the whole way—now winding dreamily over a wide plain, where the green corn-fields stretch endlessly away; now foaming and dashing over a rock-built dam, and widening into sheeny ripples below; now sheathing itself between two jutting hills, and again flashing into the sunlight, and bordering the emerald skirts of the meadows. Here and there a cabin nestles on the swell of the uplands, with the smoke curling softly from its chimney, and white-headed children playing near the door. Snow-white farm-houses dot the landscape on every side; and the gray barns loom up from yellow fields of rye and oats. Cattle are feeding in the pastures, and drinking lazily from the river, where the fences have waded into the stream, and enclosed little pools its water. Birds are making merry in all the woods and fields around. The jays call harshly to each other from the elms, and the flickers make love in the deadenings. The meadow-larks and quails pipe sweetly from the new stubble fields. The halcyon poises himself in the air above the ripple, with a loud chattering, and then darts into the water. The blackbirds are issuing from their noisy settlements in the sycamores; and pensive turtle-doves are cooing in the bosky dales. Every sight and sound is of beauty and melody.

Perhaps Walter is conscious of all this. But I am afraid his heart is not open to the gentle teachings of nature. I am afraid he is even listless, and thinks nature a bore, as the sorry nag he bestrides, trots along toward Errington.

[*Ashtabula Sentinel*, 23 November 1854]

CHAPTER III

An after-supper listlessness pervades the whole village. The heat and bustle of the day are over, and Oldbury gives itself up to the enjoyment of twilight. Little boys, in scattered groups, are launching dust-rockets into the air, and assailing the buggies as they rattle to and fro along the streets. Here and there, an easy smoker may be seen sauntering toward his evening haunt in the post-office, or pausing to hold a moment's chat with a friend on the queer turn politics have taken. On the tavern stoop several urchins, just verging into loafer-hood, are seated in the chairs which are always filled, an hour later, by a choicer coterie of thorough-bred loungers.—A bevy of serene office-holders, linger about the court-house steps, and talk together in idle clumps: and laugh uproariously at jokes which reach the sidewalk only in hoarse, indistinct whispers. It is yet too early for moon-lighting, and no merry, two-and-two strollers are abroad to crowd one from the pave. Quiet home-folk, standing near front-gates, gaze and guess at passers-by; and some, whose in-door toil ended at five, are refreshing themselves with hoe and spade among the thrifty garden-beds which flank the white houses.

Twilight is to day and night what those weeks of mellow sunniness which halo the going-out of October, are to fall and winter. The garish beauty of summer day melts into the more pensive loveliness of evening; and night with dreamy stealth dusks the valley and the hill, and seems half-mournfully to hover near the little realm of light on the plain: the rich season of red and yellow fields and woods fades slowly away behind soft veils of purple and amethyst, and winter calms his blustering gales until she breathes her last amid the bliss and plenty she has strewn around. In the gentle musings with which they fill the heart, the Twilight and Indian Summer have kin, as well. The same quiet blending of light and shade, and the same muffling of sound with melancholy stillness, invite to revery in both; and the forgetfulness of earth-life that one tastes in the twilight of the day, is drunken with a sweeter and deeper draught in the twilight of the year. If angels ever journey on errands of peace and mercy to this world, they fly nearest at such times!

I say, then, that in this twilight, among the other sights worthy of note, Mr. Gilky can be seen at work, nailing up a hole in the fence, with his wife near to lighten his toil by the charms of gossip and small-talk. It is not in my thoughts to give anything but a very brief sketch of Mr. Gilky and spouse, as that gentleman straightens his back from the painful arch into which it has been bent, and glances down upon the pride of his youth with feelings of joy and love. It is enough for me to say that Mr. Gilky is a man of some thirty Septembers, with watery blue eyes, and weak expression of whiskers. He has, moreover, a hooked and drooping nose, and puckered mouth; and is clad, at this speaking, in a dress-coat which has seen better days, a waistcoat, slightly frayed, shoes well-aired and roomy, and a pair of pantaloons very lofty in the skirts. On the other hand, Mrs. Gilky is a brief woman, in a faded calico dress and gingham apron. Her eyes have a slight squint, if I may be allowed the word, and are of a light grey. It may be from sympathy with her eyes, that the good lady's nose juts from her face with such perverse crookedness, but I am not sure. Her lips, however, may be safely deemed to have nothing in common with neighboring features. The upper rests upon two fairy tusks, and the lower slopes backward with a graceful curve.

Angelica and Moro Gilky, are a very loving couple. Their marriage was purely a love-match. A church-mouse would have been reckoned a Crœsus when compared with Mr. Gilky, in point of worldly wealth; and the marriage-portion of Angelica was leaner than the turkey of Job. Both, however, were plentifully endowed with that cheap thing called *heart*. But no base love of animal beauty entered into the etherial passion which consumed the soul of each. All was pure and spiritual: partly, I suppose, because the charms of Angelica were of the soul, rather than of the face, and partly because Moro's intellect overshadowed his personal attractions. Of a truth, there never was a worthier and plainer pair.

I have spoken of Mr. Gilky's mental greatness. Ill-natured people have been known to say that only his wife is aware of his powers

64

of mind; but I place little faith in this.—Any one who will listen
for ten minutes to Mr. Gilky's commonplace remarks will be set at
ease on this point. His use of huge words, where homely monosyl-
lables would do quite as well, is enough to prove him a savant alone.
The daw who rigged himself out with peacock's feathers, was a very
silly bird, and the donkey who played lion was a great ass: but this
does not shew Mr. Gilky to be a fool if he chances now and then
to misapply a lumbering Johnsonism, or happens to speak ungram-
matically. The shafts of study may not have been sunk, as yet, into
the rich beds of thought-ore; but Mr. Gilky is aware of his strength,
and will some day, his wife feels sure, make a splash in the world.
He has always been on the brink of doing something. Perhaps he
has diddled. Perhaps he has been kept down by a certain love of
small beer and large brandy. I cannot say; but I know that Moro
Gilky is to-night no whit wiser, nor greater, nor richer than when
he first began the world.

It is at the moment when Mr. Gilky raises himself to reply to
some remark of his wife, that he catches sight of George Berson
coming across the street toward him.

Mr. Berson lifts his hat and bows. There is crape on the hat.

Mr. Gilky returns the salutation, and Angelica smiles winningly;
albeit she has often said the sight of Mr. Berson always gave her
the nerves.

"Fine evening!" says that gentleman.

"Delightful!" and Mr. Gilky rapturously twiddles the hatchet,
which is still in his hand.

"Mrs. Gilky, I see, is out taking the air—like the rest of us.
Pardon me! My cigar is offensive." Mr. Berson makes a feint of
throwing it away.

"No, no! Don't. It's very agreeable!—Mr. Gilky smokes cigars!"
cries Angelica, with an arch look at Moro.

"And commons, I dare swear, at that," Mr. Berson thinks. "With
your leave then, I'll keep mine," he adds aloud, with an easy nod.
"The fact is, one becomes quite wedded to these little vices, after a
while. D' ye think we're going to have rain, Mr. Gilky? That bank
of clouds in the west looks like it."

"Well—the dry weather has been of such long durashin, one
doesn't hardly like to prognosticate," Moro says with a deeply meditative expression.

Angelica thinks we have no reason to complain, she is sure.

"No, we have not," Mr. Berson admits, leaning his arms on the
top of the fence.—"It might be a great deal worse than it is. Your
garden don't seem to suffer? Those are fine cucumbers."

"Yes," answers Moro, eagerly. "A peculiar speshees. Makes a
very excillent pickil." Mr. Gilky is somewhat stagy in his pronun-
ciation.

"I would like to get a few, then, if you'd sell them," Mr. Berson remarks.

Mr. Gilky says they are not for sale, but he might spare some, if Mr. Berson would accept them.

"Why—I thank you indeed," is the reply. "But don't inconvenience yourselves."

"No inconvenience at all, sir." And the cucumbers are plucked, and placed in a little basket by the ready-handed Angelica.

Mr. Berson thanks them again and again; "And now, Mrs. Gilky, I'm going to take your husband off with me, for a while. I expect you wont thank me for it."

Angelica hopes he wont keep him long; and Moro starts for the house, to change his coat, as he says. Luckily Mr. Berson will not hear of it, or the credit of Moro's wardrobe would have suffered sadly.

"Wont you take a cigar, Gilky," says Mr. Berson, when they are at last off. "Couldn't well offer you one before your wife, you know. Women pretend to like these things, but they don't."

Mr. Gilky is obliged. He believes he will take one.

"That's a pretty snug little place of yours," Mr. Berson remarks, when both cigars are lighted.

"Why-e-e," Mr. Gilky rather grudgingly admits, "it isn't mine yet. Though I intend purchasing it."

"Ah! indeed—I thought it was yours."—Which is a sly bit of humbug. "A man of your abilities, now, ought to have a home of his own in a country like this."

"Quite true, sir," Gilky says, very plaintively, "but a man who has to contend with adversitee, can't have but a poor chance in a place where land is a hundred the acre, and building materials— Lord!"

"Perhaps you're right," is the bland assent. "I should think, however, you might get some kind of work better than grubbing around at all sorts of jobs. You might, and ought to raise yourself above your present level.—Your wife, now, is a woman of mind, and she'll tell you the same thing."

"She has, on very numeris occazhins," Mr. Gilky admits.

"Not," says Mr. Berson removing his cigar and blowing a cloud, "not that I want to disparage labor, at all—Heaven knows! But I was thinking that some kind of writing would suit your turn of mind better. For instance,—and that puts me in mind of what I was going to say."

Mr. Gilky's eyes grow waterier than ever as he bends to listen.

"You know that I'm running for the legislature this fall on my own hook. I've been kind of shoved and coaxed into it: but I will do my best to come out ahead, now I *am* into it. I'm not trying to humbug you, you see—for a man of your perception wont be humbugged. I'm coming right to the point. The fact is, I want some one to go out and see how the land lies. Now, my cousin, Larrie," continues Mr. Berson, with an air of great confidence, "is doing what he can for me in that way; but I want an older head at it."

Mr. Gilky says "Just so," very nervously, and Mr. Berson goes on.

"As I said, I sha'n't use any palaver with you. I know it wont go down. If you were a common, every-day chap, now, I might go on about the good of the country, and that sort of thing. Candidates generally get the name of liars and humbugs, anyhow—so they have to be liars and humbugs when it pays. But I'll just tell you, the matter is simply this: I want to go to the Legislature, and I'm going there, if I can make the votes to send me. D—n 'em!" cries Mr. Berson, "I'll break up that infernal clique, if it breaks ME!"

Mr. Gilky grows still more nervous.

"Now, Gilky, you're a man of—the world, and I want to know if you're green enough to throw away this chance of making money? I make you the same offer I did Larrie. You are to go around the county and see my friends in the townships, write me about the feeling on the subject, and get up enthusiastic demonstrations. You are to talk privately in my favor, and see what can be done as to votes. There's no great harm in all that? Now, *will you do it?*"

Mr. Gilky does not know. He is not certain; but he thinks he will. Could Mr. Berson allow him time for consideration?

"O to be sure! Take till to-morrow.—Only don't mention it to your wife. I am a believer, I must confess," adds Mr. Berson, "in the old saw, that a woman can't keep a secret."

The talk has brought them to a fine, large house, with a grassy yard, adorned with flowers and enclosed by an iron fence. It is Mr. Berson's residence. A lady on the doorstep, and a child standing at the gate, are the only persons to be seen.

"Why Clara!" says the candidate, as the child springs into his arms, "what a little romp! Come—take this basket to aunty."

"I wont!" cries the little girl. "Let aunty come here. I'm going to stay with you."

"O now—do. That's a good girl. I'll get you some candy."

"Will you, though?" Clara asks. "I don't believe it."

"Hut-tut. You oughtn't to talk so. I will get you some."

"Upon your word and honor?"

"Yes, upon my word and honor."

"Then I'll take it," said Clara, and ran off with the basket to the lady on the steps.

"Wont you come in, Gilky?" Mr. Berson asks.

No, Gilky believes not. The night is becoming quite advanced.

Then Mr. Berson will go up town with him; and the two saunter along together, talking earnestly. When they reach Gilky's residence, he begs to know something as to "the remunerashin," and Mr. Berson whispers him, and asks "What do you think of that?" Mr. Gilky says it will do, and goes into the house, feeling very much like a man who has been knocked off cheap.

Mr. Berson resumes his walk. He is not a very bad man; and privately, would scorn to do a mean or dishonest thing. With too many others, however, he thinks honor and its kindred virtues, like dressing-gowns and easy slippers, are meant only for home use. He never dreamed of such a thing as an upright politician, and deems any stratagem fair in the game of State. "Gilky, now," he argues, "is a poor, sickly devil, really not able to work, and if I can throw a little something into his way, now and then, I ought to do it. As for its morality, I dare swear it isn't a great deal worse than the common run of—such matters. Besides, Gilky's just the man for this business. He wont know when he's playing second fiddle, and Sliprie can wind him round his finger."

What with thus musing, and hoping, and wishing, the candidate soon finds himself at the door of his office. It is unlocked, and upbraiding his forgetfulness, Mr. Berson goes in, and turns the key upon the inside.

All country law-offices are alike. There is a writing table in each, with a sheet or two of fools-cap lying upon it, a box of wafers, and some steel-pens. There are always more or less desks covered with green baize, and a book-case filled with dry-looking tomes in calf. There is, moreover, a stove in the middle of the room, which is used for heat in winter, and as a spittoon in summer. Not a great deal more is revealed by the candle which Mr. Berson lights and places upon the table.

A quire of letter-paper is laid before him, and the candidate begins to write. A very pretty hand. Very swift, too. The quick pen glances along the page, and the graceful letters are formed in rapid succession. A quiet, pleasant scratching the pen makes, and a fly upon the window, whom the light has awakened, hums drowsily.

Suddenly a sound, as of a heavily drawn breath, is heard. The writer lifts his head, peers into the gloom which has thickened in the corners, and listens. It is nothing; and again the pen is at its task. The drowsy fly is growing drowsier, and his song deepens an octave. The candle-wick grows long and droops its crown of angry red toward the writer. The night is very still outside; and the barking of the dogs alone disturbs the quiet, as some straggler hurries home.

But the noise again! Looking earnestly into one of the darkest corners he thought he could discern a wild face that stared upon him with its heavy eyes.

In the sunniest day, a vagrant cloud will hide the sun, and fling his dark shadow upon the fields below. Gay hopes and dreams of fame had bloomed in the heart of the ambitious man. But they shrunk now and withered, as the cloud hovered over them. A dim remembrance of a sad tale, half-told and half-withheld, about the doom that might be his; the recollection of certain wild freaks that he had witnessed in his father; the memory of a wretched old man, who was the terror of his childish years, and who died at his father's house, a dotard and crazed—all came thronging up.

George Berson was not a coward, and if he had deemed the noise real, he would have boldly sought its cause. But the dread that it is effect of his own fancy, and the fore-runner of a dreadful fate, unnerves him, and the pen drops from his lax fingers.

It would be a relief to hear it once more; and now it comes, mingled with a snuffling groan. The candidate's heart lightens with a bound. Of course it is the snoring of some drunken straggler, who has tried the office-door, and taken up his quarters on the floor. The candle is raised, and darts its light full upon the form of a man who has just lifted himself into a sitting posture under a desk in the corner. His clothes are foul and ragged. A bundle lies at his feet, and one hand grasps an empty bottle.

[*Ashtabula Sentinel*, 30 November 1854]

CHAPTER IV—RATHER DIDACTICAL

"Sin juramento me podras creer que quisiera que este libro, como hijo del entendimiento, fuera el mas hermoso, el mas gallardo, y mas discreto que pudiera imaginarse."
—CERVANTES, *Prologue to Don Quijote*.

Nor do I think any reader of mine need scruple to believe me when I tell him that I would like to make this the most beautiful, lively, and discreet story that ever was penned. If I do not, he will please to remember that my failure was not from lack of willingness to do better. Let him remember, moreover, that I have not the high-topping quaintness of Lippard, nor the gory skill of Emerson Bennett or Lieut. Murray, and that I shall not even attempt to imitate these masters; but shall content myself with following, at goodly distance, the less dazzling authors of *Pendennis* and *Bleak House*. Let him, I say, who is wont to regale himself with the literary blood-puddings of the great western novelist, or to gloat over the faithful pictures of sea-life which the man of pen and sword has furnished us, remember that I can offer him nothing of the kind. Unfortunately, I have neither Indians nor Pirates to deal with, and it is such a very serious thing to kill off a Christian, that I cannot find it in my heart to slaughter so much as a single character, as yet. It is true that I might have Merla fall sick of ague, or have Walter hang him with his neckcloth; I could make an end of Mr. Gilky by means of *delirium tremens*, or could drown the heir of the house of Trooze in a tub of rain-water with a mere stroke of the pen: but I would fain have these children of thought, play at foot-ball with chance for a while; and I cannot but think some kind heart would be pained to see them brought low.

"Why don't you, then," cries Old Smith, to whom I have read the foregoing, "why don't you, being so anxious to please even sanguinary readers, invent a postmaster, and have him run over by a stage-coach. I would!"

I—(in the greatest amazement)—"My dear sir!"

Old Smith—(thrusting his cane violently into one of the many holes in my carpet)—"Yes! Of all 'whom God made upright,' I do think they are the most"—

I—(hurriedly)—"Wait one moment! I see you are one of those unreasonable men who believe every justice of the peace is a Shallow, and every postmaster an"—

Old Smith—"Infernally sulky, scurvy corporal Nym! 'That is the humor of it.'"

I—"Just so. Now let me show you how ridiculous such a belief is. Here, for instance, is the postmaster of Oldbury. Not a miracle, I'll admit; but still most amiable, polite and courteous. I declare it's quite a pleasure to prepay one's letters, when one remembers it will benefit him. At least, you would not style our postmaster a Nym."

Old Smith—(grimly)—"Maybe I have been too hasty. But railing at the class as I did, is a right guaranteed us by the constitution; and if one happens to accuse one wrongfully, it can't be helped. They all seem so like a set of"—

I—(gravely and triumphantly)—"Mr. Smith whatever may be your opinion of postmasters, I certainly cannot suffer one to be run over by a stage-coach in my story. On reflexion, I am sure you regret your little burst of spleen."

Old Smith—"Well, well, postmasters aside, then. What do people say of your story?"

I—(nervously chewing my pen)—"Why the fact is, it hasn't excited a great deal of attention, yet. I read the first chapters to my aunt, who pronounced them excellent. She is so deaf, however, I'm afraid she didn't hear half of it."

Old Smith—"And Jobkins says they are very poor.—You are fond of quoting Cervantes. Perhaps you remember a little fable of Iriarte's,—The Bear, the Monkey and the Sow. If I have not forgotten, the moral was this:

"Guarde para su regalo
Esta sentencia un autor:
Si el sabio no aprueba, malo!
Si el necio aplaude, peor!"

I—"Well, how does that apply to my case? My aunt is not a fool, nor Jobkins a savant."

Old Smith—"No, but he is a man of taste, and your aunt is deaf. All things being equal, you ought to 'smell a fault.'"

I—"Jobkins is prejudiced. He regards me enviously.—I am afraid, however, that every man who ever ran for legislator will think I am trying to personify him in Berson."

Old Smith—"O! console yourself with the thought that they probably don't read your story."

It is very plain that Mr. Smith dislikes my getting the better of him about postmasters. Howbeit some new actors in the play, who have talked in dumb-show all the while Smith and I have been chatting, will now advance to the foot-lights, and represent an instructive and pleasing scene.

CHAPTER V

"When a man comes into convention," says Mr. Cuffins, raising his head, and thrusting it forward like a turkey gobbler in the act of listening, "when a man comes into convention, is balloted for and nominated, *or* defeated, he ought to abide by that decision—abide by that decision."

"Hem!" says the editor in a meek, bored way, "to be sure—certainly."

"Mr. Berson," continues Mr. Cuffins, "than whom there is no greater gentleman in the county, *personally*,—came into convention and was fairly dealt by. And now, to see him *in arms*, as it were, against the regular Whig nominee, looks bad—Mr. Doan—looks bad."

The editor chews the thumb-nail of assent.

"It is not," cries Mr. Cuffins briskly, "for me to say that convention did wrong in preferring me to Mr. Berson, by not making an effort to crown their choice with success. I shall strain every nerve to accomplish it."—And Mr. Cuffins looks like a very determined and virtuous old gobbler. "The good of the republic depends upon our putting down bolters."

"Why," retorts the editor, "in our own party—yes!"

"Exactly. Of course, we're not going to make a fuss when the locos bolt." Which is such a good joke that its worthy father chuckles over it till he is quite red in the face.

"The question now is, will the locos nominate?" Mr. Doan says, when Cuffins has subsided.

Cuffins grows very grave. He had not thought of that.

"If," Mr. Doan goes on, "they were to unite with the independents, it might go hard with us. The last Herald looks that way."

"Well," remarks Cuffins, dryly, "can't something be done?"

"I don't know what," the editor replies.—"We can't control the movements of other parties. The only chance is to chip off voters when the rub does come—one by one."

"Humph! that's a very poor prospect. We must try to have a nomination. Sliprie, of Beauville, ought to be put up to call a convention. The fact is, ours was held too soon—too soon."

"I don't know but it was. But it's a case of spilt milk, now."

The regular Whig nominee, dolt and bore as he is, cannot but acknowledge the truth of this remark; and Mr. Doan continues:

"Besides, this Sliprie has gone over to Berson already. They were to hold a meeting at Beauville last night."

Mr. Cuffins rests his hands upon his hips, and begs to know who was to address them.

"Mr. Larrie," the editor says, "a cousin of Berson's."

"Very young, Mr. Doan, very young, isn't he?"

"Young? Yes. Twenty-three, I think. Very talented, however. He has been admitted."

"Indeed! it's a pity he begins wrong," and Mr. Cuffins falls into a reverie about the future. Of a truth, however, there is nothing pleasant in the blurred and blotted picture which fancy,

"Herself the fair and wild magician,"

holds up to him, and he turns from it with a sudden start.

"There is one fact connected with the Berson family, that is not very generally known; if it were, it would surely reduce Berson's chances of success. He is liable at any moment to be seized with insanity.—With insanity, Mr. Doan, with hereditary insanity."

"Dear me!" cries the editor, almost startled out of his spectacles, "Dear me!"

"Yes—his grandfather died in the full belief that he was the man in the moon. Of course, the matter was hushed up. I saw the old gentleman very often, when a boy.—Quite polished, in his lucid moments, quite quite polished." Mr. Cuffins takes a pinch of snuff. "But the most singular antics were those of his father; really amusing. Thought he was Old Mother Hubbard, and insisted on being dressed in a frock and bonnet. A man of much intelligence; translated the ballad of Mother Hubbard into Greek."

Mr. Doan never heard of that before, and Mr. Cuffins is kind enough to relate many pleasing anecdotes of the Berson family, that will hardly bear retelling. It is enough that when he rises to go out, he remarks:

"About this matter. Mightn't it be well to suggest something—

well, hint at the danger to which the people expose their interests in voting for the son of a—a—lunatic?"

I do not think Mr. Doan was ever in such a rage before. The regular nominee fairly starts at the redness of the editor's face, as he lifts it, and fixes its sharp gaze upon him.

"No! Mr. Cuffins, not in my paper! I am a Whig from principle and choice; and I have edited the *Messenger* ten years. But I've never done any dirty work yet. I tell you no man ever insulted me with such a proposition till now. The *Messenger* is paid for, and it shall never be used as a means to blast any man's character while in my hands.—God knows the curse of hereditary insanity is fearful enough without being brought to bear against one in whom it has never appeared."

I love to see a man get angry in a good cause. I love to watch the nostril swell in hate of wrong, and the eye flash its fine scorn upon the tempter. I feel prouder of mankind for the sight!

Mr. Cuffins slinks into a corner. I believe he is afraid the editor will strike him. But there is no danger of that, for the storm has blown over already. I make no doubt he would take a scolding from Mrs. Doan without a murmur, even now.

Mr. Cuffins regrets that he should have crossed Mr. Doan. He thinks he has been misunderstood. He did not mean to suggest anything venal at all. He is very sorry.—Good day.

Sly Mr. Cuffins!

Mr. Doan would call him back, and exchange forgiveness; but Walter, travel-worn and dusty, happens in just at the moment Mr. Cuffins happens out.

There are but few office-loungers to whom printers ever take a liking. From the roller-boy up to the pressman there is a quiet contempt for pretence, in every mind, and a bitter hatred of dullness and assumption, that no care is taken to conceal. The jour., with his long, grave face, tips the wink to the 'prentice, who passes the jest to the pressman and devil, and the dandy who plumes himself upon the thinness of his legs, and struts about the room for the "editah," speedily feels his littleness, in the sphere of cutting drollery which surrounds him. Nor does the chronic loafer, who drops in morning after morning to tumble the editor's exchanges, fare a great deal better. He is taken off before his face by the shrewd little chap behind the press, with matchless humor; and is made the butt of those jokes, which speak more in a word to one of the craft, than volumes could. The pompous fellow who casts about him with the air of a man who would like to buy things is not long in finding his true level in a country printing-office.

But a gentleman, in any walk of life, is known and respected the moment he is seen. His unaffected pride of self, when tempered

73

with courtesy to those about him, never meets a sneer. His foibles are forgiven, his little ways are fallen in with, and if he choose to frequent the office, he is always welcome.—If he is a wit, he will not find any who have a finer sense of mirth than printers; and he is at once loved and caressed by the whole office.

[*Ashtabula Sentinel*, 7 December 1854]

CHAPTER VI

G. Berson, Attorney at Law, is a very good-looking man. His dead wife thought so. His eyes are black and full. His smoothly shaven face is of a purely Grecian cast.—A smile lurks pleasantly in the corners of his mouth, and his whole seeming is such as wins trust and love.

The candle-light paints his profile darkly on the wall as he stands there with his fine form slightly bowed, gazing at the man beneath the desk.

Only a quick parting of the profile's lips, betrays the change that comes upon the living face. The glance of deadly shame and rage that lightens from his eyes is not copied upon the wall. Let it be never so well-shaped, the face is not an handsome one now.

With a sudden spring, he leaps forward, and drags his drunken lodger into the middle of the floor.

"By—! and so you're back again? Ugh! I've a notion to throttle you. I don't think," adds the candidate between his teeth, "it would be murder to make an end of such a brute."

The man, swaying to and fro uneasily beneath the tightening grip of Berson, leers half comically upon him with his maudlin eyes.

"Loog 'ere—Jaw Busson—you re' go!"

But the candidate only smiles grimly, and says nothing.

"Jaw Busson," repeats the man, whose powers of speech are sadly overcome with drink, "say—re' go, now!"

He fumbles at his pocket, and draws forth a knife, which he flings open with a sullen click.

There are some men who seem to gather strength as they are tempted; and now, instead of yielding to the dark thought which the sight of the knife flashes upon his mind, George Berson only dashes the man heavily against the wall, and sinking into a chair, calms himself with a strong effort of will.

The jar, and the tumble which follows it, seem almost to sober the man who lifts himself upon his hands and stares about him like one roused from an unwholesome dream.

"Robert," says Mr. Berson in the undertone of a man who dares not trust himself to speak louder, "Robert, if you are not too drunk, I want you to listen. I am not going to recall the past to your mind.

74

This is not the time, and you are not now the man to understand all I could say. You are my sister's husband, and that alone saved me from doing an ugly thing to-night—though you killed her by a thousand acts of brutishness and deviltry. Never mind that, now. She's dead. But I furnished you money to leave this place, when you had disgraced yourself and the family, and paid you never to come back. You *did* come back. You came as you come now—drunk. You came again and again—drunk. You have haunted the best years of my life like a besetting sin, that tempted me at every turn. Now look here! What are you back for *this* time?"

"I came to see my child," says the man sulkily, "she's at your house now."

"I know that," retorts the candidate, "and, by heaven! you shall never set eyes upon her."

"I will," cries the man staggering toward the door, "I'll go now."

"No,—don't," says Mr. Berson, with a bitter sneer, as Robert Wate tugs hopelessly at the lock. "But you didn't want to see Clara. Come! You want money."

Wate's bravado has been waxing less with returning soberness, and he now turns slowly round, and rubs his hand over his puffy eyes.

"Yes, I want money. I haven't tasted anything but liquor for two days. That's gone, now, and the fire inside's burning me up.—For God's sake, George, give me a few dollars. You can have the child. And I swear I'll never trouble you again. Upon my honor, now."

"Upon your honor—*honor!*" says the candidate, toying with his scorn, "well, how much will keep your honor whole for—say, two months?" and he takes out a purse musical with gold and silver.

Robert Wate steals a glance at the open knife upon the floor, but turns again with a hopeless sigh toward the candidate.

"Robert," says Mr. Berson, "I could send you to the State's Prison for half the money I put into your hand this moment," clinking the coins one upon another into the hot, tremulous palm stretched out to him. "Robert," he adds, while the man tells the money over and over, "you drew your knife upon me. I'll take care of that knife till you call again. As for this," kicking the bottle into a thousand pieces, "you wont need it any more.—And now, in God's name, be off; and never let me see you face again."

He opens the door, and without a word Robert Wate totters forth into the peaceful night. Only the holy stars behold him as he plods along the village street, and down the narrowing road, till distance mingles the crests of the arching trees above his head.

CHAPTER VII

"Hallo, boys!" cries Walter in that pleasant, cheery voice, which wins him friends and welcome everywhere, "How d' ye do! Mr.

75

Doan." And then from all arises a cordial greeting, and the little editor shakes hands with Wat, and says, "How-de-du! how-de-du! take a chair—dear me!" till the top of his bald head glows with feeling and good humor.

"How did that speech come off?" demands the pressman, resting his arm upon the pile of damp sheets before him, and looking over his shoulder at the eloquent young person whom he supposes to have spoken in Beauville, "how did that speech come off—eh?"

"Hi-yi! Strawberry," says Walter, dashing the dust from his clothes, "you here yet! By the beard of the prophet! I should have thought a delicacy of your sort were out of season, the last of July. Don't you trouble that speech. It isn't quite made, yet."

Strawberry, who owed his nickname chiefly to a round and pimpled visage, laughs with the rest, and then wonders if the name of Larrie could not draw together the elect of Beauville.

"The meeting was postponed," Walter replies. "But you come out there next Tuesday night, and see how I'll pour the hot shot into your clique."

"I don't know anything about hot shot," Strawberry says, with a sly twinkle of his eye, "but I'd like to bet that if I go to hear oratory, I'll be 'fooled to the top o' my bent.'"

"Come, Strawberry," chuckles the editor, "don't you be too hard upon the big gun of the Independents, even if he does brag a little."

"No! let him come on. He might get injured if I were to give full sweep to my sarcasm. But I'm not 'i' the vein,' now.—There's no danger."

"Not in the vein! Vain enough, I should say, from the way you talk," retorts the pressman.

"Now look here!" cries Larker, the jour., "I can stand a lame joke, but when it comes to such a wooden-legged pun as that, I'm going to protest. Stop! Strawberry, you can't go on in that way. You wont be sustained."

"You mean," exclaims Wat, eagerly, "that if he punned for a living, he wouldn't gain his *sustenance*."

"Now by Saint Paul!" retorts Larker, "methinks you would both starve at that trade."

"Come—come! boys," Mr. Doan breaks forth, "this 'is most tolerable and not to be endured.'"

"A Dogberry come to judgment!" roars the pressman.

"Nay, by 'r lady! 'tis a most villainous inversion of the text! cousin of Strawberry. How now—mad wag! how now?" asks Larker with a laughable staginess of voice.

"A parlous jest,—i' faith!" and Strawberry prints off the first sheet since Wat's arrival.

"I'd like to bet something," observes the young person named, "that you've got a one horse theatre in town."

"Well—you wouldn't lose much on that bet," is Strawberry's reply. "Though it is not a one-horse affair—understand that."

"I cry you mercy! But now, Mr. Doan," says Wat suddenly turning on the editor who has been lapsing into an article in the Tribune, ever since his last remark, "you are going in for the Berson ticket, I hope."

"You'd better not hope anything of the sort," says Larker, "Doan never bolts."

"I'm sorry we can't meet as friends in this canvass, Walter," the editor remarks, "but it mustn't be done. You've got the best man, but the principle's on our side. Larker is right. The *Messenger* never bolts."

"Why listen here, once," says Strawberry, going up to a stand, and reading from the type:

☞ Mr. Berson.—It is with some regret we hear that this gentleman has seen fit to allow the use of his name as a candidate in opposition to the regular Whig ticket. Personally, Mr. B. and ourself are friends, and shall ever be, so far as we may control the matter. We shall not permit the great Whig cause, however, to suffer for private considerations. We shall treat Mr. B. as an enemy, therefore, to the cause, until he returns to the Whig cause.

"There!" cries Strawberry taking a fresh fingerful of fine-cut. "You see what you've got to expect. Now my advice is that you cave at once. 'Cause you see, the Errington Messenger is down on you."

"I'm obliged to you," says Wat. "However, I didn't suppose you would take up with our side, Mr. Doan. But we wont tweak each other's noses for all that."

"Six o'clock," exclaims Larker, so breaking in upon Mr. Doan's forthcoming reply to Walter, as utterly to drown it from his mind.— "Wat, you are going home to supper with me. Come! I wont take any denial."

Walter does not know. His horse is at the tavern. He supposes he ought to go there for supper.

"No sir! you go with Larker. They live well there; and I want you to see who Larker takes to the play."

"There's no need of that, Strawberry," Mr. Doan slyly remarks. "Everybody knows who he'll take."

Whereupon Larker, whose cheeks have been glowing with unwonted redness, implores Wat to be off; and laughing gaily, the two young fellows quit the office.

A few minutes' walk brings them to the little house where Larker boards.

"Wat, I'm going to shew you my Dulcinea," and he opens softly the door of the little front parlor.

In good hour I would have you know, reader of mine, that Walter is not free of the weakness, which it has been sagely remarked, young men have for seeing a pretty and new face. I say, then, that although Merla Carmin has ousted the thoughts of all other maidens from his heart, Walter feels that the presence he is about to enter, demands a slight twitch of shirt-collar, and a smoothing his clustering locks with the palm of his hand. It may be that an overweening consciousness of his own good-looks imparts a tinge of foppishness to this feeling. Of a truth, however, all his care is lost, for the young lady in question proves not to be at home.

"She went," says an old lady who is made known to Walter as Mrs. Rueford, "over to Mr. Carmin's, to see Merla."

Lover-like, Walter takes every mention of Merla for a direct allusion to himself, and he cannot help thinking that Mrs. Rueford is very pointed in her remarks.

"Harry was saying," Mrs. Rueford goes on, "that Merla expected her cousin to-night; and she wanted to see her badly, and so I let her go."

Which is gall and wormwood to our friend Wat, who writhes inwardly, and hopes that the coach may have broken down with Merla's cousin.

After a few commonplace sallies on everyday themes, Walter lapses into a mute examination of the room and its furniture, while Larker and the old lady gossip pleasantly together.

At length, Mrs. Rueford leading the way, says, "Elfred, your friend is tired and hungry, and if you'll step into the room, we'll have tea."

To his no little satisfaction, Walter finds that Strawberry has not overrated the table of Mrs. Rueford, and he is speedily divided between the enjoyment of a cup of tea, and a dread that Merla's cousin may have come.

"I tell you what," says Larker, when Mrs. Rueford leaves the table a moment to oversee the kitchen, "no!—hold up! You are acquainted with Miss Carmin?—eh? Well, it's nothing to be ashamed of," adds he, on seeing Walter's confusion. "We'll go round after the consumption of all edible and potable substances on this board, and take the girls to the play. Come, now!"

Walter shall be very happy.

"Well by Saint Paul!" exclaims Larker, with a merry laugh, breaking open a fresh biscuit, and spreading thereon the pet preserves of Harry without stint, "What a confounded simperer you are! You're a perfect sucking dove about the matter. Why I was older at fifteen than you are at twenty-three. You don't catch me reddening up, because some one happens to mention 'my true love's' name—to adopt the language of the Nautical Songster."

"That's a fact," retorts Walter. "I observed how particularly un-concerned you looked this evening when Strawberry and Mr. Doan were boring you."

"Hit!" cries Larker, taking a huge bite of biscuit and a gulp of tea, "hit."

"Perhaps, my dear Elfred, increasing years have softened your nature, till now, at the mature age of nineteen you more nearly resemble a sucking dove than you did at ten-and-five," and Walter helps himself to cheese.

"No more of that, sweet wag, an' thou lovest me," Larker says, throwing himself into an attitude.

"Or it may be," Walter continues with a quiet smile, "that you were more correctly likened to a sucking calf."

"Peccavi! which being interpreted, means I cave. Take some more tea." Larker makes a feint of pouring it.

Not any more, Walter thanks him; and at the moment of this rash speech, Mrs. Rueford returns to her seat.

Wont Mr. Larrie try another biscuit?

He could not, indeed. He has had plenty.

These preserves. Mrs. Rueford thinks he can hardly have tasted them.

Walter has tried them. They are nice, but he does not eat a great deal for supper.

A glance of droll meaning from Larker, is the only comment upon this speech; and the two young men withdraw to the parlor.

"Well!" says Larker glancing out of the open window, "I guess the girls are going to save us the trouble of going after them; for as I'm a sinner, here they are both at the gate."

Ere Walter can twitch his collar into a proper state of horres-cence, or even so much as catch a look at himself in the glass upon the wall, Merla and her friend bound into the room.

"O Mrs. Rueford! don't you think it's too bad? My cousin isn't coming to-night, and"—

Why need she stop with that air of bewitching bashfulness on beholding Wat?—Why need that young gentleman stumble over two chairs and a stool in shaking the fair hand held out to him? Why need Harry look at Elfred? Why, above all, need that unwor-thy fellow laugh?

"The touch of that little hand, dear Frank," Wat afterward wrote, "sent a thrill of foolish pleasure to my heart. I know what you will think when you have read all this! I know how you will pish and pshaw, and cry 'Nonsense!' But thank heaven and Merla, that I am proof against your railery at last. * * For the life of me, I cannot tell what was said or done during that blissful half-hour I spent with Merla in the parlor of Mrs. Rueford. I only know that I was presented to the daughter of my hostess; that she seemed to care as little for me as I did for her; that I talked to Merla; that our friend Larker talked to Miss Rueford; and that we all went to hear some strolling players mouth 'The Lady of Lyons,' to top off with.

"Well, it was near twelve when the 'laughable Vaudeville,' came to a close, and the manager returned his 'sincere and heart-felt thanks,' and I started home with Merla.—The young moon lay in a silver sleep on the bosom of the west. Cresset stars were lit along the front of heaven. The village homes, half hidden by clustering trees, gleamed whitely through the branches. The one-toned caty-dids made pensive music in the maples that lined the walk. Broad soft shadows of these fell across our path, all bedropped with moon-light, like kingly robes of velvet with flecks of gold embroidered on their rich dark ground. I used to listen as you recalled in a bitter unbelieving way, some kindred stroll, and wonder at the glow of rapture that lit up your features ere you knew it. I say I used to wonder at you. But I shall never wonder at you again. I believe I felt better then, and fitter for heaven than I ever shall while I live. Indeed, I had left earth. I was no longer a part of that very unworthy planet. I lived in a little errant world of my own with rose-colored atmosphere, and lost in immeasurable space of dream. Merla was there, too. We were never to grow old. She retained enough of earthly beauty to be still the girl I loved, and I was worthy of her.

"Though a good half mile to the residence of Mr. Carmin, (of whom I am training myself to think dutifully), I could not help thinking the distance very short; and so I begged Merla to lengthen it somewhat. By heavens! I wish that walk could have lasted forever. I shall always hold mud-puddles in the most grateful remembrance, for the sake of that over which I had to lift Merla. It gave me a good pretext for putting my coat-sleeve around her waist; and as for keeping it there, why, there might be other mud puddles in the way, and I ought to be on the alert. We had talked-up the play long before the turning-point in our saunter, and so we were silent a good part of the way. I believe that my arm clasped Merla still closer all the time; and I appeal to you, Frank, as man of 'phine pheelinks,' if I was to blame for kissing Merla (half-a-dozen times, or so) on our return? Or for accepting an invitation to sit down in the little portico, where Merla said she used to look out upon the stars alone? I·did sit down, and she sat down beside me. I took her hand in mine, and drew her nearer to me till our

—'Cheeks, like peaches on a tree,
    Leaned with a touch together thrillingly!'

"'Merla,' I said—

"Why should you want to know what I said?—you iceberg! It is enough that a ring is glancing on my finger as I write, and—that is all. To-morrow night I am to save the country in a speech to the citizens of Beauville. Heigho! I would rather spend the time with Merla in the little portico away at Errington."

What sage was it who has said that people laugh about the nonsense of lovers at first, but get awfully bored with it after a while? I quite agree with him, and therefore I conjure that mythical personage, my reader, to look for no farther letters from Wat on his pet theme.

[*Ashtabula Sentinel*, 21 December 1854]

Old men who have been wont to recall the campaign of '40 with a sigh for the spiritlessness of latter-day politics, are dumfounded at the fervor of the present contest. It is now beyond a shadow of doubt that the democrats will not make a nomination. The cat will jump in the very direction Mr. Cuffins most feared. The locos and the bolters will herd together.

> "Black spirits and white—
> Blue spirits and gray;
> Mingle, mingle, mingle,
> You that mingle may."

Blubber, the sworn foe of Cubber, will shake the political paw of his old enemy.—Rubber, who has not spoken to Dubber since that gentleman came in ahead of him for the hand of Miss McJiltem, will walk arm in arm with him throughout the canvass. The moral character of the Publican Nubber, will be so whitewashed of all stain in the eyes of Deacon Flubber, that he will bow to him on the way to church. It is easier to mingle oil and water than to make friends of Vubber and Gubber. Yet Vubber and Gubber will hobnob, if need be, for the good of the cause. And so on.

Meantime, let us to Beauville. Walter is at Beauville. He is seated in that chair, whose oneness startled him on his first advent into the barroom of the Napoleon hotel; and the last copy of the Oldbury Herald, is being read by him. The landlord's burly person fills the doorway, and the smoke from his pipe, rises in soft wreaths. But Walter, I say, is lost in the perusal of the Herald. The leader, and some half-dozen smaller squibs are fulsome in their adulation of Berson, and their abuse of the regular Whig nominee, and the editor of the Errington Messenger.

"It is a fact that we assert without fear of contradiction, that the Whig nominee is a man destitute of every ennobling trait of mind, and deaf alike to censure and to praise. He is a man in whose hands it were as dangerous to lodge power as to place a lighted torch in the grasp of a maniac. The music of a dollar is sweeter to him than the voice of prayer; and he would barter his salvation and the liberty of his country for

81

lucre. * * But what shall we say of the pitiful wretch who would fain be the pack-horse of this bundle of stupidity and wickedness? What shall we say of a man whose filthy sheet now poisons many a peaceful fireside in Ecks? What *can* we say? Shall we hint that the Messenger man's uncle was a leading member of the Hartford Convention—that his grandfather was a Tory in the days of the Revolution—that the blood in his veins is red with inborn treachery and servility? No. We scorn to attack any man because his kinsman was this or that. But we say to the people of Ecks, Beware of this man! Beware of one who comes to you in sheep's clothing, but inwardly is a ravening wolf."

"If I had Gorley by the weasand, I'd squeeze the venom out of him!" cries Wat, forgetful of his listener. "I swear it is cruel! this wholesale tirade. I'll bet," mournfully apostrophizing the mantel-piece, "that George pays the fellow ten dollars for villifying his old friend Doan in this style."

Ah! Walter, who wanted the Herald man to come out savage?

"Now look here, oncet," says John Trooze, slowly relaxing from his pipe, "I've hearn tell walls has ears, an' ef walls hasn't, Sary Ann has. Sayin' she'd ha' happened to ben standin' at the door, there, listenin'—as it's ony a wonder she wa'n't—your cousin's cake 'ud ha' ben dough in no time."

Wat turns upon the speaker in amaze.

"What do you s'pose my old woman does, bein' she overhear you? She lets them dishes of her'n lay in the pan, and bundles slap over to her dum'd old mother's. The cuss."

Walter's thoughts revert at once to Merla, and he wonders whether he shall ever call *her* an "old woman," or a "cuss."

"Women," continues Trooze with mournful sententiousness, knocking the ashes from his pipe, "is out and out cussedness, any way.—I used to think sparkin' was a mighty fine thing, but blame me ef the slangin' and bangin' and whangin' *sence*, aint enough to make up for it."

It is but fair to suppose that the Sary Ann of Mr. Trooze's bosom has been having words with her lord; and that he has got the worst of it. At any rate, Walter thinks as much, and deems a discreet silence, the safest part he can adopt.

"Why it's like this. My old woman's mother would cirkelate that 'ere report all over Beauville in two hours, and you'd find your cousin a gittin' hail Columby in the next Messenger," cries the land-lord in high key.—"I tell you women's nothin' but cussedness, any-way; and if ever you marry one, you're a dum'd fool! That's all."

This last remark appears to have been suggested of a dim belief that Wat is about to marry out of hand,

"With all his imperfections on his head,"
and overwhelmed by the direful fate in store for his young friend,
the wretched husband and father bursts into tears. Perhaps he has
been drinking, and therefore yields more easily to the melting mood,
than if he were sober.

Be this as it will, Mr. Trooze feels that tears are an unmanly
weakness, and going behind the bar, he overcomes that weakness
by huge draughts from parti-colored bottles.

It is at the moment when Mr. Trooze stoops down to draw
himself a glass of beer, that Sary Ann enters the room, bearing in
her motherly embrace the dejected Marquis de Lafayette Trooze.
That young nobleman is drowned in grief. Sary Ann herself is not
proof against the shafts of fortune, and snuffles and whimpers in
such kind as only an ugly woman can. Her dress is all awry, and
her bloomy locks are escaped the durance of comb and string. In a
word, she confronts the man of her girlhood's choice,

"In all the wildness of disheveled charms."

When the Apparition of an Armed Head Rises, it is customary
for Macbeth to retreat across the stage with a frightened straddle;
and I blush to record the fact that the puissant Walter Larrie, is
equally startled by the appearance of Sary Ann, and sneaks unos-
tentatiously into remotest corner of the room.

"O-ho! there you be—be you? A swillin' down that beer like a
great pork! Yes—a pork—a great, big, nasty por-r-r-k!" cries the
worthy little woman, italicizing every renewal of the epithet with a
spank bestowed skillfully upon the person of the unlucky Marquis.

She pauses for breath, and the Marquis pipes an interlude which
for compass and expression is very creditable.

"Sary Ann—for the Lord's sake!"—implores the unlucky Trooze.

"Quit a-swearin'! that's splendid talk to bring up a child on. You
little tormentin' skunk! I'll shake you into bits. Was any one so
bedeviled in their life? John Trooze, if you say Lord, or any other
swearing word again, I'll leave your bed and board. Now mind
that!"

I do not think Mr. Trooze was ever so tempted to profanity
before! Howbeit, he stands speechlessly with a tankard of beer in
his grasp, and very much the air of a man who is going to wait till
the shower is over.

"Bringin'," continues Sary Ann, "all sorts o' trash into your
house, and holdin' and tendin' meetin's. What do you know about
'em, you natural born, you? My old shoe knows more."

Mr. Trooze looks perfectly willing to yield the palm of superior
knowledge to Sary Ann's sandal, which to say truth, is none of the
smallest.

But Sary Ann now turns upon Walter:

83

"And you, you young scape-goat—why don't you stay to home, 'stid of scourin' the country side, disturbing peaceful families?"

"My dear Mrs. Trooze," begins the heartless foe of domestic happiness, "my dear Mrs. Trooze, I"—

"John, do you stand by and hear a strange man call you wife his *dear*, and not say nothin'? The Lord forgive you!" and Sary Ann sinks breathless and panting in that only chair.

The writer of this would not undertake to say what might have happened, if an ungainly steed bestridden of Moro Gilky, had not chanced to jog up to the very threshold of the Napoleon Hotel, in midst of the tumult. Mr. G. is a shade lanker, if anything, than when we saw him last. His dress is quite dusty, and his face is expressive of hope and hunger, having started from home without his breakfast.

He hitches the horse to the ring in the side of the house, and drags himself into the presence.

"Hem!—good day. Beautiful morning, ma'am. Mr. Larrie—how is your health this morning, sir?"

Sary Ann sweeps sulkily from the room, without so much as a nod for the astonished Moro. It is the pet belief of the good woman that every traveler is her sworn enemy.—The benign smile of Mr. Gilky is to her eyes, therefore, but the treacherous lurking-place of a merciless fondness for victuals; and his swingeing bow only too plainly betrays a villainous desire to sleep in beds, and make work for her thereby. Sary Ann sees through him.

Walter gives his hand with a very bad grace, and presents Mr. Gilky to John Trooze. Some talk is had on various matters, and Mr. Gilky at length remarks that he has "a letter of introducshin to Mister-r-r Sliprie—a legal gentlemin."

"I tell you, Frank," is the exclamation of Walter in one of those juicy epistles he used to write, "it was a situation which would have brought out Dickens' Mark Tapley 'jolly.' *I* came out jolly. Tongue-lashed by that unrighteous woman, as I had been, and smarting with the recollection of being called a 'scape-goat,' I was now urbanely requested to accompany Mr. Gilky to the office of Sliprie. I went. I left Mr. Trooze pensively seated on the beer-keg. I confess that I felt a twinge of sorrow when I thought of the rowing to which the poor wretch was doomed; but I left him, nevertheless.

* * "If heaven ever deal so harshly with you, as to meet you with Sliprie, let him prove himself the scoundrel-thief he is, by 'stealing out of your company.' He is a rugged, bluff-visaged knave, who sins doubly in belying his open, honest face. His broad, rich laugh seems to breathe the music of a generous, free-handed nature. It is as treacherous as a pitfall covered with flowers.

* * "What George wanted Sliprie to do with Gilky, I did not

know, and to tell you the truth, I cared less. I presently left the two in mutual borage, and sauntered listlessly down street. I did not go back to the Napoleon Hotel. I took up my quarters in J. Hasker's store, and there dined sumptuously on three time-honored crackers, a bit of cheese, and a sufficiency of spruce beer. I dare be sworn that Sary Ann could not have got a better meal! I was regaled during the banquet like any prince by Mr. Hasker, who gave me succinct sketches of every horse trade he had experienced in a long and brilliant course of swaps.

"Well, the day passed wretchedly enough, and when the shadows of the houses waxed fat and large upon the green, untroubled street, I wended toward the school house in no pleasant frame of mind. I meant to be early, and I foreran the faithful some hours.

"The door to the temple of knowledge stood ajar, and I strode sulkily in. The master was seated at a rough table, writing copies and renibbing pens. I fell to chatting with him, and soon found him to be a man of wider intelligence than I had vouchsafed to think.— He lacked the unhappy *selfness* of his tribe, and he talked more like a man than a school teacher. I made known my business, and we discussed politics, and books, and Beauville right pleasantly.

"The squat, low room, with its two bleared little windows, was extremely hot. The walls were plastered with straw and mud, and adorned with grotesque designs in ink. Here the youthful artist had shadowed forth the passion of Scorn in a figure whose thumb rested upon the tip of its nose, and whose fingers were supposed to be describing a contemptuous circle. In another place, 'A INDIEN CHEEF,' was depicted life size. The attitude of this sachem was one of eager expectancy. His brow was decked with horrent plumes, and the bow in his nervous grasp, was bent in the act of launching an arrow into the body of an imaginary buffalo. Over the door, a huge battle-scene caught the eye. On this the limner must have exhausted the riches of a teeming fancy, and the skill of a miraculous pencil.—Lovers of art, however, will hear with regret that the Vandal pedagogue scourged the artist from his task as he was retouching sunset in the distance with a bunch of scoke berries. The ceiling was rough with paper wads, and a halo of these graced the wall behind the teacher's desk; discharged, no doubt, with the intent of avenging on the bare head of that dignitary the countless injuries sustained at his hands.

"I could but be struck with this, and laughed heartily at it. The master took my merriment in good part, and remarked that if I had nothing worse than paper wads thrown at my head that night, I might account myself very fortunate. Now, I confess that I had not thought of my opponents in a bellicose light, and the possibility of being—ahem!—in fine, 'egged,'—had never suggested itself to me. Alas! that I should have realized that possibility.

85

"At early candle light, Mr. Sliprie, flanked by Mr. Gilky and an astonished boy, whose brimless straw-hat heightened the expression of amazement stamped upon his face, entered the school-room, which the pettifogger speedily filled with the smoke of a villainous cigar. Mr. Gilky bore a great oaken staff in his hand, whose use as a vehicle of applause might be readily guessed. I blushed for shame at the thought of being in league with two such shabby rogues. Mr. Witheron, the school-master, had been on the brink of going to supper for more than an hour, but now determined to remain; and I continued chatting with him.

"One after another my audience dropped in, and I must say they were as unworthy a gang as it was ever my lot to behold. But let me not weary you with details. It makes my very soul sick to think of it even now!—I began to speak. I reminded my hearers of the glorious deeds of the revolution, and shewed them how it would be in accordance with the dying wish of those patriots for them to elect George, Legislator. I was violently cheered by Sliprie, and the oak staff of Gilky performed a colossal tattoo upon the floor. I cannot say, however, that outside of the immediate circle of my acquaintance, I was very warmly received.

"I changed my tack. I depicted the terrible despotism of the Court House Clique. I assured the Men of Beauville that the fabric of this monstrous system of oppression would crumble into dust with the same breath that wafted into power the Independent Ticket.—I would not allude, I said, to the regular Whig nominee. I would not allude to the dastardly treachery which had brought about his nomination. I would not allude to the personal character of Mr. Cuffins. I would not allude to the fact that for long scores of years he had ground the faces of the poor.—And so on. [Renewed applause, and obstreperous enthusiasm on the part of the Astonished boy.] I grew facetious. I made puns. I cracked jokes. If there was an old line Whig in that assembly I would like to see him. I had not met one for some time, and I was a little curious to know whether such a thing existed in Beauville. I did not believe there did.

"Alas! I paid dearly for my levity. A hulking, burly, beef-butchering varlet stepped from the crowd, and remarked that he was an old line Whig. What did I want with him? I need not tell you that I am perfectly at ease when bullying and browbeating a witness. I went at this fellow and cut him up beautifully. Some chaps near the door seemed inclined to hiss; but the Independents drowned all other sounds in stunning salvos of delight. The Astonished boy, who was holding a candle near his face to get a full view of me, now thrust it under his nose, in a fit of laughter, and fell stifled from his perch on the window sill. Mr. Gilky gave himself up to a series of choking snuffles, which I suppose the poor devil meant for laughs.

"I must have been half crazy, or I would have seen that I was on dangerous ground.—But while the butcher waxed redder and angrier, I only attacked him with renewed gust. At last he burst into tears, and dashed toward me. There was not a great deal of time to think, but I did a great deal of thinking, nevertheless. There was a pitcher of water on the desk before me, and I let the butcher have that at once. I also bestowed two candles and sticks upon him and the 'Sacred Songster,' which lay within reach. I was about to launch 'Webster's Unabridged,' when my antagonist closed upon me. Somebody got awfully thrashed. I could not tell who, exactly, but I do not think it was the butcher.

"Meanwhile, the fellows near the door kept up a deafening yell, and discharged volleys of eggs at the speaker. I cried enough,—I state the fact without shame, for I might have said *plenty* with good reason—and the butcher allowed me to rise. I cast about me for my hat. I found it after a while, but it was so fearfully cocked that I could not wear it. Bareheaded and reeking, I made for an opening in that accursed room. But there was none to be found. Utterly bewildered, I ran hither and thither. At length I caught a glimmer of the night without, and dashed ahead in that direction. It was the door.—A great ruffian was stationed on the threshold after the manner of the Colossus of Rhodes. I ran between his legs, and upset the monster.

"How cool the damp night breezes were!—I breathed them as eagerly as a thirsty man quaffs the thrilling waters of a desert spring. But I had no time to sentimentalize. I cut across lots, and was soon out of sight.

"Wending unsteadily toward the Napoleon Hotel, I came suddenly upon a man who wept and smacked his fists by turns. It was Gilky. The poor knave had been thrust thro' the window, and had worn the sash about his neck for some distance. By dint of bribery, he prevailed on the Astonished boy to relieve him of the unpleasant ornament.

" 'I'd like to secure a good night's repose, for I am really quite fatigued up,' he remarked after relating his story.

" 'The deuce take a good night's repose!' roared I; 'we'll get our horses, and leave this infernal place.'

* * "My dear friend, I have not spoken in public since! Moreover, I never shall again."

[*Ashtabula Sentinel*, 28 December 1854]

For a faithful history of the never-to-be-forgotten campaign, whose first meeting resulted so disastrously to the Independents the

87

curious are referred to the files of the Oldbury Herald. Despite his determination to retire from the scene of strife, Mr. Larrie, it will be found, addressed enthusiastic crowds in several towns; and fully redeemed his name from the charge of cowardice, by the use of twice as much insolence and bravado, as marked his conduct previous to the rencontre with the Butcher of Beauville.

Mr. Gilky, however, does not appear in print, and the story of his adventures is more or less involved in doubt. The writer of this has had frequent recourse to the voluminous epistles of Mr. Larrie, in the course of his narrative, and to these he must again resort for anything like a reliable statement of Gilky's doings. He seems to have made himself very serviceable during the canvass, by stooping to such mean jobs as the loftier natures of his companions would not. Mr. Sliprie is attacked in a spirit of bitter animosity, for placing Mr. Gilky in positions where his peccadilloes are amenable to law; and I am led to believe that his employment at times was not strictly honorable.

A feeling of cool disbelief in the honesty of mankind pervades these letters, which not too plainly shews a growing want of it in their writer. Less and less frequent exclamation is made against the chicanery of political warfare; and gentle Merla is scarce mentioned. It is to be feared that Walter's fickle, headlong mind, could ill brook the guidance of her gentle hand, and that the bond between them is dissolved.

Mr. Berson has not been idle. Little vexed with "uncleanly scruple," he has directed the campaign with a master hand, and at the beginning of October he finds himself on the high road of success.

The Whigs have not been very active, dispirited by the helplessness of Mr. Cuffins, who made speeches throughout the county, chiefly remarkable for being hurtful only to himself, and weakened by a consciousness of inferiority. Berson was the choice of many Whigs in convention, and those who do not actually go over to his side, hardly care to oppose him.

This fresh October morning, then, with its strong, sweet air is thrice grateful to Mr. Berson, as he smokes his cigar on the verandah of his house in Oldbury. The broad-leafed grape clambers over the porch like a vine of gold, and dapples the floor with restless shadows. The large maples that flank the mansion on the west, blush with a thousand tints of crimson. The meadows are still green, and stretch away on every side, broken here and there by fields of rustling corn, among whose ranks the heavy wains are moving, and the farmers are heaping in parti-colored mounds, bright ears of red, white, yellow, and purple. The circling forest rises "like a thing dipped in sunset," and far beyond, where earth and sky are mixed, the outlines of the hills are hushed in softest blue.

Mr. Berson dwells upon the beauty of the scene with a dreamy enjoyment, and feels loath to obey a voice from within, which begs him to come "right away."

"George, you mustn't leave home, to-day," Annie Berson says, placing her hand upon his arm, very lightly, as if she feared to startle him.

"What's the reason, Annie?"

"Because Clara has a high fever; and I'm afraid she's going to be sick."

The self-complaisant face grows pale, but Mr. Berson gives a stout "psahw!" and says: "O not very sick. It'll soon pass off. Come! Annie, let's see her."

With an aching heart, George passes into the room where his little niece lies sleeping on a sofa.

Her mother had been his favorite sister when they were both children together.—Their love was strengthened with increasing years, and when she died, his affection was transferred to her worse than orphaned child. He was jealously alive to every danger and disease that threatened her infancy, and now that she was grown a rugged healthy child of six years, his tender, half foolish fondness for her, passed the bounds of reason. She swayed him as easily as ever mistress did lover, and nothing was too great a sacrifice, if it pleased Clara. She was a self-willed, imperious little creature enough, yet sweet and loving withal. No wonder, then, that her uncle's heart, so full of love for her, stands still as he marks her flushed cheeks, and her forehead, where the blue veins are visibly throbbing.

"Why, Annie! What's the reason you didn't tell me about this child? We must have a doctor."

Mr. Berson calls to a man who is cleaning the garden walks, and bids him fetch Doctor Wetherbee.

"And hurry, man. Don't creep along at that snail's pace."

Dr. Wetherbee comes.

He is a pleasant, cheerful man, of burly presence. His hair is sprinkled with gray, and his blue eye beams with good humor. There is health in the very screak of his boots.

"Somebody sick, eh?" says Doctor Wetherbee. "What, Clara?"

"Yes. She's quite ill," Mr. Berson replies, huskily.

"Pooh! pooh—I'll see about that." And Dr. Wetherbee bustles cheerily to the sofa.

He takes up the little wrist in his kind rough palm.

"A slight fever, merely," Doctor Wetherbee observes.

"Nothing—dangerous, then, Doctor," falters Mr. Berson.

"O no! Pass off, pass off in a day or two. And now Miss Berson, if you'll give her one of these powders once in every two hours, we'll soon have little Clara on her feet again, shining in all the dark corners like the bit of sunshine she is." And the good old fellow takes out that mysterious wallet, which all his craft are furnished with, and daintily portions certain white and brown powders therefrom with the tip of his pen-knife, upon square bits of paper. Heaven bless the man and all his tribe! They hold our lives in their hands. They lift our hearts, or sink them, as they will. They carry sunshine and happiness in their quaint phials. Their wallets are full of relief, and kindliness, and very joy. O let us think of these men as those who stood beside the bed of ones dear to us, and lifted from our souls great loads of fear and grief.

Mr. Berson grows easier as he watches the doctor's movements. "And now, George Berson, you go off up town. Your sister can take care of this child, and you'll only be in the way."—This and a great deal more from Dr. Wetherbee, who pushes the candidate playfully out of the door, and then adds: "You might stop and send Mrs. Gilky down. She could be useful to Miss Berson."

And so Annie is left alone with her charge. She sits down before the fire which is softly flickering on the hearth, and sews.

It is a beggarly kind of wit at the very best, which singles out for its victim, the woman who, from choice or chance remains unmarried. Truer, nobler, purer hearts than beat in the bosoms of Old Maids, are never found. What if they are full of odd ways and whims? What if they are nervous? What if they do affect cats and pincushions? Let them. They pass through life harmlessly, and their quaintnesses should be forgiven them.—At parties they take the dark corners, and quietly read books, and are in nobody's way. At church they are decent and devout, and are never seized with a fit of giggling because Kory will wear that fright of a bonnet. They do not stare bashful young men out of countenance; nor laugh when Dr. Anthropos happens to sneeze in the middle of a prayer. On the contrary, they are always peaceful and unobtrusive. Who cannot recall the time when that dear old maiden aunt, who sat in the rocking chair and seemed to be forever patching quilts, averted the flogging which was to have been given him, to correct an untoward love for playing hookey? Who makes as many presents on Christmas, as that same aunt? Who always gave imploring childhood a sup of preserves from that jar, of which it was sacrilege to think lightly? When we were grown great rowdy boys, and broke into mill-ponds, who gave us dry warm clothes, and stole us off to bed without letting mother know any thing about it? Who left the frontdoor unlocked, and made Cousin stop laughing at us next morning, when we had been sparking the first time?

Alas! we little dreamed of what she might have undergone! We little dreamed, that haply when her heart was young, it had been given to one who carried it up to heaven with him! Or that beneath her still demeanor, a stream of love throbbed restlessly, like a river locked in ice! We little recked what bitterness of grief she might have tasted, and knew her only for the quiet little body that she seemed.

When the curls that drooped about the cheeks of Annie Berson wore a brighter tint, and Time had not yet scrawled his autograph upon her brow, she had been called to act a part in one of those tragedies, which no curtain rises on, to let the world behold. One of those dramas wherein the actors play no studied part; whose stage is real, and whose woe sincere. They are played in our midst, again and again, and we see no shifting scenery, nor glare of lights. The story of their being comes to us only in an oldwife's gossip, which we scorn.

Why need there more be said than that fate parted two it should have joined? It does not matter how, or when, or where. Poor Annie's heart turned in upon itself, and her lover went a missionary beyond seas. That is all.

When her brother married, she made her home with him; and when his wife died, she soothed the wild outburst of grief that threatened his reason. She was his better angel. She loved him with that holy unselfish affection, which none but women can feel. What if he only half returned her affection. She never asked herself the question, but happy in the privilege of loving him, her life glided peacefully away; like a stream, which, though no longer sparkling through its old sunny channel, and lost among somber vales, still murmured contentedly upon its course. When Clara was taken into the household, the lonely woman took the child to her heart, and devoted her mind to her education and training.

The clock ticks pleasantly upon the mantle, and the fire purrs drowsily upon the hearth.

The low breathing of the child does not break the dream of by-gone happiness that Annie dreams. Her soul is lost to all consciousness of self, and wings its way back through gloomy-arching mausoleums, where the years of pain and secret suffering are buried, out into the sunshine, and bathes its plumes in the mellow light.

—Angelica, almost beautiful in her sympathy, steals into the room. The greeting between the two is cordial, and Mrs. Gilky lays off her "things," and straightway unfolds her budget of work and gossip.

Annie listens with a quiet smile.

[*Ashtabula Sentinel*, 4 January 1855]

The columns of the Oldbury Herald are adorned with a splendid array of capitals and flaunting italics. Voters are warned to beware of split tickets. There is cause to believe that tickets have been printed with the name of the Whig nominee in place of Mr. Berson's, and headed "Independent Ticket." Let the people guard against them. Our enemies are hard pressed, and will resort to all kinds of trickery and fraud. The freemen of Ecks should see that every man is at the polls. They must prepare to battle relentlessly with a foe which know neither honesty nor mercy.

"Gorley has thrown himself this time, sure," says Strawberry, conning the Herald over to himself. "I s'pose he thinks he's done it, now," and the pressman stirs the fire, with the toe of his boot. "Larker! where's Larrie, these times?"

"Lord! I don't know," returns Mr. Larker with a yawn. "He had a very large amount of building material in his hat, the last time I saw him."

"You don't say so!" cries Strawberry.

"What's the reason I don't?" retorts Larker.

Whereupon Strawberry falls into a brown study from which he emerges with the remark, "That's bad!"

"I don't dispute that," says Larker.

"Well it seems to me, you're mighty cool about it, anyway, Larker." Strawberry flings a stick of wood into the fire.

"O! I don't know. I expect I feel very sorry for him. But then, when a fellow throws himself away, who's to blame?"

"The fellow is, I suppose."

"Right, my Strawberry. I'm charmed with your penetration. O! dear," adds Mr. Larker, "I'm nearly used up. There was no use rushing the Messenger out. Those fellows will beat us. Eh, Straw?"

"I guess they will."

The conversation is interrupted by the apparition of Mr. Cuffins, carrying an umbrella in his hand. There are some men who always seem to be carrying umbrellas. Such men commonly have weak eyes, and the noise of their boots is hushed with India-rubbers. They never have their umbrellas raised. They are very tiresome to look at, and quite overwhelming to talk with. They never make jokes. They are staid and grave, and they are marked by a negative courtesy of bearing, whose bourne we seldom overstep. There was Stub, a Man-with-an-Umbrella man. Nobody ever saw him without his Umbrella. Of course, nobody ever remarked that he always had it with him. Nevertheless, he had. At church, if you beheld in the vestibule, a blue Umbrella with a narrow streak of white around the edge, you were safe in declaring that Mr. Stub was attending divine service. There was no mistaking the Umbrella. It had a meek ivory-topped handle, and an imbecile tassel dangling therefrom. I have said that Mr. Stub left his Umbrella, as a general thing, in the vestibule of the church. This, however, was sheer reverence. It is to be doubted whether Mr. Stub would have suffered himself to part from his Umbrella for any other feeling, let it be never so sacred. At a lecture, the Umbrella supported the chin of Mr. Stub, while he took aim through his goggles at the lecturer. At public meetings the Umbrella punched neighboring ribs. At market, the Umbrella invaded egg-baskets, and spilled measures of apple-butter over white napkins, and angered the dame, who buttered them. There was a touch of malice in the nature of that Umbrella. It took a fiendish delight in upsetting the cups on the stand of the Coffee-Woman, and bruising the wares of the Little-Molasses-Candy-Girl. What wonder? It was a Demon Umbrella. Can I ever forget the moment when Mr. Stub appeared on the roof of the burning house, with his Umbrella under his arm. The red flames leaped from the burning casements, as if to dash themselves upon the crowd, and roared and crackled with unearthly glee.—There seemed to be no escape; and a shudder ran through the mighty throng below, as Mr. Stub stepped jauntily to the edge of the roof. He must needs fling himself down. Everybody thought so. What was their astonishment to see Mr. Stub raise his Umbrella, and sheltering himself beneath it, jump from the eave into subtle air. He hovered over the house for a moment, and then drifting to the leeward, soared easily up toward the clouds. Every eye was strained to watch the flight of the devoted man. The Umbrella waxed smaller and smaller, and at last, with coat-tails flapping frantically, Mr. Stub faded from sight.— He never came down; and perished, no doubt, a victim to his own Umbrella!—Every Man-with-an-Umbrella does not go up like a balloon. Yet there is a dreadful mystery hanging about such people, which may well excite in the boldest heart a willingness to give them the whole sidewalk.

But to return. Mr. Cuffins, though not a confirmed Umbrella man, has, as I have said, an umbrella in his hand when he enters the Messenger office. Of a truth, he has need of one to-day, for a cold drizzly rain falling, makes a shield of this kind truly useful.

It is unmistakably election day. Mud is in the streets, and a disagreeable chilliness in the air. Teams are hitched to the awning-posts in front of the stores, where they stand motionless, with great drops of rain beading the harness, and clustering upon their manes. Horsemen, with splashed leggins, are stalking about; and the tavern-yards are crowded with vehicles.

Mr. Cuffins wants to know if the editor is in.

"No," Strawberry says, "he went down to the polls."

"Well, you have some tickets here, haven't you?"

The pressman thinks there are some left, and hands the nominee quite a roll of them, which he takes with a faint smile.

He offers one to Strawberry, who says he has voted. Mr. Cuffins looks as if he would like to know whom he voted for, but does not ask.

"Well, has Mr. Larker voted?"

"I'm not a sovereign, yet," Elfred says, half-sulkily.

"How?"

"I mean that I'm not of age. And if I were," adds Mr. Larker as the nominee bustles off with his tickets, "you wouldn't get my vote." Which declaration it is fair to state, Mr. C. does not, and was not intended to hear.

The voting in Errington goes all one way. Errington is Whig. No matter what the bone of contention is, Errington pulls Whig-wise. There are men in Errington who would scout the notion of voting for a man because his principles are right: they want to know what party he belongs to. And so, these men of Errington walk up to the polls, and cast their votes for Cuffins, who is a staunch Whig—let him be stupid and dishonest, if he will.

At Oldbury, it is different. In the palmier days of yore, when the party presented an unbroken front everywhere else in the county—even then, there was defection in Oldbury. What with a strong infusion of radicalism, and a natural inclination on part of the people for bolting, the old Whig spirit is much weakened. But now, when a man of their own place, is risen against the regular nominee, there is hardly a trace of that spirit left.

Meantime, despite the predictions and potions of Doctor Wetherbee, a gloom is deepening in the hearts of the dwellers in the fine old mansion, which looks moodily out from its stricken maples upon the dull, blank stretch of fields and miry road.—All day long, Annie Berson sits beside the bed, and watches to anticipate the slightest wish and movement of the sick child. All day long the humid sweat gathers upon the window, and runs down in little rills to the bars in the sash, where it hangs in tremulous rows. All day long, the wagons passing to and fro, make an unpleasant grinding on the road, and then slowly fade from sight and hearing. All day long, a trio of buzzards, circle lazily around the top of a dead ash, and rest themselves upon it, and battle noiselessly among themselves, and flap their foul wings, and rise and sink again, like birds in a dream. All day long, the meadows keep a monotonous simmering, and the sheep cower on the lee of stumps, and nibble the briars in the fence corners. All day long, the woodlands slumber in their robes of mist, and seem shorn of half their height.

And when the dreary night comes down, these things are seen no more, and wide, and all-pervading darkness reigns.

"I wonder why George doesn't come! What a long, long day it has been!" Annie rests her forehead on her hand, and tries to read.

The forgotten fire burns low. Shimmering, spectral glances light up the polished furniture, and play along the carpet, like the weird firelight in The Raven—

—And each sep'rate, dying ember
Wrought its ghost upon the floor.

The rain beats against the windows, with wearisome monotony as if innumerable beaks

From the Night's Plutonian shore,

were tapping there for entrance.

O! the long, lonesome Night! To lie sleeplessly, and count the life-throbs of the clocks; to cheat oneself into a half slumber; to have the golden charm broken by visions of wild, haggard forms and faces, that change and shift like the glories of the kaleidoscope; to drug Reason, and leave Fantasy and her train of grisly whims in full possession of the brain; to listen to the noises, that rise through all the house, and echo in the silent room; to weave horrible pictures that fade and brighten by turns; to be haunted by memories of dreadful scenes, that will not be laid; to rehearse the business of the day, with fantastical garnishment from Phantom-land; to sink at last in a whirl of contending fancies into an unquiet dream, only to fright oneself with new terrors. O! this is most fearful. But to Watch! When the lamp glimmers feebly; when the invalid tosses uneasily, and prates of the ghastly things that haunt his delirious moments; when the stillness aches upon the sense; when the heart sinks in deadly fluctuations of hope and fear; when the day that seemed never going to come, comes at last, and brings no relief!

Annie Berson reads till the print grows blurred and big, and bright blue and crimson lights dance before her eyes. Then closing her book, waits.

Not long.

A quick, ringing step upon the stone pavement without—an unlocking of the door and its clanging to, again—a footing on the stairs—and Mr. Berson enters the rooms.

"Half-past twelve! By heaven—I'd no notion it was that late. Returns coming kept me. I'm the man, and no mistake.—How is the child, Annie?"

There is an energy and rapidity in these words very different from Mr. Berson's usual complaisant utterance. His eyes sparkle with unwonted life, and his whole body is intense with excitement.

"Not much better, I'm afraid," Annie says, going up to the bed, and placing her hand upon the burning forehead of the child.

"Not better? That's strange. Clara hasn't been properly cared for, Annie."

"George!"

"Oh! well—never mind, Annie. I didn't mean to blame you. Has the doctor been here, to-day?"

95

"Once," Annie says, "and only prescribed quiet and rest."

"The best medicine! O heaven—quiet and rest," repeats Mr. Berson, and then adds, incoherently, "What a whirl I am in! A thousand—not less. Really!"

A pang of deadly apprehension thrills the sister's heart as she watches the movements of Mr. Berson, while he slowly paces up and down the floor.

"George—George, sit down. You're tired, poor fellow; and you are too much excited."

"I know what you are thinking of, Annie," and Mr. Berson pauses in his walk, "but it isn't that—it isn't that. Don't be alarmed about me. I tell you I'm all right."

"Not all right, George, dear. You are not well. Sit down, do. See! you will wake Clara."

He suffers her to place him in a chair, but immediately rises with the question—

"Father never told you then, that I was the Pope's nephew?"

"Never," falters poor Annie.

"Ah! I didn't suppose he had. Though it's quite as well. You needn't mention it. O! don't be frightened about me. I am all right. Eh, Annie?"

[*Ashtabula Sentinel*, 11 January 1855]

It has stopped raining. A few bon-fires which political fervor endeavored to kindle in the earlier part of the night, now blaze feebly up along the silent streets of Oldbury. The village clock is striking three, as a boisterous party rattle up to the tavern, in a light wagon.

"Why—what the devil!" cries a voice. "Everybody abed. That's great. Well, drive on down to George's. Hullor!"

Away down the road, the mud flying from the wheels and horses' feet, and the party singing snatches of a hundred songs in vigorous discord, till Mr. Berson's house looms dimly up before them through the fog.

"Everybody abed here, too!" and the party quit the wagon, and hitch their panting team. "No—there's a light. I knew it—I knew it! Right after me, now." And the owner of the voice tries the door, which Mr. Berson forgot to lock, and is soon out of sight in the darkness of the hall. The others follow him, and after various attempts to pass through a shutter by its side, the last one finds the door and closes it behind him.

Up in the room, now, where the little child lies very ill, there is a strange quiet. Mr. Berson, fallen asleep in the arm-chair, is calm at last; Annie sitting near him, not less regardful of his welfare than the child's.

But the noise in the hall below, startles her, and she rouses the sleeper. "George, there's somebody down stairs, and the Doctor hasn't come yet. O! wake up—do."

Bounding from his chair, Mr. Berson's first impulse is to go down and eject the intruders, but a sudden thought detains him. "What if he should come when I am gone, and take her?" And he turns toward the bed, and spreads his arms as if to shield the child from some fancied harm.

He hears the men groping to and fro, looking for the stairs. He hears their muttered oaths and exclamations, as they stumble over chairs and tables. He hears the door open again, and the voice of Dr. Wetherbee expostulating with them. He hears them on the stairs at last, and up the flight, and through the passage, to the door of the room. He hears an awkward hand fumbling at the latch, and the men scrambling through.

"Hullor! George—we've gained the day. Boys—give three cheers for George Berson."

Little Clara, frightened from sleep by the tumult, raises herself from the pillow, and flings her arms around the neck of her uncle. The apparition of the strange men with their muddy clothes, and haggard faces, blends with some terror of her delirium, and she sinks upon the bed again in a swoon.

"Dead!—dead!" cries the candidate in a wild voice, his black eyes flashing and his lips compressed. "You did it!" and he springs upon Walter, and dashes him to the floor.

Sobered in an instant, the young man regains his feet, and assists Doctor Wetherbee, and his man in securing Mr. Berson. There is a room near at hand which has known such inmates before, and into this the struggling wretch is hustled, and the door bolted upon him.

"Not crazy—doctor—not mad?" asks Walter.

"As a March hare!" says the Doctor, solemnly. "And now put out this gang of ragamuffins."

"God pardon me for this night's work!" Walter exclaims, remounting the stairs after sending his drunken, bewildered retinue away,—"God pardon me for this night's work!"

A golden summer evening, and the slant rays of the sun shedding a mellow bloom over the landscape. The shadows of the trees eked out upon the fields, and the gnats dancing in airy convolutions over the sunnier spots. The robins flitting to and fro among the maples, and trying the first notes of their vespers. The bluebirds chirping querulously. The garden gay with flowers and an air of cool repose about the old homestead.

There is a little company drinking tea in the verandah. The grape vine is grown much stouter, and its thick foliage almost shuts out the sun, only flecks of it stealing through here and there.

One of these rests in the clustering curls of little Clara, and turns them to gold.

"Uncle George! Have another cup?" And the proud little girl clutches the handle of the tea pot, and makes great pretensions to gravity, in her office as head of the table.

Mr. Berson smiles faintly, and looks at Annie, who nods and says, "Yes."

Then Mr. Berson's cup being refilled, he sips the tea with an air of great enjoyment, and asks—"Walter, where is he?"

"Why, uncle," says Clara, "you've been told nearly a dozen times, already. He's gone to Errington."

"Ah! true—quite true. Bad memory. I remember now. But what for, Annie, what for? You didn't tell me what for?"

"O! yes she did. He's gone to get married," Clara says, anticipating Annie's reply. "Going to get married! Don't you think it's funny, uncle George?"

Mr. Berson ponders a while, and then says: "It seems to me as if I forgot a good deal of late. But tell me this. Hasn't Clara been sick?"

"Very sick," Annie says, "two years ago."

"And she didn't die?"

Annie shakes her head.

Mr. Berson rises from his chair, half-involuntarily, and places his hand upon the child's head, as if to make sure of her reality, and then sits down again.

"Why, uncle, I hope you don't think I'm a ghost!" cries Clara.

"And Robert—Annie—and Robert?" asks Mr. Berson, turning to his sister. "He was a great trouble."

Annie nods at Clara, and makes "Dead!" without speaking.

"Ah!" Mr. Berson says, and plays with his teaspoon. "So Wat's to be married. Who is he going to marry? Clara can tell that, I dare swear," he adds with something of his old manner.

"Yes indeed!" exclaims that young lady triumphantly. "And it's Miss Carmin."

And then they talk of those matters that chance to rise faintly to the recollection of his shattered brain, and Mr. Berson at last strolls out into the twilight, and walks to and fro beneath an old elm in the yard.—It is his changeless custom; his feet have worn the grass away, and packed the pathway smooth and hard.

And his patient, gentle sister watches him, thanking heaven that he is no worse, and trying to believe that he is better.

[*Ashtabula Sentinel*, 18 January 1855]

Howells between two friends, 1855

"W. D. Howells at eighteen, with Goodrich—an organ builder—on his right, and Miller (a jeweller) on his left. These two older [men] were his literary friends in Jefferson, Ohio, with whom he talked about Shakespear, Thackeray and poetry. Miller was a friend of Forbes, the Scotch farmer in Williamsfield—near Jefferson—who offered to become one of the three to send W. D. Howells to Harvard."—Mildred Howells

CHAPTER TWO

Pictures of River Travel

All the soft, damp air was full of delicate perfume
From the young willows in bloom on either bank of the river,—
Faint, delicious fragrance, trancing the indolent senses
In a luxurious dream of the river and land of the lotus.
Not yet out of the west the roses of sunset were withered;
In the deep blue above light clouds of gold and of crimson
Floated in slumber serene; and the restless river beneath them
Rushed away to the sea with a vision of rest in its bosom;
Far on the eastern shore lay dimly the swamps of the cypress;
Dimly before us the islands grew from the river's expanses,—
Beautiful, wood-grown isles, with the gleam of the swart
    inundation
Seen through the swaying boughs and slender trunks of their
    willows;
And on the shore beside us the cotton-trees rose in the evening,
Phantom-like, yearningly, wearily, with the inscrutable sadness
Of the mute races of trees. While hoarsely the steam from her
    'scape-pipes
Shouted, then whispered a moment, then shouted again to the
    silence,
Trembling through all her frame with the mighty pulse of her
    engines,
Slowly the boat ascended the swollen and broad Mississippi,
Bank-full, sweeping on, with tangled masses of drift-wood,
Daintily breathed about with whiffs of silvery vapor,
Where in his arrowy flight the twittering swallow alighted,
And the belated blackbird paused on the way to its nestlings.
                            —"The Pilot's Story" (1860)

[Though he was certain there had been previous trips with his mother
when she had gone upriver to see her people, the earliest steamboat journey Howells remembered with any distinctness was one he had made

with his father between Cincinnati and Pittsburgh when he was nine or ten years old. Their host-captain was an Uncle Dean, one of the four brothers of Mary Howells, exceptional rivermen whose abilities remained part of the river lore as long as piloting was a vocation ambitious youth strove for. The distinction this association conferred on the two travelers was not lost on the boy, but compared to the greater attraction of the river, it measured little. Seventy years after, when Howells recalled the years of his youth, details of that ancient voyage returned with a vividness that underscores the importance of that initial venture into the world beyond the family circle. River life, like that of the region whose well-being it supported, was boisterous, idyllic, threatening, exotic, enthralling, sublimely democratic. No matter how sophisticated one's standards, the show was bound to impress.

No doubt I have since seen nobler sights than the mile-long rank of the steamboats as they lay at the foot of the landings in the cities at either end of our voyage, but none of these excelling wonders re-mains like that. All the passenger-boats on the Ohio were then side-wheelers, and their lofty chimneys towering on either side of their pilot-houses were often crenelated at the top, with wire ropes be-tween them supporting the effigies of such Indians as they were named for. From time to time one of the majestic craft pulled from the rank with the clangor of its mighty bell, and the mellow roar of its whistle, and stood out in the yellow stream, or arrived in like state to find a place by the shore. The wide slope of the landing was heaped with the merchandise putting off or taking on the boats, amidst the wild and whirling curses of the mates and the insensate rushes of the deck-hands staggering to and fro under their burdens. The swarming drays came and went with freight, and there were huckster carts of every sort; peddlers, especially of oranges, escaped with their lives among the hoofs and wheels, and through the din and turmoil passengers hurried aboard the boats, to repent at leisure their haste in trusting the advertised hour of departure. It was never known that any boat left on time. (*YMY*, pp. 26–27)

The splendor of the world where his uncles' lives were passed bestowed on these kindly, affectionate kinsmen a magical dimension, and their hap-hazard visits, or, rare and more wonderful, their treating their sister's children to passages on the river were events to be treasured in antici-pation and memory.

The occasion of his voyage in 1858, Howells afterwards remembered, was the home visit of his cousin Willie Dean, who a few years earlier had left Pittsburgh for St. Paul where he sought and, in time, found his fortune. Now as he prepared to return to Minnesota, someone in the family apparently thought it would be good if Howells accompanied him. The disappointment of his last winter in Columbus when illness had forced him to give up his appointment as legislative corespondent weighed heavily on the young man, and some such amusement would possibly help him regain his bearings.

Upon first returning to Jefferson from Columbus early in March, Howells had resumed the therapeutic regimen he had worked out with his father on those earlier occasions when his health and spirit had been unequal to his ambition. The benefits of the countryside and family life were immediate, and early in April he recorded in the pocket diary he had purchased in Columbus the year before some details of a pattern of life the older man sometimes thought approached the ideal.

Friday, April 9, 1858.
Got up yesterday morning, per resolution, the instant I awoke. Made fires, read the papers, a chapter in Conde and a chapter of Aaron Burr's Life. This latter book (by Parton whom I don't admire) appeals so successfully to the *contrary* in me, that I am quite enamoured of Burr, and cannot but think him shamefully wronged and persecuted.

After breakfast translated part of an article on "Vampires" from the Spanish; washed and went to the office, where I set up a job.

Afternoon—finished the translation mentioned; quite a lengthy affair—and read it to the women.

John and I went to the woods and brought home two raspberry bushes and planted them.

Last Monday, I cast my first vote.

Saturday 10 Got up as I have done for the last six days just at six o'clock. I find that I wake at that hour almost exactly, and then I rise *instanter*. Brought an elm from the woods and planted it in the front yard. Went to the office, filled a case, and came home. After dinner set an advertisement. Albert Ransom at the office. Carrie and Eunice both at home. Half promised to visit them today or tomorrow. But do not think I shall go till next week. Finished "Burr."—Tried to write a letter to Babb and didn't. Ashamed of this fact. Read to the women at night from the "Old Curiosity Shop."

Sunday 11 Fishing to-day. No great run of luck. Spoil—"shiners" and chubs, chiefly. Got a letter from father, enclosing one from E.A.S. No recibio su carta, basta nueve dias pasadas. Bad Spanish enough, but the truth.

But in later years, the quiet peace of country life was largely an alluring, elusive alternative, more dreamed of than lived, to the hectic and distracting demands the world made on a successful man of letters. At twenty-one, the youth could only regard his rustication as a further denial of his hopes and ambitions. The prospect of a visit with Dean relatives in Pittsburgh and afterwards a voyage on his Uncle Sam's steam packet perhaps as far as St. Paul may not have done much to assuage the terrible burden of those life questions which weighed on Howells, but it did allow a temporary respite as well as a literary opportunity.

After the custom of the day, Howells wrote letters home descriptive of the scenes and impressions suitable to the general consumption of *Sentinel* readers. Such epistolary sketches were by no means restricted to the provincial press in the mid-1800s. Even though improved means of transportation had made travel more accessible to ordinary men and women, the travel sketch remained a literary staple of enormous appeal, and few writers failed to try their wit at the form. Cooper's *Gleanings in Europe* (1837–38), Bryant's *Letters of a Traveller* (1850), Bayard Taylor's *Views Afoot* (1846), George William Curtis's *Nile Notes of a Howadji* (1851), Melville's South Sea adventures, and Thoreau's travels at Walden were modern variations of a familiar type increasingly common to Western literature since the Renaissance. But Howells's immediate inspiration for his travel letters came not from any such native durables but from the whimsical witchery of Heinrich Heine's *Reisebilder*, or "Pictures of Travel."

Howells first encountered the work of the German romantic in George Eliot's important essay in the *Westminster Review* for January 1856, an article occasioned by the appearance of the first collected edition of Heine's works which was then being published in German in Philadelphia. During a lifetime of many literary passions, none overwhelmed the Ohio poet so much as his love for Heine. With the help of *Ollendorff's New Method*, a system of language training which guaranteed that one would learn to read, write, and speak German in six months, and, more important, the kindly tutelage of an emigré bookbinder named Limbeck who had settled in Jefferson, Howells was soon engrossed in German romanticism. It would be several years before the spell of Heine paled, and at the end the success of his example was in Howells's finding his true self, "and to be for good or evil whatsoever I really was." Heine's writings showed Howells that art and life are inseparable, "that the life of literature was from the springs of the best common speech, and that the nearer it could be made to conform, in voice, look, and gait, to graceful, easy, picturesque and humorous or impassioned talk, the better it was" (*MLP*, p. 129).

Howells embarked on his twelve-hundred-mile trip to St. Louis early

Thursday morning, the thirteenth day of May. Known to the early French settlers as La Belle Riviere, the smooth flowing Ohio wound its way through what even after a lifetime of travels Howells would still think "the loveliest hills and richest levels in the world." As the elegant packet made its seemingly effortless descent southward, the warm scent of the willows in bloom along the shore put Howells in mind of Tennyson's "Lotos-Eaters."

How sweet it were, hearing the downward stream,
With half-shut eyes ever to seem
Falling asleep in a half-dream!

But some cares could not be forgotten; countering the peaceful enchantment of this mid-American idyll was the terrible fact of slavery, more felt than seen, and the division it was making in the nation. Already reality had a way of disturbing romance.]

DOWN "LA BELLE RIVIERE"

Cincinnati, May 15.

The "Cambridge" steamboat, in company with myself, arrived at this city today about 8 A.M., having made the trip from Pittsburgh (some 490 miles) in about fifty hours, which is very fair traveling in point of speed. In point of everything else, steamboat traveling is delightful. One has, to begin with, abundant room to lie about in, which one has not on a train; even when one is a double-upable person. One can sleep at ease; eat sumptuously; talk without splitting one's throat to be heard; read without spoiling one's eyes. Best of all, one is not continually aggravated by glimpses of things, but can contemplate scenery at leisure.

And speaking of scenery. One of the pleasantest features of Ohio river landscape, are her little islands. Some of them contain hundreds of acres, highly cultivated and adorned with cozy farmhouses. One is classic: Blennerhassett's Island. We all remember Wirt's paradisification of this isle, and I being fresh from the lection of "The Life of Burr," was anxious to behold the place to which so many romantic associations link his name. To my great regret, we passed the island in the night.

Below Wheeling the lovely hills that overlook the river, begin to recede, and the bottoms to wax broader. Country roads meander along with the windings of the stately stream, and more frequently, farm mansions and pretty villages adorn her banks. Of these latter (qualified by an apposite adjective) is Coalport, which some one has described as seven miles long, and extending as far back as you can see—and this is no exaggeration, the hills rising nearly bluff from the river. The solitary incident of our yesterday's journey was the leaving behind a deck passenger at this place. He had gone up into the village to imbibe a villainous species of lager-bier they sell there, and reached the landing just as the boat was putting out. Poor fellow! his tipsy look of trouble and despair, would have been droll, if it had not been pitiful.

No one but the poor foreigners ever take passage on deck. I do not think there is an American deck passenger on the boat, but there are Germans, Irish and French. One of these latter looks as if he might have sat for all the pictures I have ever seen of Napoleon's Old Guard. He is of an erect, manly figure; clad in pantaloons of indiscriminate hue, and a dirty blue *blouse*, with a slouch cap on his head. But with his keen eyes, "overwhelming brows" and gray moustache, and his soldierly carriage, he is quite the veteran; and I should be very sorry to learn that he was a mere peasant, who had never cut anybody's throat.

The deck passengers "inhabit" a narrow space behind the boat's engines, and here they, their baggage and provisions are stowed away in a marvelously uncomfortable fashion. Men, women and children, cook, eat and sleep together, and all the decencies of civilization are ignored. It is by no means "high life below stairs." Here they herd together the greater part of the time, but in the cool evening, they come forward and sit in clusters about the bow of the boat.

The cabin passenger is a limited monarch, going where he pleases, and saying and doing nearly all the things he lists. It is a deliciously idle life—to lounge about on the guards till breakfast, sharpening the appetite with drafts of sweet morning air; to eat; to talk, to saunter to and fro, to doze over a book, till dinner, with the same in the afternoon; and, supper over, to play at cards, or watch (ever-present cigar in mouth) the dun hills and gleaming lights along the shore.

Last night we laid up awhile at Portsmouth, on account of a severe storm. It came on suddenly as a lake squall, and continued with violence for nearly half an hour. This morning, in strolling about the city, I went into the U.S. Court room, where Judge Matthews (Dist. Att'y) was just preparing to make the closing argument on Connelly's case. Ex-Gov. Corwin closed yesterday for the defence. I saw the old "Wagoner Boy," (as we used to sing him,) looking as black, as good-humored and sound as when I heard him twelve years ago.

People were dropping into the court room, one after another, but there did not seem to be a great interest felt. At least I heard nothing said by spectators. I suppose that the real excitement existed yesterday.

You will hear from me again I think at St. Louis.

[Signed "W.", *Ashtabula Sentinel*, 20 May 1858]

[But Howells did not wait until his arrival in St. Louis to write again, and two days later his impressions continued.]

Evansville, Ind., May 17.
Some twelve miles below Cincinnati, there stands on the Ohio bank of the river, a modest frame mansion. Age has not roughly touched it, and its guardian trees bend over it affectionately, as if to shield it from decay. The grounds about it are neat, and nothing more. Before it moves the Beautiful River; to left and right stretch broad rich acres of arable and wood land; behind rise gentle acclivities.

In this house, lived Harrison; on one of these knolls, he sleeps now. A few evergreens mark the spot where he rests, and white pickets enclose the shaft above his grave. If, indeed,
"Death is the end of life,"
how calm must be his slumbers here!

Poor old man! he was the victim of too enthusiastic a campaign; and over much hand-shaking and barbecues, and hurrahings, accomplished what years of military service had failed to effect.— (Undigested mutton killed Wellington.)— Or he was an honest man, and suffocated in the atmosphere of Washington.

The young May grass is green upon the hero's grave; sweet Spring gales make music in the whispering leaves about it, and the singing birds soothe—"the dull cold ear of death!"

Our good steamboat yesterday descended the Falls of the Ohio, instead of going through the canal; and I must say that I am by no means satisfied with the falls. I expected to enjoy at least a sensation in beholding them; but beside a few tame looking ripples just below Louisville, I saw nothing. The river, however, is very high, and it is only at a low stage of water that the falls are a spectacle of any grandeur.

We stopped awhile at New Albany, and I strolled up into the town, which I feel no little desire to buy, on account of its beauty and location. It is indeed, one of the prettiest places I have seen. It was universally agreed by G. and me, as we paused before a small cottage, with a summer bower in front, covered with May roses, and a yard full of lilacs and snow balls, that New Albany would be a nice place to live. Taste and refinement evidently abide there; and business, I should think, also, judging from the solid, cityish blocks which adorn the principal streets.

As we descend the river, the scenery, without lacking variety, becomes tamer and less picturesque. The hills are less frequent, the bottoms wider, and the banks lower. Yet, we passed some glorious scenery yesterday, which, to use a novel expression, cannot be appreciated unless seen. I was most enamored of a rustic mill that stood under a woody bluff, at the very river's brink, and with its overshot wheel and dashing stream, that

"Rolled a slumbrous sheet of foam below,"

looked the very picture of quietude and seclusion. It put me in mind of mills in sweet old German stories.

We took on coal at a small Kentucky town, opposite Cannelton; and here, without experiencing any change of sentiment on the subject, I beheld the argument urged with such persistent dullness and stupidity by the supporters of slavery. It was Sunday evening, and the whole village, black, coffee-colored, and white, crowded the landing to look at our boat. Among the rest were some twenty or thirty slaves, dressed in gala garments, and making a very brave show in their Sunday clothes. There were big darkeys magnificent in white vests and black coats, and little darkeys grand in various patterns of clean linen. The ladies all wore hoops, which I noticed were of the largest size; and they certainly looked very comfortable and contented in their airy calicos.—The far-sighted logicians who urge that Southern slaves are better off than Northern laborers, point exultantly to such occasions to prove the truth of what they say. Is it worth while to dispute them? I think not.

I think that Hawesville, for that was the name of the place, contains, perhaps, more lazy souls than any other town in the country. Everybody looked a little lazier than the rest; if any difference existed it was in favor of some gentlemen on the shady side of the "Eagle Hotel," whose chairs were balanced at luxurious angles, with a skill that only long practice could confer. The village looked dirty and uncomfortable, and had an unbaked-brick complexion generally. The house of one of the richest residents, (Colonel somebody or other,) was pointed out to me; and if other southern grandees do not house more splendidly than the Colonel, we have nothing to envy them.

We stopped about dusk at some other Kentucky town of an unrememberable name, and while we lay there, a large Louisville and New Orleans packet landed just below, and took on some poultry and sheep. These latter were induced on board by "snaking" their leader aft, when they all followed him helter-skelter, with a blindness of instinct to be found only in sheep and locofocos. In a few moments, another of these packets, upward bound, came in sight, and majestically approached. As she drew near, strains of music burst forth, and sweet, dear, old "Lilly Dale," performed by a full brass band, enchanted the night.

It was a brave sight. The three boats were brilliantly lighted up, their bows all aglare with the flames of beacons that blazed high with resin and pine, and dropped glowing coals into the flushing waves below. Looking weird and gnome like in the light, the deck hands hurried to and fro, and the boat's guards were crowded with spectators. From the 'scape-pipes the steam breathed languidly, and out of the lofty chimneys the wreaths of smoke floated slowly away. The sky was full of fleecy clouds that dimmed, but did not hide the young moon. After a few moment's stay, the upward bound packet, slowly quitting the shore, strode out into the middle river. "She walks the water like a thing of life," I cried, and I never felt the grandeur and truth of that line before. Far away she moved with increasing speed, and when lost to view, the other boats glided away from us, and hoarsely whispering farewell, rushed down the broad, still, stately stream.

[Signed "W.," *Ashtabula Sentinel*, 27 May 1858]

"FATHER OF WATERS"

Just above Cairo, May 18.
Yesterday afternoon, we had a storm of wind and rain that would have done credit to Lake Erie, in her most exasperated moments; and indeed it took no great stretch of the imagination, to fancy oneself on some such inland ocean, with the white-caps rolling furiously, and the far off shores dimly visible through the driving tempest. The weather continued very rough throughout the night. I have the Captain's word for this, having myself retired at the reasonable hour of nine, with a trust in Providence, the crew and the "Cambridge," that no violence of the storm could shake. A few moments, (it is to be confessed,) I lay thinking what an extremely uncomfortable thing it would be, to be called up in the night to take a wagon-bed excursion to the low-lying swampy shore; or to make Cairo on the top of some drift-wood. The rain however played the sweet old tune that it plays upon the roof at home, and making believe that the roaring wind was the *susurrus* of our threshold maples, I fell asleep to dream of far-away old Jeff.

We skirted all day yesterday, the south shore of "Egypt;" and any ill-conditioned Israelite, who would long to return to the flesh-pots of that region, I should think, would have a ravenous appetite for meat. Nothing varied the sameness of the flat shores, through whose thick, clustering trees, one could see far inland, the sheen of inundating waters, whose marshy breadths looked fever and ague given "a local habitation." Nothing varied this scenery but a few squalid towns, squatted on the river's brink, or rude cabins scattered at intervals along the banks. It is a condition of things to make Mark Tapley come out jolly, and I think Chuzzlewit's 'Eden' was situated somewhere in 'Egypt,' though Dickens has placed it a little lower down on the map.

The most notable feature of a South-Western river-town, to a steamboat traveler, is the wharf-boat, against which the steamer lands. This is always a kind of amphibious craft, with a boat foundation, a house roof, and hybrid weather boarding. It invariably contains a little freight—chiefly old chairs—which no boat seems ever to take away, and swarms with loafers, of all sorts, sizes and colors; from the tender ruffian of boyish years, to the accomplished *semper* inebriate, who remembers keel-boats. Besides this, there is always a pleasing prospect of half a dozen taverns, with loafers on horseback before their doors; a harness shop; a grocery where they keep whisky and quinine; and a grocery where they keep whisky and tobacco.

I have seldom the curiosity to penetrate these pleasant villages, and indeed, the boat merely touches at most of them. There is a species of traveler, however, given to rushing ashore upon all occasions; and yesterday I had the satisfaction to see two of these left behind.—They made frantic signals of disapproval and remonstrance, and started on a very spirited run after the boat. The captain, not proof against the entreaties of their friends on board, stopped to take them on; and they came panting up into the cabin, looking heated, and excessively silly. One of them, an oldish gentleman, remarked that he felt it a good deal in his legs.

The whole country through which we passed is "flat, stale," but I should think from the looks of the soil, not "unprofitable." Impenetrable thickets of cottonwood line the shores, which are else low and flooded by the swollen stream. None of the lovely hills that make the upper Ohio so gloriously picturesque, are to be seen; and for miles and miles, the eye rests only on broad expanses of river, terminating in thick, unwholesome looking forests. Their verdure is dense and dark; but no bird songs float from it.—Stately, loathsome buzzards are the only living things that seem to frequent them; and these soar above them, as if loth to penetrate their secret recesses.

I meant, in the course of these hasty jottings, to have noted the difference in the growth of vegetation; but two weeks' absence from the Reserve, has done much to obliterate any recollections of the Spring's forwardness there. I believe, however, that peaches were just in bloom, and that little or no gardening had been done. Yesterday I saw well grown corn in Egypt, and in some of the Kentucky towns, locust trees loaded with white blossoms. Of course all kinds of forest trees are in full leaf. I cannot speak of orchards, for I have not seen more than one or two since we left Indiana. Where the timber has been more scattering, I have seen some golden wild flowers in the woods; but few of the sojourners in these unhappy regions cultivate such things about their houses. It was only at a little place where we stopped last evening that I saw evidence of a taste so common with us. It was a village on the Illinois shore, and was for the most part squalid and uninviting enough; but one little cottage of stone, built on the crest of a little knoll, redeemed the place. Shade and fruit trees embowered the house, and half its front was hidden in a clambering rose vine, crimson with roses. A few pigeons circled about the roof; and I was reminded of one of the charmingest pictures in Heine's "Reise Bilder," wherein he portrays the Italian maiden spinning at her cottage door, and the white doves resting on the jutting roof overhead. "Da saß sie und lachte," etc. etc.

This morning, about seven o'clock, we reached the metropolis of Egypt, the famed city Cairo, which was originally built at the bottom of the Mississippi river; a levee was hastily thrown up, and the water pumped out of the enclosure. It is now quite dry in spots; and the town has several respectable brick blocks, and a branch of the Illinois Central Railroad terminates there. The appearance of the place from a steamboat is unique. You see only roofs and second stories; but on ascending the levee you look down upon quite a number of houses, standing in appropriate puddles of water. The cruelest piece of irony I have seen for a long time, is displayed in a sign reading "Land Office."

The "Cambridge" had some freight to put off and some coal to take on, and ample time for a stroll through the place was afforded. G. and I, just to say that we had been there, muddied our boots, and stood upon that sharp out-jutting point of Illinois, from which you behold three rivers and three States: of the former, the Ohio, gross, swollen and bloated, like some vagabond profligate, forgotten all the grandeur, beauty and purity of her native hills; the upper Mississippi,

"From the land of the Dacotahs,
From the land of handsome women,
From the falls of Minnehaha,
Minnehaha, Laughing Water,"—

the lower Mississippi rolling a vast, turbid, unwholesome length through swamps, cotton fields and brakes, till he mingles his waters with the Gulf of Mexico.

Of States you see Kentucky and Missouri, each represented by marshy peninsulas covered with a dense growth of cottonwood; and Illinois, represented by Cairo, standing ancle-deep in the waters of the three rivers, with the Ohio before, and the Mississippi beside and behind, defended on one side by a levee and on the other by a cypress swamp. Ague is evidently king there; yet people are fighting their way into the water, and securing every inch of hard-contested ground by the erection of solid edifices.

We returned to the boat, and she presently put out again. In a few moments she had quitted the Ohio, and rounding a point of watery land, we steamed slowly and safely up the Father of Floods.

UP THE MISSISSIPPI

May 18, 1858.

Mississippi scenery for more than an hundred miles below St. Louis, has nothing of the grand or the picturesque, but a great deal of the flat uninteresting. Its distinctive features are the same with those of the lower Ohio, which I have perhaps enough described. One sees the same low banks, the same tangled cottonwood swamps; but the towns are fewer, and the river islands far more frequent. These dot the whole course of the stream, at brief intervals, for hundreds of miles, and are continually increasing and decreasing with the action of the water.

The Mississippi is incredibly swift; and boats ascending keep near shore, for the sake of the dead-water. We are hardly ever more than four or five rods from the bank, and one can sit upon the hurricane deck, and enjoy all the novelty of backwoods life, without knowing its frets and perplexity. During the course of our trip, frequent unsuccessful shots have been fired at wild ducks, "and other fallow deer;" hardly a day has passed without some exploit of the kind. This morning, a passenger fired at a wild-turkey running in a cottonwood thicket, with the usual result of not hitting it. The more sanguine among us believe the bird to have experienced a trifling loss of plumage, but this opinion is by no means universal.

About the first thing I noticed on entering these waters was the apparition of divers unpleasant-looking logs, which, fast rooted in the mud beneath, made continual obeisance with the force of the current. It may be politeness; but their nod has something defiant and mocking about it; and they brought unpleasant ideas of holes to be punched in the hulk, sinking, and solitary midnight excursions "down the Mississippi." *Sawyers,* men call them.

Gerideau, a town nearly as old as the first French exploration of these regions, we passed yesterday evening. It is a pretty place, but entirely American in appearance. The Jesuit college is its chief edifice. Several of the Society of Jesus were seen taking the air, clad in long sombre coats, and touching their hats to each other at intervals, with a stately courtesy long disused among our go-ahead people. Nearly all the settlements along this part of the Mississippi were made by the French, but their names are now almost the sole thing about them reminiscent of their founders. St. Genevieve, is one of these. A couple of saw mills are the romantic features of the village.

As we ascend the river, the aspect of the country improves. The banks are higher, the timber of larger growth; highlands appear in the distance, and now within some fifty miles of St. Louis, we have just passed rocky bluffs, which would furnish studies for all the artists in the world forever. They rise within a few yards of the river, lofty, abrupt, gloomily beautiful, all seamed and scarred, full of dark caverns, now regular as a solid wall, now scattering and broken as some old ruin; but ever crowned with luxuriant groves that wave in the cool river wind. On an interval between two of these bluffs, stands a castle-like building whose gothic style, heavy stone walls and lofty turrets harmonize finely with the surrounding scenery. It is the residence of Kennett, formerly mayor of St. Louis, and now stands unoccupied, the monument of taste and exhausted fortune.

It is, I think, the most picturesque edifice I have seen during our journey, and no extravagance mars its perfect architectural beauty. A grand flight of steps leads from the river bank up to the mansion, which is erected on a gentle knoll commanding a most enchanting prospect of stream and shore. Selma is the name of this residence. Near it, several stone houses now fallen into decay, were formerly used in the manufacture of shot from the lead abounding in the vicinity. The ruin of the proprietor of the rocks is too plainly attested by the present aspect of the place. Rank, poisonous vines clamber over the fronts and roofs of the houses, and weeds choke all wholesomer growth about them. On the brink of the steepest and loftiest bluff hangs a slender frame edifice used as a shot tower.

So much written yesterday. Last night about eleven o'clock we reached St. Louis, and this morning my ears are stunned with the roar and bustle of the busiest steamboat wharf in the United States. Frantic deck-hands rushing forth with flat iron slabs, which they dash down with infernal clangor; wagons rattling and clashing over the stones, hacks and omnibuses hurrying up and down, drays drawn by mules harnessed tandem; uncontrollable porters run down by bewildered passengers—horses, men, poultry, women, corn, kegs, bags, bales, children,—all the products of the East and West— throng the landing for more than a mile, while a forest of chimneys rise from the steamboats at its edge.

I have strolled somewhat through the city this morning, but as we are to remain here some days I defer further notices.

St. Louis, May 22, 1858.
Two days' stay in St. Louis, has made me tolerably well acquainted with the outer city; and yet my observation has been after rather a quiet fashion, than the orthodox sight-seeing mode.

The first thing for which I looked about me with interest, was some indication that I was in the metropolis of a Slave State. Not, indeed, with much belief that I should behold anything of the institution's working here; but still I had a hankering that way, which was of course not satisfied. One sees no more blacks in St. Louis than in Cincinnati, if as many. The coarse labor everywhere is performed by the Irish. The artisans are Americans and Germans. With the negroes whom I have met, "sir," is the style of address, and not "massa;" and they are not nearly as servile as the Irish, a people whom freedom does not make independent. I haunted the court house somedeal yesterday, in hopes to be present at a sale of negroes advertised in the *Republican*, but I managed to miss it.

St. Louis is a beautiful city. That is, the *residential* part. The business part is just like the business part of all other cities. But its suburban streets are lined with fine mansions, generally shaded, and with ample, flower-filled yards. Some of these are adorned with fountains; and last evening I noticed one unique and fanciful in design—a slender jet issuing from a marble column, and tossing in its attenuated stream, a little ball, that rose and sank, and danced and quivered among the crystal drops.

The public buildings of the city are not very imposing; and in church architecture, St. Louis is behind Columbus and Cincinnati. There are not indeed, a great many churches here, and the people are doubtless imperfect in building them, for want of practice.

Of saloons, however, there is no lack, from the gilded hall with its marble tables, mirrors and voluptuous paintings, to the loathsome pitfalls along the wharf. They are at every corner of the street, and in nearly all parts of the city, tempting all passers.

From the boat at night, we have a full view of the orgies in the hells along the landing. These are frequented exclusively by Irish and the lowest Americans. The German is at his Lager-Bier Haus, or his Theatre, or his Sang-Verein. At dusk, however, the "finest pisantry in the world," begins to gather around the doors of these low dramshops, and by the time the gas is lighted, they are wild with poisonous drink.—Then the saturnalia begins. A fiddle and a banjo, or hand-organ make music, and heavy heels clatter about in the dance. "The strange woman" appears. She drinks with them again and again. She dances before them, and they go mad with obscene glee. Shouts, cries, oaths, and curses issue from the dens where they are crowded together; and the uproar grows more furious, till all sounds are blended in a frightful clamor. Now let the belated passer have a care; for these men are ripe for robbery and murder; and there is much chance that he will figure in the morning papers as one of the parties in a case of "Brutal Assassination."

Immediately opposite to where we lie, is Bloody Island, between St. Louis, and Illinois Town. Ferries ply constantly back and forth; and Thursday, we crossed over, to look at a place, whose sanguinary name hints it the scene of many a tragic deed. It is merely a great sand bank covered with large cottonwood trees, each one of which is rooted in a circular terrace, several feet high, repeated inundations having worked away the loose sandy soil around. Several houses are built upon the Island, and it is occupied by a large railroad depot.

As soon as the ferry boat touched, the grove suddenly became alive with hundreds of shirt-sleeved ruffians, who rushed to the landing from every direction. They were all highly excited, and made a very unpleasant display of heavy fists and cudgels; discussing, at the same time, some occurrence in terms which exhibited a great command of profanity. On inquiry, we learned that we had just arrived too late to see a prize fight, which had taken place between The Slasher and The Shanghai. These champions were both Irish, and every soul who had witnessed the fight belonged to the same admirable people. Some dispute had arisen, and the combatants had repaired to the neutral ground of Bloody Island, where they were perfectly safe from arrest. Here the affair was, as they say in Washington, when a Congressman knocks down another honorable gentleman—amicably settled.—There were eighty "rounds," and the Shanghai was so badly "punished," as hardly to be able to walk. Everybody was delighted, the champions were satisfied, and returned to the city, gratified at the pleasant turn of the affair.

We walked about the island, and seeing nothing more notable than a gentleman firing his revolver at something or other, for his personal amusement, we recrossed to the city.

Yesterday, in passing a warehouse, I saw what yielded me more enjoyment than all the other sights of my jaunt. It was nothing but an old Spanish Bell, lately brought from Santa Rita in New Mexico, bearing the date "A.D., 808," and some illegible legend in Latin. It was cracked, and bruised and bent; and the metal seemed almost entirely copper—perhaps sweetened according to the superstition of the old founders, with silver coins and jewels. It was a brave old bell, and rang doubtless its first peal, from some convent tower in that romantic Spain where so many of our castles are built. Christian knights sallying forth to battle had crossed themselves at its sound, and the turbaned infidel had listened to it, while he ravaged the convent fields. How many beauteous saints and austere monks had knelt before the gothic shrine at its summons; how many sobs had its clangor drowned; with what laughter had its music mingled! Then it had roused the forests and deserts of the New World, calling to worship at the altars of the same magnificent faith—"whose turrets are bright and clear, whose dungeons are so deep, and dark and terrible," in the Old World. Alas! old bell, whose iron heart, throbbing a thousand years, is stilled at last.

Last night, I saw Edwin Booth in Richard III. He is not, to my thinking, a great actor.—He is quite correct, according to the canons of the stage, and ranting through his part, died with the orthodox number of flops, flip-flops and wriggles.

[Signed "W.," *Ashtabula Sentinel*, 3 June 1858]

DOWN THE MISSISSIPPI

May 26, 1858.

It has been a sore struggle with me to quit the contemplation of the panorama that unfolds its glories of rock, and hill, and tree, mile after mile, and sit down to the limning of those faint outlines, which counterfeit on paper, the live pleasures of a journey.

It is a morning of ineffable loveliness. The mild May sun pours his effulgence from a heaven of darkest and unclouded blue. A sweet gale scarcely ruffles the broad bosom of the river in which he glasses himself. The wildwood shores are vocal with the joy of singing birds. It is such a morning as makes faint all the praises of the poets, and fills the soul with a sublime ecstasy, the exquisiteness of which is almost pain. "Das Vergnuegen ist nichts als ein hœchst, ange-nehmer Schmerz."

(As I have not indulged in many of these rhapsodies, which, like the crumpets of Sam Weller's man of principle, "are so wery fillin' at the price," I venture to hope this one will be pardoned me. To resume in more sober strain:)

We left St. Louis about noon, yesterday. I confess that I saw, without reluctance, its roofs and spires fading out of sight; and welcomed the pleasant silence and solitude of the river again.— Fairer, in her rudest aspects, than the most pretentious works of man, Nature was unspeakably beautiful to me after five days im-prisonment in the dull streets and walls of that city.

Other places may be more wicked than St. Louis, but there are few in which crime is so daring and open; others may be more vicious, but in none is vice more palpable, more bold, and more offensive. A different state of things is not perhaps to be expected in a city of such rapid growth,—the congregation of so many dif-ferent peoples at one point, must always produce the same result. Hither flock immigrants from all parts of the world, bringing with them their peculiar vices, and make the place a microcosm of licen-tiousness, drunkenness and crime. Rich, beautiful and profligate, the young city wantons in every form of dissipation which belongs to the mature metropolis.

A fresh wind blowing from the South, darkened the sky with clouds, soon after we left St. Louis; and with squally suddenness, a tempest of rain and hail burst upon us, just as we had rounded a lofty bluff. A river boat is not calculated to weather a heavy storm, and the "Cambridge" lost no time in putting to shore. There, securely moored on the lee of the bluff, we watched the strong blast roughening the sullen river and tossing its waters in wreaths of spray—sweeping along the low swamps of cottonwood, and twisting the trees upon the hills like straws. It was a very entertaining spectacle witnessed from our position; but I was content that our boat did not participate actively in the ceremonies.

About dusk, we stopped at "Sulphur Springs' Landing," to take on some pig iron, and lay there all night. Dick H., the artist of our party, made a sketch of the place, while G. and I strolled up the railroad; with the customary result of picking a few flowers, throwing some stones into the water, and carrying away vast quantities of real estate on our boots. Some of the passengers went back to the Sulphur Springs, about a mile from the landing, and returned, bearing bottles of the health-giving water. I suppose it is highly medicinal. It is certainly very nasty.

By the time all were on the boat again, the moon had risen, and poured from full horns, a flood of silver light upon the scene. It was something that had often enchanted me in pictures; but never before had I beheld the glorious reality.—Serene, and still, the fair orb floated up the azure night, accompanied by a solitary star, while the far shore darkened beneath her, and athwart the swarthy river, lay a long, wide path of light, tremulous, beautiful. It seemed as if one might, leaving earth behind, walk on it, in a rapturous dream, out into the Morning Land, and forever forget the toils, cares, and vexations of life in a sweet oblivion.

While I yet contemplated this scene, a group formed underneath an old cottonwood that overhung our boat, and presently the music of violins and castanets broke from them. Not loth to turn from that which while it pleased pained, (as all perfect beauty does the human heart,) I went up and mingled with the crowd. It was one that could be found no where but on a western steamboat. There were all varieties of men, dressed in all forms of fashion, drawn together by the same languid desire to be amused, and all posed in attitudes unconsciously artistic. Here was a Missouri farmer, wan and weak with recent ague; there a Kansas man, fresh from the prairies, bearded and free in bearing; there a disappointed emigrant returning home; here a mere idler and pleasure seeker; there a son of labor, respited for a week from his doom of toil. Our *Chips*, "rare Ben" G., performed with native skill upon one violin; while a wild-looking, picturesque fellow, with a slouched hat, black hair, gleaming eyes, and raven beard and moustache, (whom I afterwards saw playing euchre with *professional* accuracy and success,) picked out the tune on another. The engineer performed on the bones. Figure to yourself this group—the dark foliage above them, on the shore the blazing beacons, throwing fitful flashes of light upon a crowd of idlers attracted by the music, and upon the forms of the deck-hands hurrying back and forth with their iron burdens—then the still river with its silver path; imagination may fill up the outlines I have given. No pen can do it.

Presently the music ceased; one by one the members of the crowd sauntered away to the euchre tables in the cabin; the deck was deserted. Slowly, as if the engines lay in a dream below, the steam breathed from the 'scape-pipe; slowly the black smoke floated from the chimneys; slowly the waifs from a thousand forests stole by upon the waters. The moon rose higher in the heavens; the quiet stars looked down, and with these images of peace and tranquility in my heart I went to rest.

Up the Ohio, May 27.

Once more, the Beautiful River!

All day yesterday we journeyed down the Mississippi, (more swollen than it had been for five years); with the falling night and rising moon, we rounded the swampy Cairene point, and entered upon the waters of the fair Ohio. Regretfully I looked back upon the broad breast of the father of floods, that had borne us so far in safety, and that now in the radiance of the full moon, glowed one vast expanse of silver.

Sweet are my last day's memories of the mighty river. For all along our course the young water-willows, thickset among the cottonwood, laded the charmed winds with delicate fragrance, and every little breeze blew as if from paradise.—So is it, they say,—at this enchanted season of the year—from the Egyptian metropolis, to the mouth of Red River. The vast region through which the river sweeps away, is a Lotus-Land of perfume, where the luxurious sense of the traveler is fed upon odors sweeter than the breath of Hybla. Lapped in a dreamy revery, I hung upon the guard and, "watching the tender-curving lines of creamy spray," almost thought to see "about the keel,"

"The mild-eyed, melancholy Lotus Eaters come," bearing in their languid hands, branches

—"of that enchanted stem
Laden with flowers and fruit."

But in reality there was little else to see than immense quantities of driftwood, with which the river was almost covered.

There was nothing at all notable in the landscape, which presents the characteristics so often mentioned. I regret to say that I left my dinner half finished, to catch a sight of the Grand Tower, and the Bake Oven, objects legitimately to be pointed out to all travelers. Of course, with an exaggerated notion of their interest, I was disappointed in their appearance. The Grand Tower is a little isle of rock, girt by the swiftest waters of the Mississippi, and crowned with trees. Nearly opposite stands the warty hillock called the Bake Oven, which is very like a bake-oven, or—"a whale." In one side is an aperture, which you may fancy, if you like, to be the hole whereat they put in the bread.

That one does not thirst to death on the Mississippi, one has to thank Heaven for a strong stomach, and a general ability to shut one's eyes to the nastinesses of existence;—for one has to drink the river water which, constantly boiling up in great eddies, is thick with mud. From the hurricane roof of a steamboat, the earthy particles are distinctly seen, glistening in the sun; and at dinner, when the water has stood awhile in the glass, there is quite a young farm deposited at the bottom. The Ohio water, which is turbid and foul enough, is crystal beside it. An Hungarian lady traveling to New Orleans remarked these facts. "Why don't you *filter* the water?" she asked. The American friend with whom she was conversing, considered awhile, and returned answer: "Well, we're such a go-ahead people, we haven't time to filter the water."

During the day, we noticed constant signs of inundation—houses deserted, and standing *knee-deep* in water; fields flooded, the tree roots sapped and trees fallen. But the remarkable town of Cairo, presented the greatest spectacle, standing, like a shabby Venice, with water, that turned its lonely avenues into canals and its environs into broad lagoons. It was as I said just twilight when we stopped there, the witching hour when the froggy denizens of the swamp are most melodious, and it seemed as if all the musical amphibia of earth were congregated at Cairo.

En passant, a Cairene who came abroad told me that Cairo was actually *healthy*. What made it strange was that he was moving away, and had no longer an interest in the place.

Up the Ohio, May 28.

Another day of beauty; (withal a little hot.) At noon, we passed Cave-in-Rock, a cavern extending into the hill a hundred and twenty-five feet, and opening upon the river above high water mark. The novelesque pen of Emerson Bennett, hath given it classic interest, making it the rendezvous of a melodramatic and sanguinary freebooting chief. Truth is, it was once the retreat of Wilson and his gang, who were wont to fire from its covert upon the hapless keel-boatmen as they passed to and from New Orleans; and to drag other unfortunate wayfarers into it, where they robbed and murdered them at leisure. How much of dreadful interest the stories of Cave-in-Rock have acquired through the mere handing down from

father to son, it would not be well, for romance' sake, to think. The obscurity of rude periods—
'Like State, makes small things grow and swell.'
The Cave is on the Illinois side, about a hundred and forty miles above the mouth of the Ohio.

Dinner over, I sat down on the shady side of the hurricane deck, in that agreeable state of sentimental languor which repletion often produces, and looked out upon "the old Kentucky shore." Descending, we took the middle river and swiftest current; ascending we keep near shore in the dead water—so near, that sometimes the overhanging boughs of the cottonwoods almost touch our chimneys. The wood bird's note floats from the cool depths of these water-loving bosks, and the fragrance of young leaves and flowers is in the air. Now we pass a clearing, where the broad, rich, arable acres, cover the whole river bottom; and ashore, as a customary thing, a dilapidated darkey is ploughing with a mule-team.—Anon, I discern between green branches and retreating trunks, many cabins of Uncle Tom. To the door of one comes old Aunt Chloe with her unruly boys, to watch as we passed. In front of others, the swarthy children of bondage were enjoying the shade, which like a type of their own life, lay deep and dark, threaded with scarce a ray of sunshine. Again we come upon some little white-washed, treeless village, hot, glaring, uncomfortable, with its inevitable taverns and groceries. Then woods, and cabins, swamps, and plough-land. So, with a pleasant book of plays *to hold*, I while away the long afternoon.

In the evening, when the sun was down, and not a zephyr breathed, of all that blew by day; and the wide calm river lay entranced, it was fitting pastime to sit overlooking the bow of the boat, and pore over the delicious scene. Softly, and but for the hoarse respiration of the engines, silently, we steal up the river. A blue heaven with rosy cloud-isles, is mirrored in its depths, and on either bank the trees bend to the water, like Narcissi, fallen in love with their own images, and mutely pining. Swift bank swallows skim, with joyous twitter, thro' the air. Some belated blackbirds, pause for a moment on the floating drift, then calling to each other, wing their way to the Kentucky shore. With these sounds, mingles the mellow cowbell's tinkle, sounding from the woody pastures on the shore.

I see the people crowd their doorways to watch the passing boat, and I hear broken snatches of their talk. There they stand, peaceful home-groups,—father, mother, and flaxen haired children. From the chimneys of their cabins floats the smoke in wavering columns and completes the rustic picture. Shadow and distance hide them, and the night falls.

Meanwhile, the women, conducted by a musical Californian,

119

have approached us. Seated, there is a little *susurrus* of discussion, and then the sweet familiar strains of "Lily Dale," float upon the still air. "Do they miss me at Home," follows; then "Old Kentucky Home," "Nelly was a Lady," and "Gentle Annie." Then again they dispute. What makes the crimson glow that fires the Western shore, and spangles a thin rack of cloud with diamond light? But while they talk, the full round moon emerges above the tree-crests, and floats up "wie ein leichter Nachen in der stillen Nacht."

"Then all at once they sang"

that sweet old song, "Lone Starry Hour."

Presently we retire again to the cabin. Rare Ben brings forth his fiddle, and quadrilles, polkas, and schottisches crown the pleasures of the day.

Dear, happy, lazy Life!

Cincinnati, May 31.

Partly from the consciousness that I cannot transfer to paper the lovely "Reisebilder" I have beheld; and partly from the fear that however much one may like to talk about these pictures, another may possibly not like to hear so much about them, I have forborne my scribblements for a longer space than usual. Indeed I could but again and again describe the lovely hills, fair vales and fertile plains, or the beauties of which I have already dwelt; and no one but Hawthorne can hope to make a "twice told tale" anything but "weary."

Of our indolent life, I have spoken—Within the last four days nothing has happened to vary it. When breakfast is eaten, we lounge upon the guards, and follow the lines of the dizzy water, or gaze with vain *Sehnsucht* upon the beautiful shore. If we stop at some rustic wood yard, we are languidly alive to the appearance of the women who look from their log cabin doors; if at a town, we are fairly aroused, and stare the wharf boat idlers out of countenance. When a stately boat appears in sight, and shouts to the "Cambridge," whose replying note startles the dreaming echoes of the hills, there is a faint movement of curiosity in our group which subsides as soon as we ascertain the name of the stranger.—Then we watch her on her downward way, dashing the water from her prow and making mimic breakers on the shore, till distance lessens her and her chimneys, "bearded with plumes of smoke," fade out of sight. Perhaps some venturous lady has waved her handkerchief to us in passing, and we discuss the incident, and the probable good looks of the lady for a minute and a half, when we return to our former quiet, which we interrupt only with laconic expressions of opinion in regard to the value of a horse or mule, or country seat upon the bank. An argument is an impossibility; and an ardent German Turner who proposed to prove the fallacy of the Bible and the virtue of Lager bier, positively languished for want of an antagonist.

Of course the most thrilling event of the day is dinner, which is dispatched with a species of frenzy peculiar to American travelers, and then we all take a *siesta*, or lounge upon the guards as aforesaid.

For three or four nights past we have had dancing; but the number of our saltating ladies is now reduced to three, and hereafter we must fall back upon "forfeits" or some other game—which, without osculation, are rather stupid than otherwise.

So goes our life.

At Louisville the boat stopped an hour, and I took a walk through the town. It is full of gay shops and well dressed people, and everybody there seems to have *plenty of time*. I saw more negroes in my half hour's ramble than I did the whole time I was in St. Louis.

"I hate to leave Louisville," I said to my companion, "without seeing the greatest man in it."

"Who? Jim Porter?"

"No," said I, a little ashamed of my want of interest in the Kentucky Giant, "I mean Prentice, the poet."

"O," said my companion.

But we didn't see Prentice.

Just below Cincinnati, the Ohio hills are really vine clad, from the river shore to their very crests. The vine dressers' cottages are cosy places, with abundant gardens about them. There were no ruined castles to be seen, but these hillside vineyards looked very picturesque and quite like the scenery of the Rhein, (as I imagined it.) I said as much to a traveled friend in Cincinnati. But he pooh-poohed the notion to that extent, I was fain to hold my peace. Your full grown travelers are so arrogant.

[Signed "W.," *Ashtabula Sentinel*, 10 June 1858]

Wheeling, June 3rd.

Last evening, just before the night fell, and while the dew and calm of twilight were on everything, we passed the romantic island of Blennerhassett. The garish light of mid-day would have discovered it more fully, but the twilight made a pleasant mystery of the place; as chance and time have made of the man whose home once adorned it.

('If thou wouldst view Melrose aright,
Go visit it by the pale moonlight.')

Three miles in length, but so narrow in places, that one might almost leap across it, the island lay half hidden in the 'soft brown gloom' of the elms and willows that fringe its shores. At intervals I caught glimpses of farmhouses and cultivated fields—for the soil hallowed by misfortune yields excellent corn and potatoes. Near the head of the island stood Blennerhassett's mansion, of which there now remains no trace, except a hole said to have been the cellar. The vandals who sacked the house at first, did not destroy utterly, but conflagration and decay have fairly completed their work.

As I stood looking upon this storied isle, it seemed as if all the years between then and now were nothing, and Burr was but mooring his pleasure barge to the lofty sycamores upon the water's brink. 'On such a night,' saith history, like another 'pretty Jessica,' and then comes the old story of weakness and refinement fascinated by ambition, and ending with the old catastrophe.

But 'Blanny's' (as steamboatmen call it), has weird as well as classic interest. An old pilot who has been on the river more than a score of years, never passes the island by night, without seeing the headless ghost of the ill-starred dreamer whose beloved home it once was. This acephalous spectre, sheeted in a flowing robe of ghastly white, descends the Ohio shore to the water's edge, and then disappears with a wild and piercing shriek. The superstition involves a bull, and betrays otherwise a slight confusion of ideas—but the venerable navigator to whom it is peculiar, is so firm a believer in it, that he would quit the wheel rather than pass the haunted place without a companion in the pilot house.

—As these pleasuring days of mine draw to an end, I linger with regret on what has made them so delightful—the beautiful hills whose bosks are sweet with all the birds and flowers of June, the broad, rich plains, waving with grain,

'The bowery hollows crowned with summer sea,'
the farmhouses, set in little expanses of garden, and looking from rose-latticed windows, upon the Fair River; all the trees that whisper one another as we pass, the lovely river isles, with their groves of elms and sycamores; the river sights, the stately and picturesque steamers, the grim coal barges, the slow and lazy rafts!

But not these alone have made the month pass like a pleasant story read in some incredible book. Many warm friends are to be parted with, many kind hands are to be shaken good-bye.

—What if a little mist obscure the good old boat (come, in these few weeks, to be another home), and make dim the smiling faces that look from her guards? Those with whom we have been happy even for an hour, may claim a throb of regret at separation; and earnest friendship is not so vulgar a thing in the world that we should ignore its severance as an unconsidered trifle.

[*Ashtabula Sentinel*, 17 June 1858]

CHAPTER THREE

Something Literary in the Line of Journalism

None, indeed, who have ever known it, can wholly forget the generous rage with which journalism inspires its followers. To each of
those young men, beginning the strangely fascinating life as reporters and correspondents, his paper was as dear as his king once
was to a French noble; to serve it night and day, to wear himself
out for its sake, to merge himself in its glory, and to live in its
triumphs without personal recognition from the public, was the
loyal devotion which each expected his sovereign newspaper to accept as its simple right.

A Modern Instance (1882)

[In the fall of 1858, the *Ohio State Journal* was purchased by a partnership of prominent and well-to-do political journalists who wished to place
the chief organ of Republicanism in the state "on a firm footing after
rather prolonged pecuniary debility" (*YMY*, p. 125). Henry D. Cooke,
formerly the owner and editor of the Sandusky *Register* and one of the
new partners in the Columbus venture, was made editor of the paper,
though he had little interest in the routine tasks of producing a daily
newspaper. He was intent on image, however, and immediately instituted
several material changes which gave the paper a smarter as well as somewhat larger format. In keeping with its assumed political prominence, the
time of publication was shifted from the evening to the morning, but in
matters of political responsibility there was no place for change, and the
paper continued as before "a reliable exponent of the principles and policy
of the Republican party in Ohio." It was the new proprietors' intention
"to make it a first class NEWSPAPER [in every department], in order
that it may possess value and interest, not only for the politician, but for
the general reader" as well. It was also announced that "experienced and
competent assistants" were to aid the editor in the venture, and in this
capacity Samuel R. Reed and William Dean Howells were hired. The
choices could not have been better; both were eager young men of uncommon qualities and abilities, experienced in the practical aspects of

journalism and true through and through in their Republicanism. The ironic, mocking Reed young Howells greatly admired as a guide and partner, remembering him afterwards as "a man of high journalistic quality, of clear insight, shrewd judgment, and sincere convictions. . . . I do not believe that in the American press of the time he was surpassed as a clear thinker and brilliant writer" (*YMY*, p. 128). The feeling was undoubtedly mutual, and it soon became known that the two younger men were the real voices of the *Ohio State Journal* and Cooke merely the titular head, more than willing to leave the writing to his assistants and interfering only when he thought they went beyond the limits sensible Republicanism dictated.

Because the new proprietors intended the *Ohio State Journal* to be much more than a political sheet, Reed and Howells worked hard to give the paper "a metropolitan character." "There were no topics of human interest," Howells remembered, "which we counted alien to us anywhere in the range of politics, morals, literature or religion" (*YMY*, p. 127); and both junior editors were suffered their way on a great variety of matters. Good society in Columbus enjoyed the "new journalism" offered in the *Ohio State Journal*—a light, sarcastic, slightly cruel, mocking style, moral in point, and always hopeful in its satiric wish to righten the world of its wrongs—and the doors of the prominent and influential were opened to both young men, an attractive daughter or two frequently there to greet them. For a while it was very heaven.

Howells's salary in Columbus was only half that which he had given up when he left the Cincinnati *Gazette* the year before, and, as first conceived, his duties were to be nearly the same as those he had found so odious and onerous in Cincinnati. But Columbus was a smaller and much pleasanter town, and Howells had come to feel at ease there during his several years of association with the political and journalistic personalities who made up its leading citizens. Then a change in assignments gave Howells a far more congenial job on the paper than that he had first been called for, and his new situation was entirely to his liking.

First among Howells's tasks was to compile a digest of news stories from the many newspapers that were received in exchange in those days before the wire services and associated presses. It was a common practice in the period, providing editors with points of view against which to play off their own, and, best of all, the copy was free. Howells approached his department with typical imaginativeness and interest.

> I had been made news editor and in the frequent intervals of our chief's abeyance, I made myself the lieutenant of the keen ironical spirit [Reed] who mostly wrote our leaders but did not mind my

dipping my pen in his ink when I could turn from the paste and scissors which were more strictly my means of expression. My work was to look through the exchange newspapers which flocked to us in every mail, and to choose from them any facts that could be presented to our readers as significant. I called my column or two, "News and Humors of the Mail," and I tried to give it an effect of originality by recasting many of the facts, or when I could not find a pretext for this, by offering the selected passages with applausive or derisive comment (*YMY*, pp. 126–27).

The serious and the comical, stories of virtue and vice, the very enormous variety of the real: nothing, apparently, which others thought fit to print was Howells disinclined to copy or censure. Politics, fashions, domestic and foreign disasters, gossip of the theater and the literary circles of Europe and the Atlantic seaboard, news from California, technological and scientific developments of general interest, the barbarism of slavery and the utter folly of most Southern folk—the "news and humors of the mail" encompassed the great, round world itself, and Howells was the ever-present puppeteer, arranging and coaxing, making the simple facts tell the truths he saw in them. Sometimes he tended to be overharsh, as young men generally are whose experience of the world has been happy and wholesome, and cynicism before the condition of human frailty was something that had always to be fought off, not always successfully. But the failure at least provided a good deal of fun.

The few dozen squibs from Howells's column printed below have been selected to provide some sense of his work at its best and most original. In these, Howells's own face and values shine through the occasions provided by others, and in their indirect way are truly as original as the stories and sketches he was also writing at the time.]

NEWS AND HUMORS OF THE MAIL

[Rules pertaining to intellectual ownership were somewhat more roughly regarded a century ago than today, though the offended party was just as apt to smart in his or her wrong as those do now who find their good things claimed by others. Paragraphing and itemizing naturally led to this offense, especially in understaffed newspaper offices nearing their weekly date of publication. Distance and the unlikelihood of being found out diminished the moral guilt, but sometimes the truth was brought home with a vengeance.]

Not a few highly respected contemporaries have fallen into the pernicious custom of stealing our editorialettes.

We think that the business of itemizing, has a tendency to blunt the keen edge of the sense of honesty; and we make every allowance to our fellow creatures in this respect; well knowing the temptations by which they are beset. It is often, moreover, a matter of some difficulty to indicate the original proprietorship of an item, and requires a prodigious effort to hunt up the pencil, and affix a credit. But we try to overcome these adversaries in our dealings with others, and we mildly request, with what pathos we may, that our friends and admirers will be equally upright.

It is but a few days since our local came into our sanctum, holding up an exchange,—his sensitive features suffused with indignation, and his slender form agitated with emotion. We begged him to state the cause of his feeling, and he pointed to a certain paragraph in the paper he clutched. It was credited to the Toledo *Blade.* "That paragraph," he remarked with miraculous calmness, "is the product of my own pencil. It was endeared to me by a long and arduous pursuit through storm and mud. It is a local item. I chased it down; caught it; dressed it; presented in attractive guise to an enlightened public. The *Blade* cut it out, and, O! 'most unkindest cut of all!' neglected to credit it. I will be moderate and say, *forgot* to credit it. The item came back, and was copied into a Columbus paper, and erroneously attributed to the *Blade.* And with this false credit, it has gone the rounds." Our local (a person of the most delicate physique,) was quite overcome. But we consoled with him, telling him how we had, one evening at the dead hour of half past seven, fallen upon an attractive idea; how we had elaborated it; how in the enthusiasm of the moment, we had read it aloud to the seniors, who "laughed demnibly"; how we had printed it; and dwelt upon its leaded countenance with delight; how, alas! we had since seen it going the rounds of a predatory press—tossed upon a newspaper sea, a helmless boat, with no clearance papers abroad.

Our local was but partially consoled; and requested us, at some time when we felt particularly dyspeptic, to pitch into the heartless editors who would thus steal the children of the brain, and sell them into a course of itemical slavery, unnamed, and forgetful of their fathers.

But we think we have chosen the better course, in appealing as we have done to that candor which is in every soul, however whity-brown it may have become by a life of editing. [22 December 1858]

#

ANOTHER VIOLATION OF THE COMMANDMENT.

We have before us a most melancholy proof of the depravity of the editorial heart, in some paragraphs stolen by the local of the Wheeling *Intelligencer* from our article on "The Beautiful Weather."

The wretched appropriator (we desire not to be harsh in our characterizations,) has not only stolen the paragraphs, but badly mangled them in the act of unrighteous violence. We trust that this local may come to no evil end. He is evidently a person of taste, and it were lamentable if such an one should suffer the extreme penalty attached to his acts. We must say, however, that if we were in his place, we should not like to be much out at night, and should always whistle very loudly in passing through a grave-yard. [24 December 1858]

#

[These spunky Westerners were also apt to be riled when there was implicit in an exchange some demand other than the courtesy of reciprocation. The *New York Mercury* was a popular Sunday newspaper of general entertainment and information, its columns filled with pulp fiction and unremarkable essays on exotic travel or the otherwise curious.]

The New York Mercury
    Sends us a prospectus that would occupy about half a column of the *State Journal*, with the munificent offer to exchange with us a whole year, on condition that we publish their prospectus six times. It is an ungrateful thing to fly in the face of active benevolence, and reject a blessing, when it is offered on such favorable terms, but having consulted with the young gentleman who "sets up," "works off" and "carries" our humble publication, we have concluded not to "insert" the *Mercury's* prospectus. We know—indeed, do not the publishers assure us? that we shall be cut from the *Mercury's* exchange, but we have condescended to make the sacrifice. It is hard, for many reasons, to part with the *Mercury*. In the long days of summer when we were aweary with looking over the exchanges, we felt perfectly secure that we should find nothing in the *Mercury*, and never opened it. A person of fine literary taste, who is compiling a scrap book, is always eager to have the *Mercury* on account of its stories—so long, and so easy to cut out! The elderly Hebrew youth who lays in his stock of wrapping paper from our exchanges, has frequently spoken in high terms of the *Mercury*, as being large, and extremely convenient to wrap the other papers in. We say we regret to part with the *Mercury*. We know we do our feelings a violence, but duty before pleasure. Adieu, wing-footed god! Adieu, "corpse" of talented contributors! Adieu, Dr. Robinson, Ned Buntline, Bayard Taylor and the rest! With tears, adieu!
    P.S. A collabrateur suggests that Mercury may feel more keenly than ourselves, the severance of the ties which have bound us. If this be the case—we would be generous, let the *Mercury* publish a column prospectus of the *State Journal*, and "notice" our paper every week and we will continue the exchange. [7 December 1859]

[Although it is true that the young editors of the *Ohio State Journal* tended to eschew personalities in their news stories, the public faces and attitudes of politicians and journalists were fair game, all the more so when there existed some difference in taste or political belief. One must also remember that rivalry among newspapers was one of the first spectator sports in America, and the more pointed and witty one's attacks against one's competitors, the greater the appreciation both in and outside editorial rooms. Democratic assumptions have always included the bathetic, and the great newspaper editors of the nineteenth century, powerful and influential in the political positions they held, were common targets of the provincial press.

Ever since the founding of his New York paper in 1835, James Gordon Bennett had displayed in the *Herald* an extravagant and exploitative relish that made the fraud and hypocrisy he attacked more interesting than the reforms he proposed. "Spicy" and "saucy," the paper was one of the most widely read journals in the country, and Bennett was with some justification referred to as the "Barnum" of journalism. John Bigelow, on the other hand, William Cullen Bryant's partner in the New York *Evening Post*, was the very image of Republican respectability. As for the other papers and persons noticed by Howells, the context makes his meaning unmistakably clear.]

INTO BENNETT.

Bennett of the *Herald* is going into the boot and shoe business. He has long accumulated a stock of hides, fully understands tanning, and will use his own bark in the process. [17 December 1858]

MR. JOHN BIGELOW,

Who has conducted the New York *Evening Post* with such distinguished ability, was tendered the compliment of a public dinner, before his late departure for Europe, by the most eminent Republicans of the city; but he declined with a modesty which speaks far more for him than any "remarks" he could have made
"Across the walnuts and the wine."
Vive Bigelow, and Bryant and their noble *Post*—the truest steel of all the good metal of the Republican Press! [17 December 1858]

The Washington correspondent of the New York *Times*—a journal that by dint of the vilest *toadying*, has achieved access to sources of information closed to others—writes the press of that city, that a report of his appointment to the governorship of Nebraska is unfounded. This patriotic individual "desires to hold no official station not conferred by the people." Any nice little thing in that way it is but reasonable to suppose he will take. [23 November 1858]

#

An Editor Turned Missionary.

Mr. W. E. McLaren, formerly attached to the editorial corps of the Cleveland *Plaindealer*, is preparing to depart for Japan, where he will hereafter devote himself to missionary service.

It would take purification by fire to fit an editor of the *Plaindealer* to preach the Word of God; and Mr. McLaren can hardly have gone through this ordeal. It is true that there is forgiveness for sinners; but the depravity of a man who has once written for a locofoco newspaper must be so great, as almost to forbid the idea that there is pardon in his particular case. Certainly, he is not prepared to teach the gospel to the heathen. Mr. McLaren had best stay at home. [27 April 1859]

#

A Poetical Local.

The Cincinnati *Enquirer* of Sunday, announces that a poetical contributor of that paper, "has become permanently connected with its City Editorial Department." He is evidently a fine writer, if we are not mistaken in attributing to him the item, "Suicide of a Young and Lovely Girl." The concluding paragraph is as follows:

"The shining waves that in the sunbeams dance and ripple o'er her coral lips, have hushed a voice which erst made sweeter music far than they, and sing a lowly requiem to the summer winds which sigh their pity back again into the waves, and bear to her gentle spirit in a happier world their sympathy and love." [24 May 1859]

#

[The "humors" of the news were oftentimes notices of oddities of incident and character; but literate Americans at mid-century also had a passion for verbal puns, a weakness that in Oliver Wendell Holmes's opinion bordered on the criminal. But even Holmes was a proven master of the art of "verbicide," which in large part accounted for his popularity. Amusing or absurd, the human condition was a marvelous matter.]

American humor is first in the field of startling and extravagant absurdities. Here is an instance:

In Arkansas, when a man desires to say that he would like to drink, he declares that if he had a glass of whisky he would throw himself outside of it mighty quick. [1 December 1858]

"Assault on the High Seas,"—Is the heading of an indignant item in a Baltimore paper. But why not a salt on the high seas? Where else would he be more at home? [3 March 1859]

#

Not very Bad.

We find the following in the Wheeling *Times*. We don't exactly credit it to that paper, for we are a little suspicious of the way they get up editorial good things in Wheeling, but we think it well enough to state where it came from:

A Prophecy.—The Hon. Stephen A. Douglas was once a cabinet maker. He never will be again, though he may dream that he will. [11 January 1859]

#

Droll Mistake.

An exchange, noticing that the Mexican city of Tobasco had fallen into the hands of the Liberals, prints the word *Tobacco*. Not so bad, since it is probable that the inhabitants were badly chewed up. [16 December 1858]

#

"By Jimminy!"

Hon. George P. Marsh traces the vulgar expression "by Jimminy" to the invocation of the strange celestial brothers, the Dioskuri of the Greek, the *Gemim* of the Latin faithful, and the Castor and Pollox of Dr. O'Toole's "haythen conchology."

The erudite Johannis Phœnix says that the term Rotunda, as applied to the interior of a dome, is a corruption of 'Wrote Under," such being the ejaculation of a Roman emperor who found the walls of the circular apartment in question, inscribed with an infinite number of names. A courtier, one Naso Snekellius, caught up the phrase, and affectedly repeated "Rotunda," which presently came into vulgar use.

It only remains now, for Mr. Marsh or Mr. Phœnix, to account for the origin of the popular imprecation, "Gee Whittaker!" It is used by vast numbers of thoughtless young persons, who, we feel quite certain, have no adequate notion of its meaning. An unspeakable benefit would be conferred upon the cause of general knowledge, could this expression be traced to a rational source. [22 December 1858]

Something Literary in the Line of Journalism

AFFECTION UNLAWFUL IN CHICAGO.
The virtuous police of Chicago lately arrested a man and woman for kissing on the street; and the immaculate justice fined them $10 and costs. [18 January 1859]

#

A MATURE VICTIM.—In Albany, a lady of 83, has entered complaint in a court of law against a young man of 18, for "leading her from the path of rectitude." [3 March 1859]

#

AFTER A MARRIAGE CEREMONY
Had been performed in one of the churches in Adrian, Michigan, the bride, when receiving the congratulations of her friends, shed tears, according to the custom, at the sight of which the groom followed suit and copiously. After his friends succeeded in calming him, he said he couldn't help it, for he felt as bad as she did. [10 January 1859]

#

The St. Louis *Democrat* contains the following singular advertisement:
PERSONAL.—I would like to know what is going on; I would sooner be hanged than live in this way.
JOHN JACOB SCHWAGLER.
St. Louis, December 7th, 1856. d8 dl*
[10 December 1858]

#

[New York lowlife was already a subject of common knowledge about which everyone was an authority, and even the lack of firsthand knowledge did not prevent Howells from speaking humorously of the dangers of metropolitan life. Psychologists might infer here a case of sour grapes.]

Evacuation day, (Nov. 25,) was duly kept in New York. It will be remembered that it was on this day the British withdrew from Manhattan, gracefully making over the city to the rowdies, who have there maintained undisputed dominion ever since. [29 November 1858]

#

Thanksgiving day was observed in New York city by the usual sermons, at the churches, at the Five Points' Missions, and the other benevolent institutions. Business was generally suspended; and one man was murdered. An infamous and cruel hoax was played off on the poor by some soulless and brainless scoundrel, who announced

131

through the *Herald* that food would be dispensed *gratis* at certain points.—Thousands of starving wretches assembled to be disappointed. [22 November 1858]

\#

EXODUS OF GAMBLERS.
In Sacramento and San Francisco, indictments were being found against professional gamblers, and they were generally fleeing to escape arrest. Many of the most pestiferous of the tribe had made good their escape to the South and to New York by the latest steamer. [21 December 1858]

\#

DISEASED PORK AND MUTTON
Are said to be sold largely in New York markets, just now. Where is the great curdler of swill-milk, Frank Leslie? Here is an undeveloped field of art and literature. [26 January 1859]

\#

[*Frank Leslie's Illustrated Newspaper* was just one of many offenders against public taste in literature. Far worse, however, and the target of many slings in Howells's "News and Humors" was Robert Bonner's *New York Ledger.* Purchased by the extravagant and colorful Irishman in 1851, the *Ledger* soon became the most successful weekly literary miscellany in the United States, its circulation claimed at times to be in excess of one-half million copies. Although such well-established authors as Bryant, Tennyson, and Longfellow on occasion contributed to the pages of the tabloid-sized paper which proudly advertised itself as "Devoted to Choice Literature, Romance, the News, Commerce," it was hack writers like Sylvanus Cobb, Jr., E. D. E. N. Southworth, Emerson Bennett, and popular, sentimental poets like George D. Prentice and Alice and Phoebe Cary who maintained for the *Ledger* its large readership. Howells may not yet have been entirely certain in the way his art was eventually to develop, but it is clear that the avatars of market-place acclaim held nothing for him. Time has of course proven him right, and the names of John G. Saxe, a humorous poet of enormous popularity, and Lydia Howard Huntley Sigourney, called by her thousands of admirers the "Sweet Singer of Hartford," are as forgotten as their works.]

The determined and indefatigable Bonner, has written a letter to the New York *Times* in defense of his *"Ledger."* He is actually preposterous enough to assert the excellence of Cobb as an author. [22 November 1858]

Bonner announces a volume for the relief of "neglected poets." It is intended not to interfere with Dana's Household Book of Poetry, but to embrace such American writers as are not recognized in that collection. If the editor does justice to his subject, it will be a voluminous work. [4 February 1859]

#

AN ADMIRER OF SAXE
Spreads himself in the Richmond (Indiana) *Broad-Axe*, saying that "Saxe stands first among America's noblest poets;" and that he is "prominent among those great intellects who have labored successfully to elevate the literature and refine the poetical taste of the American people." [19 January 1859]

#

Fearful Retribution.
John G. Saxe has been lecturing in Virginia. [13 December 1859]

#

Mrs. L. H. Sigourney, of Hartford, Conn., furnished fifty poor families in Boston with turkeys or fowls and pumpkin pies, of the best quality, too, for a Thanksgiving dinner.
A deed so noble, that we easily forgive her all the verses she has ever written. [29 November 1858]

#

[When Charles Dickens sold a story to the *Ledger*, the first engagement he had ever made with an American editor to publish his work, Bonner capitalized on the coup, and Howells, in turn, capitalized on Bonner's publicity. This group of items constitutes the entire "News and Humors of the Mail" for 3 February 1859, the only complete reproduction of one of Howells's columns in this collection.]

Charles Dickens writes for It!
It is asserted positively that Dickens has been engaged to write a series of papers for the New York Ledger. Now, who next? Shall not the Ledger advertisements within the next month read?
Thomas Carlyle writes for it!
Alfred Tennyson writes for it!
Bulwer writes for it!
Macaulay writes for it!
Browning writes for it!

133

Nay, shall it not even come to pass that—
Tupper writes for it?
We hope Mr. Bonner, after having obtained an immense circulation through the contributions of Cobb, will not desert the great genius for any other writer. What would the Ledger be without a story from Cobb, though all the intellectual wealth of the world should enrich its columns? Manifestly no longer the Ledger. Have Dickens, and Everett, if you will, Mr. Bonner, but—O, keep Cobb!

Milton,
We observe, has been writing some very indifferent verses for a paper down in Kentucky. We are sorry that Milton has done so. "Paradise Regained" was not a distinguished success, and the author will add nothing to his reputation by the emission of verses on "Friendship," such as we copy below:

> Oh, how desolate and dreary,
>   Would this sinful world appear,
> If the heart when worn and weary
>   Knew not friendship's kindly tear!

> Hopes bright flowers, how soon they wither!
>   Love is an illusive dream,
> They may fade and die together,
>   At the evening's fading beam.

> But friendship is a priceless treasure,
>   Richer than the finest gold;
> Source of every real pleasure,
>   All its sweets can ne'er be told!
>   MILTON.
> Hillside, Shelby County, Ky.

Several Mistaken Gentlemen
Met at Albany recently, to consider the feasibility of buying out slavery. Of course they did nothing. The plan of the ingenious dreamer, Elihu Burritt, was properly rejected, and the Convention adjourned without delay.

Gold at Topeka, Kansas.
The correspondent of the New York *Post* writes that gold has been found at Topeka on the Kansas river. Three pans of dirt yielded eleven cents of gold.

134

$22,250 for a Husband

Mrs. E. Shaw, whose husband was killed some years since by a train of the Boston and Worcester R. R. colliding with his carriage, has recovered the above sum in damages.

Good Fortune at Last.

The Cleveland *Plain Dealer* is reliably informed that Robert J. McHenry, whose trials for crimes committed by the notorious Townsend the public are painfully familiar with, has lately come in possession of a handsome fortune, left him by an uncle, who recently died in Scotland.

If ever a man underwent diabolic persecution at the hands of a vigilant police, and a corps of virtuous reporters, McHenry was that man. The sanguinary locals of Cleveland were bent upon having him hanged by way of testing his identity; and when it began to appear that he was not Townsend, they wanted him hanged for crimes which a man of his physiognomy would probably commit.

Decoration for Lieut. Maury.

Walewski, Louis Napoleon's Minister for Foreign Affairs, has directed the French Minister at Washington to ascertain whether our government will allow Lieut. Maury to receive the Order of the Legion of Honor from the Emperor, as a recognition of the great services, which Lieut. Maury has rendered to the navigators of all countries by his works upon ocean currents and winds. No officer of our government can receive such testimonials without the permission of Congress.

Cranberries at St. Croix.

The Stillwater (Minnesota) *Messenger* is credibly informed that the cranberry trade of St. Croix valley amounted to ten thousand dollars.

Who is it?

The Boston *Traveller* contains the following paragraph:

SPIRITUALISM AND DIVORCE.—We regret to hear that a gentleman of this city, of distinguished literary and scientific attainments, one who bears a venerated name, and whose genius and science has given an important improvement to the cities of the United States, has been so far bewildered in the mazes of spiritualism, as to believe that he is wrongly mated with an amiable and devoted wife, and has found his spiritual affinity with another young lady. As we have been informed, the wife, though heart-broken by the development, and having one child, has assented to the request of her husband for a separation, and he has gone to Indiana to procure a divorce in order that he may marry his new affinity, who, we believe, is, like his wife, a lady of intelligence, amiability, and irreproachable in character.

Important if True.

Banvard, the panorama man, says the *Home Journal*, can trace his pedigree to Bonnivard, who was imprisoned in Chillon Castle on Lake Geneva, and whose sufferings suggested to Byron his poem, the "Prisoner of Chillon."

Saved by a Newspaper.

A few days since Mr. R. H. Martin, who is in the employment of John H. White, Esq., as one of the superintendents of the laborers at work at the new Washington Spring, Saratoga, being engaged near the steam pump, by some means slipped so that the skirt of his coat caught in the cogs of the pump. One bite of the cogs on his coat, and it commenced drawing him in pretty fast. He had no time to give any alarm before he was brought up with a prospect of being maimed by the cogs, but fortunately he had a copy of a newspaper folded tightly together in his pocket, and when the cogs came to that they stopped, throwing the band off the pullies.

The moral of this is, that everybody ought to wear a newspaper in his coat pocket. We hope this will be done, and the circulation of meritorious literature thereby extended. [3 February 1859]

#

[True to Howells's notion of the satirical in the "humors" of the news, he frequently assumed the role of moral censor, wagging an ironic finger at the foibles and failings of civilization in the nineteenth century. Owing to the temporal variables of morality, or as the modern temperament might put it, the complacent smugness of middle-class Protestantism in "Victorian" America, Howells's voice is at times foreign to many of our concerns and values today, and it certainly possesses the rigidity and certainty of proprieties in which young men of good conscience are always apt to fail.]

A bill is now before the Senate of Arkansas, which provides for levying an annual tax of one hundred dollars on the harmless luxury of carrying a pistol or bowie knife. Of course, the weapons worn by officers of the law are excepted. Civilization is dawning, even in Arkansas. We shall next hear that its beams have penetrated to the halls of Congress. [8 December 1858]

136

Henry Ahlbright, of Baltimore, tried at Norfolk for shooting and wounding a female, has been convicted of unlawful shooting, fined ten cents, and imprisoned in jail two days. From this, it appears, that "unlawful shooting" is not a very costly amusement at Norfolk. Reading this, one is naturally curious to know what kind of shooting is lawful in Virginia. [27 November 1858]

#

Afternoon of the Nineteenth Century.

A man was recently hanged in North Carolina for a murder which he was incited to commit through a superstitious belief in witchcraft, believing that the old lady he killed had the power to conjure his wife and child to death, and while in a state of intoxication he committed the deed under an erroneous notion of self-defense. [18 November 1859]

#

Some absurd fellow writing to the newspapers about the proposition to send out missionaries to Japan, suggests that a better way to Christianize that country would be for Christians going thither to practice Christianity in their lives and dealing with the Japanese. [25 November 1858]

#

[Although Horace Greeley's immensely popular New York *Tribune*, a journal of national importance and firm Republican principles, was in most respects a model of journalistic decorum and propriety, its editor's penchant for fads and sensations sometimes caused his friends regret and misgiving. John C. Heenan, an American-born prizefighter whose sobriquet was the "Benicia Boy," had gained considerable prominence in a much celebrated bout against the champion John Morrissey earlier in 1858. Though Heenan lost on a technicality, he was thought by most the better fighter, the man American contenders like Tom Hyer should challenge and the British champion, Tom Sayers, should be matched against in a fight that had obvious nationalistic dimensions. Howells remained unimpressed by these strenuous aspects of American life, but he was disturbed by the apparent moral primitiveness he saw manifest in the rising passion for fistiana in the United States. Still the most effective rebuke would have been silence, and Howells's protests may have served his readers' interests in a way he did not intend. Or does this assumption undervalue his journalistic savvy?]

PRIZE FIGHTER'S ORGAN.

The *Courier and Enquirer* appropriately applies this term to the New York *Tribune*. That journal, once the purest and best in the country, is no longer fit reading for the family circle. [27 December 1858]

\#

BASELY DECEIVED.

The editor of that moral and virtuous quotidian publication, the New York *Tribune* is justly outraged that he should have been led into publishing a forged letter of challenge from Thomas Hyer to the pugilistic Youth of Benicia. It seems that some ill-conditioned person, knowing the eagerness of the journal mentioned to supply its readers with edifying intelligence of all kinds, took this method to hoax it. Well, it was a cruel deception, certainly; but we cannot say that we are sorry for the *Tribune*. It seems to us that an editor sincerely regarding the morals of community, would not publish cards from prize-fighters. It seems to us that the *Tribune* is doing much to foster the spirit of the ferocious ruffianism in New York, which it affects so much to deplore; and is certainly prostituting its columns to a very vile purpose. There is no excuse for it, even as there is in the publication of obscene divorce trials, and harrowing murder-cases. No matter of actual event is concerned; and the printing of Mr. Heenan's card, or Mr. Hyer's card is a very palpable mode of patting blackguardism on the shoulder, and telling it, as it rolls up its shirtsleeves and meditates fresh assaults upon decency and religion, to go in and win. [28 December 1858]

\#

The following remark from the *Sporting Life*, a paper which is the delight of the royal family, nobility and gentry of England, gives a partial list of the accomplishments of Sayers. He has had thirteen regular fights, and been victor in twelve of them. To offset this, our champion has had one defeat in the ring, and considerable active service in managing democratic conventions in New York:

"The victories he has obtained over such powerful, active and experienced pugilists as Harry Orme, Tom Paddock, Jack Grant, the 'Tipton Slasher,' and the game and scientific Bob Brettle, compel us to believe that in Tom Sayers we see a man who possesses, in an extraordinary degree, certain natural qualities essential to a successful gladiator, and which have, by cultivation and experience, attained a high degree of development and perfection." [28 November 1859]

\#

The P. R.

Tom Sayers, the champion, is in fine condition. The English "fancy" do not approve of the attitude of Heenan, the Benicia Boy.

"He holds his hands up like a girl," was the remark of a renowned *ci-devant* bruiser of the light-weights, and added: "Tom will find his work cut out easy." [27 February 1860]

#

[Much more enjoyable was the game Howells and Reed made of making hits at locofocos, doughfaces, and F.F.V.s. They called it "firing the Southern heart," and while Howells afterwards thought that the pleasure he took in shredding the texts of proslavery contemporaries "into small passages and tagging each of these with a note of open derision or ironical deprecation" was neither wise nor well, he couldn't help but admit that it had been amusing.

To come upon some inviting fact, or some flattering chance for mischief in an exchange, above all a Northern contemporary with Southern principles, and to take this to [Reed] and talk it or laugh it over and leave it with him, or bring it back and exploit it myself, was something that made every day a heyday. We shunned personalities, then the stock in trade of most newspaper wits; we meant to deal only with the public character of men and things. It seems to have been all pleasure as I tell it, but there was a great deal of duty in it too; though if burlesquing the opposite opinions of our contemporaries happened to be a duty, so much the better. If it were to do again, I should not do it, or not so much; but at the time I cannot deny that I liked doing it. (*YMY*, pp. 128, 131–32)

Actually, when these words in *Years of My Youth* were written, Howells at eighty was no more gentle in attacking moral ignorance and political blindness than he had been at twenty; he had merely learned to be more subtle and indirect. Old or young, however, he never forgot the human suffering that was, in the words of his favorite Tennyson, "the riddle of this painful earth."]

THE BIRTHDAY OF DANIEL WEBSTER,
The first day of the New Year, is to be celebrated in grand style, at Boston. Caleb Cushing and Rufus Choate are selected to do honor to the memory of the man, whose errors are the only things they venerate in him. [25 December 1858]

#

Fun at Ashland.
Our readers will remember a distinguished Cuban gentleman, who had so great a disregard for the proprieties of the Spanish language as to call himself Joan Don Pedro, and who attempted to

lecture in this city a few weeks ago, on the subject of the *siempre fiel isla*, and who, being spoken to in Spanish, was found lamentably deficient in his native tongue, and who backed out of the back door of the City Hall, thus effecting the salvation of his bacon from the wrath of an outraged populace, at the expense of his personal dignity.

Joan Don Pedro's career has been somewhat eventful since he quitted Columbus, and has illustrated the fact that Castilian blood enables a gentleman to live by his wits as easily in the nineteenth century as in the sixteenth. The most amusing incident of his lecturing progress occurred a few days since at Ashland, where the Democratic party took him under their wing of our common spread eagle, and organized a meeting, and listened to his lecture with the greatest earnestness. Joan Don flourished under this treatment, and gave another lecture in which he attacked the Republicans for their opposition to the taking of Cuba. He was immensely popular with the Democrats, and his last lecture was a triumph.

Will it be believed that this Cuban gentleman ran away with the nut-brown chambermaid of the village tavern? We regret that such was the case, on the very evening following his glowing panegyric on democracy. [2 July 1859]

#

Unspeakable Flunkeyism.

Howadji Curtis, the brilliant essayist and lecturer—one of the most successful literaturers of the day—who has been the editor of the "Lounger Column" of *Harper's Weekly*, and the "Easy Chair" of the *Monthly*, is no longer connected with those periodicals. His well-known anti-slavery and progressive opinions made him obnoxious to the South, and the Harpers'—always the meanest of toadies—dismissed him. This act of pitiful persecution cannot, of course, enhance the virtue of Mr. Curtis' writings, but it will endear him personally to the North. But who, after such flunkeyism on the part of the Harpers, will buy one of their publications? [15 February 1860]

#

Inter-State Amity. . . .

Mr. Perley Seaver, of Oxford, Mass., who went to North Carolina, to take charge of a saw-mill, has returned. He read the Bible and had religious service at his house on Sunday, and made himself distasteful to persons of fine feelings. They directed his attention to the North Star, and Mr. S. yielded to the beneficent attractions of that planet. [26 January 1860]

#

Dreadful State of Society.

A Henderson (Ky.) paper in describing the hanging of a negro in McLean county, by a mob, says that "at least one hundred of the *most respectable gentlemen* of McLean were engaged in the mob!" [20 October 1859]

#

A duel was fought last week on Staten Island, by two medical students, from the chivalric state of North Carolina. After firing four times at each other with the most wretched success, they shook hands and made friends. It was about a lady, of course.

They are very funny people—our Southern brethren; and must acquire from their local journals, singularly correct and lucid notions of what Northern statesmen say and do. Here is an extract from a Mississippi paper's report of Senator Seward's speech—which will surprise those who thought themselves acquainted with the sentiments of that gentleman:

"Having supposed these facts, [the incompatibility, in the long run, of free and slave labor,] he, [Senator Seward] then proceeded to prescribe a line of action for the North, as follows:

"*Let us anticipate the blow by invading the States of South Carolina and Georgia, and emancipating the laborer who is toiling on the plantations there.* The two principles cannot live. Either slavery must triumph and become universal, or *emancipation must be carried into every State. If the South lives, the North must die. Then down with the South. 'Delenda est Carthago.'* And if the compact of the Confederation stands in the way, *tear it to pieces. There is no faith to be kept with slaveholders.* In politics, that only is obligatory which is expedient." [25 November 1858]

#

The Free South "Wiped Out."

The citizens of Newport, Ky., have abolished the only free press in their State. We published yesterday an account of an attack upon Mr. Bailey's office on Friday evening. On Saturday the work was completed. A meeting of the most "respectable and orderly citizens" of Newport resolved to transport Bailey's ruined type and broken press to the Northern side of the Ohio. The mob formed, beat in the door of the office, and carried the material to the river bank, where suddenly changing their purpose, they threw it into the river, and a committee was appointed to prevent the re-establishment of the "Free South." The paper was not one of great force, and the North can better afford to lose its assistance, than the lawless cowards of Newport to destroy it. Mr. Bailey is an honest and earnest man, whose property has now been four times destroyed by violence. He deserves the material sympathy of all good and just men. [1 November 1859]

SENTENCE OF A SLAVE ABDUCTOR.—"Hugh Hazlitt, a white man, charged with enticing and persuading slaves to run away from Dorchester county, Md., was tried this week, at Cambridge, and found guilty on seven indictments. He was sentenced by the court, on the first indictment, to the penitentiary till May, 1867, and on each of the others for six years—making in the aggregate, forty-five years."—*Baltimore Sun.*

A most just judgment! In this country one may destroy a man like Sumner, one may massacre abolitionists in Kansas, one may pistol Irishmen—but to tell negroes of liberty, and counsel them to run away from their beloved Massas, is monstrous! Hazlitt escapes too easily with his forty-five years' imprisonment. He should have been burnt alive. They would have managed the business better for him in South Carolina: though the Marylanders have been very prompt in other instances. [23 November 1858]

Reckless Destruction of Property.

A slave girl drowned herself at Nashville, on Thursday, by sticking her head in a puddle of water. The deed is supposed to have been done in a fit of resentment, because she had been chastised. [22 September 1859]

#

Whipped to Death.

It is "a melancholy pleasure" to present to our readers the evidence that great wrong is possible even under the blessed system of slavery; it forms some excuse for an unnatural fondness for liberty which animates our paste and scissors. We read in the St. Joseph's *West*, a pro-slavery journal, published at St. Joseph, Missouri, that a slave girl belonging to Mr. Wash, of that place, was recently beaten to death by the amiable lady of Mr. Wash, and an Irish friend. The suspicion of the public was aroused by the hasty interment of the victim, and her body was exhumed by the Coroner. Let American Snobdon, which hates "Abolitionism" look upon this picture! The *West* says:

"We are informed that the body was literally covered from head to foot with marks of cruelty. There were stripes which had healed, were healing, which were beginning to suppurate, which were in the height of suppuration, *and others again fresh as if they had been inflicted the day previous.* A more horrible spectacle it is difficult to imagine."

The editor of the *West* is glad to have "it in his power to do the South the justice of stating that one of the parties implicated was born and raised in a Free State, and that the other was a foreigner." But an emancipation journal published in the same city, denies that Mrs. Wash's son lived more than three months in a free State, and declares that she was a Kentuckian. It matters little; but if there were no positive evidence to the contrary, we would incline to think the *West* right. The recreant are always the cruelest; and from apology for slavery beyond its influence, it is but a little step to savage oppression within. There is no where anything so meanly tyrannical as the northern man with southern principles. [30 September 1859]

#

Auto da Fe.

A negro was burned to death, near Grand Cane, Texas, recently, for killing his master. The newspaper account of the cremation, says that he did not believe he was to be burned, even when the fire was kindled about him; and did not struggle until he was involved in the flames. This thing happened in the year of our Lord, 1859, in the sunny south of this glorious Union, which God preserve. [25 May 1859]

#

[When John Brown and his companions attacked the Federal Arsenal at Harper's Ferry, Virginia, on 16 October 1859, Howells looked on the event with wonder and bold admiration. Not surprisingly, Brown's plan for instigating a slave insurrection in Virginia was an utter fiasco, and after several days of battle against the federal forces, Brown and his surviving followers were captured and held over for trial on the charge of treason. On 20 October 1859, Howells wrote his father in Jefferson: "I suppose you are all dreadfully stirred up about the Harper's Ferry business. Reed and I are getting off any amount of [one or more words missing in typescript copy] on the subject. In some respects, it is the most absurd and laughable event of the age; but I'm sorry for poor crazy Brown." And when the *Ashtabula Sentinel* failed to work up something appropriate to the enormity of the affair, Howells chastised his father for the elder Howells's reserve. Before Brown's execution on 2 December 1859, a sort of cult had grown up in the North which venerated him for his courage, if not for his prudence, and Howells committed his art to the cause of

143

the martyred hero. Like Melville after him, he saw the emergence of John Brown in the nation's consciousness as a portentous "meteor of the war," "gigantic, colossal," filling "the sky at Harper's Ferry."

> Some thought it a myth, some a joke, some a miracle; but as it resolved itself into a reality and began to reveal itself in its full material absurdity, its spiritual magnificence, every detail of the man's personality lent it an increasing impressiveness, and increasing persuasiveness.

And like Melville, Howells found his fittest expression in verse. One of his poems, first published in the *Ohio State Journal* a few weeks after Brown's execution, appears to have been widely reprinted in the periodic press and was eventually included in James Redpath's *Echoes of Harper's Ferry*. Howells never reprinted the poem in his own works, though he apparently revised it for Redpath's volume.

OLD BROWN

I.

Success goes royal-crowned through time,
    Down all the loud applauding days,
    Purpled in History's silkenest phrase,
And brave with many a poet's rhyme.

While Unsuccess, his peer and mate,
    Sprung from the same heroic race,
    Begotten of the same embrace,
Dies at his brother's palace gate.

The insolent laugh, the blighting sneer,
    The pointing hand of vulgar scorn,
    The thorny path, the wreath of thorn,
The many-headed's stupid jeer,

Show where he fell. And by-and-by,
    Comes History, in the waning light,
    His pen-nib worn with lies, to write
The failure into infamy.

Ah, God! but here and there, there stands
    Along the years, a man to see
    Beneath the victor's bravery
The spots upon the lily hands:

To read the secret will of good,
  (Dead hope, and trodden into earth,)
  That beat the breast of strife for birth,
And died birth-choked, in parent blood.

II.

Old Lion! tangled in the net,
  Baffled and spent, and wounded sore,
  Bound, thou who ne'er knew bonds before:
A captive, but a lion yet.

Death kills not. In a later time,
  (O, slow, but all-accomplishing!)
  Thy shouted name abroad shall ring,
Wherever right makes war sublime:

When in the perfect scheme of God,
  It shall not be a crime for deeds
  To quicken liberating creeds,
And men shall rise where slaves have trod;

Then he, the fearless future Man,
  Shall wash the blot and stain away,
  We fix upon thy name to-day—
Thou hero of the noblest plan.

O, patience! Felon of the hour!
  Over thy ghastly gallows-tree
  Shall climb the vine of Liberty,
With ripened fruit and fragrant flower.

Howells's bewilderment at Brown's folly and outright wickedness in the name of right eventually tended to undercut his feelings of reverence and affection for the man and his deed. But not entirely. Writing fifty years after the momentous event of his youth, Howells found it incredulous that any good men had remained unsullied by the evil of slavery, and without condoning Brown's actions at Harper's Ferry, he still found reason and value in them. Brown might be no saint, but he would always be for Howells a hero and martyr.]

Adding Insult to Injury.
  One of the amusing features, (and these, unfortunately for the cheap patriots, are so many as to make the whole thing laughable,) of the late insurrection at Harper's Ferry, is the report that old Brown, after having taken a number of slaveholders and workmen

prisoners, added to their sufferings by making them an abolition speech. It was hard enough to be restrained of liberty, but to oblige them in addition to listen to the incendiary sentiments of the crazy "Commander-in-Chief of the armies of the Provisional Government," was the refinement of cruelty. We are half inclined to believe that poor old Osawatomie's principal object was not to command an army, but an audience, and his method of securing attention to his harangue, was ingenious, to say the least. The hint may prove useful to Democratic orators in the free States, where scarcely anybody listens to them willingly. Let a secret band of vigilants be formed to capture every loose man on the streets when a Democratic speech is to be made, and bring him before the orator; and we shall have no more such disagreeable demonstrations as in the late campaign, neutralized the efforts of Senator Pugh to do good. [21 October 1859]

#

"Vigilance at Washington."
Ridiculous performances of the patriots at the Capital when the news of Brown's Rebellion first reached that devoted city, continue to become public. The Capitol Buildings were watched all night; and Buchanan actually hurried to the depot on a dog-trot to see the marines off. Everybody, particularly if colored, was ordered to be searched. As an evidence of the rigor with which this order was carried out, some watchmen arrested a colored man soon after 10 o'clock, and proceeded to search him, when he cried out, "Bress God, massa, no use to search dis nigger; I'se been searched free times afore to-night." He was cautioned to make tracks for home, and released. [26 October 1859]

#

Wendell Phillips.
Some absurd person writes to the New York *Times* over the signature of "Republican," proposing that Wendell Phillips shall surrender himself to the Virginia authorities, on condition that they give up old Brown. This absurd person has no doubt "that Brown will be, upon those terms, forthwith pardoned and suffered to end his few remaining days in peace. In that event the Virginians will doubtless find some way of visiting upon Phillips the punishment which is now in store for Brown."
We venture that if such a proposition were made to Phillips by the Virginians, he would instantly accept it; and then we should see the beautifulest fight in the world. [31 October 1859]

* * *

LITERARY GOSSIP

[Cast in the same format as "News and Humors of the Mail" was a column titled "Literary Gossip" that appeared occasionally in the *Ohio State Journal* during the early months of 1860 and again in January and February of 1861. Usually made up of synopses or long quotations of reviews and articles that had appeared in other newspapers and literary magazines, the column did not allow Howells the opportunity for fun and wit that "News and Humors" did, and many of his paragraphs are, as one would expect, baldly derivative. Still his point of view is unmistakable, and in addition to giving evidence of Howells's reading and literary standards, as they were developing during this crucial period of his later youth, they reveal the future "Dean" of American letters in the role of critical arbiter, educating and guiding his readers in the matters that most mattered to him. Then, too, he was given ample opportunity in the pages of the *Ohio State Journal* to review new books and to essay literary topics; these longer pieces, some of them collected under the title "Western Poetics and Literary Prejudices," form a later chapter of this volume.]

The *Edinburgh Review* for January opens with a curious and entertaining article on mortality in the different trades and professions, which startles the reader with the facts it presents. Civilization, indeed, would seem to be hardly worth the waste of life which is required to maintain it; and one is rather inclined to desire a relapse into that state of nature where nobody is required to dry-grind steel, or dig coal, or work in lead or quicksilver. There is one trade largely followed in England, which is as absolute death as consumption or cancer—this is the dry-pointing of needles and forks, the sharpening of these instruments on a dry grindstone, by which process fine particles of flint and steel are constantly emitted, and received into the lungs of the workman. At twenty-nine he dies of what he calls the *grinders rot*. His lungs examined after death are found perfectly black, and cut like a piece of india-rubber—having none of that spongy character of the healthy organ. The English coal miner works for the most part in a horribly cramped position which any gentleman can illustrate for himself, says the reviewer, by getting under the table, and striking at the board with a pickaxe. This brings on heart disease. The coal dust and bad air the miner inhales, clogs his breathing apparatus. He dies at the average age of thirty. After death a black fluid taken from his lungs, and put through the gas-making process, afford a brilliant and cheerful light. The artisan whose skill gilds the interior of your silver cup, pays for this "giddy pleasure of the eye" with his life at an early age. The most terrible disease, to which St. Vitus' dance is repose, twitches and tortures every muscle of his body. The quicksilvering of mirrors, produces a similar malady. The workers in lead suffer from paralysis. The printer dies from want of exercise and ventilation at about thirty. And so on through the whole catalogue. But by all means read the article. . . .

A rich treat to book-collectors—especially to those who prize antiquarian literature—will soon be offered in Boston, at the sale of Dr. Percival's library. Not the least interesting thing about it is the large number of autographs of the poet, which will thus be scattered; for he wrote his name on the fly leaf of every volume, and was so jealous, in his later years, of those who sought to lionize him, that he would not give his autograph even to intimate friends. Of course he was cursed, like all popular authors, with incessant demands for his handwriting. In looking over his MSS. recently, the *Boston Traveller's* correspondent came across a most impudent example of this, on the part of a young man out West, who sent a note to Percival, inclosing postage, and requesting him to copy one of his more characteristic poems, and, having signed his name, to send it out to him. The letter lay among the poet's papers, just as it had been opened— not even the enclosed postage having been taken out.

Among the recent announcements of trans-Atlantic publishers is that by the Blackwoods of a new novel, by the authoress of "Adam Bede." It is called "The Mill on the Floss," and will appear in March. . . .

Mr. Hawthorne's new romance will be issued simultaneously by Messrs. Smith, Elder & Co. of London, and Messrs. Ticknor & Fields of Boston. Its title will be "The Marble Fawn; or, the Romance of Monte Beni." . . .

Thackeray, according to a rumor afloat in London, contemplates a continuation of Macaulay's "History of England."

Goethe's Faust has been translated into Hungarian, by Stephen Nagy.

[*Ohio State Journal*, 27 February 1860]

Among interesting announcements is that of the establishment, in New York, of *The National Quarterly Review*, the first number of which will be shortly issued by Rodney & Russell. It is to be neutral in politics and religion, and (funnily enough) it is promised that, while it will contain theological and political articles, it will attack nobody's opinions. The question of slavery will be let alone entirely. So this review will be neutral without doubt—as neutral as skimmilk thinned with warm water. "Mr. Edward J. Sears, A. B.," who is spoken of as one of our best writers, but who has certainly, so far, succeeded in keeping himself out of public notice, is to be the Editor.

Chapin's extemporaneous sermons are hereafter to be regularly published in book-form.

The essayist, Tuckerman, has a taste of celestial celebrity, in the republication at Macao, China, of his paper on "Art in America." It first appeared in the *Cosmopolitan Art Journal*: in China, it is printed in pamphlet form.

A recent letter from Rome states that Theodore Parker is looking very well, and has strong hopes of his recovery.

It is said that very few of Macaulay's good things, dropped in conversation, have been remembered. We think very few deserve to be, if they are no better in quality than this:—It is said that he met Mrs. Beecher Stowe at Sir Charles Trevelyan's, and rallied her on her admiration of Shakespeare. "Which of his characters do you like best?" said he. "Desdemona," said the lady. "Ah, of course," was the reply, "for she was the only one who ran after a black man." . . .

The Boston *Atlas* has a very favorable review of "Adela, the Octoroon," just published by Follett, Foster & Co. The editor says:

"In this volume the lawyer-author has laid aside his brief, to indulge his taste for literature and romance; and certainly few of his profession could have done it so gracefully, or so successfully. He has made a very beautiful and interesting story; and interwoven with it an argument—no doubt a sincere one—and as effective a one probably as has ever been made—in favor of African colonization. But he advocates colonization not in the Southern spirit— not from a wish to get rid of a dangerous and offensive population— but because he honestly believes that, in view of the prejudices, against which they here struggle, and the consequent disadvantages under which they labor, those who can go to Liberia, will improve their own condition by doing so, and also, by building up a free and prosperous nation of their own, will elevate their race in the estimation and sympathies of mankind."

Other eastern journals granting the work to be elaborately written, object to many of the incidents as injuriously improbable. . . .

[*Ohio State Journal*, 22 March 1860]

MRS. JAMESON.

Since our last gossip, two more have been added to those great names of literature, which death has eclipsed within the last year.

With that of Mrs. Anna Jameson, every reader of culture is familiar. Her clear, tasteful and delicately appreciative works on art have been appropriately *set* in this country, by Ticknor & Fields, in their blue and gold; and no author's thoughts and best paragraphs have enjoyed among us such wide newspaper quotation as Mrs. Jameson's. She was born near the close of the last century, with an hereditary love of art—her father being painter-in-ordinary to the Princess Charlotte. In 1824 she was married to Mr. Robert Jameson, late Vice-Chancellor of Canada, with whom she never lived. About the time of her marriage she published her first work, the *Diary of an Ennuyee*, which was followed in 1829, by the *Loves of the Poets*; in 1831 by *Lives of Celebrated Female Sovereigns*; in 1832 by *Characteristics of Women*, and *Handbook to the Public Galleries in and near London*, and *Companion to Private Galleries of Art in London*; in 1845 by *Memoirs of the Early Italian Painters*; in 1847 by *Sacred and Legendary Art*, of which *Legends of the Monastic Orders*, and *Legends of the Madonna* are the sequel. These were followed by *Essays on Social Morals*, and lectures on the *Sisters of Charity, Catholic and Protestant*, and on the *Communion of Labor*. Her last work, which was not quite finished at the time of her death on the 17th ult., is the "History of our Lord, and of his Precursor, John the Baptist, with the Personages and Typical Subjects of the Old and New Testaments, as Represented in Christian Art."

J. K. PAULDING.

The other death is that of James Kirke Paulding, who closed a long life of various labor, at his home on the Hudson, on the 6th inst. He was first known in connection with Washington Irving, as a writer of the *Salmagundi*; then he gained a temporary notoriety as a satirist of the English. His writings extend, in time, from the beginning of this century almost to the present time, and embrace every variety of subjects. He has written political articles, essays, poems, histories, novels, and one work of scriptural argument in favor of slavery. In Van Buren's time, he was Secretary of the Naval Department, but has since lived in retirement, dedicating himself to books and friends. He had entirely outlived his fame. His works are no longer read, and his name has almost passed out of literary mention.

REAL LIFE IN FICTION.

Already the charge of studying from life in the "Marble Faun," has been brought against Hawthorne. Residents at Rome, it is said, think themselves able to identify American female artists now living there, as the originals from whom Hawthorne has taken traits of character, both for "Hilda" and "Mariam." It is a nice question (which we have never been able to decide for ourselves, and cannot attempt to answer for anybody else,) how far an author is justifiable in drawing upon the traits of living persons for the characteristics of his fictitious creations. In point of mere artistic wisdom, it does not seem to be best to make characters of a book too much like actualities of human life, for what the imitated character gains in depth and intensity, it loses in that breadth and universality which make the personages of Shakespeare real men and women, and not copies of men and women. In an ethical aspect, it is very questionable whether the interests of literature transcend individual rights, and whether an author does not commit an unpardonable trespass upon another man's nature when he applies his traits to the formation of a character uttering thoughts and doing things of which the original is incapable. We know that the practice has the sanction of Goethe, Charlotte Bronte, Dickens, and others.

THACKERAY

Is said to be engaged on a historical work of the time of Queen Anne—the Augustan age of English literature. He has already revived the life of that period in fiction and his essays on "English Humorists," and his history of the time would be delightful. It is not probable that his work will appear in sequel to Macaulay's, as has been announced.

SWEDENBORG.

Admirers of Swedenborg will learn with pleasure that Mr. Elihu Rich, a gentleman known for his researches in mystical lore, and author of a book on "The Occult Sciences," has just completed a classified analysis, and arrangement in the order of instruction, of the great work of the Swedish Seer, the *Arcana Celestia*. It will form two bulky volumes of one thousand and four hundred closely printed pages, and has been executed as a labor of love in moments snatched from pressing daily avocations.

THACKERAY'S CORNHILL MAGAZINE.

The fourth number of this periodical contains an original illustration by Sir Edward Landseer, and a posthumous fragment by Charlotte Bronte. . . .

[*Ohio State Journal*, 12 April 1860]

Redpath's "Echoes of Harper's Ferry,"—a collection of notable sentiments in prose and poetry, touching Brown's Conquest of Virginia—has appeared. The title-page is adorned with the Virginian coat-of-arms, as it was—the prostrate despot, and the triumphant genius of liberty, with her motto, "Sic semper tyrannis;" the last page has the coat-of-arms as it is: a seedy gentleman on his back, with a cow rampant, and the motto as before.

It is denied that Humboldt said of Bayard Taylor, that he had traveled more, and seen less, than any other person. We have no doubt, however, that he thought it.

Appletons, of New York, have in press a book called "Three Hundred Sonnets," by the irrepressible Tupper.

151

A new edition of Coventry Patmore's singular poem, "Angel in the House," has been published.

Walt Whitman's "Leaves of Grass" are to be published in sumptuous style by Thayer & Eldridge of Boston, about the first of June. It is possible that Walt Whitman may become the fashion; and that we shall have Walt Whitman hats; and all the band-boxes will be lined with "Leaves of Grass." On the whole, however, we doubt the success of the book in a splendid dress even. The reading of it is utterly bamboozling, if without offence, we may so speak; and you have an unpleasant doubt whether the author is sublime or a beast, with an inclination toward the latter belief. His likeness, which accompanies the work, does nothing to relieve the painful impression. It is that of a man-about-horses—slouch, insolent, 'cute, coarse.

Story, the sculptor is making a bust of Theodore Parker.

It is a great pity that M. de Lamartine cannot rest content with the measure of contempt he has already achieved by his system of mendicancy. But he has a new project on foot for raising the wind, in the shape of an edition "personal, definitive, unique," of his complete works. It will be composed of forty volumes of from 500 to 600 pages each, to be brought out in four years, at the price of 300 francs, if paid in advance, otherwise every yearly course of ten volumes will cost eighty francs. Every subscriber will receive Lamartine's portrait with his autograph. . . .

That *Purgatorio* of authors—the search for a publisher—would be shorn of half its difficulties were every writer as clear and candid in the enunciation of his views as the inserter of the following advertisement, now to be found in the London journals: "Wanted, a publisher for 'The Bazaar,' a poem with notes, about 40 pages, the object of which is to illustrate and reprehend the incongruous and mischievous effect of fancy fairs, in connection with religious objects. Any person willing to accept and publish this essay at his own risk, and for his own profit, may address a line to X. T. N.," &c. As the grievance complained of is not totally unknown here, X. T. N. had better try the transatlantic market, should his liberal offer fail of acceptance at home. . . .

[*Ohio State Journal*, 21 May 1860]

The temptation to say first something about the progress of Dickens' new story, is not so easy to resist. The interest, so far, has not been intense, but those who love the quieter delights of thought and style, must deeply enjoy "Great Expectations." The style seems to us the perfect development of all that was best in Dickens' earlier manner. It is racy and full of life and spirit, but not exuberant. The ideas rise and float down its strong, profound current, that never breaks from the channel. The style is even better than that of "The Tale of Two Cities," which Dickens is said to regard as the best of his works. As to the thought in this new story, nothing could be fresher, as far as relates to outer life, nothing could be subtler in relation to the strange inner world of man's consciousness, about which so little is known. The transfer of vague mental impressions to paper—the impressions that really form so great a part of life and thought—has been accomplished with rare success by Holmes, but he deals with them in a scholarly way, and with somehow the air of one that makes interesting discoveries in physiology as a science. But Dickens gives them with an unconsciousness most like their own occurrence to us. There is something of this sort in the last chapter of "Great Expectations," which is worth a fortune in silver and gold—that in fact nothing could buy if such thoughts could be sold.

The wife of the blacksmith Joe is a terrible shrew; and has a quarrel across Joe's good nature with his surly journeyman, which ends in Joe's beating the journeyman, and in Mrs. Joe's falling into insensibility.

"Then," says the narrator Pip, "then came that singular calm and silence which succeeds all uproars; and then, with the vague sensation which I have always connected with that lull—*namely, that it was Sunday, and somebody was dead*—I went up stairs to dress myself."

Is not this inestimably precious? It makes you altogether better acquainted with yourself—your instinctive self. It recalls to you innumerable vagaries of the sort, which you have striven vainly to grasp before. It is the magic lens by which your infusorial ideas become visible—formless, as they are, but inhabiting your unconsciousness by myriads. It does not explain why, for instance, you always thought the odor of long-closed rooms to be of a brown color, related to a sense of preserves in a closet—but it excuses that extraordinary absurdity.

(We are perfectly aware that all this is not sensible, and having begged the reader to observe our consciousness on this vital point, we propose to lapse again into unconsciousness.)

De Quincey says that the idea of the glowing splendor and abundant life of midsummer noon, and the idea of stark and frosty death, were always inseparable in his mind. It is the grand principle of Plato's philosophy, and we believe of all other philosophies, that we think by opposites—that there is an occult equality, a sameness in the most antagonistic things, so that we cannot imagine anything without its opposite—difference being the appearance of which we are secondarily conscious. But this principle of equality explains to us only the grosser facts of mental operation. The subtleties of cogitation elude its touch, and remain for revelation by the accidents.

That inveterate imitator, and man of wonderful talent, George Augustus Sala, commences a new story in the February number of the "Temple Bar" Magazine, which he calls "The Seven Sons of Mammon," which exhibits original ability. It is in the manner neither of Dickens nor Thackeray, but is racily Sala's own. The adaptableness of Sala to the style of others, has been remarkable. While writing for "Household Words" and "All The Year Round," he wrote exactly in Dickens' manner; as the author of "Hogarth Papers" in the "Cornhill Magazine," it was impossible to distinguish him from Thackeray. He is now the editor of "Temple Bar," a magazine which is in nearly every way the equal of "Cornhill," but with a flavor of imitation in the very title.

Harper's Magazine for February contains a poem by George Arnold, called "Introspection," which is embarrassingly suggestive of Owen Meredith's "Last Words," recently published in the "Cornhill Magazine." Mr. Arnold is a poet of authentic power, and need not be like any body else to be good. Is it impossible that the work of our young poets should not be flavored by the sentiment and manner of the elder poets whom they admire? J. Ross Browne's "Peep at Washoe" is concluded. These papers have not had the abundant humor that characterized Browne's former writings, but there has been still a raciness in them that made them very pleasant. . . .

[*Ohio State Journal*, 18 January 1861]

* * *

[Howells's duties on the *Ohio State Journal* involved much more of his time and talents than simply the snipping and framing of items from the exchanges. It fell primarily on him to write the "cutting criticisms" of new books received in the office, and he afterwards hoped he would be "forgiven by the kindness which I sinned against without winning the authority as reviewer which I aimed at" (*YMY*, p. 132). Too, he was always ready to help Reed with editorial and general news commentary which the daily schedule of the newspaper constantly demanded. In memory it seemed that he had always been writing poems, sketches, and criticisms for the *Ohio State Journal*, and a casual perusal of the newspaper for the several years of Howells's association reveals a great number of items that can be ascribed to him with little reservation or fear of error. It is unfortunate that when his friend and successor at the *Ohio State Journal*, James M. Comly, sent Howells a file of the newspaper in 1868, Howells did not initial those items he recognized as his; but he didn't, and the tone of his letter of thanks to Comly suggests that he may not have wished his youthful work remembered:

Many thanks for the files of the Journal, which I've not time now to do more than acknowledge. I've been looking over my performances somewhat, and on the whole I rather wonder that I wasn't drummed out of Columbus for them. Their innocent wickedness dismays my experience, and is the greatest evidence of youth in the writer. They bring up old times with the greatest vividness, and I've lived great part of my life again in reviewing them. Thank you again for your very kind gift.

Several of the reviews and articles on literary matters published in the *Ohio State Journal* during Howells's tenure which appear to be his are included in the next chapter. In regard to the authorship of the items printed below, there is no doubt, as Howells either mentioned them in letters written at the time or later recalled the youthful pieces in his literary memoirs. Or, as in the case of "The Day We Celebrate," internal evidence reveals it to be Howells's work. Whatever disregard the older man may have had toward his writings for the *Ohio State Journal*, to our disinterested eye they appear fine examples of good journalistic writing, an unquestionable testament to Howells's mastery of the essayist's art.]

The Old and the New Year

Shall we be humorous or didactic? Or shall we be at once instructive and entertaining? Take that other chair, good reader, and listen to us. We are not going to talk long; and if we break this excellent promise, you can avenge yourself by falling asleep, in the midst of our improving remarks.

Did you go out yesterday, Sir, or Miss, or Madame? Then you noticed what a delightful day it was. We think you must have remarked how bright the sun was, how fresh the wind, how pure the air! And then, doubtless, when you had remarked these very prominent features of the weather, it occurred to you that it was the last day of the year—easy, graceful and natural transition! In your reflections on this theme (which we venture were of the proper, pensive and sombre kind,) did it strike you that the dying year was extremely hale and well-looking for a moribund twelve-month? Did he not seem rather like a year just starting on his journey, with his three hundred and sixty-five days before him? And yet he was standing with one foot upon the threshold of eternity. His journey was done, and the smile that you saw upon his face was not one of hope, but rather of gratification at a task accomplished. To-day he is dead. We speak of him thus, for memory haunts us more like that of a human being, than the recollection of a mere thing of weeks and months.

It is true that there were some things in this defunct old year that were not just as we could have wished. But taken all in all, we

155

shall look back upon 1858 with regretful pleasure. Is it not always so? Whether the mountain lie before us, or whether we have left it in the distance behind, still there is enchantment lent to it—still it is robed in azure.

And standing here, upon the threshold of the New Year, are you not puzzled to tell whether memory or hope be sweeter? If the thing might be, would it not be pleasant just to repeat in the coming time, all that you care to remember of the past? But

"Time driveth onward fast,"

and there is but one joy and one sorrow of its kind. We may, however, amend our future by our past.

Therefore, O friends, resting here in this pausing place of time, count up your errors and failures, as well as your successes, and study the causes of both. And while you study them, think it is not alone in you to will and to do; but also in One who is above us all. Most fit is this season for thought of things beyond the world and time; and every heart should take the lesson of the transitory day to itself.

But "we would not be a death's head to you," nor set any skeleton at your festive tables to-day. Eat your turkeys and mince pies, and be the hours as happy to you all, as we wish them to be.

[*Ohio State Journal*, 1 January 1859]

The Day We Celebrate

We rather like that title. Being obliged to write a Fourth-of-July Article, which shall destroy two fowls with a single fragment of rock—that is, content the Local, who is gone away, and wants something light and spicy for his column,—and please the Senior, who is gone away, and wants something grave and patriotic for his column—we think it well enough to have a title which permits us to be light and spicy, and grave and patriotic, without the smallest damage of its titular integrity. Indeed this heading will allow ample latitude, in which the vicarious pencil may slide

"From grave to gay, from lively to severe."

There is no reason now why we should shy off from saying an amusing or an instructive thing (as we are very often forced to do under ordinary headings) simply because it has nothing in the world to do with the subject in hand. Everything, we conceive, bears upon the subject in hand. The flood, Noah's ark, Aspasia, the Mother of the Gracchi, the French revolution, the patent shoe-pegging machine, the Atlantic Telegraph, the slave-code for the territories, Mr. Cass's letter, Pike's Peak. Indeed, what not? Fuzzyguzzy has all these things in his oration, and a thousand others too tedious to mention.

156

Then, besides this agreeable latitude, we like the novelty of this title. You think, friend, that you have heard the same sentiment offered before? You think you can remember having heard it in laughing childhood's hour, when, a very sweaty little Sunday School boy, you attended a Fourth-of-July Sunday School Festival, and were made miserable by a long, hot ride, and ate a wild-wood dinner, where a bug fell in your water, and you underwent unspeakable torture in the spectacle of an unattainable roast pig, with an orange in his mouth? When, after dinner, a lively clerical person amused the infant mind with stories of Hindoo ladies who cooked themselves in company with their dear departeds—and of deluded Indians who made a habit of being run over by an immense car of Juggernaut, and of heathen mothers who cast their offspring to devouring crocodiles. When you marched up and down, and to and fro, and bore banners, and sang, and had a sense of being in a patent flame-encircled oven. When some secular person got up, and said, "Children, I'll give you a toast,—The day we celebrate." In the most obliging manner, as if he had said, "Children, I'll give you fire crackers and ice cream all round." When you drank this toast (which the gentleman was so kind as to give you,) out of your glass of water with the bug in it, and were very skillful in avoiding the bug. You think you have since heard this sentiment, which innumerable obliging gentlemen have continued to give you, at a vast number of Fourth of July dinners, all like the first, a delusion and a snare.

And what then? Is not the sentiment a thing of beauty, and consequently a joy forever? Love is as old as Eden, but who forbears to make love because the thing is rather hacknied? Cupid is quite an old boy, and yet he is as much an infant phenomenon as ever. The fact is, friend, there are a few things that do not grow old; as we accept the term in the sense of mature unmarried ladies and gentlemen.

And this sentiment is one of them. *It* (like a few other things) grows old in the sense of

"Old wine, old books, old friends."

It will bear repeating, and we give you again, "The Day we Celebrate," and here's wishing you many returns of the same.

We know, that you are too wise and incredulous to take delight in childish things, as some simple folks do about you; but nevertheless, let Bobby have his firecrackers; and turn out yourself to see the bold defenders of your common country go by, with streaming flags, and bristling arms and dusty boots. Let your heart thrill again, (it will, if you let it,) at the dreadful sound of the Captain's voice; let your foot keep time to the throbbing of the drum, and the squeaking of the fife. Nay, make an excuse to yourself that you want to go up town, and mingling with that crowd of joyous urchins, keep the soldiers in sight as long as you can.

157

Try to feel a little patriotic; and when you go to dinner, don't say anything disagreeable to your wife, about a republic where freedom is a privilege and not a principle. Bobby is there with his bright eyes and believing soul, and it is best he should not learn that our boasts are somewhat ornamental and meretricious. He and the boys have just been talking it over, in solemn boyish conclave, and have come to the conclusion that if Louis Napoleon would send for a few of our citizen soldiers, he could readily sweep the Austrians out of Italy. They have also come to the time-honored conclusion that America can whip the world. Because it's free.

Well, this is better than disbelief. It is better even than hope in the ultimate freedom of mankind.

Bobby is anxious to hear the oration, and we trust you will take him. Listen to the reading of that bundle of "glittering generalities," (there is something of it yet, that stirs the heart like a trumpet,) listen to the singing of "Hail Columbia," ("by all, standing,") listen to the oration. We doubt, it shall do you no harm.

It is a good thing to keep the brave old day in remembrance; for after all, (and patriotic bluster aside,) it is the most glorious day time ever knew. If it were but for the holy-day's sake, it were well kept; but we think we may solemnize it with a deeper thought. Looking back at the past, we may well take courage, and looking forward, we need not despair. The republic is freer, and worthier to be free, than it has ever been, and the democrat need not falter with the fear that universal and perfect freedom shall never be ours.

And so, we give you again, "The Day we Celebrate," to be remembered and celebrated in all time, even to that poetic future
"When the war drum throbs no longer, and the battle
    flag is furled
In the Parliament of Man, the Federation of the World."
[*Ohio State Journal*, 4 July 1859]

[Situated on the Scioto River, eighteen miles north of Columbus, the Ohio White Sulphur Springs opened for the summer season in June 1859 under the new proprietorship of Andrew Wilson of Cincinnati. Patterned after the White Sulphur Springs, a popular spa in Virginia, the Ohio resort promised the usual medicinal benefits of its waters, combined with the best amenities of a pastoral retreat. Under Wilson's direction, a new hotel building, numerous cottages, bowling alleys, and bath houses were constructed, accommodations altogether for six hundred persons. As a member of the press, Howells was a guest of the management, seeking to establish its goodwill. He announced his good fortune in a letter to his sister Victoria written during the morning of July third: "I am going to White Sulphur, this afternoon, on a reporting expedition. It will cost me nothing, and I shall not have much to do; so I expect to pass the fourth pleasantly enough." But for some reason his departure was delayed, and the early morning hours and the chill of the day that followed had unpleasant consequences for the young reporter. As he wrote a few days later to his friend J. J. Piatt, "'Me and the other fash'nables,' as Yellowplush says, spent the Fourth at White Sulphur, and I haven't yet got over a violent cold I took. It was a most confoundedly cold morning, frost and things." Indeed, the unpleasantness of his discomfort was a fact he never forgot, and he thought the incident of sufficient interest to warrant mention in *Years of My Youth*:

> I was in those thinnest summer linens, with no provision of change against such an incredible caprice of the weather, and when I reached the hotel, there was no fire I could go to from the fresh, clean, thrillingly cold chamber with its white walls, and green lattice door, which I was shown into. No detail of the time remains with me, except what now seems to have been my day-long effort to keep warm by playing nine-pins with a Cincinnati journalist, much my senior, but as helpless as myself against the cold. There must have been breakfast and dinner and supper, with their momentary heat, but when I went to bed I found only the lightest summer provision of sheet and coverlet, and I was too meek to ask for blankets. (Pp. 169–70)

After a lapse of many years, he had little notion of the newspaper account he had given of his day at White Sulphur Springs, "but no doubt I tried to make merry over it, with endeavor for the picturesque and dramatic" (p. 170). Appropriately he signed the piece "Chispa," as was his wont at this time, the name of the rogue servant in Longfellow's dramatic poem, *The Spanish Student* (1843).]

A Day at White Sulphur

"With your love of nature," said somebody, "you'll be delighted by the picturesque drive from Lewis Centre to the Springs." This, of course, was said without any supposition that I was to be shaken as with a tertian ague while gratifying my love of the beautiful in nature. It was certainly very unseasonably cold. I saw the frost on the fence rails as I rode along, and the woodland road was chill and damp—all the chillier, I think, for glimpses of sunlight I caught between the trees, mixing with the gold of near lying wheat fields. It is odd how a little thing will change us. You think Marianne the prettiest girl in the room. She curtly refuses to dance with you. The ridiculous thing! She has a pug nose and cat eyes. Nature is very fine while nature does not rain on you of a sudden, or unexpectedly freeze you. When she does that, she loses a great deal of her attraction. Sitting in the smallest conceivable space in the most expedient corner of the coach, and giving thanks to heaven for every jolt that outshook my own individual shivering, I conceived an undying hatred for nature; and ceased not to quote in bitter derision and "grim silence," the words of Mr. Squeers, on witnessing the parental enthusiasm of Mr. Snawley for the ungrateful Smike—"Natur is a rum 'un."

I suppose the drive really *is* charming. I can understand how, on the breathless day of—what month?—I was going to write July—the shadows of those great trees, and the far-felt coolness of the forest depths, must be exceedingly delicious; how the succession of gentle acclivities, tempered with stretches of level, forms a romantic and picturesque road; how the little streams, and the pleasant farms heighten its charm. On Wednesday morning, however, the *coup d'oeil* I most enjoyed, was that of the long, dormir-windowed, green-shuttered hall, and clustering cottages of White Sulphur Springs. Here was nature, to be sure, but her marriage with art had softened her old maiden asperities.

Of course, with a whole day before me, I did not begin to do nothing till I had eaten breakfast, which I recommend everybody to do, especially after being called up at three A. .M., and made to travel the streets of the city in an omnibus for an hour, and then wait half an hour in the cold for the train, and then ride twelve miles on the cars, and then ride six in the coach. After breakfast you may stroll down and taste of the White Sulphur, which you will instantly acknowledge to be medicinal, if medicine and an extreme evil savor are associated in your mind. The spring gushes up crystal clear, and brims a mighty marble chalice, in the center of an exquisite pavilion. To a person in robust health, a fountain of not medicinal properties would be pleasanter; but the virtues of the White Sulphur are so great, that we can readily forgive its bad taste, which is what we frequently have to do with good people. Everybody who makes a stay at White Sulphur drinks of these waters, the resident physician, Dr. Dawson, told me; and the reader will doubtless take occasion to drink every sort on the place, during the summer. So we will on (if I may borrow an expression from the heroic drama) to more congenial themes.

If you are a little romantic (and have anybody with you), you had best ramble through the beautiful grove, while the dewy freshness is yet in the air, and while you are yet too languid for ten pins. I noticed numbers of young persons of both sexes, engaged in this agreeable and profitable diversion—so eminently calculated to develop the finer feelings of our nature. If, however, you are not romantic, and have nobody with you, go to ten-pin alleys at once. Speaking from the depths of experience, I suggest that you will find the pins very dexterous in avoiding the balls, and that you will probably lose every game you play.

For one who never saw the White Sulphur, under the *ancien regime*, it is difficult to understand how much money and time have been expended in bringing it to its present perfection. The new-comer finds a fine piece of wood land cleared of all under growth, and zoned in a smooth and level track two miles in length, pretty white cottages peering out between the trees; new buildings going up, and everywhere visible the work of taste and lavish care. The open grounds are dotted with spring pavilions and summer houses, and planted with thrifty silver leaved poplars and maples. All is new, but it has the advantage of newness without its unpleasantness. There are billiards, horses, ten-pins, and walks and dancing and health-giving waters. What more can man, sick or well, want? The main hotel and the cottages are thoroughly and sumptuously furnished—

But this is not the Complete Guide to Little Peddlington, I hope?

Owing to the general prevalence of the Fourth of July, and the coolness of the weather, there were not so many people at the Springs, but that in one's walks and talks, one could feel that delightful sense of joint-proprietorship, which one used to experience at our poor, dear, shabby little theatre, last winter, on taking seat with the snug dozen of good sinners, who attended the performances of that wicked, wicked place. After awhile, when the heats of summer have surely set in, it will not be so at White Sulphur; though if there were a thousand guests, Mr. Wilson would make each one feel himself the object of his sole attention. But just now, before the crowd has thronged to the Springs, it will be pleasantest to visit them; that is, if you love not much company. If you care greatly for society, go then, and you will find abundance of it.

I ought to say that at dinner the tables "groaned"—as they are accustomed to do in newspaper accounts—"under their weight of good things," but I really have not the conscience to represent the tables as doing any such lugubrious thing. Jolly tables!—they *laughed* beneath their loads—laughed in a vast variety of substantials and ephemerals, solids and liquids, dainties and "delicacies of the season," of course. We had Senator Reid there, and drank his compliments to that extent, that the Ohio Senate was not missed at all. You think you had a noisy time here on the Fourth, with your cannons and things; but that is because you did not hear the cork-explosions at White Sulphur.

After dinner, when reasonable rest had been taken, we began to have it debated whether there should be a speech in the grove, or a dance in the great hall, and the question being put, it was decided in the affirmative—that is to have the hop. So the light fantastic was agitated; and what with dancing, and rolling ten pins, and rambling over the grounds, the afternoon passed so rapidly as almost to make one regret supper time.

In the evening we had fireworks, and the dancing, and so—sleep. A full day of pleasure crowned with tranquil slumber.

I suppose that I ought really to say something (for the sake of those who have not been there) of the scenery about the springs. It is very charming—hardly picturesque, if you understand that word to imply sublimity. Looking across the Scioto—which brawls in sunny ripples at the foot of the grounds—you see rolling uplands—field and wood;—gold of wheat mixing with emerald of meadows, and all held in the embrace of dark, green forest. The Scioto is guarded with elms and water loving trees, and the banks slope gently to the stream.

When you go to White Sulphur from Columbus by buggy, fail not to drive toward Delaware on that road which the liberality of Mr. Wilson has made one of the best in the State. It brings you in view of beautiful and constantly varying scenery. If you can have the morning sun slanting over the hill-crests into the stream, all the better.

When you go to White Sulphur—but you will find out all these things of yourself, and innumerable others which cannot be mentioned in any reasonable space. You will find recreation of all kinds. You will meet pleasant and refined society. You will find delicious little solitudes. You will find the best "accommodations" at the hotel, and the promptest attendance. Indeed, to close this epistle general, with proper flourish, you will find every attaché of the establishment, from Mr. Wilson down, to be "gentlemanly and accommodating" in the widest newspaper sense of the word.

[Signed "Chispa," *Ohio State Journal*, 6 July 1859]

[Little did the citizen soldiery that encamped on the State Fair grounds a short distance outside Columbus on Monday, 29 August 1859, realize that the game they played would soon be in deadly earnest. But even these militiamen had a better idea of what they were at than did Howells, who looked on in wonder and bemusement. What bothered him was the absence of pomp and grand ceremony. Those would have been easy to poke fun at, or at least to describe in picturesque terms. But instead he found the commonplace reality of military camplife, and he was disturbed.]

I Visit Camp Harrison

I have not, that I know, (for if it is not safe to say that a man is happy till he is dead, it is a greater imprudence to say what he has had,) a military genius; though I once certainly broke out, morally speaking, into a warlike rash, at a very tender age. I say that I have not a military genius, and yet I am a friend to the gallant spirit which occasionally prompts the American citizen (defiant of The Gaze of Europe,) to doff the apron and the cap, to drop the needle, the awl, the pen and the yardstick, and involve himself in hot clothes and carry a large gun, in honor of his country. I like to see it, and think it ought to be encouraged. With a view to countenancing the matter, I have, at a remoter period of my history, listened to the reading of the militia bill; and yesterday, being already much enthused by a perusal of our local's noble sketch of the history of Camp Harrison, I determined to visit the spot hallowed by so many patriotic associations, and celebrated by so great a man.

The hands of that time-piece which has acquired a repute among the people of the sanctum, for keeping time in a manner equaled only by the chronometer of Captain Cuttle—were pointing the hour of nine, as I sallied forth. The air was bracing and salubrious, and the fruit and melon stands were peculiarly suggestive of cholic. It is a fact that I did not want to walk, though I didn't like to mention it to myself. When therefore an acquaintance, going to Camp Harrison, offered me a seat in his buggy, I had not the heart to refuse his offer.

(The reader will observe that I am making this relation as dull and egotistical as possible, in order to give myself the air of a real traveler. It does not so much matter how far you go, and what happens, as how you tell the story of it. If you bully people with a long account of nothing, they will be very apt to think you a wonderful fellow of vast experience.)

Arrived at Camp Harrison at a moment which I cannot exactly give, by reason of the unaccountable conduct of the watch, (Captain Cuttle aforesaid,) which had not moved a tick since I looked at it before, I felt that my first duty was to explore the camp. A person in a military dress (in whom it was difficult to distinguish the peaceablest civilian of my acquaintance,) denied this privilege on the ground of "orders." I felt a thrill go through me of exquisite satisfaction. Come, I observed to myself—Come, now, this is something like. Here is a gentleman who knows that I couldn't carry off any tent or camp kettle upon the ground, and he boldly refuses to admit me. I like that. Deuce take it, it's Discipline.

This in bitter irony. But I remembered, in justification of this too faithful sentinel, that if he admitted me, he would be obliged to admit the whole campful; and I forbore to tempt him with a massy wedge of gold that I had in my pocket for that purpose.

I fell back a reasonable distance, and surveyed the camp. It is a fine piece of ground for the purpose. The tents are pitched on an elevated plateau, among numbers of beautiful elms, through the dark foliage of which they show at a little way very picturesquely. The camp fires were yet smoking, but breakfast had been eaten, and presently the drums began to summon the soldiers to parade, and the camp was alive with the clash of arms. It was at this moment that we were invited within the lines, and witnessed the dress parade of the battalion. The companies were by no means fully represented, but the men on the ground were well disciplined; and their easy and soldierly-execution of command was a *cosa de ver*.

And yet, I couldn't realize the fact that this was a "muster." I missed the gorgeous uniforms, the white pantaloons, the splendid coats, the mighty plumes, that made "ambition virtue" in

"Life's morning march when my bosom was young."

Here were gentlemen dressed in a uniform so modest and sensible, as to be absolutely as unimpressive as citizen's dress—gentlemen who didn't think it was necessary to wear an absurd costume in order to be a soldier. I was disappointed, and I think I read a like sentiment in the countenances of small boys about, whose starved eyes evidently hungered after a more magnificent display.

After the parade, a stroll through the neat little camp was entertaining enough—made yet more pleasant by the courtesies of the officers. Everything was calculated to impress one favorably with the affair. Perfect order reigned; and during the night before, no disturbance whatever had taken place. Good feeling and satisfaction seemed universal.

And why is it not a pleasant and a wholesome thing for those merchants, and clerks and artisans to take this week, and renew themselves by a few days of hardy, wholesome, natural life, made zestful by exercise and novelty? Say nothing about the rheumatism, and the possibility of the camp's being rained upon, and I contend for Camp Harrison. I know that it would be easy to be facetious upon the militia men. I know that I might quote of

"Mouths without hands maintained at vast expense,
In war a charge, in peace a weak defense."

But I think we do wrong to discourage the spirit that shows itself in the training of the slender bodies and hardening of the feeble muscles of our young men. Let us stay at home, and sleep in our beds, but if any of the neighbors want to try straw and a tent for a little while, in heaven's name let them.

This is too dreadfully earnest. Let us have a well-ordered retreat to the descriptive again, and leave the didactic to our betters.

The undress parade by companies took place at ten o'clock, when the troops were marched out of the camp, and down the knoll, and formed in line, and in column an agonizing number of times, to the music of the ear-squeaking fife and spiritspiring drums; and marched about over a very large bed of "Jimstown weed" till it smelt to heaven.

Before noon, numerous carriages appeared on the ground, and the usual occurrence of fair women looking upon brave men took place. It was then that a uniform—but I will say no more.—Let it pass. It was then I bade farewell, to Camp Harrison, and returned to the city in the carriage of another friend whom a special providence called up at the critical hour.

It is a remarkable fact, that though I was conscious of having been absent several hours, Captain Cuttle still maintained that it only was nine o'clock when I returned.

[Signed "Chispa," *Ohio State Journal*, 31 August 1859]

[Howells was much more at home at the Ohio Editorial Convention which met in January 1860 in Tiffin, in the north central part of the state. Here "hard-working country printers and busy city journalists" gathered to talk over the issues and problems they faced in their profession. Politics, government patronage, and complaints against the post office were the chief topics of their discussions, but a few minutes had been set aside for the delivery of some verses, and Howells was asked this time to be the poet of the day. Though the practice must appear to some as quaint, poetry in nineteenth-century America still performed an important social function, just as it had in the classical world for which these antebellum democrats felt such a kinship. As a public event, it gave expression to the values, the aspirations, and the pride of the guild; as ritual it dignified the proceedings; and as language it had the power to inspire and entertain. Whether he succeeded—and he afterward had his doubts about the effectiveness of his performance—Howells very much meant to inspire. His model was Tennyson's "In Memoriam," whose form and mood he had also drawn on at this time for his lines on "Old Brown"; his vision, that of a journalistic future that would rise above the venal prejudices of the day. He put it best in the third or final section of the poem.

> O not of us, but after us,
> That talk to-day, and jest and dine,
> And view the future through our wine
> Red with the dawn and glorious—

> Shall come the man. For us the toil
> To fell the trees, to clear the land,
> With steadfast heart and willing hand,
> To plough the field, and sow the soil.

> Slow moves the work. Our hands are fast
> In manacles of Prejudice:

We will not that, we dare not this,
We doubt and falter to the last.

On tongues that else would speak in sooth,
   The palsying touch of Fear is placed—
   On many opening lips is pressed—
To lock within the rising truth,—

Want's bony hand. The sepulchre
   Of Custom many a living heart
   Holds in its narrow dark, apart,—
To vainly beat, and dumbly stir.

Envy, and Avarice, and Wrong
   Betray us in ourselves; and Doubt
   Fills all the unknown place about
With phantom shapes—and ponders long

Whether the golden grain will be
   Of greater value than the mast
   Shaken to swineherds by the blast
That rocks the moss-grown, dark'ning tree.

The work is great. Ah! clasping hands,
   Be here the ancient trust renewed,
   Be here the ancient hate subdued,
Here strengthened all fraternal bands!

Still striving forward, let us laud
   Our avocation with our deed—
   Not perfect words, but actions plead
Of good intents to man and God!—

Remembering, while the dollar flames,
   And ever up the nightly skies
   The calm and patient stars arise—
To look above with loftier aims;

Remembering, when we fear to move,
   Our way is safe to onward tread—
   Behind us quake the sands we dread—
The rock is firm we shrink to prove;

Remembering, in sore need and pain,
   The struggle is the victory—

For none that struggles to be free
Deals any lightest blow in vain!

In spite of whatever difficulties they encountered—moral or linguistic—Howells's auditors were apparently in a forgiving mood. He described the occasion a few days later in a letter to his sister Aurelia:

> Last week, you know, I delivered my poem before the editorial Convention at Tiffin. There was an audience of some four or five hundred present; and at first my knees smote together like Belshazzar's, the kings, when the exciting proclamation appeared over the side board in his dining-room. I, however, went through pretty well, and was cheered, congratulated and complimented in due order. That was Wednesday night. The next evening, we had a grand banquet and dance; I taking down to supper a matron of the first consequence in Tiffin, and proving myself as to the young ladies, a perfect *mangeur des coeurs*. There was one young person there, looked just like Kate Jones, with whom I fell violently in and out of love. (Mem. Don't mention to Sis.)

How he must have shined. Were man in control of his fate, young Howells perhaps could have been content with his lot and possessed of the good sense to see the virtue and value in a life of journalism in his native state. But as he eventually came to know, fate has little care for the whims of one's good sense. His dreams appalled in their boldness and commanded a courage and perseverance that must ever baffle those of safe hearts. In declining an invitation from his sister Victoria to accompany her on a visit to family in Martin's Ferry, Howells spoke the truth and hardship of every ambitious youth: "I am working very hard—reading, studying, and scribbling constantly—aside form the drudgery I perform on the Journal. So that I grudge myself even the time it will take to go home. O, it's such a long way up! But I have my eye on the temple that 'shines afar,' and I will fall uphill, if I must succumb."]

The Editorial Convention at Tiffin

The State *Journal* was there. In fact, (and there would be little use in attempting to conceal this from the world, which had its eyes upon the Convention,) the poet of the occasion was selected from the State *Journal* office; and as no scribbler ever loses an opportunity to read his verses when one or more are gathered together, the bardling went—with his effusion and free pass in his pocket, a neat and portable newspaper bundle containing articles of wardrobe under his arm, and a very, very heavy heart in his bosom. For he has all the ingenuous shame of people with his infirmity, (who are said,

167

when not tipsy, to be the modestest and dullest in the world,) and he was not sure, as he phrased it to twenty of his confidential friends, that his poem was "adequate."

At the Urbana depot this youth expended a great part of his ready money in the purchase of a copy of *The Ohio State Journal*, and during the journey read the heavy man's editorial (which the heavy man himself had read to him the day before,) as well as his own verses on the fourth page.

He does not remember any other incident worthy of record that occurred until he arrived at Mac-a-Cheek, where "J. J." of the *Press* came on board the train, and Mr. Donn Piatt also. It was half-past four o'clock on Wednesday afternoon, when in company with some thirty (or forty) editorial gentlemen, he stepped from the cars upon the ground at Tiffin. And here let him say it to the honor of the profession, that not a soul of all that goodly company took the omnibus, but rather repaired to the hotel on foot. A baffled conductor-and-trunk-boy attached to the hotel, was the sole passenger. Him we viewed derisively, as we trudged along, enlivening the way with gushes of that easy wit which springs eternal in the editorial breast.

Let the enemies of Tiffin delight to bark and bite at the reputation of that beautiful little city, if it is their evil nature to; but I maintain that it is one of the most charmingly situated of places, with an immense capacity for being beautiful in the summer time. Even in the dead winter, this was perceptible, though the effect was marred by the bustle of the business streets—painful to one just from the elegant repose of the State Capital. But I come to bury the convention not to praise Tiffin, which like the hair restorative that is "not to dye," speaks for itself.

In the evening, we "had the Literary Exercises," at the Loesser Hall. A cornet band of Germans were in attendance, and between the bursts of poetry and eloquence, we had bursts of music a great deal better than either. Our good Teutonic friends, also sung us several songs, and if the immense audience which crowded the hall were disappointed in the quality of *some people's* verses, it could certainly not complain of the singing, which being of Tiffin was admirable. The truth is—and we would not hide a rushlight of that precious flame under a bushel,—that when you like the people of a place, you are very apt to think the place itself rather marvellous, and the Editorial Convention brings away from Tiffin the most unbounded regard and respect for it; and one at least, would like, if his limited means had not forbid him, to have bought Tiffin, and presented it with the compliments of the donor, to the citizens, who alone are worthy of it.

But I wander.

The band came first. Then the poem. Then the band. Then the oration, by Mr. W. H. P. Denny. Then the band. Then a song from the Bruderbund. Then somebody called Mr. Donn Piatt out; and Mr. Donn Piatt made a delightful little, droll speech, in which he rehearsed his experience with a Democratic campaign paper, published at Mac-a-Cheek, in 1840. After Mr. Piatt, was another song, and then the Convention adjourned to the Shawhan House parlor at nine, on Thursday morning.

It did not appear, after the convention met, in the morning, that there was a great deal of business on hand. Resolutions were drawn up, recommending a general adoption of the cash subscription system; and the best method of conducting country newspapers was discussed—the discussion resulting in the discovery that every publisher had to adapt himself to the circumstances in which he was placed, as regarded advertising and subscription. The interchange of views and information on the subject was useful, and will end in good. The Convention selected officers for the following year, as well as poet and orator. (Owing to an unaccountable disappearance of a memorandum of these gentlemen's names, I am reluctantly compelled to defer their publication.)

In the afternoon, the gentlemen of the Convention, with the exception of two, visited the schools of Tiffin. An eye-witness of their embarkation from the Shawhan House, in a magnificent chariot drawn by six milk-white horses, describes it as the most gorgeous spectacle which he had beheld since the happy days when he used to go forth to meet the circus wagon. They were indeed a gay and goodly company, delighting the eyes of the youth of Tiffin, and glorying in their impressive equipage. But when did not Pride, since Poor Richard pronounced against it, have its fall? It is the truth, that these editors returning to their hotel, pleased with the Tiffin public schools, and elate with their own appearance, so puffed up the heart of their driver with vain-glory, that he yielded, in an evil hour, to a desire to make a yet more splendid show, and turned a corner of the street with such sharpness and suddenness that a wheel broke down, and the controllers of destinies were strown like autumn leaves about the street. (A beautiful figure, which the country press are requested to credit.) Of course, a scene of that kind would reduce the descriptive powers of an eye-witness to mendicancy, and how can one who was not there to see, describe it? It is reported that every soul in the wagon was spilled out, but on questioning each one separately, it appeared that each had clung to his seat, while all his neighbors went overboard.

In the evening the festival came off, which had been prepared for the Association at the Shawhan House, by the hospitable people of Tiffin. Bounteous tables they were—laden with everything to tempt the appetite and distract the mind.

The fairest ladies of Tiffin graced the occasion with their presence, and the talent and consequence of the place were fully represented.—The speeches in response to the toasts were what such speeches are always described to be,—and the dinner passed off, how?—pleasantly, harmoniously, delightfully. After dinner, the dance—which was kept up till the larger of the smaller hours, when the company dispersed—very regretfully on the part of the guests—not unreluctantly, it is to be hoped, on the part of their kind hosts.

There was little to do on Friday, but pass the usual votes of gratitude, which were passed with unusual sincerity, and at ten, yesterday morning, the Convention adjourned to meet at Sandusky, on the last Thursday of July next.

Several little incidents of the Convention, like the great mass of the N. Y. *Ledger's* answers to correspondents, "stand over for our next." I must not omit, however, to allude here to the excellence of Mr. J. J. Piatt's poetical response to the toast of the "Rural Editor," which I hope will see the light in the pamphlet report on the Convention's proceedings. All the other responses to toasts—some by editors and some citizens of Tiffin—were excellent-good.

The editorial fraternity are much indebted to the activity of the profession in Tiffin for their share in making this Convention one of the pleasantest that has ever been held.

[Signed "Chispa," *Ohio State Journal*, 21 January 1860]

[The profession of journalism has never been one to insure permanence. Nowhere was this more true than in the middle-western states before the Civil War, and in a short while the happy company of newsmen of the *Ohio State Journal* was scattered, quite literally around the globe. Samuel Reed was the first to leave when in the spring of 1860 he took a position with the Cincinnati *Gazette* where he immediately struck Moncure D. Conway as a "brilliant writer," a leading journalist in a city noted for its excellence in that respect. Asa L. Harris was the next to depart the capital city. Though he mattered far less in Howells's mind than either Reed or Reed's successor, Samuel Price, Harris had been responsible for the "Local News," as well as a number of odd jobs about the office. Late in 1860 he purchased the Coshocton *Age*, a weekly newspaper of Republican sentiments published at the seat of Coshocton County, sixty-five miles east-northeast of Columbus. That left only Howells and Price and the usually absent Cooke, and when the senior editor decided to sell his interest in the paper to Isaac J. Allen in July 1861, the younger men waited for the inevitable. They tried to dislike the new proprietor, but he gave them no cause other than the fact that he had no need of them, and early in August the two young friends, ever hopeful before their uncertain futures, walked together to the Miami Depot and bade each other and the city whose society they had so enjoyed a final farewell. Several weeks earlier, Howells had made his valedictory in the *Ohio State Journal*, a singular display of personal affection and youthful pride. Before him lay the uncertain promise of a Roman consulship; around him, the disarray of a people in the process of mobilizing for war. "The future is all confusion to me," he had written to his mother earlier in May; "I guess, however, things will straighten out and I shall get through (*LL*, 1: 34)."]

CHANGES IN THE STATE JOURNAL.—With a heart almost affected to tears, we have read in the Coshocton *Age*, a notice of the editorial change in this journal, and a retrospective glance at the career of the paper during the last three years. The editor of the *Age* is justly praiseful of the editorial *corps* of able and eloquent writers who took charge of the *State Journal* in November, 1858, and inaugurated a new era in Columbus journalism. They discovered to a delighted populace, that the Capital of Ohio possessed metropolitan facilities, and they improved them. The *Journal* became a name—yet more, a sensation; it was read, quoted, admired. With a marvelous degree of fearlessness, it advocated the cause of humanity, good morals and religion.—Of its Republicanism, we can say that it was anti-slavery, without doubt, and never halted in its noble career, because the good seemed a long way off. The *Journal's* leaders were full of life, of principle and power, and it is melancholy to think that the brilliant spirit that flashed them forth, should now be engaged in trying to glimmer through the Cimmerian darkness of the Cincinnati *Gazette*. The news department of the *Journal* was full of spice and information—a *ragout* of original talent and attractive clippings. Of the miscellaneous selections we can say that they were at once useful and ornamental in their nature; and of the poetry habitually printed on the fourth page, that the ladies cried for it. The present writer feels the more freedom in speaking of this department, because he himself had charge of it, and is modestly conscious of then wielding scissors of metropolitan brilliancy.

Yes, in those days the *Journal* was a power, and without affectation we hold that it has continued to be so up to the present time. In the hands of the incoming editor, this retiring writer begs to assure the editor of the *Age*, that the *Journal* will be worthy of its former greatness.

We have spoken merely of what were falsely called the leading departments of the paper under the *ancien regime*. The Local Department of that great day remains to be noticed. It was conducted by no less a person than the present editor of the Coshocton *Age*.

He was at the same time partially mailing clerk, and the hand writing with which he inscribed the wrappers of the *Journal*, was gall and bitterness to the envious postmaster under whose eyes it passed. He was perhaps the best local editor we ever knew in our life. Chaste, yet at times passionate in his manner of describing the arrest of disorderly persons, his style possessed a charm which we remember with tender regret. In notices of fires and runaways, he wielded a pen of lurid and graphic power. In the invention of those pleasing fictions with which the local column is occasionally eked out, he displayed a genius not less wonderful than that of Nedline Buntwin himself. But his grand efforts were made when he rose superior to the envious combinations of his journalistic seniors, and soared into the discussion of moral topics. His defence of a bill to punish seduction will live as long as social purity and fine writing are popular. Of course, he was not without his defects, but as he is now editing a country newspaper—*de mortuis nil nisi bonum*.

But alas! why do we recur to the past?

"For now, the whole round table is dissolved
Which was an image of the mighty world, .
And we the last go forth companionless,
Among new men, strange faces, other minds."

Let us drop the curtain, as they used to do at our poor little theatre, when the powers of the actors gave way; and let the new play be put up on the stage.

[*Ohio State Journal*, 20 July 1861]

CHAPTER FOUR

Western Poetics and Literary Prejudices

[One of the more welcomed features of the "new journalism" with which Howells and Reed dazzled Columbus was its sophisticated literary tone. Unlike country newspapers, such as the *Ashtabula Sentinel*, there was no need for the metropolitan journal to fill empty spaces with serial novels clipped from other papers and magazines. But the poetry corner had an honored place, and literary gossip and reviews of new publications were regular departments of the *Ohio State Journal* following the new dispensation. If not in name, then certainly in practice, Howells became known as the literary editor of the *Ohio State Journal*, and in a prospectus of the paper's weekly edition printed on 10 December 1860, it was announced in bold type that "a due proportion of space is devoted to literary matters, under the special charge of Wm. D. Howells, Esq., which is ample evidence of the taste and skill with which it is managed." These literary items for the weekly edition appear always to have been reprinted from some previous number of the daily *Ohio State Journal* where Howells's association had won a respect the publishers felt worth advertising. But as with all the unsigned newspaper items, without either Howells's recollections or some contemporary admission to the authorship of a particular piece, we can only speculate regarding the particulars of his critical writing for the *Ohio State Journal*. The absence of a byline or of the name of another newspaper from which some piece is reprinted, along with the collaboration of opinion and style with those of articles known for certain to be his, do recommend a goodly number of reviews and literary essays as his work. And, although speculation is always liable to error no matter how cautious and considered one be in his or her judgments, the gain made by recovering a little more of Howells's literary apprentice work than we should otherwise have just may outweigh the danger that any one or more of these pieces was in fact written by another.

That the leading Republican newspaper in a state of such emerging importance as Ohio should have devoted so much of its space as the *Ohio State Journal* did to literary and cultural matters was not so unusual as it might appear to the modern reader. The West was, as Howells later remarked, romantic in peculiar ways, and it valued the person who had some poetry in him so long as it did not interfere with his practical worth and abilities. Literary culture, too, was taken rather seriously. If anything, the region sought too strenuously to excel in that regard, as later generations of ardent handmaidens of art and learning give shrill testimony to. What began as merely an understandable and altogether human response to a sense of cultural inferiority became in time an excuse for that insularity and bluestocking morality that Sherwood Anderson and Sinclair Lewis found an easy mark for satire and ridicule. But the sins of the children should not always be charged against the parents, and on the whole the literary culture of the antebellum world of Howells's youth must be regarded as wholesome and supportive. All that was missing was sufficient talent to maintain the region's growing sense of itself. But in time that too came.

In his account of a visit he made with his father in 1871 to the home of James A. Garfield, then a rising figure in the United States Congress, Howells records an incident that may only reveal the quality of Garfield's mind and imagination, but may also reflect the conditions of that culture and region of which Garfield even more than Lincoln was typical. Seated one lovely June evening on the Garfields' veranda overlooking the lawn, Howells was holding forth on the close association and friendships he had made with the New England worthies. But before he had really got started, Garfield stopped him, ran to either side of the grassy space that separated his house from his neighbors, and called those within hearing over. "He's telling about Holmes, and Longfellow, and Lowell, and Whittier!" and a small crowd gathered to listen to Howells's talk (*YMY*, p. 176). Their mute homage was something he had known and shared from his earliest youth, and in time Howells was wise enough to realize its true measure. But during his years at the *Ohio State Journal*, he had been content merely to serve this need, and in turn he was amply rewarded.

Howells was at this time passionately a poet, and he gave much thought and time, as well as a considerable part of his talents, to the matters of his craft. The romantic revolution was still being fought in the backwaters of Western civilization, and the generations as well as individuals were sharply divided on questions of taste and style. But among those promises which the great majority of Americans of every age and aesthetic persuasion remained steadfast in believing was that of a great national literature, a new poetry free of the limitations and impediments of European art and civil immorality. Its scale might not be epic, as earlier thought, but in grandeur and sublimity it would somehow suit the landscape and people it celebrated. Grandest and most sublime of all was to be its essentially democratic character, an ideal Howells never, during his long life, abandoned. It was, for example, Henry Wadsworth Longfellow's common and universal appeal which justified in Howells's estimation *The Courtship of Miles Standish*, published in October 1858 and noticed soon afterwards in the *Ohio State Journal*. Half a century later, Howells reiterated his earlier belief in "The Art of Longfellow" (1907), the years between having effected very little change.

The poet has nothing to tell, except from what is actually or potentially common to the race. He will realize, so far as his process is conscious, that the thing in which any one thinks himself singular is the thing by which he is one with all other men, that the personal within is the universal without. This courage in frankly trusting the personal as the universal, is what made Longfellow not only sovereign of more hearts than any other poet of his generation, and more than any other poet who has lived, but now, on the hundredth anniversary after his birth, when a generation has passed since his death, has established him a master of such high degree that one who loves his fame may well be content without caring to ascertain precisely his place among the other masters.]

Why We Believe in Miles Standish

The man who ventures to say what is poetry, and what is not, is a very foolish and audacious man. And yet, how full the world is of just such people—who are forever treading on the tender toes of each other's literary preferences, and boxing the ears of each other's poetical pets! What right has middle-aged Mr. Brown, who believes in Cowper and Pope, to insult young Jones by pishing at the grace, tenderness and beauty of Tennyson? Or, why should our thundering friend Smith, abuse the taste of Tompkins, because Tompkins likes Longfellow and Browning, and not Byron? Why should we be bullied because we love old Chaucer better than all the moderns that ever wrote? Is Johnson obliged to call Stubbs a fool, because Stubbs dotes upon Heine to the utter exclusion of Pollock? Tupper has admirers—shall we knock them upon the head? (as we confess, in the sacred privacy of parentheses, we would like to do.)

One could hardly meet one's friend on common literary ground. "It is very fine, but—" and straightway you are outraged by what you think the most stupid notions. Ah, who shall say he is right about these things? And after all, what does it matter, whether all hearts respond to the same touch so that they respond to one? If it were possible, we would have everybody love our poet—but shall we deny the sacred knowledge of poetry to him who does not?

175

We have admired Miles Standish—and we assert our admiration in spite of "Punch," who sums up the objection and ridicule of the critics, by calling it Ink-standish. We cheerfully permit Jones to say that the measure is hobbling; Smith has our leave to call it prosy; Tompkins may say it lacks depth, and complain that Longfellow has added no new thoughts to our life worth the keeping; Stubbs may call it defective in passionateness. What of it all?—We go back to Miles Standish and linger with renewed delight over the dear hobbling, prosy, shallow, passionless lines, and forget that they are such. In our heart we congratulate ourselves that we are right and the critics all wrong—that Miles is the bravest hero, and Alden the tenderest lover, and Priscilla the sweetest maiden that ever lived! None can deny us our belief, in which lies the fact that Miles Standish is a poem.

The simple ballad that touches the heart of the sailor, makes the dilettante to laugh. How bald and insipid are the ditties that made us cry when children! How turgid the ranting rhymes that fired our boyish blood! How ineffably maudlin are the verses that we languished over when we were in love with Matilda Araminta! And yet these ditties, ranting rhymes, and lovesick verses shall affect our children after us, as they affected us. The true fire of poetry was in them, but it no longer reveals itself to those who are grown callous to its heat.

A poem which, like Miles Standish, has charmed so many thousand souls, cannot be a failure, even if the world should willingly let it die. Its beauty has mixed with their lives, if it has given them an hour's harmless pleasure; and though it be but a little rill mingling with the great river of life, its waters will have dropped some sands of gold, to brighten secretly in that river's bed forever.

[*Ohio State Journal*, 24 November 1858]

[Howells's critical measure was assuredly more than the mere yardstick of popularity. John Godfrey Saxe, now virtually forgotten, was an enormously successful poet and humorous lecturer who during the decade before the Civil War rivaled even Oliver Wendell Holmes in the public's opinion. It was of course wrong, and Howells never tired in his attempts to burst the bubble of Saxe's reputation. Walt Whitman's poetry, on the other hand, genuinely and disturbingly drew Howells's admiration, and it is remarkable that in spite of the repugnance he felt before some of its more earthy and sensual elements, Howells nevertheless addressed on a number of occasions during the early years of his critical journalizing the overwhelming questions posed by Whitman's strange verse. It would have been far more judicious for him to have overlooked this "liberating force, a very 'imperial anarch' " (*LFA*, p. 68) that was making itself heard in the land, but to have done so would mean his keeping shop with the Mrs.

176

Grundys and Miss Nancys of critical taste, something Howells resisted doing throughout a long career of service for the True, Good, and Beautiful. Though he never overcame his failure to see the profound artistic worth of Whitman's poetry, Howells at least tried to see the problem of Whitman's art in its aesthetic dimensions. As a result, his views are still of value, apart from any biographical or historical interest they may possess.]

John G. Saxe

"A feeble imitation of Hood's worst manner."—*Bedford Standard.*

Not so much because this characterization of Saxe is felicitous, do we copy it, as because it is in some sort a protest against a shallow and spurious merit, which is too often mistaken for the real article.

Perhaps in no other field do we display our national characteristic love for humbug so much as in that of literature. We gull each other, the more readily, in this matter, because, though an intelligent people, we are by no means a critical people. We have general opinions about books and book-makers; but individual opinions, we have very few.

We do not of course, speak of that very large class who feast on
—"the gross mud-honey"
of such ephemera as the New York *Ledger*; but of those who profess to have a more refined taste. How many among these have more than a "view" of Longfellow, or Read, or Curtis, or Mitchell, or Taylor, or Saxe? They have all read authorities on these authors; and will *quote* any amount of opinion. They buy their books, and they read them. When any of these gentlemen lecture, they take their families to hear them.

To these people is chiefly attributable the crying sin of Saxe, a person, who has afflicted this nation with more vile *funny* verses than any other. Of course, critics who from laziness, or good nature, or from anything else, have suffered him to exist almost undisputed as a poet, are greatly to blame; but the fault lies chiefly with those who *take authors for granted.* Seeing him first endured, then pitied, then embraced—seeing him quoted and praised—hearing him read his smooth shallow poems—shining with inexpensive wit and cheaply gorgeous as a player's robe—they have formed ideas of his powers, with which no man could candidly read him. They have the impression that he is a fine writer and cannot get rid of it. It is the most natural thing in the world.

We went once to hear a distinguished orator—a Kentuckian, who having taken a sufficient quantity of drink, is generally thought to be a very eloquent man. We listened in company with a person, for whose taste we had vast regard, and in whose enthusiasm at the lecture, we shared voluntarily, but came away with a distinct consciousness of having been bored.

Saxe, considered a poet, can only rank among the least considerable. *Funny* poetry is always detestable. There is something absurd in the very nature of the thing. The snicker is constantly at war with the rhyme. The joke jolts to the metre terribly. And Saxe is nothing but a *funny poet*. Humorist he is not, for he is never genial nor touching; wit, he is not, for he is not epigrammatic; satirist, in the best sense, he is not, for he punches and hits, rather than cuts. Who ever felt the tear softening his laugh over Saxe, as over Hood? Whose brain was ever cleared by the sharp lightning of his *esprit*? Whose eyes were ever dazzled by the glitter of his satiric blade? He selects those whom people already despise for the display of his prowess, and fires volleys of purposeless puns at them. Long-haired reformers and silly, crack-brained women, are his game. He cannot grapple a great wrong and fight it.

And this punster is actually ranked among our poets! The fact is not at all surprising, yet it is very hard to acknowledge. A man whose coarse mental fibre is betrayed in the texture of his verse; a man so destitute of poetical instinct! Yet we all listen to him when he lectures, and come away, and say to each other, "Wasn't it good?" Wasn't *what* good? A rhyming farrago of stale jests, rough with unseemly puns, and cruel with blows at the foolish and the helpless! And that is all, as surely as there *is* poetry in the heart of man.

[*Ohio State Journal*, 30 November 1858]

"Bardic Symbols"

Walt. Whitman has a poem of this title in the April *Atlantic*.

Swift denunciation comes always from either ignorance or prejudice, or passion—no less in literature than in any other living affair; and it carries no force with it except to the ignorant, the passionate, and the prejudiced.

It is a pity that criticism should ever forget this; but criticism does; and the newspaper critic particularly seems to think that so long as he makes a great wind in his angry scoop, he carries conviction with him, and strikes dead the poet whose heart he cannot understand, and cannot find.

Walt Whitman has higher claims upon our consideration than mere magazine contributorship. He is the author of a book of poetry called "Leaves of Grass," which, whatever else you may think, is wonderful. Ralph Waldo Emerson pronounced it the representative book of the poetry of our age. It drew the attention of critics, but found no favor with the public, for the people suspect and dislike those who nullify venerable laws, and trample upon old forms and usages. Since the publication of his book, Walt Whitman has driven hack in New York, and employed the hours of his literary retiracy in hard work. Some months ago he suddenly flashed upon us in the New York *Saturday Press*, and created eager dissension among the "crickets." Now he is in the *Atlantic*, with a poem more lawless, measureless, rhymeless and inscrutable than ever.

No one, even after the fourth or fifth reading, can pretend to say what the "Bardic Symbols" symbolize. The poet walks by the sea, and addressing the drift, the foam, the billows and the wind, attempts to force from them, by his frantic outcry, the true solution of the mystery of Existence, always most heavily and darkly felt in the august ocean presence. All is confusion, waste and sound. It is in vain that you attempt to gather the poet's full meaning from what he says or what he hints. You can only take refuge in occasional passages like this, in which he wildly laments the feebleness and inefficiency of that art which above all others seeks to make the soul visible and audible:

"O, baffled, lost,
Bent to the very earth, here preceding what follows,
Terrified with myself that I have dared to open
　my mouth,
Aware now, that amid all the blab, whose echoes
　recoil upon me, I have not once had the least idea
　who or what I am,
But that before all my insolent poems the real me still
　stands untouched, untold, altogether unreached,
Withdrawn far, mocking me with mock-congratulatory
　signs and bows,
With peals of distant ironical laughter at every word I
　have written or shall write,
Striking me with insults till I fall helpless upon
　the sand."

If indeed, we were compelled to guess the meaning of the poem, we should say it all lay in the compass of these lines of Tennyson— the saddest and profoundest that ever were written:

"Break, break, break,
　On thy cold gray stones, O sea!
And I would that my tongue could utter
　The thoughts that arise in me!"

An aspiration of mute words without relevancy, without absolute signification, and full of "divine despair."

We think it has been an error in Whitman to discard forms and laws, for without them the poet diffuses. He may hurry forward with impulses, but he is spent before he reaches the reader's heart through his bewildered understanding. Steam subject, is a mighty force; steam free, is an impalpable vapor, only capable of delicate hues and beauty with the sun upon it.

But O, poet! there is not a sun in every sky.

[*Ohio State Journal*, 28 March 1860]

LEAVES OF GRASS.—BY WALT. WHITMAN.—Thayer and Eldridge. Year 85 of the States. (1860–61).

Who is Walt. Whitman?

The person himself states his character, and replies to this question in the following general terms.

> "Walt. Whitman, an American, one of the roughs, a
> kosmos.
> Disorderly, fleshy, sensual, eating, drinking, breeding.
> No sentimentalist—no stander above men and women,
> or apart from them.
> No more modest than immodest."

This is frank, but not altogether satisfactory. From the journals therefore, and from talk of those who know him, we gather that Walt. Whitman lives in Brooklyn, that he has been a printer, and an omnibus driver, that he wears a red flannel shirt, and habitually stands with his hands in pockets; that he is not chaste nor clean, despising with equal scorn the conventional purity of linen, and the conventional rules of verse; that he is sublime and at the same time beastly; that he has a wonderful brain and an unwashed body. Five years ago, he gave to light the first edition of the "Leaves of Grass," which excited by its utter lawlessness, the admiration of those who believe liberty to mean the destruction of government, and disgusted many persons of fine feelings. We remember to have seen a brief criticism of the book in dear, dead *Putnam*, by a critic, who seemed to have argued himself into a complete state of uncertainty, and who oracularly delivered an opinion formed upon the model of the judge's charge in Bardell and Pickwick. Ralph Waldo Emerson, however, took by the horns, this bull, that had plunged into the china-shop of poetical literature, threatening all the pretty Dresden ornaments, and nice little cups with gold bands on them; and pronounced him a splendid animal—and left people to infer that he was some such inspired brute as that Jove infuried, when he played Europa that sad trick.

But presently the bull—being a mere brute—was forgotten, and the china-shop was furnished forth anew with delicate wares—new-fashioned dolls, bubble-thin goblets, and dainty match-safes.

Nearly a year ago, the bull put his head through the New York Saturday Press' enclosure, and bellowed loud, long and unintelligibly.

The mystery of the thing made it all the more appalling.

The Misses Nancy of criticism hastened to scramble over the fence, and on the other side, stood shaking their fans and parasols at the wretch, and shrieking, "Beast! beast!"

Some courageous wits attempted to frighten the animal away by mimicry, and made a noise as from infant bulls.

The people in the china-shop shut and bolted their doors.

Several critics petted and patted the bull; but it was agreed that while his eyes had a beautiful expression, and his breath was fragrant with all the meadow-sweetness of the world, he was not at all clean, and in general, smelt of the stables, and like a bull.

But after all, the question remained,—"What does he mean by it?"

It remains yet—now when he stands again in front of the china-shop, with his mouth full of fresh leaves of grass, lilies, clover-heads, buttercups, daisies, cockles, thistles, burrs, and hay, all mingled in a wisp together.

He says:

"I celebrate myself,
And what I assume you shall assume,
For every atom belonging to me, as good belongs to you."

And so proceeds, metreless, rhymeless, shaggy, coarse, sublime, disgusting, beautiful, tender, harsh, vile, elevated, foolish, wise, pure and nasty to the four hundred and fifty-sixth page, in a book most sumptuously printed and bound.

If you attempt to gather the meaning of the whole book, you fail utterly.

We never saw a man yet, who understood it all. We who have read it all, certainly do not.

Yet there are passages in the book of profound and subtle significance, and of rare beauty; with passages so gross and revolting, that you might say of them, as the Germans say of bad books—*Sie lassen sich nicht lesen.*

Walt. Whitman is both overrated and underrated. It will not do to condemn him altogether, nor to commend him altogether.—You cannot apply to him the tests by which you are accustomed to discriminate in poetry.

He disregards and defies precedent, in the poetic art. It remains for Time, the all-discerning, to announce his wisdom, or his folly to the future.

Only this: If he is indeed "the distinctive poet of America," then the office of poet is one which must be left hereafter to the shameless and the friendless. For Walt. Whitman is not a man whom you would like to know. You might care to see him, to hear him speak, but you must shrink from his contact. He has told too much. The secrets of the soul may be whispered to the world, but the secrets of the body should be decently hid. Walt. Whitman exults to blab them.

Heine in speaking of the confidences of Sterne, and of Jean Paul, says that the former showed himself to the world naked, while the latter merely had holes in his trousers. Walt. Whitman goes through his book, like one in an ill-conditioned dream, perfectly nude, with his clothes over his arm.

[*Ashtabula Sentinel*, 18 July 1860]

[Polite, literate society in Columbus was clever enough, Howells trusted, to be amused by the raillery he directed against Saxe, the poet manqué of the lecture circuit; regarding his opinions about Whitman's poetry, probably few of his readers knew enough about the subject to care. When, however, it came to the question of a Western literature, the public's view was decidedly unified. Cultural nationalism had important regional implications, and it was an ardent belief of many good, caring, intelligent Westerners that their region would produce a literature which for the first time would speak in the American idiom and whose themes would adequately reflect the American ideals. Hawthorne was merely giving his personal authority to a well-established notion when he celebrated the West to Howells as more purely American because it did not have cast over it the damned shadow of Europe. A generation before, James Hall had written in his *Letters from the West* (1828) that, owing to the Westerners' removal farther from their European origins, they were more apt to display in their culture the "national character," whatever that might be. Or as Lowell later so well expressed in his eulogy of Abraham Lincoln in "The Harvard Commemoration Ode" (1865), Nature had in the instance of the Illinois statesman, the preeminent Westerner, thrown aside her Old-World molds:

> And, choosing sweet clay from the breast
>   Of the unexhausted West,
> With stuff untainted shaped a hero new,
> Wise, steadfast in the strength of God, and true. . . .
>   Nothing of Europe here,
> Or, then, of Europe fronting mornward still,
>   Ere any names of Serf and Peer
> Could Nature's equal scheme deface
> And thwart her genial will;

Here was a type of the true elder race, . . .
New birth of our new soil, the first American.

Undoubtedly, it was such a life as that of Lincoln's that Moncure Conway had in mind when he tried to convince Howells "that the West was to live its literature, especially its poetry, rather than write it" (*YMY*, p. 152). But Howells was not persuaded: "My affair was to make poetry, let who would live it, and to make myself known by both the quality and quantity of my poetry" (*YMY*, p. 152). Already he was enough of a poet to realize that true art inevitably transcends the merely autochthonous. Celebration of the local might be a civic virtue, but it was folly to make it a literary standard. Still, Howells was somewhat reluctant to speak his opinions on this score so openly in public as he frequently did in private. His sentiments, he knew, would appear ungracious and might diminish in the estimation of many whose friendship and respect he valued the work he was attempting in the *Ohio State Journal*. But the resentment was there, and sometimes he could not resist making light of the cultural boosterism that surrounded him.

When Howells again returned to Columbus in November 1858, his old acquaintance, William T. Coggeshall, the state librarian and a man of considerable energy and intelligence, had already begun assembling the materials for his anthology, *The Poets and Poetry of the West*, which the Columbus firm of Follett, Foster and Company was later to publish in the summer of 1860. Apparently the germ for the volume had been in an address Coggeshall had delivered at Ohio University in June 1858 "on the Social and Moral Advantages of the Cultivation of Local Literature," or, as it was titled when later published as a pamphlet, *The Protective Policy in Literature* (1859). Coggeshall drew on this discourse when he reviewed Charles Anderson Dana's *Book of Household Poetry* in the *Ohio State Journal* on 20 November 1858, a few days after Howells's acceptance of the position offered to him on the editorial staff. Coggeshall objected to Dana's slight of Western poets which led one to question, "Have We Household Poetry in the West?" But Dana was not alone, Coggeshall pointed out, in his error: it was the common treatment which the West had come to expect from Eastern critics and compilers of anthologies.

It is acknowledged that the West has rude strength—it is confessed that there is vigor and vivacity in it; it has some reputation for boisterous oratory, but the canons of criticism, in courts recognized at New York and Boston are against it, if not for art, at least for literature. Revolving in a small circle, which is a great centre for opinions and for intelligence, editors, critics and compilers who write and print "down east" are unwilling to take notice whether anything deserving of regard, among cultivated men, may be found outside of the sphere of their local sympathies. A spirit which is recorded, on the highest authority, as having once been prominent in the region round about Nazareth, has found its way frequently into our books which assume to represent the literature of America—of the whole country.—We deprecate sectionalism in whatever guise it may signify itself, but we defend local pride in local worth, and for these reasons may justly complain of Griswold's Books on the Prose Writings and on the Poets of America—of Duyckinck's Cyclopedia of American Literature—of Burton's Cyclopedia of Wit and Humor, and of Moore's Cyclopedia of American Eloquence.—They all, either out of ignorance, or out of sectional spirit, do injustice to whatever there has been of talent for good prose, good poetry and stirring oratory in the valley of the Ohio and the Mississippi.

Howells knew enough to fear the result of Coggeshall's uncritical and ponderous compilation and confessed his reservations in a letter to Piatt some months before the volume's appearance: "I suppose we shall all be put into Coggeshall's book. A prodigious man, with a fine faculty for feeding the public on sawdust" (*SL*, 1:43). Or as he somewhat later put the problem in a letter to James Russell Lowell: "For myself, I believe that so far as Western Poetry has deserved recognition, it has received it. The sad error has been on the part of its friends, the belief that cockle and cheat with sufficient cultivation will turn to grain, and they have delved and dug about in fields, that would never have yielded anything but weeds, whether upon the Ohio, or the Charles" (*SL*, 1:60). Industry and desire could not by themselves make up for the lack of talent and performance, and in the community of art boundaries were often far other than those political men and women imagined. But Howells supported Coggeshall's venture, even so far as allowing a number of his poems to be included and by contributing at Coggeshall's request several biographical sketches of other poets with whose lives he apparently had some familiarity. Early in May 1860, when the first proofs of the book were available, Howells announced the volume as forthcoming, explaining to *Ohio State Journal* readers the rationale of Coggeshall's compilation.

The plan of the editor seems to have been to exercise discrimination in his selections, rather than the severest critical taste; so that while every poem of positive merit which the west has produced, will be included in the book, the work will be made representative of what is respectable in our poetical literature, and no writer of reputation will be passed over, because his verse cannot be tried by the highest criticism. No other plan, probably, could have been adopted with success. The rhymings of the west have nearly all been desultory. Few western men have made literature a profession; and most of

the poems in the forthcoming volume are the offspring of muses
wedded to commerce, to law,
"To labor and the mattock-hardened hand."

When the anthology was finally made available to the public in August
1860, Howells muffled whatever private criticism he had of the venture
in his review, also printed in the *Ohio State Journal*, and soon after even
planned to make the volume the occasion for a series of "brief papers upon
the later poets of the West." But either the material was too thin or
Howells's real interest too slight, and after the appearance of only two
essays he forgot his promise and turned his eyes eastward to more verdant
fields. Though later in his career Howells was to reveal a remarkable gift
in his assessments of unknown but genuine literary talents, one finds in
his estimates of the poetry of William Wallace Harney and Helen Bostwick, the subjects of the two papers, as much taffy pulling as critical
judiciousness and restraint, and only that piece on Harney, a fellow journalist and occasional writer of verse, has been retrieved.]

THE POETS AND POETRY OF THE WEST: with Biographical and Critical Notices. By W. T. Coggeshall, Columbus. Follett, Foster &
Co.

In this superb volume of nearly seven hundred pages, we have
evidence that Western Poets and Poetry certainly exist as to quantity, whatever else may be said of them. The contents of the book,
indeed, are like the quality of mercy, in one respect, and its mag-
nitude is partially attributable to the motive which we had better
let the editor explain himself.

"It has been the intention of the editor," he says, "to include in
this collection, every person legitimately belonging to the West, who
has gained recognition as a writer of reputable verse."

He has therefore, with this catholic intention given us poems and
biographical notices of one hundred and forty-two writers of the
West, of which number sixty-nine were born in the West, and
thirty-nine in Ohio alone. In poet-bearing, Kentucky comes next,
Indiana next, Michigan and Illinois next, after Ohio.

When this book was forthcoming, we said (glancing at the advance sheets,) that the rhymings of the West had nearly all been
desultory; that few western men had made literature a profession,—
that

"In almost every locality of the vast region from which the materials of this book have been drawn—Kentucky, Ohio, Indiana,
Illinois, Wisconsin, Michigan, Iowa, Kansas—some bird has piped
his songs in the spring of youth, and as the summer of life advanced,
has taken to the more practical business of building nests, and sub-

185

stantially beautifying and peopling the primeval solitudes, that echoed to his earlier strains. Whatever is good in the 'airy nothing' of such singers, Mr. Coggeshall has caught and given in his work 'a local habitation.' Then, again, those people who have 'never got over it,'—through whose lips the divine afflatus has never ceased to breathe—who despite the jostling, and punching, and pushing, which must disturb the reveries of star-gazers in the streets of our go-ahead towns and cities—these are represented here in full, and the best that they have written is offered to us, who 'have not time' to read *all* they have written. The younger poets—the bardlings, of both sexes,—who make our present poetical literature, are gathered from the four winds of the newspapers and magazines, and put in this book, to which no doubt, if

'They love to read their own dear songs,'

they will turn hereafter with more tenderness than pride."

Looking over the completed work, we do not find cause to vary the estimate formed of it above; but have rather to express our satisfaction with the thorough manner in which the editor has discharged his task. It is one, indeed, for which he has been peculiarly fitted by his earnest belief in the excellence and the wrongs of Western literature, as well as his peculiar talent and industry. Few men in the country could have brought so much patience and ardor to the work—no other man in the West could have done so. Eager to render justice—perhaps too eager to encourage—yet keeping the endurance of his reader in view, he has made a book entirely creditable to himself.—And we think it creditable to the West, too.— One constantly encounters pleasant surprises in turning over its handsome pages. Here is John Finley's "Bachelor's Hall," which has crossed and recrossed the Atlantic, as the humorous extravaganza of Thomas Moore; here is that wild and powerful poem of John M. Harney's, "The Fever Dream," which was one of the horrible delights of our boyhood; here is Perkins' "Young Soldier,"—

"O were ye ne'er a school-boy,
And did you never train,
And feel that swelling at the heart,
You ne'er can feel again."

God bless us! Were we not, indeed? What else should give that rare and subtle music to the refrain,
"March, march away."
But the fact that we used to do it?
Then we have all that is best in Gallagher's verse, all that is best in the poetry of the Cary sisters, Mrs. Nichols, Amelia Welby, Fosdick, William Ross Wallace, Coates Kinney, and then later, Wm. W. Harney, (whom we account among the best,) Piatt, "Ruth

Crayne," "Mary Robbins," and a score of others to whom we must deny mention.

The critic writes to little purpose, if he fails to show wherein he is wiser than his author, and we are tempted to tell Mr. Coggeshall and the public how much better we could now make this book. But it is a good book as it is—a very good book, and we refrain from a display of superiority at once proper and inexpensive.

Nay let us be lavishly generous, and give the publisher his due, for issuing one of the handsomest volumes which has appeared from the American press. We greet it with pride—and we trust that it will meet that abundant success, which it deserves. There is an historical value in the work, which though a secondary merit, should not be overlooked. The biographical notices, following each other in chronological order, form a complete history of poetical literature in the West, and present many facts of interest, as well as a large amount of information, in regard to personal history nowhere else to be found.

We believe the book is sold entirely by subscription.

[*Ohio State Journal*, 1 September 1860]

SOME WESTERN POETS OF TO-DAY

Wm. Wallace Harney

Mr. Coggeshall's book of "Poets and Poetry of the West," is such a remarkably suggestive book in so many ways, that it is hard to keep the animadversive pencil out of it. Indeed, the present impulse is to write a series of brief papers upon the later poets of the West, who are also the best with one or two exceptions, but who are crowded into such a narrow space at the close of the volume, that the general effect is that of a bird-fancier's shop, rather than the well-known wild wood grove, in which songbirds of all kinds are supposed to disport themselves in the most expansive and advantageous manner. It is the generous impulse to give these thronged, half-throttled singers an airing, one after the other; but the impulse hardly amounts to an intention, and this series of brief papers may open and shut in the first essay. The business is not without dangers and risks. There are plumes that may be ruffled; there are performances that must be criticised, and out of the same beaks often come piping and pecking—with here and there a dash back at the benevolent critic. Nevertheless!

And the first poet in our mind, and one of the first in the book, is Mr. William Wallace Harney. We account him among the first, because he has shown in one or two poems that he possesses that poetic art, equally divine with the poetic impulse, which many of the earlier, and many of the later western poets have lacked. They

187

have forever enacted the fable of Icarus, mounting on pinions of wax, that melted from them whenever they rose to the fervor of the upper skies, and let them down with ungainly falls, alike uncomfortable to themselves and their readers. Or if a western simile is insisted upon, (we are good at any kind,) theirs are the wings of the flying squirrel, useless except to alight with from some height already scrambled up to. It could not perhaps, be altogether otherwise, for western poets are workers as well as singers, and their performances are all more or less furtive and hurried. Yet, because we hope there shall some day be a different order of things—because we trust that after while the poet shall cease to hunger amid the abundance of our sea-wide cornfields—because we believe he shall not always be regarded as an alien in his own land,—we speak these words of kindly criticism that he may be worthy of the future that awaits him. Yes, in that Some-day, where we have all "located" our happiness, we like to think that the Western poet shall be the first of American poets. But they found that the sweetest grape of Italy soured upon the hill-slopes at Cincinnati; and they had no good wine till they took the harsh vine of their own woods, and mellowed its blood with generous culture. And the wine of western poetry must have the life and strength of a native past in it, mellowed by that light and warmth which must always come from the orient.

There has been much vain talk about Western poetry. Some who have contrasted its rude graces, its aboriginal audacities, with the exquisite faultlessness of its elder sister of the east, have been ready to deny its claim to kinship. Its native beauties are forgotten in the grotesqueness of some of its rhetorical finery, which hangs upon it like the cheap splendor borrowed from a dubious civilization, on an Indian girl. On the other hand, (unluckily for western poetry,) there has been a number of ill-advised friends, who have insisted that it was already a literature, and have made themselves uncomfortable about the fancied slights and wrongs it has suffered at the hands of eastern criticism. It has been shut out, they say, from eastern collections of poetry; and eastern magazines have smothered all the babes of western song, in the secrecy of those dungeons appointed for the reception of rejected contributions. These enthusiastic, but mistaken persons, have insisted in many cases upon cultivating wild gooseberries instead of wild grapes; and when the eastern, or other critics, have made wry faces over the dreadful juice of that abominable fruit, the indiscriminate friends of western succulence have cried out: "Good Heaven! here is a nice-stomached man for you! His prejudices, sir, his *jealousy* won't let him acknowledge that this well-flavored drink is sparkling Catawba."

But this is an article on Mr. Harney, of Kentucky, we believe. Persons who wish to know him biographically will go to Mr.

Coggeshall's book. He is now the editor of the Louisville *Daily Democrat*, and is a native of Indiana.—He is represented in the book of "Poets and Poetry," by five poems: "The Stab," "The Buried Hope," "The Suicide," "The Old Mill," and "Jimmy's Wooing." The first of these poems is the briefest and the best. It is so good, indeed, that we quote it—though many of our readers are doubtless already familiar with it:

THE STAB.

On the road, the lonely road,
  Under the cold white moon,
Under the ragged trees he strode;
He whistled and shifted his weary load—
  Whistled a foolish tune.

There was a step timed with his own,
  A figure that stooped and bowed—
A cold, white blade that gleamed and shone,
Like a splinter of daylight downward thrown—
  And the moon went behind a cloud.

But the moon came out so broad and good,
  The barn fowl woke and crowed;
Then roughed his feathers in drowsy mood,
And the brown owl called to his mate in the wood
  That a dead man lay on the road.

There is one figure in this poem, which may have pleased some persons by its audacity, but which is entirely false and bad, and mars terribly a poem in which there is no other defect. We mean the comparison of the knife to
  —"A splinter of daylight downward thrown."
The poem is eminently suggestive, but it suggests no possibility by which daylight can be splintered. The raggedness and *tearing* emotion suggested is well, and has its proper effect upon the nerves; but why daylight, *how* splinter of daylight? We doubt if Mr. Harney approves this image himself, but he was probably loth to touch in correction, a poem that must have had a movement all its own and seemed to end without his volition, and had in it at afterglance an inscrutable perfection and symmetry, unfelt while it flowed from his imagination. It belongs to that class of poems which impress the reader like the glimpsed career of a cataract which is seen and is not heard to fall, but which thunders ever after in the heart. It is of the "wayward, modern" school; it is German. It does not belong to the arithmetical three-into-nine-go-three-times, or the Jones-is-dead-but-he-is-in-heaven-and-therefore-we-won't-cry, lyrical school. It

doesn't pin a poetic moral to a cork; but the shadow it casts upon you is winged.

"The Suicide," is an attempt in the same spirit with the poem we have quoted, and we think a failure. There is a lamentable inadequacy of expression here and there; the imagery is occasionally revolting, and it is rather the Corpse than the Horror of a suicide that the poet presents.

"The Buried Hope," is tender and touching, and though treating of a dead child, has none of that loud varnish-smell, with which coffin-poetesses perfume their mortuary verses.

"The Old Mill"—ah! we have been there! If we shut our eyes, we see it where it stands,

> "The lichen hangs from the walls aloof,
> And the rusty nails from the ragged roof
>   Drop daily, one by one.
>
> "The long grass grows in the shady pool,
> Where the cattle used to come to cool,
>   And the rotting wheel stands still;
> The gray owl winks in the granary loft,
> And the sly rat slinks, with a pit-pat soft,
>   From the hopper of the quaint Old Mill."

Now and then the elevator in Mr. Harney's mill breaks, and the ground wheat does not reach the cooling-flour, and is not bolted; but for the most part it remains all right in the Old Mill.

We account "Jimmy's Wooing" one of the sweetest little idylls that has ever been written. It is full of country summer scents, and rainy sights, and breezy sounds, and there is an old ballad simplicity in it, most dear to us. Not even Drayton's "Dowsabel," who—
"Who went forth to gather Maye,"
pleases us more. It is one of the few popular poems which has deserved the newspaper celebrity it has attained; and it suffers reperusal marvelous well.

It is customary, we believe, to wind up a criticism with a few general observations—a sort of "May-Heaven-have-mercy-upon-your-soul" address to the poet, and some remarks by way of warning to the reader. But as nothing particularly novel in this way occurs to us, we will offer in reference to Mr. Harney, the comprehensive sentiment, "Many returns of the same."

We like Mr. Harney's poems, because he shows an individual power, even when his themes are not original. The poetic impulses of the time are palpable in what he does—in his felicity of expression, his aversion of a really prosaic word, and his daring recognition of poetry in the commonest ideas; and in his suggestive style. He has not yet published a book; and is now so "absorbed in his duties as a journalist (his biographer tells us,) that he has not that leisure for the cultivation of his reputation as a poet that his friends could wish, and the pure spring of Helicon has been neglected for the dirty pool of politics."

Looking to Mr. Harney's future, are we not sure that he is not wiser than his friends, in giving himself for a while to politics and journalism. The pool of politics is dirty or not, according as it is a cleanly or uncleanly person immersed in it. We cannot forget that Dante (not to mention lesser names) was a fervid politician. The profession of journalism, too, with its wide opportunities of knowing men and things, may teach the poetic nature, prone to look back and sigh,

"Ah! well-a-day for the dear old days!"

that no age has been so grand as our own, and that none has been so falsely and stupidly called prosaic. The poet dreams of yesterday and to-morrow; journalism can teach him to value to-day. His art is the sublimest when it is true to his own time. There has been no time so great and earnest as this. If he remembers the world's grandeur now, it shall remember his hereafter.

[*Ohio State Journal*, 25 September 1860]

[*Poems of Two Friends* was published just before Christmas in 1859, and Howells lost no time in puffing his friend Piatt's performance in their common effort while demurely passing over his "subordinate part" in the venture. Perhaps Piatt served Howells in like fashion in the *Mac-o-cheek Press*, but since copies of Piatt's paper do not appear to have survived, it is doubtful we shall ever know.]

New Publications

POEMS OF TWO FRIENDS. [J. J. Piatt and W. D. Howells.] Columbus, O., Follett, Foster & Co.

The greater part of the verses in this little volume are from a hand not unfamiliar to the readers of the *State Journal*, and not unknown to the readers of newspaper poetry throughout the west. Mr. Piatt has written much, and achieved an undoubted measure of success. The stepmother West has been kind to his effusions, and we have encountered them in nearly all our exchanges—inhabiting the attics where benevolent landlord-editors permit poets to starve in peace. A good breath of praise at starting, does much to set verse afloat, but after all, it falls heavily without wings of its own. Mr. Piatt, seeing his fledgelings sustain themselves so well, may be justified in caging them for better advantages of exhibition. But the bird-fancying public must judge for themselves.

We like best among the poems presented here, "The Morning Street," originally printed in the *Atlantic Monthly*: "Ghosts," "Moonrise," "In the Orchard," "Frost-Bloom," "The Buried Organ," "To—," "Prairie Fires," and "The Western Pioneer."

Of the first, we need not speak: all, doubtless, are familiar with the beauty of that. It is characterized by the author's peculiar faults and excellencies—his imagination, his frequent felicity of imagery and expression, his involved diction and obscurity. In other of his poems these merits are more prominent, and in still others, these defects are exaggerated.

The little rhyme called "Ghosts" is full of poetic beauty. It is a winter night, and the poet lies in an olden mansion "that has known him long ago," while

> "The moon so close by the window
>   *Freezes in the trees with her light,*
> *A glitter of motionless silence*
>   *All the ice-lit branches bright.*"

The diction of this striking passage is faultless, and the picture it flashes upon the mind has a starlike sweetness, distinctness and truth.

Then he speaks of the ghosts:

> "Working at the drowsy silence,
>   There are footsteps on the stair."

They advance and recede—

> "They have left the *ghosts of their silence,*
>   *Walking in my brain.*"

In "Moonrise," the poet describes the slumbering city:

> "With dreaming heart and closed eyes,
>   The giant's folded hands at rest,
> *Like Prayer asleep are on his breast.*"

In "The Orchard," we find equal felicities of thought and expression. It is a breezy October morning, and the children climbing up the trees, and shaking down the mellow fruit,

> —"are happy to listen
> The noises of the mill and the flail,
> And the waters that laugh, as they leap and they glisten,
>   From the dam that is *lighting* the vale."

Then, is not this exquisite?

> "The *wild flutter of bells* that so *breezily* rises
>   From glades where the yellow leaves blow,

And the laughter of faces in childish surprises,
    If the wind fling an apple below."

"Frost-bloom" has already appeared in the *State Journal*. "The Buried Organ" typifies, doubtless, the religious feeling that haunts every heart, and rises in music, at moments of solitude and silence. There are not so many detachable gems in this as in other poetry, but the poem itself is a gem. There is a Schiller-like purity and sweetness in it; and it affects one with the magic of the rare German songs.

"To—," is a charming apostrophe to the ideal woman of the poet. We quote two stanzas:

Oft have I trembled with a maiden near,
    In the dear dream that thou wast come at last,
Vailed in her face; but I am dreaming here—
    Sweet dreams woke in the past.

May be thou never yet hadst mortal birth,
    Or childhood wings to Heaven with thee have flown,
My Eve in Paradise! O'er all the earth
    Must Adam walk alone?

In "Prairie Fires" we find the same vividness of imagery as in "Ghosts," together with a wanton tautology, and occasional obscurity. In some poems, this obscurity almost destroys their effect. The reader, annoyed and enraged at not being able to catch the author's meaning, fails to receive the impression of *unity*, which a poem should make; and feels like sacrificing palpable beauties, to his outraged perception. Take this stanza from "The Forgotten Street:"

Where are they vanished? Here an hour ago!
    The hiving purposes that hum no more?
Napoleon-wills that made the Alps seem low?
    To Dream-land—what far sunrise finds that shore?
To that New World—who but Columbus knows?
    Where are the homeless exiles? Gone to dreams!
To the green lands the love of Heaven blows;
    Laugh in their eyes green England's village-gleams;
The German all-forgets he left the Rhine—
Sings in the Past—the golden hills of wine!

It is evident that from the noble line—
    "Napoleon-wills that make the Alps seem low,"
that there is meaning in every word of this; but it is not apparent without many readings. There may be readers patient enough to search for it. We trust there are.

Goethe says: "Whoever would reproach an author with obscurity, should first be sure that he is himself perfectly clear. A very plain manuscript is illegible in the twilight."

Let Mr. Piatt console himself, and the reader be ashamed. In every one of his poems some passage of power and beauty will start out of the darkness to dazzle the grumbler into silence.

Of the subordinate part of this volume it is not for us to speak. It is to be hoped that of the poems which compose it, some will be found not so bad as others.

The style in which Messrs. Follett, Foster & Co., have issued this volume is extremely creditable. With its fair, clear type, beautiful tinted paper, and tasteful binding, it is typographically charming. No book of the season has a more "goodly outside." There are several errors in it of proof-reading—incorrect punctuation and omissions of words—but if the whole volume be not a mistake, lesser blunders will be excused. . . .

[*Ohio State Journal*, 26 December 1859]

[Just as Howells in his "News and Humors of the Mail" and "Literary Gossip" columns had used articles and items in other newspapers and journals as occasions for his own animadversions and reflections, so too in his longer critical essays he frequently relied on the leading journals and Eastern newspapers to provide him with literary topics. An article in the *North British Review* by Coventry Patmore, for instance, lead him to express his own views in the *Ohio State Journal* in December 1858 regarding the "Decay of Modern Satire." Some months later, a letter written by an American woman to the New York *Home Journal* reporting her interview with the French poet, Alphonse de Lamartine, caused Howells to return to a subject which the *Ohio State Journal* had several times before given space when copying from other publications articles and comments critical of the means to which the Frenchman was willing to resort in order to repair his fortunes. For example, a "justly severe notice of the whimpering sentimentalist" which had appeared first in the Philadelphia *Press* was reprinted among Howells's "Literary Matters" in the *State Journal* on 17 December 1858.

Lamartine, the poet, has been unable to raise the money to pay off his debts. He threatens to quit France, and pass the remainder of his life in England, unless his debts are liquidated by subscription. This threat, coupled with this expectation, is very much on the true brigand "stand and deliver" style. In his excessive vanity, Lamartine thinks that Frenchmen cannot do without him, that, if he expatriated himself, France would be "a world without a sun." Louis Napoleon put 10,000 francs ($2,000) into the Lamartine begging-box, and certain sympathizing noblemen and rich landlords in England gave £500 (or about $2,500) for the same purpose. What Americans have given literally seems "nothing to nobody."

When "Lamartine and American Litterateurs" appeared in the Columbus paper two years later, Howells could assume his readers knew fully the circumstances of his remarks. "Diagnosis of a Poet," published in the *State Journal* on 27 November 1860, was a report on an article about Edgar Allen Poe by Henry Maudsley, a British alienist and the medical superintendent of the Royal Lunatic Hospital in Manchester. Maudsley's extravagant bit of psychologizing had first appeared in the *British Journal of Mental Science*, April 1860, and was afterwards reprinted in the *American Journal of Insanity*, October 1860, where undoubtedly Howells made its acquaintance.]

Decay of Modern Satire

Some one we have read, thanked God that Satire had never held the first, nor even the second place in English poetry. It was a good deal like thanking God that rose-trees did not bear Dead-Sea Apples, but the devout Satire-hater was not without any cause of gratitude. Even in its worthiest form, (as defined by the author of the paper whose heading we have adopted,) it seems to us that there is something more diabolic than divine in the fashioning of Satire. Those who have been our severest satirists have not been our best poets, nor have their satires been the best among their poems. The feeling with which the reader rises from the perusal of a poem is a test of its worth,—better than any analytic criticism. And certainly the emotions raised by the finest satire are not elevated or sublime. The sense of the absurd is sharpened; but it is not always best to have too keen a sense of the absurd—it makes people eminently disagreeable to their fellow creatures; the sardonic in man's nature is appealed to, but it were better if some other principle had been awakened; and all the ungentler faculties are called into play. "For my own part," says an eccentric friend, "I never speak ill of people with so much satisfaction in the mere evilness of the thing, as when I have done reading some fierce satire, which has given tone to the inherent wickedness of my soul. I am then quite certain to say enough unkind things to cool all my friendships for a week."

The writer in the *North British* correctly classes mere personal satires with lampoons, and declares that the only true satires are those directed against parties or principles. Therefore, every body finds most satirical poems very hard reading. Their Attic salt cannot save them from the internal taint of decay. It is no great pleasure to behold people spitted, who have been dead these hundred years, even on the rapier of Pope. Who reads the Dunciad—best of its

195

kind—beside the student of metre and antithesis? For ourselves, if we were obliged to choose between Byron's "Hours of Idleness," and his "English Bards and Scotch Reviewers," we should take the former, and think ourselves lucky, dreadful as the alternative might appear. Our reviewer takes notice, in his remarks, chiefly of Canning's "Anti-Jacobin" and Lowell's "Biglow Papers," throwing aside Festus Bailey's "Age" as "flabby" and unprofitable; and, oddly enough, not even mentioning our great Saxe! It struck us, that as his theme was the decay of modern satire, the verses of the latter gentleman might have been alleged in melancholy proof of the correctness of his views.

"The Anti-Jacobin" is a collection of papers published about the time when the doctrines of the French revolution, were most popular and prevalent in England; and its wit and sarcasm were directed against them. The contributors to the "Anti-Jacobin" were among the most eminent and learned tories of the day, but the life and soul of it was Canning, whose "Needy Knife Grinder" burlesque of poor Southey's sapphic "Widow's Complaint," is one of the jewels that will "sparkle upon the outstretched finger of all Time." Despite the reviewer's prophecy that it will hereafter be one of the pleasantest of our classics, we think differently. The men who hated the Revolution with all its principles were as far wrong as those who loved them. Their errors are graves in which the world will bury their wit out of sight.

To the "Biglow Papers" the writer gives great praise, placing them far above any English satires since those of the "Anti-Jacobin," wherein we think him right. Doubtless, he says, there are abuses enough in English society and government to give employment to the satirist, but they have no such glaring fiction as a popular profession of freedom and support of slavery; therefore the Americans have the advantage in this respect.—The jest is grim; and the readiness with which Lowell's superiority is conceded hardly compensates for its perpetration.

We do not see however, that the writer proves the decay of satire in English literature. The mere migration of the acidulous muse to our shores, seems to have increased the number of her votaries, and her voice speaking the same tongue, seems to have been heard across the sea. In admitting the excellence of the "Biglow Papers," as legitimate satires, we think the reviewer defeats his own argument.

[*Ohio State Journal*, 17 December 1858]

Lamartine and American Litterateurs

Some gossiping woman went to see M. de Lamartine the other day; and then wrote a letter to the New York *Home Journal*, relating the words that passed between herself and the poet.

It was the last excess of vulgarity to do this, for the public has no more right to be present at a social interview with a great man, than with the obscurest person. The gossiping woman, who reported M. de Lamartine's remarks upon Americans was guilty of as gross ill-breeding as if she had called upon Jones and recounted his petulant speeches to Robinson.

Nevertheless, this kind of key-hole acquaintance with fame is what Americans like. The nation seems to have a passion for looking down the chimney, and peeping in at windows.

Whoever among ourselves, rises above the mass, is subjected to the most impertinent inquisition. The history of all his affairs is published; and we know if his second cousin has turned out badly.

But we do not insist because we personally are virtuous there shall be no cakes and ale, and so we printed the gossiping woman's letter about M. de Lamartine, and our readers had the pleasure of learning what a distinguished beggar thinks of money-getters.

M. de Lamartine infers—because Americans did not help him to pay his debts by subscribing for books which they did not want, that they know nothing but the Almighty Dollar, and cannot appreciate poets; that consequently poets do not exist here; that consequently affairs are in a bad state, with the Republic.

It seems impossible that a person whose manhood has been debauched like Lamartine's by the charities of a despot whom he hates, should understand the literary situation in this country.

In America literature is not mendicant, and there is no tradition of a mendicant literature, to confuse an author's instinctive feeling that it would be his shame, if he received anything but the love and admiration of the people, after they have paid him for his books.

Here as in Europe, the publication of a poem or a novel (which is the modern poem) is an affair of business—between the author's agent and the public. There is no sense of patronage received or conferred.

In this country it has never been otherwise, and we trust never may be otherwise.

But in the old world there is a literary past as mean and as odious as the religious or political past.

There the poet, in the earlier centuries was protected, and patronized by kings and princes, and as stupidly undervalued as he could be by any dullard who insults him in a newspaper now. Think of Dante made the jest of the buffoons who partook, with him, the insolent hospitality of a petty prince! Think of Ariosto's menial services to his patron cardinal! Think of Tasso's imprisonment by the Duke of Ferrara! Think of Spenser complaining that Elizabeth forgets his poverty!

After this age of protection and insult comes that of patronage

197

and neglect; and we have the picture of Johnson dancing attendance upon Chesterfield, of Cervantes making obsequious dedications to grandees, who gave him the splendid condescension of their friendship; of Goldsmith blundering out his adulation to my lord's valet; of Chatterton poisoning himself to escape the starvation to which his noble patrons left him.

In the present literary system of Europe, no trace of these degradations (which nothing but genius could survive,) remains, but the pensions awarded by government with a sparingness that makes them of little value or detriment.

M. de Lamartine, who seems to have been born some ages too late, thinks it the duty of his readers to pay his debts, and render that assistance which the state no longer gives. The author of *Confidences* trusts that the publics with which he has wept, will restore to him the fortunes he has squandered. He remains, therefore, upon the brink of ruin, and has forever an execution in his house, for the purposes of pathos.

It is vain; and the mendicant cries out upon the meanness of those who will not contribute to his standing charity.

The truth is that the public owes nothing to the author after it has bought his book, but fame—gratitude and admiration. It would be equal shame to both if this debt were discharged in money. "When you have bought a book," says Longfellow, "you have not purchased the right to abuse the author." It is true. Nor when the author has sold us his book, has he right to take largess out of our purse.

Enlightened criticism—above all, journalism—has contributed to place the author and the reader in true relations to each other. The one writes a book. If it is good, the other buys it, and there is an end to all pecuniary obligation.

As to the larger debt of love and esteem which we contract for an author who has pleased us, do we not pay it with a free hand?

In no other land is literature held in such esteem by the people as in this. It is false that we starve our litterateurs. It is absurdly false that we do not appreciate them. They hold the first place in the hearts of a people—who earn money, and do not beg it—and who, properly, or improperly, look upon charity as a humiliation which they cannot offer to those they respect.

[*Ohio State Journal*, 3 November 1860]

Diagnosis of a Poet

We remember to have read somewhere, a learned paper in which the case of Lady Macbeth's lunacy was considered in the light of medical science, and all the symptoms of her disorder dwelt upon with the minuteness and earnestness of a veritable professional investigation. We believe that the paper was meant only as a *jeu d'esprit*, and it was a joke no less profound than successful. Taken seriously, however, it might be as profitably received as some critical inquisitions which have been made to prove that Shakespeare was a lawyer, or a physician, or anything else, according to the humor of the critic. It might, indeed, be defended as a thing eminently appropriate, in view of Shakespeare's supposed medical attainments; the episode of Lady Macbeth's madness is certainly useful in shewing the unreasonable expectations formed of the profession at that day, and the rude insult with which occasional failure was visited. The lady's royal spouse is made to ask of the attendant practitioner:

> "Canst thou not minister to a heart diseased;
> Pluck from the memory a rooted sorrow;
> Raze out the written troubles of the brain,
> And, with some sweet, oblivious antidote,
> Cleanse the stuffed bosom of the perilous stuff
> That weighs upon the heart?"

To which the physician responds:

> "Therein the patient
> Must minister to himself."

Whereupon Macbeth retorts—

> "Throw physic to the dogs, I'll none of it."

Thus showing himself to be very little better than an anachronistic Dr. Holmes.

Shakespeare apparently took a medical view of poetry when he said,

> "The lunatic, the lover and the poet,
> Are of imagination all compact."

And it is doubtless proper for a physician of the present day to take a similar view of poetry. At any rate, it is very natural for him to do so, and we have to thank one of the most learned of modern writers on insanity for a clear and able diagnosis of the poems and character of Edgar A. Poe.

Dr. Henry Maudsley is the medical superintendent of the Manchester Royal Lunatic Hospital, and his paper is contributed to the Journal of Mental Science. It is written in that tone of liberality and enlightened charity, which characterizes the speculations of medical science when dealing with those physical disorders, which are so intimately allied with the difficulties of the psychological problems.—Dr. Maudsley carefully considers the race, parentage, childhood and education of Poe, before he advances to the contemplation of developed evils in the man. The diagnosis necessarily involves a biographical sketch; and the paper concludes with an analysis of Poe's principal poems, which are criticised in their relation to his life only.

We all know the salient—for they were salient—faults of Poe's character. He was weak, drunken, ungrateful, mendacious, vindictive and cowardly—capricious beyond caprice, impulsively an angel, and very deliberately a devil—apparently destitute of honor, and yet loved by those who knew him best with most ardent affection. He charmed and wronged all his friends—nay, antithesis exhausts itself in the characterization. Unless one is oneself shriveled out of form by passion, and warped by brutal indulgence, it is impossible to love the character of such a man; it is an effort even to compassionate his sufferings.

In the light of Dr. Maudsley's diagnosis, however, one arrives at a very Christian and merciful view of Poe. He was the son of a marriage, in which one parent abandoned prosperity for a beautiful woman, and the other abandoned the stage for solid respectability. Slight *désagréments* diversified the life of this loving couple, and their child was born and fostered amid influences calculated to destroy the balances of self-control, and render him irresponsible for the sins of his career. No authority seems to recognize more reverently the inexorable law that the children's teeth must be set on edge by parental indulgence in grapes than medical science, and none questions more boldly the propriety of punishing inherited evil, as the highly respectable, the world punishes it.

Poe's education was of the kind to exaggerate every defect of his character, and to do little for the development of its latent good. Throughout life he seems to have suffered in his own individuality, the results of causes, many of which were wholly anterior to himself. To every man there is a compensation in kind: good for good, evil for evil, is the stern law of nature, which has no Bible. But here was a man who was compensated, not alone for his own wrongdoing, but for the errors of those who went before him—the errors which became a part of his spiritual organism, and weakened all his purposes for good—the very errors out of which his own sprang. The instance is not singular, and questions result from it all, that are not pleasant ones to answer. Does the ultimate bad man of this time, represent anything but a sum of follies, shames, passions, sins, which had their root in his own race, when its blood warmed the hearts of ancestors long since dead, and now flourish in him with a growth and strength beyond his control? This seems to be the scientific view of the case. If it be correct, does divine justice consist with the pangs suffered for the indulgence of inherited frailties? And how much individuality is there left us, when the dead so possess and torment us?

Dr. Maudsley is charitable to Poe, while he recognizes all his sins and their consequences; but after stating all the facts of his life, and discussing the composition of his genius, he draws on his gloves, and takes leave without summing up. The anomaly of this wild and miserable career remains. "Is no explanation possible?" the Doctor permits the reader to ask him; and he sorrowfully admits there is none; leaving you to infer what he will not say, that Poe was crazed—a madman.

[*Ohio State Journal*, 27 November 1860]

[Among the reviews and notices of new publications which appeared with some regularity during the period of Howells's association with the *Ohio State Journal* are several that reveal his critical acumen and developing interests more fully than others. His remarks, for instance, on William Cullen Bryant's *Letters of a Traveller, Second Series* (1859), foreshadow the problems he soon would face in his own experiments in the genre of travel writing. In his notice of "The Atlantic for March [1859]," he focuses on Oliver Wendell Holmes's *The Professor at the Breakfast-Table* which had begun its serial publication in the Boston magazine two months before. What seems not to have been so clearly noticed as it should be is that Howells's warm admiration and frequent quotation of Holmes's writings during his youth are trustworthy indications that the New England writer mattered more in the young man's literary growth than he afterwards remembered when confessing his "literary passions." Hawthorne's *Marble Faun* was published in March 1860, and its critical reception during the ensuing weeks was a frequent item of "literary gossip" in the *Ohio State Journal*. As one might expect, it was not long before Howells added his own thoughts regarding the meaning of Hawthorne's troubling romance.]

New Books

LETTERS OF A TRAVELER. Second Series. By Wm. Cullen Bryant. New York: D. Appleton & Co. Columbus: J. H. Riley & Co.

Mr. Bryant's letters from Spain, published in the New York Evening Post a year or two since, afford perhaps the best notion we have yet had of that country. "Cosas de Espana" was an admirable book, so far as it went, but it did not go a great way, and an "Attaché at Madrid," spoke only of the capital. These letters are full of a pleasant and quiet interest; the author is good-natured in his descriptions of Spain and the Spaniards; but while he is not captious, he never sacrifices fidelity for the sake of an agreeable picture. You feel, all the while that you read his book, as if he were talking to you, and recounting the incidents of his tour, in an easy and genial fashion; being humorous and sufficiently picturesque, and yet candid. He tells you more of what he sees and hears, than what he does; which is an excellent thing in a traveler; people of that kind commonly fancy themselves to be the only objects of interest in foreign countries.

The letters were written during a journey from France to Naples by way of Spain, where the author made his principal sojourn; he visited also the States of Northern Africa, and was a while at Rome. Altogether, the work is most entertaining.

Mr. Bryant says that these letters "are laid before the public without material correction." This is true, even to a typographical error which we remember to have noticed in one of them, as published in the *Post*. The Spanish word *cobarde* (coward,) is twice printed *codarde*: and in the notices of Granada, that word is invariably spelled "Grenada." These errors are trifling, but they are just of that sort which should have been corrected.

[*Ohio State Journal*, 16 April 1859]

The Atlantic for March

It was a perilous thing for the "Autocrat of the Breakfast Table" to venture upon a second series of papers kindred to that in style and purpose. Every one he had charmed felt jealous of the "Autocrat's" excellence; and the "Professor" was very sharply criticised. We think, it would have been rather pleasant than otherwise, to find him a falling-off; so well were we content with his predecessor. If the "Professor" had first occupied that chair, no doubt we should have thought him a marvelous fine talker; but after the "Autocrat" he must be silver-tongued to please us. We weighed his fancies against the choicest of the "Autocrat's;" we picked his philosophy carefully to pieces, anxious to detect something stolen from that illustrious ruler of the feast; we shrewdly scanned his verses.

"The Professor" has stood the test bravely. He comes out better and better, every time we sit down at table with him. We nod applause at his good things; and neglect our coffee. For does not every reader board at the same place with the professor?

He is peculiarly felicitous in his last essay. He talks with the reader, and with a score of chatty little episodes, tells a young girl's story. Her story he does not finish. But that of her father, the Latin tutor (whom you remember, wrote "Aestivation,") he does finish, in a manner exquisitely humorous and touching. There is no tenderer bit of coloring in the whole language. It is almost as skillfully wrought as the picture in which poor old Colonel Newcome says "Adsum!" The claudent verses (as the gentle tutor might have said,) are "The Opening of the New Piano."

"A Plea for the Fijians," is pleasant and wholesome reading. The author advocates the introduction of the ancient and honorable custom of eating men and women, on the same grounds with the arguments in favor of reviving the slave-trade; and we think he is quite as reasonable as the friends of that Christian measure. "The Waterfall," is a beautiful poem. "The Double-Headed Snake of Newbury" is by Whittier, we suppose. Doubtless its moral is pointed enough; but we found it rather hard reading. As for "Achmed and His Mare" we wondered how either got into the "Atlantic." Mrs. Stowe's story of "The Minister's Wooing" continues; so does that of "Bulls and Bears;" so does "The New Life of Dante." Sawyer's Translation of the New Testament is causticly reviewed; and the remaining articles are "Holbein and the Dance of Death," "Lizzie Griswold's Thanksgiving," "Charles Lamb and Sydney Smith," "The Winter Birds," "The Utah Expedition." Kennedy has handed us the magazine.

[*Ohio State Journal*, 22 February 1859]

Hawthorne's "Marble Faun"

The people who have read this beautiful book will hardly wish to have the story feebly rehearsed. Those who have yet the pleasure of reading it before them, could only be vexed by glimpses of its incidents.

For the reader's sake, therefore, we repress whatever desire we have to tell Mr. Hawthorne's tale again, and permit ourselves only allusion to the idea of the book.

Of all this author's romances, "The Marble Faun" is the most darkly sad, the most subtly mysterious. In it you glide forever through a dream of exquisite sorrow, with the dim life of antiquity vaguely haunting the shadowy groves, and mixing with lives of the present, so far exalted out of the common-place and vulgar. Hawthorne, indeed, seems to have wreaked his soul upon the expression of the emotion which rises from the thought of Death, and the story, fine and precious as it is, is but the clay in which he shapes and moulds the idea to make it palpable to coarser vision.

In no other atmosphere than that of Rome is such a work possible, and there the scene is laid—in that city, where life, constantly confronted with eternal Art, seems so cruelly brief and little, and where old Nature is ineffably sad with the secrets and sorrows of her dead children, the Generations.

Yes, the Idea of the book is Death. Not that ghastly thing which triumphs over our joy, and shows itself grinning and hideous at our feasts—but Death, the old attendant of our race, inevitable, and universal, standing in wait for us at the end of the journey, and embracing the beggar and the prince with wide arms that know no difference. Death the moss-bearded,—death the vague but not the terribly mysterious,—death the rest but not the punishment,—death the inexorable but not unkind—venerable, serene.

The little stream of life and love that goes glimmering through this Valley of the Shadow is sweet enough; the flowers of our common delights spring upon its banks, and kiss its waters; and the woods that group themselves along its course, are full of sylvan creatures, and gleam with exquisite works of art.

Kenyon the sculptor is a real and noble man; Hilda is marbly pure and tranquil as a saint, preciously carved out of stone; Miriam is—Miriam—and Donatello, the poor Faun, who found a soul in sin—there is only one other man like him that ever lived, and he lived in "The House of Seven Gables"—Clifford Pyncheon, in whom destiny annulled all the rich and beautiful purpose of nature, and mocked with the terrible earnestness of grief, the soul that was born for enjoyment and happiness.

[*Ohio State Journal,* 24 March 1860]

[A few years later, Howells and Henry James would frequently be denounced by the American press for savaging "the American Girl" in their fictions. But Lydia Blood, Daisy Miller, and Isabel Archer were not the first to annoy American readers in their less than ideal characterizations. William Makepeace Thackeray drew fire when two-thirds through his novel *The Virginians,* which he had begun publishing in monthly numbers in November 1857 and was being reprinted in America in *Harper's Monthly,* he introduced Lydia Van den Bosch, a wealthy heiress from Albany, New York. Pretty, but also ignorant and pretentious, the flirtatious American girl comes to London to find a suitable husband. Her eventual marriage to Eugene, Lord Castlewood, does not prove to be happy, however, and in time she loses both her beauty and youthful innocence. Howells might have had a less volatile career had he learned from Thackeray's example the strength of American journalistic outrage, but he did not. Already his art and his thinking about his art were determined in a course which afterwards seemed inevitable.]

Unworthy Mr. Thackeray!

There are a great many stupid people in the world; and we regret to add, stupid editors.—Candor, however, compels the admission. When Mr. Thackeray began publishing his "Virginians," there was a vast deal of patriotic virtue ventilated, because the satirist did not approach the "Father of his Country" (see our last 22d of February address,) in the hat-in-hand, low-louting, Weems-y fashion of American writers, but actually ventured to treat the great man as a human being. A number of able and intelligent editors, who commonly devote the whole of their valuable time to enlightening their readers upon political topics, suddenly turned their attention to literature, and exposed Mr. Thackeray's ingratitude to a country through which he had traveled, with a great deal of vigor. It was not necessary for them to have a conception of the author's peculiar genius and humor. The fowl of our national independence had been disrespectfully squinted at, and this was enough.

Mr. Thackeray, however, by dint of making "The Virginians" such dull people that scarcely anybody cared to pursue their acquaintance, finally over-lived this patriotic *furor*, and might have proceeded unmolested to the end of his chapter, had he not ungraciously attacked The American Female!

In the last numbers of his story, he introduces a little coquette who has been born and "raised" in the American colonies, but is come to reside in London. She flirts desperately, involves two characters in a bloodless duel, and finally marries a profligate old Peer. The common mind may not see anything so very dreadful in this, but an editor who has cherished the American eagle in his bosom, and constantly fed it with the elevating and lively sentiment that 'Mericans must rule America, sees a good deal in this colonial coquette business. A stab, a secret assassin-like punch (so to speak) at the reputation of American women for virtue and modesty!

The coquette and her grandfather, like a great many of the first families of Virginia, have just a little negro blood in them.

"Beautiful origin for an American girl!" exclaims the editor of the Baltimore *American*:

"Mr. Thackeray is not content to make the American girl a shameless tuft-hunter at sixteen or seventeen years old, he must also make her ignorant and ungrammatical, in a word, ridiculous. He makes her talk. We give a specimen. Lydia is talking to George Warrington, who has made some remark about her lips. She says:

" 'They don't tell nothin' but truth, any how!—that's why some people don't like them! If I have anything on my mind it must come out. I am a country-bred girl, I am—with my heart in my mouth—all honesty and simplicity—not like your English girls, who have learned, I don't know what, at their boarding-schools, and from the men afterward.'

"The 'Americanisms' in this little speech of Miss Lydia's are the least objectionable feature in it. Grant, as every true Briton will take for granted, that American girls are in the habit of saying 'I'm a country-bred girl, I am,' that is a small matter. But there is positive indelicacy in the closing lines of the American girl's reply to Warrington. Concerning this we might say much,—we will say but little."

Is not this an alarming state of affairs? True Britons, from an expression put in the mouth of a vulgar little colonial girl, will conclude that American ladies habitually say "I'm a country-bred girl, I am."

As for the "indelixy" hinted at, in Miss Lydia's speech, we cannot discover it, though it may be plain to any nice people upon this well-known theory of Dean Swift.

"Mr. Thackeray must settle with his own conscience for this slander. Doubtless there are silly girls in America, and not only silly but indelicate in thought and speech. But the average, as Mr. Thackeray well knows, is far otherwise."

We wish Mr. Thackeray joy of this settlement with his conscience. We don't believe he'll be able to "effectuate" it. He has been guilty of an abominable thing. It is true that his English women are not angels (the more acceptable for that,) but why could he not put us a pair of wings on Miss Lydia's plump shoulders? He had been in this country. He had seen what a great and noble people we are. He had lectured to highly intelligent and fashionable audiences, and was very much hunted up and looked at. Yet he goes home, and maligns American female character! O, Mr. Thackeray! Compliments are not in your line, but we did expect to be buttered a little! You did better than Mr. Dickens, who once told us so many disagreeable truths, to be a disgust to the patriotic stomach ever since. You did better than he, but you did not do enough. Nay, we are afraid that you really do not look reverently upon our old colonial society, and thereby offer disrespect to these States.

It will be a difficult matter for the satirist to get over this, and we say in all sincerity, with the *American*, "we are truly sorry it has come to this."

[*Ohio State Journal*, 14 May 1859]

CHAPTER FIVE

Town and Country Sketches

[As a literary form, the sketch emerged during the eighteenth and early years of the nineteenth centuries in response to the needs of magazines and newspapers, and by the time Howells came to his craft in the 1850s, the miscellaneous essay was without question the most common and available form of literary expression, at least among American writers. Its simple outline and its demand on the powers of expression rather than the imagination make it an ideal form for apprentice authors, just as its counterpart in drawing makes the artist's sketch preliminary to composing on grander scales. Its weakness tended to be just that which Emerson had found lacking in so much of Hawthorne's work: "there was no inside to it"; or, to put it another way, the sketch was satisfied with the surface charm of "the meal in the firkin, the milk in the pan" and did not work to find the sublime in the common as Emerson expected of the poet. Much of what later passed for literary realism was merely an adaptation of those sketches of commonplace scenes which the earlier nineteenth century had taken such enormous pleasure in. Lamb, Hazlitt, Leigh Hunt, Thackeray in England, Heine on the Continent, Hawthorne, Holmes, Curtis, and the largely forgotten Ik Marvel at home each, in his distinctive way, provided young writers like Howells with examples and . solutions to the problems of style and expression, and he looked to their work with the attention and ardor of the disciple whose aim is not imitation but possession and independence.

The study of languages itself was for Howells a necessary means to master their literatures, works against which he knew in time he must be measured. "I loved form, I loved style, I loved diction, and I strove for them all, rejecting my faultier ideals when I discovered them, and cleaving to the truer." Always he tried "for grace, for distinctness, for light," willing to be satisfied with nothing "less than final perfection so far as I could imagine it" (*YMY*, p. 102).

The fact is that in those days I was bursting with the most romantic expectations of life in every way, and I looked at the whole world as material that might be turned into literature, or that might be associated with it somehow. I do not know how I managed to keep these preposterous hopes within me, but perhaps the trick of satirizing them, which I had early learnt, helped me to do it. I was at that particular moment resolved above all things to see things as Heinrich Heine saw them, or at least to report them as he did, no matter how I saw them; and I went about framing phrases to this end, and trying to match the objects of interest to them whenever there was the least chance of getting them together. (*LFA*, pp. 18–19)

Howells's enormously good fortune was that from early youth he was able to rid himself in print of his more successful experiments. Oliver Wendell Holmes later quipped to him that, so far as one's writing goes, the pudding is in the proof, a characteristically charming way of reminding one that the cold distance of type gives our words an existence apart from us, unprotected by our best intentions and private understandings. Although they may falter and die, at least we are free to grow and leave the past where it belongs. In addition, Howells had from the very beginning of his literary life the costly encouragement of an audience that demanded to be pleased, and in return, was eager to show its appreciation, at least in praise, if not in wealth. These literary opportunities are something the young writer of today must find hard even to imagine. The business of authorship, which Howells came in time to understand profoundly, is, like other businesses, conducted in the marketplace, and here in Ohio just before the Civil War the young writer found ample opportunity to display his goods and benefit from the remarks and interests they might draw from those who passed by.

"Boots," the earliest of the pieces gathered here, was published in the *Cincinnati Daily Gazette* in February 1858. For it, Howells received five dollars in payment, an amount equal to half his weekly salary from the *Gazette* for his legislative letters. More importantly, the sketch probably contributed to the Cincinnati publishers offering Howells shortly afterwards a position on their paper's staff. "Bobby" appeared in the *Ohio State Journal* ten months later, early in the tenure of Howells's association with that paper. It is in every respect the strongest of these early pieces and invites interesting comparisons with Howells's mature writings on the child. The Columbus bookseller who told Samuel Reed that the sketch "was enough to make anybody's reputation" apparently knew what he was saying since country editors eagerly copied the piece in their papers (*SL*, 1:21).

All these early performances of Howells succeed well in displaying his versatility both as a literary stylist and as a civilized wit, qualities his time undoubtedly overvalued but without which no literary culture can exist. It is difficult to imagine such apparent talent going unrecognized in any time or place, and impossible in the capital of Ohio during the late 1850s.]

BOOTS

By Octavius Augustus Jones

"STIEFEL—STIEFEL!"—GŒTHE.*

There is not, as some stupid people have been led to think, a great deal of expression in the eye. The nose, however scrupulously followed by a second person, will not bring one acquainted with a man's character. The mouth, the brow, are often deceitful; and for those traitors that lurk under the hair of the head, what man, not Fowler-mad, would have faith in them? How then, it is asked me, is one to judge of a man. Partly by letting him discover himself; chiefly by his boots. In them the whole mental man is glassed.

I know very well that there are witty persons enough to say to this: But what if he wear gaiters? I am talking of men, not milk-sops. Only milk-sops wear gaiters. But women? Fie, sir! let the ladies' feet alone.

(I was nothing astonished at the presentation of boots in this singular psychological aspect by Phillip Clare, knowing him as I did for a bundle of eccentricities; but I was a little startled to hear a man denounce others as milk-sops for wearing what he then had upon his feet: gaiters. I stated as much in words.)

Tush! I bought them to ease my curb-stone corn. My feet are more fertile than the Miami bottom lands. Forbear that jest about their having an equal depth of soil, or I shall stop talking.

It is a truth, as little to be questioned, as that learning is remembrance, that the inanimate articles of daily human use and wear, assume the look and characteristic expression of their wearers. I mean, that being accustomed to see a man in a given hat or coat, you know them for his, wherever you come upon them, by a certain resemblance they bear to him. Strong minds impress this *ipsisimilitude* upon their weaker ones about them; and there is, under a wise Providence, force enough in every man to imbue his clothes with himself. Sometimes, this influence extends to his horse or dog; and if you have ever noticed, a widow's cow always looks like her.

---

*This sentiment will not be found in the commoner copies of Gœthe. Indeed, it is only to be met with in a very rare edition, published by Schnelleryungermann at Nirgends am Rhein.

Young girls are apt to bewitch their bonnets into a personal resemblance, and I once saw a foolish fellow adoring a *hood* upon this principle. (O *cara mia*! who ties your hood under your chin now? It is a good minute's work, even when one's nerves are firm.) Little boys usually confer their impression upon the cuffs and elbows of their jackets. But never does this mysterious quality of likeness fail to be seen in *boots*.

Were I writing an essay on this subject,—(you are glad I am not, are you, sir? Go to grass, then, for an unenlightened Nebuchadnezzar!) I should pass over as unprofitable, any speculations on the puerile *selfnesses* of youthful stogas; and treat only of human character as illustrated in the adult, or grown-up-boot. I should approach the theme, too, rather as a moralist, than as a savant, though I have long regarded and pursued boot-psychology as a science, depending upon my great paper, published with the transactions of the Stiefelgesellschaft, of Germany, to sustain me against the charge of superficiality. (You are a Scotchman, Andrew, and I forgive you. But if you interrupt me again I will apply the poker to you. What does it concern science, whether you ever heard of the Stiefelgesellschaft, or not?) My sphere of observation has been as extended as that of most men, with a theory, and I should expect to carry conviction with my words. I have, indeed, contemplated boots not as a convention of Society, but as a great principle in Nature. The penetralia have been opened to me; and I speak, as it were, from the loftiest blacking-box of truth.

It would be great folly in me to pretend that I am acquainted with all varieties of boots, for they are as infinite and various as men. There is a manner of boots, I believe, as peculiar to every people, as their manner of speech or hand writing. Thus, there are nationalities of men and of boots; and there are individualities of men and of boots. The German boot, a quaint mixture of solidity, profundity and transcendentalism, is as unlike the boot of the gallant, cowardly, virtuous, vicious, faithful, false Irishmen, of whom love is said to be the soul, as those two people are unlike. The Frenchman's boot—

> "Long, narrow, light—the Gallic boot of love—
> A kind of cross between the boot and glove,"

is only so when worn by a Frenchman, as their language is never French except when spoken by themselves. The English boot sympathizes in all the prejudices of its wearer, and announces him everywhere, in a stiffly, haughty, bullying fashion; while the American boot is full of vanity, pretence, pluck, *dash*, and humbug as the American himself. The Scotch boot—pah! Andrew, it smells of brimstone and mercurial ointment.

As to boot-individuality, you have but to go upon the street, to

remark it on every man you meet. There is not any need that you should look further up than a man's foot to see whether he is proud, insolent, vain, cruel, generous, kind, ruffianly or gentle! Tennyson, whom you quote to weariness, Octavius Augustus, understood very well that "Maud's" brother could never have gorgonized her lover with a stony British stare, had he not been at the same time,
"Leisurely tapping a glossy boot,"
which must have contemptuously inflicted the lover's slovenly misanthropic Wellingtons. If you are a weak, undetermined vacillating man, be sure your boot will betray you; for to-day it will be shapely enough, and to-morrow run down at the heel, with a tendency to lop over, when set outside your door at night. If on the contrary you are a strong, resolute man, your boots will be miracles of self-respect, uprightness and brilliancy.

The politician's boot is observable for a faintly audible, insinuating and conciliatory screak, which it has learnt, by walking into office.—Nothing can be more complaisant than its lustre, which seems to be borrowed from the boots of everybody else, and is yet decidedly peculiar; and it is a boot capable of assuming many different phases of character, without ever ceasing to be shrewd, careful and reticent. Sly boots! yet with the frailties common to boots and men; believing themselves inscrutable, yet exhibiting their weakness to every philosophic eye. We behold in them too plainly the man who has scrupled at nothing that would advance him; the shuffling foe, the false friend, the dangerous ally. Withal they are boots that baffle verbal description, and perhaps they could no more be painted than "a dying groan."

The editor's boots! what stories of unrequited labor, thankless striving, wasted health, are written in every seam and wrinkle! They are never bright, like the boots of other men, even on a Sunday; and they have a quick, nervous, eager look, that betrays their wearer's anxiety to make an article or an item out of everything they bring him upon. I cannot regard such boots without emotions of the most painful kind; for to me the mute leather is eloquent of an insane devotion to a calling that wears out soul and body—nor makes robust the purse; of long nights of scribbling and scissoring; of wanderings among uncouth people and strange places; of singular sacrifice of self for the sole satisfaction of being held answerable for unanswerable articles!

(Here the Cincinnatian blew the nose—either of emotion or meditation; and being approvingly regarded by Phillip, attempting to tell his single story of an exploit of the steam fire-engines, "When the Pork-house of Pork, Packer & Co. took fire"—Phillip's philosophic eye sternly silenced him.)

Boots, not hose, are the theme of our present talk. When this company wish to listen for the thousand and first time, to a paltry tale, of a burning pork-house extinguished, they will, perhaps, interrupt a psychological discourse on boots. Wait till they do. That is all.

As I had said before rudely broken in upon, boots are as infinite in their variety as men; and it were as vain to attempt to classify them. Indeed, there is one boot, (never on the right leg) which might of itself, form the text of a sermon. It is often seen on the backs of seats in the pits of the theatre, where it disputes popular applause with the darling actress of the hour; it is frequently heard to tap snatches of tune on the door-steps of saloons, and to perform extempore and fragmentary shuffles within saloons. It is a shabby, dashing boot, patched and run down, yet with an irresistible expression of good fellowship about it; and, indeed, it belongs to a man who is known as a *good-hearted fellow* among his acquaintances—a weak, kind, well-natured creature, hurting no one but himself; honest when he may be, and always generous and partly drunk. Such a boot wore Dick Swiveller, and such men will always be known by such boots.

Then there is a calm, negative, methodical boot, as unworldly as it is coldly-conceited and self-conscious, small, but not shapely, thin, but not flexible, which is only to be found on a certain species of clergymen—a man of whom you feel, when you see him, that he is only chaste because stone, only gentle because afraid.

"With lips depressed, as he were meek,
    Himself unto himself he sold;
Upon himself himself did feed;
    Quiet, dispassionate, and cold."

I should weary you, Octavius Augustus, (for even now, you nod more than acquiescence to what I say,) were I to animadvert at equal length upon the farmer's boots, yellow, and coarse, and stiffened and deformed by "sore labor," the merchant's boot, solid, smooth and respectable; the vagabond's boot, exaggerated in its raggedness, run-downness, and redolent with the unwholesome presence of unwashed feet; the lover's boot, pinching and pretty, dashing and cruel; the father's boots, that seem to have been made to play music upon the home-threshold; the grand-sire's boot, paralytic, tottering, broad and slow.

When I first came hither, I was a timorous, abstracted, unassuming man, and it was for this reason, perhaps, that I was put into No. 999, and made no row about it. But I had complacency enough to carry a bold face upon most occasions. I had actually the temerity at dinner one day to reject the proffer of a cold turkey drum-stick (forgive me the childish aptitude of phrase) and to demand white meat in its stead. I spoke to the gentlemanly proprietor without trembling; and I do not think I was afraid of the clerk or of the chambermaid, certainly not of the porter, who is an extremely good-natured man. In the presence of the boot-black, however, (though I failed not to propitiate him with frequent dimes ill to be afforded) I stood abashed and crestfallen; for I felt that no affectation would serve me with him, that he knew me as well as I knew myself. He must, if he be the man of genius I take him to be, have read my poverty and helplessness in every peg of my boot soles as he nightly chalked upon them "999." I doubted not but that he perused my little history in them, and learned my character as from a written book.

Strange being! There is, indeed, something weird and unholy in thus passing one's life among the boots of many men; and though I have heard this boot-black whistling about the halls, with as light-hearted and care-free a sibilation as any meadow lark, yet I knew the dreadful secrets that he acquires, whether he will or no, from constant communication with boots, must make mankind a loathing, and life a burden to him. I would not fathom his turbid thoughts; as in the hush of night, when all the hotel is whist, he places at each man's door his voiceless other self. Very solemn and preter-natural seem the long rows of boots, as they flank the narrow pas-sages, and wink knowingly on such as seeks his room belatedly, who, if he be not drunk, must shudder at their revelations.

Unriddlers of the riddle, Man: mysterious mirrors of the inmost soul, mute monitors and teachers, they stand upright or hang their crimson or azure tops, while the gas light trembles overhead; and the Marvelous Black steals slowly away, down, down to that lowest cellar deep, where, secret as an Alchemist, among his drugs, he polishes the mystic boot!

If you don't bring me a pitcher of drinking water within two minutes, my hesitant bell-boy, I shall be hanged for your murder.

(Unless you can plead insanity, said Andrew, waking up at pre-cisely the right moment.)

[*Cincinnati Daily Gazette*, 23 February 1858]

BOBBY
STUDY OF A BOY

Bobby is twelve years old. He has, therefore, survived the mea-sles, the mumps, and those repeated and obstinate attempts at self-destruction, which boys are very well known to make in their first half score of years. He tried falling into a rain-barrel, at a very tender period of infancy, but was rescued after an immersion of ten minutes, and restored to life. He next made violent efforts to break his neck upon all practicable staircases, both by rolling down the steps and falling off the banisters. These efforts, as well as determined endeavors to be run over by wagons, proved futile. A descent from the top of a tree, under circumstances peculiarly favorable to the accomplishment of his apparent object, resulted in nothing worse than the fracture of an arm; and Bobby has passed unscathed through the successive rejoicings of Christmases, New Years and Fourths of July, with all their facilities for the destruction of juvenile life. In spite of himself, then, Bobby is now twelve years of age.

The human animal at this age is perhaps less attractive than at any other. He—I am speaking of the male—has long ceased to be the delight of uncles, and the plaything of aunts; and the only being to whom he is as dear as in the palmy days of babyhood, is his grandmother. His uncles who made so much of him once, are now married, and are full of advice tending to his personal chastisement, on the broad ground that he is a bad boy—instead of the caresses and half-dimes in which they formerly abounded. His aunts, who used to make nice clothes for him—utterly impracticable for any other than Sunday School purposes—are grown shy and wary of the stoga-booted young rogue, who, if they are married, is hard to be restrained from thrashing his younger cousins, or if they are single, is utterly defiant of their authority, and savagely indifferent to appeals of tenderness. To his little sisters, he is the griffin, who appears suddenly at their mimic feasts, and in their play-houses, devouring and destroying everything before him. Gifted with a diabolical instinct in regard to beaux, and a fearful cunning as to *affaires de coeur*, he is the terror of his elder sisters, with whom he is perpetually at war; returning any aggressions in the way of boxed ears, with a direful retribution of kicks and thumps. He incessantly runs away from little Johnny, with whom it has been solemnly determined in family council, that he ought to play; and he is a poignant thorn in the side of brothers who are just beginning to shave and to fall in love. His mother sighs when she looks upon him, and his father pronounces him the most worthless fellow in the world. To whom, then, is he tolerable, but to his grand-mother? She, in beautiful and touching remembrance of the times when his feet, clad in daintiest shoes, would not reach the floor, from her lowest chair—feeds him with cake, when he comes to see her, and refuses to believe in his faults. In return for which, Bobby actually has been known to scrape his feet at her threshold, and to perform her errands with incredible promptness.

At present, the principal object of Bobby's life is to stand upon his head, and play the bones at the same instant. This admirable feat, he practices on all occasions, in all companies, and under all circumstances, dashing down upon his head, and remaining in that pleasing posture, if not assaulted by friends in unprotected quarters, until quite purple in the face. Of course, he is joint proprietor of a boy's circus, in which his accomplishment is to be turned to practical account. At table, he breaks in upon a polemic skirmish between his father and oldest brother, with the announcement of the names of clown, master of the ring, and principal performers, and the fact that you can come in for three pins. Which, in view of the variety and excellence of the spectacle, he thinks to be prodigiously cheap. He is not at all out of heart that all former establishments in which he has been concerned, have resulted disastrously, either being suddenly broken up by the man in whose barn the exhibition was secretly given, or crushed at their inception by parental tyranny, or even when successful in other respects, reduced to bankruptcy by the door-keeper's absconding with all the pins. Bobby remembers none of these things, but places his whole heart in the present venture. The only points on which he is at all dubious, are those of costume and tenting. Tights are but partially possible of attainment by stuffing his pantaloons legs inside his socks. The upper part of the attire may be managed by turning his jacket. The tent, however, is yet quite unattainable, and Bobby's sweetest hopes are embittered by the thought of it. Paper will not do, and how to get the canvas! Ah!

As yet, Bobby has had no such troubles as will grieve his heart, hereafter; and little girls are a loathing to him. He is particularly rude to a demure little damsel whom he used to walk to school with, (while he was yet under the refining influences of home,) and who still acknowledges an ardent passion for him, and an unalterable determination to marry him when she comes to be a woman. In secret she makes the tenderest romances about Bobby, in whom is not the least sentiment in the world. She writes affecting notes to him at school, and slips them into his jacket pockets, where they are found when he comes home, and read aloud to the intense delight of injured brothers and sisters, and the unspeakable rage, mortification and disgust of Bobby. In the first transports of his anger, he threatens to kill that girl! and on his mother's saying, "O, Bobby!" he repeats the threat, when his father declares that he will box his ears if he says that again, which is so little inducement to its repetition, that Bobby declines the offer.

At his lessons, Bobby is not distinguished, learning them, as it were, in spite all his efforts to the contrary. But Bobby is by no means a dull boy, and at the end of one term he comes off with flying honors and a little prize book, to the everlasting astonishment of his family and the rapture of his grandmother. Of all his studies, Bobby likes history the most, and has got a description of the battle of Bunker Hill by heart. He admires all military exploits, and thinks the soldier's calling, after that of the circus actor, the most gallant and laudable in the world.

As has been hinted, Bobby is of a very pugnacious temper. Of his own invincibility in personal contest, he has no doubt; holding it to be impossible that a boy of his skill, adroitness and bravery, *could* be vanquished by any odds whatever. He has general ideas of what he could do in case of unequal combat, which always have reference to the overthrow of his teacher, should that person, in an evil hour, attempt to chastise him. He thinks the manoeuver of suddenly stooping down, seizing the teacher by the legs, and tossing him over his shoulder, would rather astonish that gentleman. Rehearsing this measure to a group of admiring friends, he informs them that if the encounter should result in anything dangerous to Old Smith, it is his deliberate intention to run away; darkly hinting at some future re-appearance in his native place as clown of a circus.

In spite, however, of his swelling notions of himself, on all points that concern him as a boy among boys, Bobby is bashful. Company is his terror; and when his mother has visitors, he is seldom to be found at home. If maugre all his precautions, he is captured, and presented to the company, he is exquisitely awkward and quiet, being little more than a disagreeable sensation of muddy boots, glowing cheeks, and hoarse whisper. At times, when goaded to desperation by the requests of friends he will declaim "Bozarris," casting up his eyes, twiddling his thumbs, and supplying with inarticulate sounds, all defects of memory. As a general thing, however, he is proof against all entreaties, and maintains perfect silence, which is also motionless if girls are present.

Of robust health and stout-knit frame, Bobby enjoys keenly the pleasures of mere animal life—playing, eating and sleeping. In the summer, he spends a great part of each day in the water; in the fall he goes on nutting and wild grape excursions, and roams about the grand old woods, dreaming wild blissful dreams of the savage life he would like to live; in the winter, he revels in sledding privileges, and is the first boy to see whether the ice will "bear." Fraught with exquisite enjoyment to him, are the warm, languid days of early spring, (that so melt down and soften you and me,) when he first takes off his shoes, and leaps over the ground in his tender bare feet. Ah! blessed time! Ah! happy, happy Bobby!

As for looks, Bobby is neither ugly nor handsome. He has a wide mouth, (most boys have,) hard red cheeks, gray eyes, an indefinite nose, and a head of light brown hair, that is coarser to the sight than to the touch. He may be generally described in respect of person, as a cast-iron boy.

What Bobby is to be when a man, he is yet uncertain. Of course, the dearest wish of his heart is to be a circus actor; if not that, then a soldier; and of common-place callings, he would choose that of a storekeeper, as involving the possession of unlimited pocket cutlery.

But whatever Bobby is to be, that he will be with his whole heart, which is a great and a good heart, as I say in defiance of his relatives.
[Signed W.D.H., *Ohio State Journal*, 14 December 1858]

["Dick Dowdy" and "Hot," two sketches published in the *Ohio State Journal*, apparently represented in Howells's estimation standards to which his journalistic essaying should attain. At least when a decade later he came to think "of making a book of some of my Atlantic papers, and a few of my old newspaper scribblings," Howells asked his friend James M. Comly at the *Ohio State Journal* office to send copies of the newspaper letters Howells had published during his literary pilgrimage to New England in the summer of 1860, as well as "some sketches like an article called 'Hot,' and another, 'Dick Dowdy,' which I'd like . . . to recover. I was such an ass as never to keep a file of the Journal for myself, not supposing that [it] should ever at a future time be money in my own pocket." Comly was happy to comply with Howells's request, but his kindness did nothing to diminish Howells's disappointment upon rereading the pieces which memory had somehow improved, or at least made more of a piece with the work he was trying at the time to do in the *Atlantic Monthly*. Finally on 5 September 1869, Howells threw the matter back into the corner of his Columbus friend:

I'm much obliged to you for the trouble you've taken in looking up that old rubbish of mine; but I don't think any of the articles worth booking. There was one, very short—half a column or three quarters in length—called 'Hot,' and published sometime in the summer of 1860, that I thought I might do; but if on reading it over it doesn't strike you favorably, I don't care even for that. I'm ashamed, really, to have made you so much trouble, and shall hold myself ready to be commanded by you in anything I can do here.

Either Comly did not offer encouragement or Howells himself decided the sketch of the Ohio heat was too slight for his collection of *Suburban Sketches*.

Howells again recalled this piece when in July 1901 his old Ohio poet-friend, John James Piatt, asked him to contribute something for *The Hesperian Tree*, a handsomely produced "annual of the Ohio Valley" which Piatt and his wife were attempting to establish. Howells made a few, minor corrections and verbal improvements in the sketch when he gave it to Piatt but otherwise had the wisdom to leave all that the years between had irreparably changed. Except for a few snatches of poetry in *Years of My Youth*, this was Howells's only attempt so far as we know to retrieve the literary work of his youth.]

Dick Dowdy

STUDY OF A FIRST-RATE FELLOW

We *thought* we knew that figure, so unpleasantly *distingue* even at the distance of half a square; but when, on near approach, we discerned the intensely vulgar calico shirt-bosom, and sanguine collar, we felt quite certain that it was Dick Dowdy. He favored us with one hand, (which was not over-clean) and smote us jocosely upon the shoulder with the other. He has the engaging custom of thus beating the breath out of his acquaintance on meeting them, even after the briefest separations. He lugs you back and forth as he shakes hands, and peers very closely into your face, that he may announce in terms of pleasantry, his gratification at seeing you. During the utterance of his greeting, and from the attendant agitation of his clothes you become sensible of a mingled odor of beer and cigars, about which there is a vague remoteness, as if those luxuries had been drunken and smoked in a previous state of existence. The honest fellow will account for this to you, if you will but listen to him; and he will tell you many of the choice things that he said over his cups and tobacco last night. Should you offer to *stand* either of those for a present consumption, this generous creature will hardly refuse to let you do so. He will even direct you to a desirable place for procuring them; for though but young in years, and something new to the city, he is by no means deficient in matters of polite local information.

Dick's outward appearance, it must be confessed, is not pleasing. Being of a short and dumpy figure, he of course wears a raglan coat, which heightens the effect of his peculiar *tournure*. His inelegant legs are cased in a pattern of cassimere, which is not of the quietest sort; and his *chaussure* consists of a pair of extravagantly stubbed boots. His broad chest is adorned with a vest of lively colors, and we have already hinted that he wears the colored bosom and collar to which his species is addicted. For his face, it is of a ghastly yellow, relieved, it is true, by a prevailing pimplyness of expression, and a chin-growth of thin and wiry beard. His hands, when not hidden in a pair of gloves, (which it is once believed were saffron, but which are now of no particular hue,) appear adorned with rings of indifferent quality, but of vast quantity. Set in one of them is the miniature of Mr. Dowdy's "woman," as he ordinarily phrases it; in his mellower moods, the sentimental and tender hearted fellow, has been known to kiss at it tipsily, and to address it in terms of intoxicated affection; then it comes out that the picture is that of his sister.

It has been intimated that poor Dick has a general habit of pleasantry. Indeed, this may be regarded as the distinguishing characteristic of his mind. He is forever saying the archest things without the least occasion, and of laughing at them with much enjoyment. Dick is not foolishly sensitive, and it does not at all annoy him that his listeners fail to see the point of his sayings. As the merry fellow often remarks, "What the angel is the use of getting off a good thing, if you're to wait for every blessed fool to laugh at it first?" It is not, however, in pleasant sayings alone that our humorous friend's *forte* lies. He will play you the merriest tricks of any body—draw your chair away as you are about to sit down in it; dip your cigar in the water; lock you in your own room and go off with the key, and so forth. If there is anything he likes better than this, it is throwing out some catching phrase, and when you have asked explanation, to turn upon you with some coarse retort. And the beauty of this is, that the coarser his retort, the more you are expected to enjoy it. The wit will clap you on the back in his engaging manner, and cry out, "Got you that time, old fellow."

It may well be supposed that this agreeable young person is not destitute of peculiar opinions even on matters not connected with the subject of saloons. He is an ardent admirer of the noble American drama, for he believes with our most excellent people, that the theatre is the school of virtue. Of course, he thinks Mr. Forrest the greatest actor, sir, that ever lived, by jings!—Among actresses, his preferences are for Maggie Mitchell, whom he does not hesitate to pronounce sweet. When he goes to the theatre, Dick does not appear to be greatly amused, until little Zephyr Frisk comes out in her favorite dance; for be it observed, your true ardent admirer of the drama likes the dancing better than any thing else.

Mr. Dowdy, in literature, has a fondness for the Ledger school. Of course, Sylvanus Cobb is the best writer for that journal; though D. has his private impression of the excellence of Fanny Fern; and Saxe—"Why confound it, sir, I read a most infernal mean thing about Saxe in your paper, the other day. You can't appreciate true poetry! Why next to Emerson Bennett, Saxe is the greatest writer that ever lived. Here is a thing I found in a paper uses you up on that question," and the laudator of Saxe reads us from a dingy little journal, the most sarcastic notice of our late article, in which notice we are severely designated as "young," and otherwise adequately reproached for not liking Mr. Saxe.

We take up our exchanges in self-defence, and after the emission of further indignation, Dick takes the hint and his leave.

Richard is not without a certain dignity of manner, and as he walks down street, he twitches his hat into a majestic angle, and sways his person along the pavement in a very attractive style. He will go buy one of his favorite cigars, and smoke off his agitation. Perhaps, somebody will stand the beer. In which case, he will quite forget the wrongs of his literary favorites.

Poor, coarse, cheap, shabby, shallow, aimless, foolish young fellow! We can moralize about you, Dick, sitting apart in the awfulness of editorial sanctity; and say, that though there is not much about you that is very bad, there is still less that is good. We marvel at you, (having pinned you to a cork for the better convenience of inspection,) and wonder what heaven intended you for. In the celestial wisdom of creation, everything is said to have its use; but yours, we confess, we cannot divine.

Did it ever enter your tobacco-smoke be-clouded mind that you were intended for any specific purpose? a purpose alien in its nature to saying foolish things and thinking them witty; to drinking lager-bier and believing yourself fast; to wearing Jew's clothing, and fancying yourself well-dressed.

Our pity for you is greater than our contempt. You are indeed, a most melancholy study, Dick; and you sadden one. A human being, popularly believed to have a soul, living a from-day-to-day life, whose objects are all so mean, whose enjoyments are so base; whose present is so blank, whose future is so hopeless! Alas for you! whom nature has made so dull, that you even mistake your existence for a true living. To your soul, has never come any thought of the beautiful, the lofty, the good! You are hopelessly shut out from all gentle joys, all quiet sweetness drawn from books, all communion of God's beautiful creation, all the sun-crowned summits on which others stand, commanding wide prospects of pure and worthy happiness!

Thus musing, poor Dick, we almost forget that you are Dowdy; we forget that you are this moment in the "Retreat," making a night of it with those other first-rate fellows, and clapping on the table with your dirty cards and crying, "More 'logger,' here, Katrine!"

Ah! poor Dick Dowdy!

[*Ohio State Journal*, 6 December 1858]

Hot

Happy the man whose vocation it is in these days to drive an ice wagon. Though the ardent sun blaze pitilessly upon the glaring street, and melt the dust till it runs liquid from the white-hot hooves and wheels, and the pavements glow with intolerable fervor, and the houses look out through the languid trees, with half shut, sleepy windows—yet the ice-man, in the shelter of his covered wagon, breathes an atmosphere not merely tempered by dreams of winter, but the actual presence of that blessed season. We dare do anything in our present desperation and we stop not at comparing the ice man, under all the circumstances, to the cool core of that incredible custard that the Chinese bake, which being properly prepared, is thrown into the oven, and comes out done, with a heart of ice in a breast of fire.

Happy the ice man, we say. Happy even the milk man. Happy all men who have to do with pumps or water, in any guise, so that it be cold. Happy that cool, radishy German who stands behind the counter, in a little galaxy of parti-colored decanters, and mixes the iceful lemonade, the soothing and beneficent cobbler, the odorous, life-giving julep, with its garland of leaves, crowning depths of joy, and its crystal spire of slender tube. Happiness, to hear all day the murmur of pleasant liquids, the gush of the drink dashed from glass to glass, and the faint, bell-like clinking of the ice-particles against the tumbler-sides!

Miserable those who peck the blinding stones with iron beaks, in the unspeakable desolation of the full sunshine. Miserable all who shingle houses, who paint signs, who broil at furnaces, who sit on boards and sew heavy cloth.—Miserable all cooks, all bakers, all persons in the soap factory and tallow chandlery line.

Miserable who ride abroad on cleaving saddle seats, in open buggies, in crowded carriages, in dusty cars.

Happy those who lounge beneath trees, and have books, but do not read. Happy who sit in inmost rooms with darkened windows, and doze in lazy reveries, on sofas not hard nor soft; who abide in the far depths of cavernous shops, amid groves of "thinnest lawn," and airy muslin; who in unfathomable groceries, regale their souls with cool damp smells of spice, suggestive of ocean-embraced isles, where the people bathe perpetually in

—"dark purple spheres of seas,"

and only come out occasionally for a lunch of bread fruit, and a bite of cold roast missionary.

So float the vague thoughts through the drowsy brain. Dreams of inexpressible bliss, visions of unutterable horror, haunts us forever, and the sun rises, and flames up the east, and burns upon the brow of noon, and sinks, and the night comes close and sweltering, with a handful of stars drowning in the warm blue—like another Cleopatra dissolving jewels in her cup, for the coming day to drink.

People meeting each other in their involuntary walks abroad, and at their places of business, say to each other, "It is hot," and without waiting for an answer, languish away, and go and perspire in secret. All vests, thicker than gossamer are thrown aside; collars and cravats stand open, and

"The fruit of Adam ripens in the air,"

on all masculine throats. Coats are thin, and hats, and pantaloons. Yet these things cling to the frame as

"The dead leaf clings to the mouldy wall,"

in proportion as they are fragile, and if hoops were a possibility, and not a treasonous desertion of principle, many grave citizens would be tempted to adopt them.

Du sublime au ridicule il n'y a qu'un pas. We have endeavoured to make this an earnest treatise, and here we are about to fall into levity.

But a breeze comes in at the window, and we recover ourselves in time. Look how that aspen over there,

"Shakes all its loosened silver in the sun."

Cool, eh? Not at all. The wind that moves it is hot as the breath of a furnace.

Across the way, a few horses are tied in the sun, which, if not soon removed, will be fit subjects for hippophagy. (Don't try it, dear reader, if it is any trouble, *we* can't pronounce it.) In the shade of the awnings lie several dogs that carry their tongues a great way out of their mouths, and are occasionally interested in phlebotomy. (A pun. We may as well explain the jokes as we go along.) Now and then a languid shop-man comes to the door, but presently retires as if disgusted with the aspect of things. An express wagon rattles by—a buggy, a wagon, a carriage—the watering cart—that beneficent one-horse shower, scattering its cheap diamonds.

The sun blazes more fiercely against the walls, the dust turns whiter and whiter, the pavements glow with a triple heat. The smoke from the black smith shop in the alley, where they are playing the Anvil Chorus, comes athwart our window. The Chorus grows fainter and fainter. The smoke thickens. It hides the street, the dogs, the stores. There is nothing but milk-white space. The Chorus dies away, the wheels and horses feet are muffled, the—

"What!"

"Copy."

"O, here!"

[*Ohio State Journal,* 29 June 1859]

[Already Howells was developing the ability to take his work with him, a fortunate talent for a man who, in spite of his great gift of years, would rarely have a room he could call a study. Unlike some of his more romantically inclined contemporaries, he knew better than to wait for inspiration and the perfect hour. Art might descend on gilded wings, but craft was earned through effort and practice. Even visits to the folks at Jefferson during these Columbus years provided the wonderful opportunity of leisure, and that, in turn, a time to write and to shape his varied impressions into the comprehending form of an essay.

Among the earliest of Howells's published writings had been "Letters from a Village" in the *Ohio Farmer* in 1854, and for years afterwards rural scenes and village life, common enough American subjects, were frequently the focus of his occasional pieces. Undoubtedly the "village virus" is as old as villages themselves, or at least as old as that moment when one village grew large enough so its inhabitants were able to make their more rustic neighbors feel somehow inferior, provincial. But in middle-western life, the disease has been especially severe—as is evident in the many Main Streets on Middle Borders that make up its literary geography—and among its earliest victims was Howells. But he did not suffer alone. In June 1857, Edmund Babb of the Cincinnati *Gazette*, realizing the smug pleasure the paragraphs would give the readers of his newspaper, cut out a passage from a private letter that Howells had written to him and published it as an item in the columns of the Cincinnati paper.

INVITATION TO THE COUNTRY—As this is the season when denizens of the city are sighing for the green fields of the country, and many are seeking localities in which to rusticate, the following invitation from an occasional correspondent, who resides in a village in northern Ohio, will be read with interest from its truthful picture of country village life:

"If you have any rusticating to do this summer, why not come and see us? We would be cordially glad to have you do so. It would kill you here in a day or two, but you would be intensely rustic as long as you held out. There are about three hundred people in town, half of whom are fools, the rest would take great interest in finding out all about you. Then you would not be troubled by noises in the streets, our main avenues being thickly coated with a most vigorous turf. You could have the advantage of one mail a day, and you could be as entirely uncomfortable and *ennuyé* as at Niagara or a watering place."

"I escape from the chronic stupidity of village life by reading. Just now, I am fitting myself to be peculiarly useless in the world by studying Greek."

Now in 1859, Howells again returned to this wonderfully commonplace theme and made from it two attractive essays. The first was written for William Henry Smith's *Odd-Fellows' Casket and Review*, a monthly magazine Howells's Cincinnati friend had bravely begun in November 1858. The other was a series of letters he sent to the *Ohio State Journal* from Jefferson during his rustication there in June 1859. In both, one sees young Howells grasping to find whatever poetry the poor, real life of a country village might possess. His discovery at this time was an ironic nothing, much after the fashion of his treasured Heine.]

A Summer Sunday in a Country Village
as Experienced by an Ennuyé

C'est Sunday.—*French Play.*

"*Toujours, jamais! Jamais, toujours!*" says the clock upon the mantel, in that solemn monotone of warning that clocks of a somewhat gloomy and meditative mind, are so fond of using. If the clock has not a very large audience to preach to on the flight of time, it has at least an intelligent and appreciative one, (I hope I am not plagiarizing from your notice of the last lecture,) for I am its sole hearer. It is the hour of four in the afternoon, and the "folks" are gone to meeting, which according to the sensible custom of the place, is deferred in hot weather till the cooling off of the day. In brief, I and the clock, and a very loud and shrill cricket, are the only people about.

For the clock and the cricket, they have ticked and chirped with admirable diligence the whole day long; for myself, I have nothing so complimentary to say. Sundays are a burden heavy to be borne, in the country, and I do not set up for a very patient person. Therefore I am chiefly employed in wishing that it were Monday, which employment I vary by reading, and eating so large a dinner as to utterly unfit myself for supper.

One from another, Sundays do not differ here, from young June till doting September. When I wake in the morning, I know that it is the Sunday light streams in at my bed-room window by its seeming to be white-hot. For the sunshine of each day of the week is unlike that of the other in quality and complexion, as it lies upon my bed-room floor, unbroken by shadow of shutter, or tracery of waving creeper. Your Monday morning sunshine is of a golden, rich hue, full of the promise of a pleasant week, and rather glows than glistens. Tuesday is known by a light yet more fierce and heated, and it seems to wax sultrier day by day, till by Sunday it is white and deadly hot. A fly buzzes back and forth, dull in the shade and silver in the sun; and half a dozen flies creep slowly and silently along the ceiling, on which the imaginative eye can trace in the lines of the cracked plastering, a reliable map of the great State of Ohio. My clothes are strewn about the floor in picturesque disorder, and the chair at my bed-side is occupied by a candlestick, to the socket of which my scant taper burned last night, leaving me in utter darkness, and the midst of a thrillingly interesting chapter. In one corner is my washstand, and thereon a basin and water jar whose quaint shape and fantastically painted oriental scenery, have more than once assisted me to a proper understanding of the Nile Notes of an Howadji; as the study of the antique in classic architecture and sculpture, (as well as the "old pots and kettles" of the Kentuckian traveler's indignation,) assists the ignorant of Greek to a fair appreciation of the sublimity of Æschylus, and the correctness of Sophocles.*

In these modest appointments of my room, as I open my eyes at the unreasonable hour of nine, I behold Sunday hinted no less un-

*Schlegel.

mistakably than in the glare of the sunshine upon the floor. The fly *volant*, makes a hum-drum, drowsy sound with his wings, as if he were buzzing a sermon, and the flies *perrepent*, move lothly, as if they were going to church. My Egyptian pitcher looks half ashamed of its heathenish palms, and mosques, and seems to insist at least on an Hebraic cast of spout. Even the candlestick, where the guilty witness of my forbidden practice of reading in bed, expired at midnight, darts a brazen glance of hypocritical reproach at me; while the several fragments of my attire, as if to resent my contempt which familiarity might have bred in me, or to prevent its exhibition on this day, at any rate, severely address me in the mute language of their cloth, saying: "It is Sunday. Get up, sir—it is Sunday."

The shadows of dreamland, dissipated by the laconic sternness of this announcement, fly from me; and I become fully awake to an awful sense of Sunday. I dare not fall back upon my pillow, as I do of a week day, to muse upon the transitory visions of sleep, or anticipate the probable pains and pleasures of the day. Though I have had the most wonderful adventures by sea and land, with people whom I have known in the world of men, and the world of books; yet I may not pause to take up the threads that subtly connected these adventures; neither speculate upon that strange condition of the sleep-enchanted mind, to which nothing marvellous is marvellous. Truly, it is Sunday; and I must forth from its dismal presence in my room, at least.

When I have breakfasted, however, and stand on our little front stoop, in clean linen and lustrous leather, I find a consciousness of it to hang no less heavily upon me than before. The fragrance of the honeysuckle at the gable of our home is blown to me by a light wind, that has come frolicking over an hundred miles of summer lake, and twenty miles of summer land; toying with the billowy grass and grain, as it did with the rippling waters; and singing to our threshold trees the same song that it sang to the ships.

Yet for all this idle wind may do, Sunday pervades all nature. The birds do not seem to sing gaily as on the mornings of other days. The robin only pipes at long intervals, as he gluts himself in the cherry tree; the wren chirps not from the sleeve of the old coat where his nest is built; the meadow larks sing but as they rise to fly from stump to stump, and do not sit upon the boughs of the meadow elms, pouring forth sweet, wild lays in streams and gushes of song as their wont is; and even that arch rogue and hypocrite, the bob-o-link, pretends to a sanctimonious silence; which, I am gratified to observe, he is obliged to rebuke himself for breaking now and then, by stopping short in the middle of a thoughtless strain. It is Sunday in the fields, where the yellow wheat undulates in the wind, and the bearded heads nod heavily and bow themselves as if smitten with sudden contrition; where the glittering leaves of the maize shine like the arms of a puritan army marching to conventicle; where the stubble of the newly mown grass preaches a mournful homily on the vanity of life, and hints the sharper scythe and grimmer mower that lays low the ranks of mankind. It is Sunday on the roads that stretch into the country, whence arises the columned dust with the coming of heavy waggons full of heavy souls to the churches. It is Sunday in the long village street, where no urchin sports in the burning dust; and it is Sunday among the village people, none of whom are to be seen, except some sinner like myself, who speculates on the probability of his getting through the day, or goes manfully about the business, newspaper in hand.

Presently the stillness is broken by the clangor of the church bells, calling, warning, appealing; and now, one by one, and family after family, the villagers come forth, in the cumbrous splendor of Sunday dress, and seek that sanctuary to which inclination or habit leads them, for they are not a devout people, and have no religious prejudices. There are but two churches in the place, and private feuds and public discussions have so evilly wrought among their members, that there are not left enough of both to make one small congregation. Not the less, however, is the formality of separate worship kept up by the few remaining faithful, who unite only in lamenting their weakness and the decay of the Lord's work among them. Two starving pastors lead these lean flocks by diverging paths, into the same desert, wide from the fields where they both might feed under the care of a single shepherd; and pipe dismally apart, while the wolves devour their sheep. Year by year, the lambs have disappeared, either lured by the gambols of the goats seen afar off, or removed by death, and now only the feeble fathers and mothers of the flock remain, old, weary, and broken by their wanderings through the desolate places.

As the villagers approach the churches, they find the country people, who for the most part compose their congregations, already there. Heavy wagons and carriages, which possess all the qualities of ugliness and discomfort, are ranged around the sacred edifice, with the day's dust upon their curtains, and the year's mud upon their wheels, while the horses are sheltered beneath the long sheds at the end of the yards, or hitched to the trees and fences, where they stand with half shut eyes and faltering underlips, and vainly flap the flies with ineffectual tails.

I know very well how it seems now inside the church, where Elder Brown is to hold forth. Rows of red faced women sit on one side of the aisle, and rows of red faced men on the other. These fan themselves, some with fans, some with books, and some, O, wretched shift! with folded handkerchiefs, that make no motion of

226

the air, and beat flabbily against the face. Those study the testaments which the Sunday School children have left, and the inscriptions upon the pew backs: inscriptions oftener savoring of an errant mind in the writer than of a devotional spirit. For it may there be seen asserted in haggard capitals, all the Ls and Rs fronting the wrong way, that "She is a sweet one," and in another place, that "Julia Smith is smitten with,"—some one whose name can not be deciphered. Sometimes, these inscriptions are little better than blasphemous, as "O, Lord, what a long sermon!" and "Hurry up that prayer, Elder."

The interval between the coming of the people and the rising of the minister is one of painful stillness and suspense. For interminable moments they regard with fitful impatience the top of the Elder's bald head, dimly visible above the pulpit; from which they are distracted by the arrival of a young lady who has come late, and who walks up the aisle with a little mincing step that makes her silks rustle, and sets all the tremolants upon her bonnet aquiver, and sinks down upon the cushions, just as the Elder gives out the hymn. Being pretty, and fashionably dressed, she excited so much angry and envious attention, that it is hard for the congregation to estrange their thoughts from her sufficiently to pay heed to the psalm, but they all rise and go through the graceful ceremony of turning their backs to the preacher and their faces to the choir. After the psalm is the prayer, and then the sermon. But why should these be more to me than to any deacon who sleeps through them? The services are at last concluded with a benediction which the Elder's forcible delivery converts into a defiant admonition, and the overheated throng quit the church. Slowly the heavy wagons and carriages rumble away, and the villagers hurry from the noonday garishness of the streets into the cool twilight of their shady yards, and take final refuge in their dim "best-rooms"—sacred to Sunday and company!

Sauntering home, with a desperate resolution not to quit the precincts of the limited family possessions for the rest of the day, I await with fearful appetite the hour of dinner. Another day, I would take my chair, and planting it in the shade of our sun-impervious maples, read Lope, nor weary of following the wonderful fortunes of his dramatic heroes. Or with Irving, or quaint and marvellous Perez de Hyta, I might lose myself in the fountain-cooled chambers of the Alhambra, or wander along the "silver windings of the Xenil," beneath "arboles agradables." Or with Tennyson or Longfellow, I could pass the time most pleasantly, or even sleep it away over Tupper. But "C'est Sunday!" and with the habit of doing nothing upon that day, I am driven to the miserable resource of doing it, the wretched prey of the conflicting emotions of hunger and ennui.

Dinner! of hot beans, hot bread, hot tea, hot potatoes! *"Por mis pecados,"* I am ready to cry with the ever-sinning, ever-sorrowing *Lazarillo de Tormes.* These are very good things, but they don't cool one off at all. Was it this for which I longed? O, take me hence to some boundless lake of lemonade, dotted with fairy isles of ice-cream!

Slowly the hours of the afternoon wear away, and almost breathlessly. But as the sun drops down the burning west, a breeze rising up from the great inland sea on the north, gives consistence and shape to little fleecy clouds floating along the occidental horizon, and the old day makes his bed in crimson and gold. How glow the lofty hangings of his couch, showing their purple linings, and where tossed aside, giving glorious glimpses of the land beyond where the great sunset city is, whose towers and roofs and walls shine faintly and mockingly.

With the coolness and tranquility of the twilight, the languid pulse of life quickens, and we cluster about on the porch, congratulating ourselves on having survived, and talking about our neighbors and discussing such other themes, as interest villagers, till the full, round moon floats up the east, *"wie ein leichter Nachen in dem wiederschein des abendroths."*

[*Odd-Fellows' Casket and Review*, April 1859]

In the Country

I

Es is lieber nichts zu schreiben, als nicht zu schreiben.—Gœthe.
Translation (for the Vulgar Unlearned)—It is better to write naught than to write not.

HOME, JEFFERSON, Sunday Evening.
When one comes to the country, one naturally expects to make a moral Nebuchadnezzar of oneself; and I had planned I don't-now-know-what rural engagements to be crowded into one week of holy-days. I should walk forth in the morning perfectly reckless of the fact that the Northern mail was in; express papers should vex me not; books to be noticed might remain with unperused prefaces and title pages; but I would be perfectly emancipated from writing any article on any subject whatever.

I suppose you all remember Dr. Johnson's sonorous allegory of "Sigismund, King of Ethiopia," the deluded potentate who proposed to live ten happy days; and you remember, too, doubtless, the melancholy result of all his experiments in the art of felicity. He failed because contentment is not an art, and will not be achieved by idle people. It is a sad mistake to think you are at ease when you

228

are idle. You are most content when you are busiest. Those early agriculturists, who made the interdicted experiment in vegetable diet, which revealed to them the fact that their clothing was rather light, even for summer wear—deserve the everlasting gratitude of a numerous family of great-grand children. Felicity lies in being employed, and in thinking of what you could do if you had nothing to do. (Now, I suppose there are numbers of young men and women who do not believe this at all.) This is peculiarly true of one used to perform the same duties every day. I think, therefore, the most wretched creature in existence must be an old horse which has turned a bark mill a long time, and is at last turned "loas in the deestrick." "One gets set to one's work, and cannot do without it." This may be a mental deformity. If you are used to go bowed, it is not pleasant to stand erect, though it may be elegant to do so. Leisure may be a fine thing for people who know how to be lazy— but for myself—No, thank you, really, I had rather not. It is such a fearfully long while from breakfast to bed-time. Let no body put more faith in the sincerity of the present moralist than may be helped. He is really indolent, and enjoys *far niente*, well enough, but he thinks it best to preach the contrary. Cakes and ale do not hurt him, but some people may abuse them. Therefore—total abstinence.

I left Columbus, on Friday, exulting in the thought of quitting the city's dust and heat, and reveling in anticipations of long rambles in the butter-cup *dorados,* and cheese-bearing meadows (*casifera*) of old Ashtabula. For certain, I left the heat with you. As we flew northward, the cold lake air struck chiller and chiller upon us, and by the time we stepped out of the cars in the Cleveland depot, the weather was decidedly and uncomfortably cold. The afternoon sun lay white and thin upon the rough surface of water, that, dirty green near shore, showed a bar of blue further out, melting into gold at the horizon. A frown of ragged clouds hung low over the lake, and the sail of a solitary ship was sinking out of sight. The scene was so dispiriting, that I went and bought something to eat.

From our railroad station I rode home in the hack, between long stretches of sunset meadows. One bit of landscape was delicious— though rather chilly—a visual ice-cream, if one may so speak. The sun dropping behind an open piece of woods, struck bright across rolling meadows, and poured gold and crimson upon their emerald, and illuminated the dark green of the forest beyond. All the mean details of the landscape were transfigured. The uncouth farms were enchanted into something beautiful; barns and dairy houses threw back a blinding light, and farm house windows
"Burned like one burning flame together."
A flock of sheep pastured on a rising ground, added picturesquely

to the scene; and a bob-o-link came and lighted near the road, and sang to us as we passed. If I had been an artist, I can't say what I should have done. Not being an artist, I remarked, in an excited manner, that it was glorious, which nobody disputed.

It continued gloomy all day yesterday, until late afternoon, when the clouds broke away, and it cleared up, (like Miss Sally Manchester after a cry,) cold and breezy. With the fall of night, the wind fell, and the frost. People who had gardens covered their tomatoes and other plants with boxes, pots, papers, and every other material and utensil which could be pressed into the service, and went to bed with apprehensions which the event proved to be only too well founded. This morning, the frost was thick and white on everything, and fruit and vegetables almost totally destroyed. Potatoes and corn are cut down like human beings; and the whole face of verdure looks as if it had been served up for greens. Water was frozen in the pools, and the plants, which people had tried to protect, were destroyed as utterly as those fully exposed. Wild grape vines are blighted, and even the leaves of forest trees are nipped. One gentleman told us that he went out after nightfall to see to his garden, but he broke off a plantain leaf, and found it frozen stiff. He desisted, and "let nature take her course," which I am bound to say, was a most unnatural one. If your peaches and apples are killed, look for none from the Reserve. Farmers will be glad if their wheat, even, has escaped destruction.

The robin is singing his vesper in our elms, and the twilight swallows are flitting. So I have to subscribe myself, yours, before candle-light,

CHISPA.

II

HOME, June 7.

People have not nearly done talking about the calamitous frost, yet. In the country we are frugal of topics; and when we get a good thing we keep it, keep it—as some unknown person was directed to do in some song, of which I have forgotten everything else. When we meet each other we inquire, in a thrilling voice, if *all* the things have been killed; and receiving for an answer, "Nearly all," we branch off, and look at the great collective injury in its individual aspects. We talk of the tomatoes, and their cruel fate; how they were cut down in the flush of a most promising youth; we lament cabbage plants and potatoes; we bemoan us for our snuffed-out hopes of apples, and peaches, and cherries and plums, and grapes; and with bated breath, we speculate upon the probable injury to wheat. Then we look at the thing in a financial light, and conclude that should the war in Europe make flour very dear, and should we have no fruit or vegetables, people will have great ado to live. From this, we turn to the religious aspect of the matter, and wonder whether it was a Providence? And if it was a Providence, what sin are we to repent of? Reminiscent remarks follow, as how, in 1845, a frost came on the 11th of June, "chilling and killing" the wheat, and cutting down the grass as close as if by the teeth of Ball and Aultman's mower. (This is not an advertisement.) Finally, we summon our philosophy, and dismiss the subject with grievous reluctance.

Is it not really a lamentable thing? Even the wild berries, raspberries and black berries, are killed, and the prospect for pies is utterly blighted. It is a fact worth remembering, that plants sheltered beneath earthen ware of any kind, were killed, while those protected by wooden boxes, or several thicknesses of paper, passed through the frosty ordeal with comparative safety.

I think I will take back part of the virtuous things I said on the difficulty of doing nothing. I find it a great deal easier than writing nothing, for these letters which I compel myself to write, that I may not lose the art altogether, are become rather hard to get up, already. Addison is said to have written a paper on Nothing, and a certain preacher once pronounced a discourse before Frederick the Great, upon the same inspiring theme. But I confess that I never read the ingenious essayist's performance, and the divine's sermon only differs from some other preachments, in that it was *of* nothing, and they *are* nothing. (This is not spoken of the minister of *your* church, excellent Sectarian, beloved Christian reader. "I know my duty better," as the old Castilian beautifully and affectingly remarks in the play of Pizarro, in the representation of which so much infant histrionic talent is annually employed.) So, these instances establish hardly a precedent, and afford me no model. I do not deny that the thing can be done. I have been in the newspaper line too long to be guilty of such folly. Travelers (those reliable people) tell us that polite Chinamen keep up a conversation for an hour at a time, without imparting to each other a solitary idea. But, indeed, the Chinese do not much excel some people among us in this regard. The fact therefore may be considered established, that we can very readily talk and say nothing; and I have pretty nearly argued myself into the belief that one can write and say nothing too. And, indeed, why not? We are so frightfully unreal, as Mrs. Skewton justly observes. Unreality is next to nothing. Therefore we are almost nothing. A sect of German philosophers prove to you that you neither feel, see, taste, nor hear, and Shakspeare says,

"We live on such stuff
As dreams are made of, and our little life
Is rounded with a sleep."

Or, if you like it better, "Our lives are rounded into a little heap," as I once heard a distinguished artist very seriously quote the sentiment, in his most thrilling chest-tones.

One of the most amusing things I ever read, is a little comedy by Cervantes, called "*Los Dos Habledoros*, or the Two Talkers," in which the principal and finally triumphant talker is a Don Vagamundo, a character such as is to be found only in Spanish literature of the sixteenth century. A gentleman is afflicted with a talking wife, (not an uncommon disorder in any country, if we are to believe Brutes and Wretches,) and falling in with this decayed cavalier, and discovering his wonderful capacity for conversation, he procures him to come and out-talk his wife. He does so; the lady swoons out of sheer weariness and despite; but recovers perfectly cured of talking. The ingenious method in which Don Vagamundo skips from topic to topic, and unites them in the most absurd relations, is only equaled by the dexterity of honest Sancho in stringing proverbs. I confess that my recollection of this play has been of service to me in the composition of the present epistle, and that I owe Don Vagamundo a debt of gratitude, which I will repay in that other life, when we are to meet all the pleasant people that ever lived in books as well as in flesh. Why not? The thing is eminently reasonable to me, and—but I will leave off convincing you, "till a more convenient season," as somebody has observed.

I really meant to have said something about birds, and flowers "and things," but this letter is overgrown, already.

III

BIRDS AND THINGS

HOME, June 8.

I notice that the bobolink is become very common in the meadows, here, where a few years since he was not to be heard at all. Bryant's poetic celebration of him, seems to have enlarged his sphere, and made him ambitious to see

"—New faces, other climes,"

for I remember that it was about the time that pretty poem appeared that I first observed him in these fields.

The bobolink is a droll bird, and like most of great musical geniuses, full of eccentricities. He has a fashion of dashing suddenly out of the grass, joying for an instant in the bland wind and sun, and then sinking upon the slenderest stalk he can find, and while it rocks to and fro with him, pouring his heart out in the most enchanting strains. A peculiarity which Holmes humorously describes, in his charming poem of "Astræa."

232

"The crack brained bobolink courts his crazy mate,
Poised on a bulrush *tipsy* with his weight."

I think it is opera-music Bobolink sings—he is so dramatic withal.
Another feathered eccentric is the little brown wren—a most
pugnacious and determined creature—building her nest in the most
exposed positions, and maintaining it there with the resolution and
pertinacity of a lady defending her opinion. Last year, our household wren nested in the sleeve of an old coat which hung outside
of the shed; but this year she is more pretentious, and has built in
an empty oyster keg put up in a tree for the accommodation of
bluebirds. Her husband makes rare music whenever he has occasion
to approach the family possessions, and our locust tree tenants are
objects of great favor and solicitude.

There is no lower form of life so full of beauty and attractions
as the birds; and the charm which ornithology has had for natural-
ists, is easy to be understood. Religion has clothed the sublimest
things with the bird-attribute of wings, and poetry has gifted all its
loveliest creations with the power to fly. It would be a curious thing
to discover to us how many of our commonest ideas and expressions
are related to the songs and flights of birds, and doubtless the result
would astonish. However, I do not propose to do it, nor to take up
the study of ornithology extensively; but hereafter to devote myself
with renewed energy to the noble avocation of clipping news and
chronicling events of the day.

Should "any young man, out of employment," however, desire
"to engage in light and honorable occupation, requiring but little
capital," I respectfully recommend ornithology.

(I suppose some people will think this is easy writing because it
may be very hard to read, but I can assure them of their mistake.)

"To him who in the love of nature holds communion with her
visible forms, she speaks a various language."—*So Bryant.*

Yesterday morning I had a very pleasant chat with the venerable
lady. Taking my way across meadows, golden with butter cups, to
a well known haunt by the side of a stream that bounds through
the little valley in the spring, and dries up in the summer, I held a
very pleasant pic nic under an elm that overhung the water. We
were a very select party, consisting of myself and a small basket,
and though we had not brought anything to eat, there were wild
strawberries on the hill-side to be had for the picking, and we were
quite gay. I used to come to this place geologizing, last fall, and
made a most astounding collection of curious rocks, which after
occupying all the spare space in the library for a week, were finally
thrown away at nocturnal cats. I remember sketching certain remarkable strata, exposed in the bank, with tree above and water
below, quite natural and easy to be told apart, I thought at the time,

though I dare say a nice artistic taste would have carped at the work. To the best of my recollection the sketch was pre-Rafael-itic in character, for I don't think anything else of the kind has been done since that master.

Now, however, I was quite recovered from my geologic attack, and more inclined to study (in the easiest possible attitude) the formation of the clouds overhead, than the rocks underfoot. One very readily acquires habits of luxury. I had been only a few days doing nothing, and I was already become a connoisseur in the matter. It *was* very pleasant incumbent *sub tegmine*, to watch the slow and stately clouds float through the bluest sky, so white and thick, it seemed they must be palpable to the touch, then to drop the eyes to the meadows, and see the long grass blown silvery in the wind; to hear the laugh and whispers of the stream mingling with the *susurrus* of the leaves above; and to think—for O, I am but human, and have my touches of selfishness, that somebody else was making up the "News and Humors," and wading through that ocean of exchanges, in the *Journal* office.

Why not? All our happiness is enjoyable only as we compare it with the infelicity of others. Around the winter fire, we hug ourselves the closer, when we think of some one without, facing that blinding storm of snow.—Dives likes his money because he has it, and Lazarus has none. Do you suppose that Uxorious does not delight more keenly in his wedded bliss, when after you have been spending the evening with him, he sees you to the door, and mentally compares the dismal boarding-house room you are going to, and the cosy little parlor he has just stepped out of?

"We are ashes and dust,"

as Mr. Tennyson has remarked in Maud, and there is so much of those unpleasant substances in the better part of our nature, even, that we may sometimes well doubt.

However, this is moralizing, and I see very plainly (though everybody else may not) that I shall be led into a theological discussion, which would be disagreeable to all parties. So, here an end.

[Signed "Chispa," *Ohio State Journal*, 9, 10, and 11 June 1859]

CHAPTER SIX

The Matter of Dulldale

There had been the ranging of the woods in autumn for chestnuts and in the spring for wintergreen; there had been the sleigh-rides to the other villages and the neighboring farms where there was young life waiting to welcome us through the drifting snows; there had been the dances at the taverns and the parties at the girls' houses with the games and the frolics, and the going home each with the chosen one at midnight and the long lingering at the gate; there had been the moonlight walks; there had been the debating societies and the spelling-matches; there had been the days of the County Fair and the Fourths-of-July, and the Christmases rehabilitated from Dickens; and there had been the impassioned interest of the easily guessed anonymous letters of St. Valentine's day. But these things had passed, and with a certain disappointment suffered and yet prized there had come the sense of spent witchery and a spell out-worn, and I chose to revolt from it all and to pine for a wider world and prouder pleasures.

—Years of My Youth (1916)

[Among the unfulfilled ambitions of Howells's long literary career was a work of fiction which would treat with frankness and fidelity the "village motives and village realities" (*YMY*, p. 109) that he had known during his early years in Ohio. But this proved a task beyond his command. Though "distance in time and space," he believed, eventually set "in a truer and kinder light" (*YMY*, p. 91) the village life he had early wearied of, Howells was never able to transform fully the memory of his lost Midwestern world, its shapes and scenes, into the forms of fiction. In the end even he seemed aware of the cause of his failure, aware of that profound am-bivalence village life and values represented in his imagination. The point of view his public well-being insisted upon was too idyllic; that nostalgic longing for veracity of conduct and stability of being which comes in time to belong to every generation was in Howells's instance largely of one piece with his sense of antebellum Ohio. Though neither a Golden Age nor an unsullied Eden, the years of his youth nevertheless became hal-

235

lowed and protected by the disappointment that was his price for success. Increasingly, he came to idealize the Ohio village as "the place of social and economic equality," in the words of one commentator, "of sweet brotherhood, of literary and intellectual stimulation, of rural simplicity, of warm, quiet, sleepy stillness." The vision was pretty enough; but it was also lacking in all human interest and complexity, offering at best scenes for pleasant genre pictures, not the materials for the kind of fiction Howells spent his lifetime defending. As we have come finally to see, Howells was not one to avoid stern reality—those unsmiling aspects of common, ordinary American life—even when his perspective revealed truths alien to his hopes and expectations, but he was never able in his maturity to focus directly and sustainedly in his fiction on the village life he had known as a youth. Instead, when it is encountered in his fiction, as it frequently is, the Midwestern village is a point of origin, the important foreground for so many of his characters—Basil March, Kitty Ellison, Shelley Ray, the Dryfooses—who, like their creator, have left their sweet Auburns in search of their fortunes and identities.

But in his earliest fiction, not surprisingly, Howells wrote almost exclusively about the world of Midwestern villages and towns, a place he suggestively called Dulldale. Long before the revolt from the village became a commonplace theme in American letters, Howells was there exploring the field for whatever fictional possibilities it possessed, and though this is apprentice work, it is remarkably successful and satisfying in its muted way. Fifteen years later, safe in the editor's chair of the *Atlantic Monthly*, Howells expressed his admiration for Edward Eggleston in the courage he displayed in using his native Midwest as the setting of his stories: "Mr. Eggleston considered the vast fields of fiction lying untouched in the region of his birth and the home of his early manhood, and for his plots, scenes, and characters, he acted on Mr. Greeley's famous advice, and went West." But Howells did not follow the Indiana writer's example, at least not until the very end of his career, and Kitty Ellison's life back home in Erie Creek remained unwritten, probably even unimagined. Rather than following the fate of the young heroine of *A Chance Acquaintance* (1873), who had so won the hearts of his readers, Howells turned his gaze instead to Europe and the progress of another provincial heroine, Miss Florida Vervain of Providence, Rhode Island.

We shall, doubtless, continue to regret that, after having come to know the world better than he did during these final years of his youth, Howells never returned in his fiction to the village of Dulldale and its environs. But for years following his escape to Italy in 1861 the memory of "the meanness and hollowness of that wretched little village-life" he had known in Jefferson haunted him to the point of abject dread (*SL*, 1:76). No doubt it was his own feelings he later attributed to Ford in *The Undiscovered Country* (1880), whose "hatred of the narrow and importunate conditions of the village life" which he had known in youth made him so much "an impassioned cockney" that he refused to leave the city even during the dog days of summer. Dreading the slender prospects fate seemed to offer, Howells wrote to his father from Venice shortly before he was scheduled to return to the United States in 1864: "I have not yet in three years shaken off my old morbid horror of going back to live in a place where I have been so wretched. If you did not live in J[efferson]. and my dear Johnny did not lie buried there, I never should enter the town again. It cannot change so much but I shall always hate it" (*SL*, 1:197). But with the perspective rendered by time and success—and with these gains, the guarantee of his place in the great world—these negative feelings figured less and less in Howells's recollections. By then, the memory of those young lovers about whose innocent ordeals he had written so fondly a generation or so before—Arabella and Charles; Arthur, Fanny, and the victorious Job Green; Clementine and young Clumsie; Angelina and Edwin—must indeed have made Dulldale sometimes appear a happy place to have lived.]

The Valentine

She said that she did not believe she would get any.

We have therefore no doubt that she meant just what she said; for if there is any one thing certain in this wretched world of incertitude, it is that young ladies always say just what they mean. This is a fact which has been noted by all observers, and is founded on a principle of the female mind, perfectly known to every philosopher. If any ill-advised person disputes it, we refer him to the young ladies themselves.

It is barely possible that in the most sacred secrecy of her own heart, the gentle Arabella cherished a little trembling hope that she would get a Valentine; for if there is anything certain in this world, it is that young ladies do not say all that they mean; which, we conceive, does not in the least conflict with the great truth we have just put forth.

Arabella, we say, may have had some such hope, but assuredly none with reference to the Charles of her untold affections. It is true that in the morning she had confidentially charged Jimmy to put in the post-office a delicate billet addressed to Charles; and had corrupted her brother to silence with a bribe of silver. It is true that she had spent the most of Sunday night (we lament to relate this fact, but a regard for the verity of history demands the sacrifice,) in writing some verses, which she burned, and that finally she had

237

quoted from Tennyson one line, of such tenderness and significance, that Charles, if he had any sentiment in his soul, must be charmed with it, and must have some idea that it came from her. These things are true, but any person of ordinary discernment must see that they formed no ground for the belief that Charles would reply.

Arabella sat at her window and looked out upon the street. It was rather a dismal spectacle. There was really nobody out. To be sure there were plenty of people out; but they were none of Arabella's acquaintance. The snow was fast melting from the middle street; but it still lay in dirty patches on the gutter-slopes, and encrusted the south side pave with treacherous ice. Arabella, sitting pensive and expectant in the solitude of her room, smiled to see the droll little dances the people performed in order to keep their feet. The boys had smoothed the ice with their abominable sleds till it was absolutely quite dreadful to walk upon. Young ladies were peculiar sufferers, having to manage their silks and preserve their balance at the same time; which it was hard to do; and old gentlemen, austere members of anti-saltant churches, waltzed about in the most unseemly and undignified way. But Arabella never did more than smile faintly, till a plump, pompous middle-aged person, in attempting the passage in a manner to combine skill and elegance, unfortunately lost his footing, flung his arms about him "with wild rejection," jostled the reproachless hat from his head, and then came down instantaneously, and all over, with his shawl spread out like the wings of a giantly bat. It was then that the gentle Arabella broke into a silver shriek of laughter, that was repeated till her ringlets were quite out of curl.

But was Arabella happy? Ah! no. The one thought haunted her. She had dismissed it certainly, but it came again, this impertinent thought. She did not believe she would get any, but yet—that—is—if it might be—Charles. So she trembled with charming trepidation at every step on the stair, thinking it was Jimmy with a valentine. We blush to record this fact, having perhaps led the reader to suppose that this young lady had no expectation of the kind.—The truth is she hardly confessed it to herself, and it was only through that mysterious power that people have who write stories that we found it out, even so late as this.

At last Jimmy came, and knocking, thrust in his head, and with a look of the profoundest importance and a wink of unspeakable astuteness, gave her a letter.

"Then fled she to her inmost bower,
And there"

broke the seal of the daintiest envelope that ever wrapt a perfumed soul of gilt-note.

"Pshaw!" cried the gentle Arabella, with a very prononcé stamp of the high-heeled infinitesimal shoe; "it's from that goose of a"— Who?

We regard the feelings of the unfortunate young person. We spare him. He is wretched enough.

The afternoon wore wearily away. The slippery pave attracted not, neither did the antics of the involuntary dancers delight. The poor young lady put one of her fingers in her mouth, and actually bit the nail. She refused supper with a melancholy air of the most poignant sadness, and remained at her window till the shadows fell upon the street. Then she was startled by another knock at the door. It was Jimmy again, with a second letter. She snatched it wildly from the astonished youth who inserted the hands of surprise in his pockets, and whistled the sibilation of bewilderment.

Ah! this time it was from Charles. The dear, *dear* fellow had written in some passionate verses of his own—

But why need any one know? It is merely the affair of Charles and Arabella. Mrs. Grundy would frown, if she knew what was in that Valentine; all the Misses Grundy would lift their hands in virtuous abhorrence. But we protest that it is none of their business, neither ours, gentle and patient reader. We do not believe in those novelists, poets and play-writers who impertinently follow their hero and heroine to the very threshold of wedded life, feasting an unnatural curiosity on all those tender and enrapturing scenes which they would have us believe take place when Peter swears to Susan that he would die for her, and Susan assures Peter that dissolution for his sake, would be preferable to any other luxury.

Were we of a different thinking, we might, perhaps, reveal what occurred when Arabella went down that evening, and found Charles in the parlor, waiting for her. But no, we inexorably shut the door between them and the world, and put our back against it.

[*Ohio State Journal*, 16 February 1859]

NOT A LOVE STORY

I

Arthur yawned.

He had been lounging on the porch for half an hour, hanging upon the slender railing, and twirling a bit of honey-suckle between his fingers; slowly sauntering back and forth, and picking at his hatband; impulsively sitting down beside Fanny, (who had a pretext of sewing in her hands) and impulsively getting up again.

The languor of a dry July morning was in his veins. Not even the presence of Fanny could inspirit him; nor a recent breakfast make him sentimental—one is always more sentimental immediately after meals than at any other time.

"What, sir!" cries Fanny. "A yawn! I declare I'll box your ears."

I have been told that there is always something peculiarly pleasant to a lover in this menace, when coming from the young person adored. I have had it from one of experience that there is not the least cause for uneasiness at it; that he never esteemed the threat as any expression of displeasure, but only as a coy fashion of letting him know that he was worth while to be provoked with (*provoked*, in a feminine sense;) that on the occasion of its first use towards him, he resisted an idiotic desire to go down upon one leg of his trowsers, and falter in an absurd ecstasy, "Box them, darling, and make them ring with heavenly music for ever."

At any rate, Arthur was not at all dismayed. Calm, indolent and impassive, and calmer, more indolent and impassive that morning than ever, the threat tickled his vanity into a smile of defiance and purpose. Think of *purpose* at such a time! The dusty road bleached dead-white; the meadows close shorn and the air above them quivering with heat. The corn-fields unmoved by any breath of wind, and even the leaves mute upon the trees. A few "light clouds smouldering," in a sky from which blazed intolerable light.

But the little porch on the west side of the house was always a cool place. Perhaps that was the reason why Arthur had the energy, when Fanny turned upon him with bright indignant eyes, and lifted the hands of chastisement, to seize them both in one quick grasp, and (such is the depravity of our fallen nature,) kiss her twice on pouting lips.

I have a theory that novelists find the caresses enjoyed by their heroes, nearly as pleasant as those themselves receive. There must be a vast deal of gratification in writing—"She twined her lovely arms about his neck, and pressed her burning lips upon his brow;" or, "Springing from his steed, he strained her to his bosom, and, etc;" or, "With one furtive kiss, snatched from her unconscious lips, he, and so forth, and so forth." The old monks, whom cloister life shut out from all knowledge of the rapturous passion, composed the most melting tales of love,—seeming to find in the ecstatic contemplation of the happiness they created for others, a compensation and a solace for that they were never to experience. To have their heroes blest, was nearly as good as being blest themselves.

"E—e—e—e! O, you wretch! O, O,—dear!" screams Fanny, and runs off to her room, where she laughs being pleased, and cries being vexed; and then laughs and cries together, being both pleased and vexed. Finally, she bathed her face, smoothed her hair, and went down into the parlor.

Arthur was not there.

II

"So the old fellow's sold out, and gone West, has he? Illinoy, hey?" demands Arthur's uncle.

"Yes," says Fanny's mother, "bag and baggage." This worthy person is fat and fifty, with a red face, and an expression of countenance like a picture in *Punch*. She wears spectacles, and has a wart on one side of her nose.

Fanny looks like her father, now dead, who was some years younger than her mother. If you want to know what kind of a life *he* led, ask any of the neighbors.

"And young Green," pursued Arthur's uncle, to whom all the things he ought to have thought of before, are just beginning to occur, now when his guests are so soon to leave him. Which is the way with some people. "What about *young* Green?"

"Dead," says Fanny's mother in an abstraction of new potatoes and peas.

"Dead? The devil. You don't say so? what of?"

"Consumption. They say," remarks Fanny's mother, poising a prodigious quantity of vegetables, upon her fork, "that he was disappointed. Mrs. Biggs, I'll thank you for them molasses."

"Hullo!" cries Arthur's uncle, turning his apoplectic neck so as to bring his eyes to bear upon his nephew, and then bestowing a fat wink of intense cunning and sagacity on that young person. "Look out my boy." And to make his meaning yet more apparent, he punches his great head in the direction of Fanny. "Dead, is he? Lord bless me."

Fanny, from under drooping lids, steals a glance at Arthur, in which theft her mother detects her. Arthur is eating new potatoes, and seems not at all concerned in the fate of the ill-starred young Green, as why should he?

"The unfeeling wretch!" cries little Fanny to herself, and then mentally rebukes herself, and excuses him with a thousand sufficient excuses.

"Well, there was his cousin. He comes into his property, don't he? He was a stupid fellow, though, a perfect block-head."

"Job's very much changed sence you knowed him," says Fanny's mother. "He's quite the gentleman. But Fanny ken tell you more about him then I ken."

"O ho!" cries Arthur's uncle.

Fanny "wanned and shook."

Arthur took some more new potatoes.

III

They were walking together in the garden; and temptation has haunted gardens ever since Eden. The leaves of the bushes were

gray with heavy dew, and all the flowers were wrapped in a fragrant sleep. Heaven was blue, and soft and near, stars—
"Few, large, and bright,"
hung lovingly about the moon, whose full orb showed a broad silvery expanse, with a faint tracery of rock and mountain.

A little wind from the river, woke the leaves upon the elms, and set them whispering in gossiping undertone about the rose's flirtation with the peony.

"See," said a shriveled old leaf, which an insect sting in early bud-hood had made prematurely dry and shrill in tone, "see, how she leans upon him. If he kisses her, I shall faint," continued this virtuous leaf, yet watching for the shameful consummation with intense eagerness.

"Hush—sh—sh!" said another, "he is whispering to her."

"I wonder," said a young leaf upon a bough that, drooping earthward, and swayed in the wind, almost touched a tall and slender hollyhock, "I wonder," said this gay young leaf with a tender look at the nearest hollyhock, "if he is saying, 'I love you!'"

Was it really the rose and the peony?

Arthur's younger brother, whom Fanny has invited to accompany them, was yawning sleepily.

"Go back and get my veil, wont you, Charley?"

Kind-hearted girl! She knew that as soon as Charley got into the house he would crawl to bed; and took this delicate method to let him know that he might do so without offence.

"What a beautiful night!" she said to Arthur.

"Yes, beautiful, indeed!" said he to Fanny.

"What is it somebody says about twinkling stars and 'hour of night?'"

"You are so indefinite, I can't guess. A good many poets have made observations to that effect. But it is dangerous to quote poetry upon certain occasions," continued Arthur, sliding a treacherous arm around her, and taking her hand in his.

"You are going to be rude again, are you, sir?" faintly demands Fanny. It is notable that she makes no effort to displace the arm or release her hand. "I haven't forgiven your conduct of this morning," she whispers, bending dewy eyes upon him.

"Then I'll have to fight the valiant Job Green, who will be sure to challenge me," cries Arthur with a sneering laugh.

"Sir!"

"Do I offend again? Farewell, then, my chance of being invited to your nuptials, when Job will probably cut his best cheese, and I'm so fond of cheese, too!"

I do not give these expressions as being severely sarcastic, though Arthur intended them as such. *I* think they were merely clumsy.

"If you wish to insult me, sir"—

"By heaven! I intended no insult. The grocery business is highly respectable, and Mr. Green"—

"O, Arthur, how can you torture me?" falters a broken little voice, from lips that hide themselves upon his shoulder. "I hate that great goose of a Job, who *will* come to see me,—and mother worries my life out about him."

"Do you hate him?" cries Arthur, and it is a fact that he was by no means shocked to hear that the gentle Fanny cherished this un-christian sentiment towards Mr. Green. "O Fanny! how I have wronged you, forgive me, my darling, and believe that I always, always"—

A wild shriek, the greeting of the down train to Blank Station, tore the silence of the night.

"Fransus, Fransus J-a-n-e!" screams Fanny's mother from the house; "come here at oncet, or you will be too late for the cars. Hurray, can't you?"

And Fanny ran.

L'ENVOI

Did Fanny marry him? Certainly not. She married Mr. Green, who kept store. If you go to Dulldale, you can see her. She is grown fat, and slaps her children when they are bad.

And Arthur? Arthur has a taste for geology—a fine cabinet of specimens—quartz, felzpar, stalactites, *etcetera*.

[*Odd-Fellows' Casket and Review*, February 1859]

[Concluding each issue of the *Odd-Fellows' Casket* was an editorial miscellany titled "Our Monthly Gossip." Here Howells's next piece for the Cincinnati periodical appeared in April 1859, preceded by these introductory remarks and a letter purported to have been written by Howells.

And we very readily and naturally make the transition from Spring to the ladies; not that we can talk as intelligently of the latter—but partly because it is the province of man to talk of them. We have been endeavoring to master their vocabulary, but so far with but meager success. There is one phrase, which from its varied use by them, has greatly puzzled and vexed us. Finally, after having heard it applied to us in several different senses, by as many different individuals of the other sex, we rushed to the room of a philosophic friend, and laid the case before him. He quietly said he would investigate it; how well he has performed his duty, may be determined from the following:—

"Dear Gossiper:—I have investigated the question you propounded to me, with the following results. I embrace them for the sake of perspicuity in the form of a dissertation.
                                                                    Yours, &c."]

A PERFECT GOOSE

I do not apply the epithet, I do not attempt to define its use. I hereby give the observations of an impertinent, though ingenious person, who has been at the pains to note several instances of its employment; and has attempted to attach some fixed meaning to it. I need hardly say, that this attempt has been a failure. The phrase is purely feminine, and if there is any trait in the female mind more prominent than a certain logical sequence of ideas and words, it is a beautiful versatility in the appreciation of the phrase. With women, my friend insists, it is significant not only of every passion of the soul, but of many nice shades of emotion. It may be said to range in meaning, from "darling" to "wretch," though this explicative again, is not so clear as could be wished, because of the uncertainty attending the use of these terms of endearment.

Charles and Arabella have one of those dreadful disputes, which now and then darken the sky of their happy wedded life. What is the expression in which the quelle Arabelle vents her anger, just as the storm is about to burst in tears? "Now Charles, don't be a perfect goose." The sprightly imagination figures the flashing eye, the curled lip, the pink nose, with which these words are spoken. You can very well guess what unkindness have led to them; but the prudent spectator declines to be a witness of what follows. If Charles is a sensible fellow, he immediately throws down his paper, and yields to the wishes of his Arabella of his bosom, which of course are reasonable and just. If he is not a sensible fellow, he prefers defeat after the battle is fought. "Don't be a perfect goose!" means a challenge of tongues, in such a case as this, and the Charles is a very great goose indeed, who accepts it.

Clementine and young Clumsie are dancing "Les Lanceurs" together. Clumsie is quite *spirited*, (the poor fellow thinks) in his remarks, and the dignified Clementine rewards his efforts with inapplausive smiles. Unluckily when they come to that figure where you make such profound obeisance, poor Clumsie is trying to make a joke, while his whole soul is absorbed in admiration of Clementine's bewitching curls. He doesn't see where he is putting those "horrid great feet" of his, and when Clementine resumes a perpendicular, there is a prodigious tearing of silk. Clementine receives the apologies, with sublime blandness, and dances out the figure, with one hand holding up her robe. In the dressing room her sister finds her, and inquires with sororal solicitude, "Who tore your dress, Clem?" "Why, that perfect goose of a Clumsie." Ill-starred Clumsie! Do you know that Clementine is lost to you forever? "Perfect goose," means renunciation, rage, wounded vanity, contempt. Chat away, poor youth, as you promenade with Flirtilla, and be as dead-lively as you may. There is one pinning up her dress, would like to make a pin cushion out of your whole stupid person.

When the lovely Clara, and the enamored Frederick, by one of those miraculous chances, which can never be accounted for, in the deep window recess, vis-a-vis, it is two to one they take to looking out upon the tranquil stars, which unconscious planets have always been interesting to young people in their state of mind. Slowly Frederick withdraws his gaze, and fixes it upon the charming creature at his side. The charming creature returns his gaze. It is very embarrassing, and he pretends to admire a ring upon her finger. He takes the finger, and pleads for the ring. It is not denied, and he presses it rapturously to his lips! "O, Fred, what a perfect goose you are!" Which speech, delivered with a melting look of the dark eyes, sends such a thrill through the poor fellow, as causes him to quake from head to foot with foolish delight, and to approach a condition of mental infirmity, greatly resembling that of the bird of which he has been given the name. Does "perfect goose" mean here, reproach or contempt? Far from it. Duck, darling, delightful man, angelic young gentleman. This is the meaning. It signifies that if such a thing were at all possible or proper, she would not struggle violently against a transfer of that eloquent lipservice to her own pouting mouth. *N'est ce pas, mes demoiselles?*

If any young lady has been anticipated by another young lady, in the matter of a bonnet, a spring silk, in what terms does she announce her determination not to wear anything of the same style? On referring to my friend's note-book, I find that he has written down *verbatim*, a reply which he received: "Why, I did intend to get something like it, but that perfect goose of a Julia Tompkins,"—tableaux.

A person of the *belle case*, is being teased by another of the female persuasion, about such or such a gentleman. She probably giggles a delighted disclaimer, and pronounces that Henrietta is a "perfect goose;" which means, "keep teasing me, that's a good dear, do."

In effect, as my friend declares, a perfect goose means anything or everything, as the case may be. There is much in the circumstances, and much in the tone to decide its signification. To be a perfect goose, is perfect happiness, wretchedness, or any intermediate state. If you have done anything absurd or puppyish, O good young gentleman, and should hear yourself called a "perfect goose," beware! On the contrary, if you have really sparkled, (and I am bound to say you are not often brilliant,) take the smiling "perfect goose," of your interlocutress, as a compliment of the greatest worth, for it has probably been uttered in a moment of unregarded sincerity, when the lady means just the opposite of what she said.

These are, of course, merely the speculations of the masculine brain, in regard to this feminine phrase. They may therefore be all wrong. For the gentle beings, after all, are a very jolly bit of slyness, and doubtless have a profounder meaning than man can fathom, when they declare that any one is A Perfect Goose.

CHISPA.

[Another contribution by Howells to "Our Monthly Gossip" in the *Odd-Fellows' Casket* in May 1859 was introduced with this editorial reference to the heroine of William Allen Butler's popular satire, "Nothing to Wear" (1857):

Ah! well, the world of full of foplings and Flora McFlimseys; and we think that the picture given of two fair creatures—ornamental appendages of society—by "Chispa," is truer to nature (as we now find it,) than many good people believe. Here, as our friend has drawn it, is the picture of the . . .]

ROMANCE OF THE CROSSING

They had not spoken for—days.

It is known how terrible are the quarrels of lovers; how easy are two fond hearts to be estranged; and how hard to be reconciled. People in love are always the most reasonable creatures in the world. They demand nothing of each other, in which there is not the most beautiful propriety. Never impatient, never annoyed, never disturbed, absurdities of every kind are foreign to them; and their conduct is marked by a placidity and rationality entirely charming. I know that some philosophers have held the contrary of this; but I do not account their opinions of any worth.

The quarrel of Edwin and Angelina was about a ribbon. In the esteem of a world wise in its own conceit, the color of a ribbon may seem a trifling matter; but upon occasion it may be a very serious one.

Angelina was showing her new bonnet to Edwin.

"Isn't it a love?"

"It would be a *lover*, if it could know how much beauty it crowned," said the gallant Edwin.

The philosophers for whom I have indicated my contempt, would say that the weakness of this pun was evidence of Edwin's enfeebled condition.

"But don't you think that blue trimming would become you better?"

"Blue? Pooh! Edwin, how foolish you are. It would make me look a perfect ghost."

"But—"

"Now, don't be a bear."

"Why, you don't know what I wanted to say."

"Yes I do."

"But—"

"Now, there again!"

"Do listen to me, Angelina."

"I won't. You're cross, when I wanted you to be pleased."

"You are unreasonable."

"I am not."

"I don't think—"

"No, you never do."

"Why, you are sarcastic?"

And so on. It is well known how amiable conversations of this sort end. I think the present one concluded in the statement that Edwin was a wretch; with accompaniment of tears.

The broad street swam with mud, and the crossing was broken and perilous. Many wheels and feet bringing their contribution of mud, had almost hidden the stones from sight, and people were obliged to poise themselves as daintily in the passage as the souls of the faithful, who walk into heaven on a bridge no wider than the edge of a sabre.

Edwin stood at one end of the crossing, and a lady at the other. Her face was obscured by one of the black vails of the period, and even had the unhappy Edwin lifted his gaze he had scarcely recognized his Angelina.

He, however, no less absorbed in deep thought than intent upon preserving unblemished the splendor of his boots, stepped from stone to stone, his brow abased, and his looks downcast.

There are many kinds of blacked boots, between which the cunning eye readily discriminates. There is quite as much difference in the mellow radiance of the gentleman's boots and the vulgar gloss of the boot of the fast man, as there is between the wearers themselves. The hotel-blacked boot betrays itself by a negligence and inequality of polish, and the boarding-house blacked boot by a miserable starveling air as to paste, which is part of the boarding-house system. I know that my position is a bold one, but I unhesitatingly assert that the only truly blacked boot is that which has received a loving lustre from the affectionate hand of its owner.

Edwin had that day blacked his boots, and was now come forth to lose his thoughts, if it might be, in the thronged streets.

He had been thinking of the cruel scene between himself and the beautiful, obstinate Angelina, and his heart had been torn with anguish. Frequently while dashing the glowing brush along the delicate uppers of those boots, had he paused to wipe the tear of secret woe, or sniff the sniff of unavailing regret.

247

All night long his dreams had been of her, she filling his sleep with horrid visions of bonnets trimmed with objectionable ribbon.

For Angelina, she too knew little of peace. Her dear little temper had been marvelously acidulated, and in a moment of extreme sentimental depression she had boxed the ears of a young and tender brother.

And now, fate was bringing these separated beings together again. Should it be to part in coldness and haughty scorn, or to meet with forgiving and sunny smiles?

When Edwin at length lifted his eyes, he found himself face to face with a young and beautiful lady. They had encountered each other like strange ships on that sea of muddy life (I think this a tint of Alexander Smith,) borne together by the breadth of inscrutable fortune.

The keen glance of misery and love penetrated even the black vail.

"Angelina!" exclaimed Edwin in a thrilling whisper.

Angelina made no response. She made a motion, as to pass him, and Edwin, with rage and mortification saw that he must step aside, and blemish those boots!

For an instant he hesitated. He was but human. The angry lover struggled with the gentleman, but the struggle was only an instant long. The gentleman triumphed. He deliberately planted one foot in the mud.

Angelina noted the sacrificial act, and her hard little heart was melted. Her eyes filled with generous tears, and before Edwin had time to pass her, she had whispered "*Dear* Edwin!"

Oh! happy young people!

The blest Edwin smiled intelligence; and when he called upon Angelina that very evening, did she tell him with tears and eloquent looks, how his grandeur of soul had prevailed over her resentment?

I think so. But, who knows?

CHISPA.

[Encouraged by the warm, personal reception he had enjoyed in New England and New York during his visit there in the summer of 1860 and by his success in placing his work in magazines and journals, Howells eagerly sacrificed his Columbus socialities before his overwhelming literary ambitions upon returning from the eastern pilgrimage. But his enthusiasm soon waned following that inevitable change of luck, and he found himself measuring his time and sacrifices by a succession of rejection notes. To his youthful dismay, his artistic aloofness was made all the more terrible and lonely by the neglect of those hostesses whose invitations and parlors he had earlier shunned.

Chief among those unwanted or aborted compositions which occupied his talents was a story of village life which he had begun sometime before and which James T. Fields, upon hearing it described by Howells in Boston the previous August, had encouraged him to finish. The most ambitious portrayal of the world of Dulldale he was ever to attempt, the novella was completed in the early spring of 1861. But to Howells's great disappointment he failed ever to find a publisher willing to hazard support. According to the author's own memory of the events, the story was rejected by Fields when he found its first chapter published as an independent sketch, titled "The Dream," in the *Knickerbocker Magazine* in August 1861 (*LFA*, p. 71). Some years before, Howells had sent the story to the New York magazine where, unknown to him, it had been tossed into a barrel of accepted contributions. Forgetting or discounting this earlier attempt at publication, he had, at Fields's suggestion, taken the sketch and continued the story from it. But the *Atlantic* editor's dissatisfaction with the finished story appears not to have been based on its partial publication in another journal. While that would have been sufficient reason for refusal, a letter from James R. Osgood, Fields's assistant, to Howells on 27 July 1861, in which he mentions the firm's having only then noticed the story's appearance in the August issue of the *Knickerbocker*, alludes to an earlier letter, now missing, concerning the story's refusal. Undoubtedly Howells permitted his memory—in that unwitting way the ego compels one to do—to preserve ever after those hopes his youth had suffered.

Later, shortly after the sketch's appearance in the New York magazine, Charles Godfrey Leland related to Howells how he, upon his accession to the editorship of the *Knickerbocker* early in 1861, had discovered Howells's contribution among the backlog left him by his predecessors. Though the years were past when it had been essential for youthful writers to cultivate the *Knickerbocker* as a sure introduction to the American reading public, the journal still, even in these years of final decline, held a lingering authority that it had enjoyed in literary matters during the years following its founding in 1832. Lewis Gaylord Clark, editor (together with his brother) of the monthly for nearly the whole of its existence, had encouraged contributions from the West, and probably it was he who had put aside Howells's sketch for future use. Leland, eager for copy that might redeem his magazine's fortunes and happy to encourage younger, relatively unknown talents (who would also not prove so demanding in the matter of prompt payment), had shown himself in both his works and editorial comments even more sympathetic than Clark to those same impulses and literary ends that motivated Howells's youthful heart, and it is not surprising that he should have retrieved Howells's "Dulldale" sketch from the editorial barrel. Known primarily as the author of "Hans Breitmann's Party," an Irvingesque bit of dialect humor in verse published in 1857, and as the first important translator of Heinrich Heine's work, Leland was in the habit of advising those who would write for him to avoid imitating the sentimental and allegorical romances of old. What he wanted instead were "novels absolutely, perfectly, and vividly true to daguerreotype-like studies of life," stories and sketches that would depict in a kindly light the customary, the American common, the life of ordinary days and men.

While "Geoffrey: A Study of American Life" is no worse than most other first attempts by genuinely talented writers, it suffers from the faults common to all apprentice work, and it is probably fortunate for Howells's career that its publication should have been delayed until now. Just as with another "first novel," *A Modern Romeo* by Percy Bysshe Shelley Ray in Howells's *The World of Chance*, the story doubtlessly seemed to its author "fresh and new, in spite of its simple-hearted, unconscious imitations of the style and plot of other stories": "He was always polishing it; he had written it several times over, and at every moment he got he reconstructed sentences in it, and tried to bring the style up to his ideal of style," something, he imagined, a little between the style of Thackeray and the style of Hawthorne.

Like Ray, Howells's understanding of the problems of fiction at this time was influenced primarily by his reading of Hawthorne and Thackeray, and, to a lesser extent, by the examples of Charles Reade, Charles Dickens, Edward Bulwer-Lytton, and (perhaps surprisingly to the modern perspective) Oliver Wendell Holmes. The "psychological" or "subjective" novel was then the new wave in fiction, and these the acknowledged masters. Evert Duyckinck was one of the first to call attention to this type of fiction, at least in its American manifestation, when in 1850 he described Hawthorne's *Scarlet Letter* as "a psychological romance, . . . a study of character, in which the human heart is anatomized carefully, elaborately and with striking poetic and dramatic power." In a similar fashion, a decade later, Thackeray's *Virginians* was praised by a writer in the *Christian Examiner* for its "faithfulness of the revelation of interior life," an evaluation Howells shared. And though he later remembered Charles Reade as a transitional figure, "a man who stood at the parting of the ways between realism and romanticism, . . . content to use the materials of realism and produce the effect of romanticism," in the heyday of his popularity it was Reade's "rare insight into human motives" that drew most critics' praise (*MLP*, pp. 144–45).

In short, during the years of Howells's coming of literary age, romance, plot, catastrophe gave place in the serious writing of fiction to "the study, analysis, and development, of the passions, motives, and impulses" of character. As a critic writing in the *North American Review* in October 1857 observed: "Novel-readers now-a-days are not satisfied with pictures of external and social life, however brilliantly colored they may be, or however various in style. . . . We ask for deeper insight into character, for the features of the mind and heart rather than of the face and figure. . . . The author plays the part of anatomist, and dissects heart, brain, and nerve, to lay them before the reader for examination and analysis." It was its "subjective character" that most distinguished the modern novel, according to George William Curtis in the *Harper's Monthly* two years later, "its constant tendency to explore the secrets of action." Certainly this was Howells's understanding of his own story, and if his imagined readers should fail to realize his intention, he made the matter clear at the end of the twelfth chapter: "but in a subjective story like this, everyone understands that this bit of reasoning was one of the unconscious operations of the brain." And it was this aspect of character development that Howells prized in Dickens's *Great Expectations*, which was appearing serially at the very time Howells was most involved in completing his own tale and which he reviewed in the *Ohio State Journal*; what he wished Dickens's readers most to notice was the British novelist's subtle depiction of "the strange inner world of man's consciousness, about which so little is known":

> The transfer of vague mental impressions to paper—the impressions that really form so great a part of life and thought—has been accomplished with rare success by Holmes, but he deals with them in a scholarly way, and with somehow the air of one that makes interesting discoveries in physiology as a science. But Dickens gives them with an unconsciousness most like their own occurrence to us. . . . It makes you altogether better acquainted with yourself—your instinctive self. It recalls to you innumerable vagaries of the sort, which you have striven vainly to grasp before. It is the magic lens by which your infusorial ideas become visible—formless, as they are, but inhabiting your unconsciousness by myriads (see above, p. 153).

It was to Oliver Wendell Holmes's son, with whom he had struck up a friendship the previous summer, that Howells rather grandly confessed in November 1860 the "frightfully analytical" nature of the story upon which he was hard at work. Recounting in his letter to Holmes a discussion he had had with an artist friend "upon the analytical tendency of the mind—the critical, uncreative nature of modern thought," he repeated for Holmes's sake his belief "that all literature tended to the development of the philosophical speculation, the subjective poem, and the analytical fiction—the fiction as written by Hawthorne, Thackeray and Bulwer, and 'The Autocrat,'" that is, the elder Holmes. And, he added, even by himself, in the story of Geoffrey Winter: "I sometimes think it bears the same relation to a romance, that an accurate print of the human heart would bear to the picture of a soul-illuminated face" (SL, 1:66).

There is no doubt that Howells's story did become too analytical for his abilities and experiences at the time to manage, that he took too much to heart the lessons learned from Hawthorne, Thackeray, Bulwer, and Holmes; but he was convinced that the direction in which he worked was the true way. And the lessons he had learned from them were mostly exercised with care and youthful distinction in his narrative. But the fable of the story was so baldly borrowed from Goethe's Elective Affinities that the American story could not but suffer by comparison. Recalling years later his reading of the German novel in 1859, Howells was convinced that he had failed ever to grasp the work's meaning, and that after thirty-five years he could "remember little or nothing of the story," which at the time he had "tried to find very memorable" (MLP, p. 133). But clearly Howells had found enough in his reading of Goethe's story to satisfy his needs in 1860, just as many other writers before and since have discovered in the same book the inspiration for their early ventures in literature.

But "Geoffrey: A Study of American Life" was no masterpiece, a fact of which young Howells was more than comfortably aware. "In some respects I like it," he confessed in a letter to his sister Victoria in March 1861, "but I encounter so many faults, that I have to struggle continually against impulses of disgust" (SL, 1:76). He would have to console himself, he reasoned, with the money which the book's sale would bring him and the pleasure that financial reward would enable him to give to others. But there was to be no sale. A year after its rejection by Fields, Howells tried the story on the editor of Macmillan's Magazine in London, but that gentleman, or more likely his assistant, kindly declined the favor Howells offered. Whatever further attempts he made to place the novella are unknown. After the return of the manuscript by Macmillan's he may have attempted to strengthen the sixteenth chapter; at least that seems the simplest explanation for its disappearance. Soon his schemes and aspirations turned to other projects, and the story of Geoffrey Winter was lost in the oblivion of a storage warehouse. This failure, along with that a half-dozen years before with "The Independent Candidate" (which was much more public and thoroughly humiliating), deeply discouraged Howells's ambitions in fiction for the time, and for nearly a decade it was as a poet that he preferred showing himself to the literary world. But in afterthought he suspected that, should he ever come across the manuscript of the old story of Dulldale, he should find himself "respecting it for a certain helpless reality in its dealings with the conditions" he knew best

I.

It was broad daylight when Geoffrey awoke. His dream was the merest vagary, and none but an idle man would have given it the thought with which he rose, and pondered upon that vision of his sleep. It was the sudden apparition of his cousin, whom he had loved. She seemed somehow to be breathed forth upon his perception in a tender light, that took her form and features and expression. In his dream, she leaned toward him, her glowing and profound eyes looking unutterable passion and sadness into his own; but when he made a movement as to embrace her, with a quick action she held him away. In his dream, he remembered that her gesture was one which he had often seen young girls use in frolic with each other — a lifting of the arm, electric, peremptory, but always followed by flight or submission. As sometimes happens when one dreams lightly, he commented in his sleep on the naturalness of the event, with a smile that he felt to play upon his lips. Thus, holding him away, his cousin seemed to search his soul with looks of ineffable yearning, and then, as if more from weakness than confidence, fell with a sob upon his heart. That was the end of his dream.

The first page of the manuscript of "Geoffrey: A Study of American Life" (title cut away in original) at the time. And, as with so many of the matters dealing with his past life, in this assessment Howells was not greatly mistaken.]

GEOFFREY: A STUDY OF AMERICAN LIFE

I

It was broad daylight when Geoffrey awoke. His dream was the merest vagary, and none but an idle man would have given it the thought with which he rose, and pondered upon that vision of his sleep. It was the sudden apparition of his cousin, whom he had loved. She seemed somehow to be breathed forth upon his perception in a tender light, that took her form and features and expression. In his dream, she leaned toward him, her glowing and profound eyes looking unutterable passion and sadness into his own; but when he made a movement as to embrace her, with a quick action she held him away. In his dream, he remembered that her gesture was one which he had often seen young girls use in frolic with each other—a lifting of the arm, electric, peremptory, but always followed by flight or submission. As sometimes happens when one dreams lightly, he commented in his sleep on the naturalness of the event, with a smile that he felt to play upon his lips. Thus, holding him away, his cousin seemed to search his soul with looks of ineffable yearning, and then, as if more from weakness than confidence, fell with a sob upon his heart. That was the end of his dream.

The robins were singing in the maples at the threshold, and the martens were gossipping noisily about his window, for it was in an upper chamber, and the house of the martens was set in the sharp angle of the gable above his lattice.

The farmer was mowing the grass in his dooryard, and the long, hoarse sweep of the scythe smote pleasantly upon the ear, and brought at every stroke a sense of purple hay-bloom, pearly with dew, and golden with sun.

It made Geoffrey think of old days; and it was with a tender pain that he glanced about the room, and found it scarcely changed since he had slept there a child. It looked older and narrower; but there was still the geographical outline of the United States suggested in the lines of the cracked plastering; and noting this, he recalled that he had heard, in the first half-conscious drowse of the night before, the ticking of the death-watches in the wainscot, as distinctly as in those dreary nights of boyhood, when the sound filled him with terror and foreboding.

Breakfast was already on the table, when he entered the familiar square-room below, and he recognized with due appreciation, the honor which the farmer's wife had done her guest in setting the meal in that place sacred to ceremonious and formal feasts. Embracing nearly the whole space between the wings of the house, this room opened by doors on every side into parlor, chamber, kitchen and stoop. Here the family sat at night; here the children conned their lessons, and had their games; here the women, in their hours of respite from heavier drudgery, bent over their tasks of sewing. But the square-room in Dulldale was never used for any purpose of eating and drinking, except when the stated hospitality of the house-wife called her neighbors, twice or thrice a year, together over cups of tea, and the other viands, which at such times come forth from multitudinous little pots and jars, long inaccessible on upper shelves of secret presses.

Geoffrey took his place at the table, and while the farmer sat voraciously taciturn, he gossiped and chatted with the wife. She told him who was dead, and who was married, and who was gone west.

He remembered that in his earliest boyhood, this woman had been one of his little playmates, and that he had felt a childish passion for her. It may be that she too remembered this, for she sighed when she glanced from Geoffrey's handsome, gentle face, to the low front and sordid visage of her husband. A dash of querulous asperity tinged her talk, and when the baby put its hand first into the butter, and then laid hold of her dress, she forgot the polite calm of hospitality in the maternal instinct, and shook the baby with violence.

Till now, Geoffrey had not seen Dulldale for seven years.

It is hard to say with what feeling a young man goes back to the home of his boyhood after so long an absence. With his tenderest sentiment for the things of the past, is mingled a half contempt of them. The events of that time are grown mysteriously and indefinably mean, as the distances and houses of the old place are shrunken and dwarfed.

With some sense of all this, the recollection of a play seen long ago, joined itself in Geoffrey's mind. As he passed through the street of the village, so strange and so familiar, he felt like that buskined hero of melodrama, whom he had seen step upon the stage out of the effigy of an inn, far too small for a far less emotional personage— he felt so deeply his resemblance to this character, that he could scarcely resist the absurd impulse to repeat his speech, and to declare in a loud voice: "After an absence of some fifteen years, I am at length r-r-returned to me nyative village!" For the whole scene about him, so oddly diminished, and suggestive rather than representative, was full of illusion and theatrical effect.

The thick-leaved maples that shaded the one long street of the village, were the only things that seemed to have grown greater during Geoffrey's absence. The people whom he encountered in his

255

walk from the farmhouse to the heart of the village (feebly pulsating with the languid life that clung about the door of the post-office and the stores of barter and ready pay,) were all somehow fallen away from a former grandeur. Few remembered him, and this did not grieve him, for he was one to whom greetings, when they represented nothing but acquaintanceship, were always an unspeakable weariness.

I think the consciousness of change in himself flatters the vanity of a young man, however much the appearance of change in others may pain him; and this was another reason why Geoffrey was loath to be known to the villagers, whose recognition would recall to him some part of his former self. He felt that if he spoke to them, he must resume something of the manner with which he had been wont to meet them, lest he should seem affected to the jealous scrutiny.

In this way we are all servile to our mere acquaintance. You subtly feel that the person to whom you are formally made known, expects you to be this or that, and your unconscious effort is to realize this ideal, and you are forever a hypocrite to that person. I mean, only, you of the average, sensitive nature. There is a coarse texture of soul which does not receive the impression of another's expectation, and is therefore rudely insincere. The great man also can be himself in defiance or indifference, or that simplicity which crowns greatness. But as for you and me, dear reader, we must seem whatever the various Mrs. Grundy thinks us.

From a sentiment of that elusive dishonesty, which is so common that I am tempted to applaud it, Geoffrey had constantly refused to acknowledge to himself the reasons of his coming again to Dulldale.

The event which he once believed must desolate his life, had not afterwards seemed so disastrous, for it left behind it none of the picturesqueness of ruin. In those moments of utter unbelief which come to young men, and make the past equally uncertain with the future, the gloomy import which he had attached to that event, seemed the most incredible, the most impossible of all bygone follies. Finding his days so blank and commonplace, he laughed to remember the interesting wretchedness which he had intended for them. But this levity was no wiser than his earlier despair had been: it was itself an unrecognized effect of that which it derided.

When the stroke of fate first descended, Geoffrey had thought there could never be sunshine in the world again. Men, not altogether foolish, think such preposterous things with less cause than he. Later, he perceived that it was not eternal night which had obscured the sun. Yet it was with emotion that he received the news of his cousin's marriage.—He read the announcement with a smile, but it was with a sigh of relief that he laid away in a package of her letters, this last writing that came from her hand.

There was sunshine again, but it had more glitter than warmth in it; and Geoffrey Winter knew no second passion. His regret for the past was not poignant; but it imbued with deeper sadness a temperament naturally pensive; and as his thought became more subjective, and dealt in that fashion with events, his pain grew to be an abstraction of melancholy and ennui. It ceased, almost, to relate itself to one cause; and the man waxed vague and languid in his purposes, though he did the work that lay at hand, and remained faithful to the duties that enslave and support us all.

From this apathy, which was like a heavy dream without the comfort of repose, he was at last aroused to a bitter and positive exultation by the death which widowed his cousin. Too gentle or too timid ever to retaliate the pain he had suffered, he exulted in this event as a vengeance of destiny. He pictured her bereavement with a fierce, self-torturing delight, that quickly yielded to compassion and remorse. He would see her once more.—He invented a pretext; and he was now in Dulldale.

It was a day of early summer, and the wind came across the meadows with fragrant whispers of June. The leaves of the maples in gossip overhead, clashed softly and mysteriously together, and deepened the revery into which he lapsed. He went absently along, plucking the heads of the timothy grass that thrust themselves through the pickets of the fences, and he did not know that he had walked so far, when he stood with his hand upon the familiar gate.

He smiled to see so little change. There had been new ladders made for the doorway honeysuckles to clamber upon, and the house had been repainted. That was all. The old fence, grown a trifle more decrepit, remained; the straight and formal flower beds on either side of the brick walk from the gate to the door, were gay with their accustomed blooms; the old housedog that lay coiled and sleeping on the threshold stone, seemed never to have moved in seven years.

In small country places, the ladies are jealous of the few spectacles that the street affords, and economize them by ingenious devices. The ladies of Dulldale sat to sew in those rooms which commanded the best views of the thoroughfare, and made much of every passer, debating his identity, business and good or ill looks.

From the front window where she sat with her work, Geoffrey's aunt peered out over her glasses in shrewd study of the stranger, but failed to recognize him; while the old dog sprang up with an angry defiance, none the less determined and vehement, because it seemed directed rather at abstract evil than any embodied form of the principle—a favorite method with very old watchdogs and moralists. Bounce's mistress came to the door to silence him, and then, scanning the stranger more closely, she knew Geoffrey. She greeted

257

him with awkward warmth, as if the transport of affection into which he had surprised her were something to be ashamed of. It is a form of the puritan rapture, observable at home among the hills of snow and granite, or in degree, half-thawed and softened in the broader sunshine of the West.

Moreover, Geoffrey's aunt was naturally a cold woman. She had loved him with one of those illogical affections which such women conceive; but she had always masked this affection, with her other emotions, under a frigid calm, and had never discovered it so much as now.—He remembered afterwards her unwonted tenderness at this time, and a certain air of reverie in which she seemed lost, and the wistful looks of doubt she cast upon him as he talked in a fashion new to her, and dashed with unfamiliar bitterness. But now, he rather felt than noted these things.

At last, it seemed to occur to her with the visible sense of relief of one who remembers a long-pondered, but troublesome, elusive thing, that he would wish to see his cousin.

"I took you for a peddler at first," she said. "My eyes are so bad. But you have got to be a fine-looking man, and not at all like a peddler—close by."

Geoffrey smiled, remembering the cherished belief of his aunt that the race of peddlers was a faithless and truculent race, not to be trusted, but to be warned away from every threshold with fierce looks, stern speeches and biting dogs—a Pennsylvanian prejudice curiously engrafted upon the stock which has given washing-machines, and clocks and grindstones to a suffering world through generations of peddlers.

"Sit here," she said, "and I will go and tell Clara that you have come."

From some vague motive of hospitality, she had led him from the square-room where they had been talking, into the grim parlor, and left him there as she spoke. She had regained her composure, but now he saw for the first time that she walked infirmly, holding her hand against her heart, and breathing heavily. At the door she turned again with that air of having forgotten something that she would have said, and then passed on without speaking.

How the past rushed back upon him here, like a cold draught, chilling him! Everything was so drearily unchanged, even to the smell of the room—a gloomy, oppressive odor, which seemed to add to the darkness and desolation of the Best Room, and mingled with which in Geoffrey's remembrance, was always an absurd and wandering impression of preserves and pickles, in a closet. On the table that stood beneath the looking-glass, lay the family-bible, and a dismal treatise on theology, hallowed but not read, and near these crouched unrebuked by their reverend company, an impertinent pup-dog in china, with crimson ears, and a very black nose. On the other wall hung the picture of Washington crossing the Delaware, with a print of Andrew Jackson upon the right, and the portrait of Geoffrey's late uncle upon the left hand. Either end of the black mantel-piece was graced with a vase of tomatoes in red and green plaster; and a plaster figure of the infant prophet Samuel prayed between them, while a forest of asparagus-boughs flourished in the fire-place.—Geoffrey's aunt was an old-fashioned woman and retained with obstinacy the tastes she had imbibed in ruder times. She submitted to many changes in the house which the nicer instincts of her daughter suggested, but she at last intrenched herself in the parlor, and successfully defended it against the aggressions of modern ideas.

In certain foolish moments, Geoffrey had thought to surprise and confound his cousin by his superior self-possession. For was it not as much his unconscious desire that she should regret him, as it was his wish to behold her again, that had brought him to Dulldale?—Was not his wounded vanity to triumph in the moment when he should look upon the face that had been so dear and cruel to him. Geoffrey was honest, and commonly indifferent enough to mere effects. But he was also a young man. He had been crossed in love, and his own past and present were to be confronted in the eyes of her whom he had loved.

Some women without having mingled with the great world, have yet a natural grace and certain style that match the unconsciousness of society. Clara, whose mental gifts were slender, had these instincts. When therefore she entered the room, and gave Geoffrey her hand with unaffected kindness, she confused him, and for an instant made him feel very young and boyish as she used to do.—But this was only for an instant. Asserting his maturity somewhat stiffly, he listened to her words as she talked, and eagerly regarded her face.

What was it had come to pass? Clara's motherhood sat most gracefully upon her; the woman was fairer than the girl had been. She was habited in a dress of that color which makes a woman most adorable. She wore black, and played with her child at times in a delicious, tender way that was altogether charming.

But not to Geoffrey, for he felt here how miserable it was to look upon this face which he had once loved in vain, and had now ceased to love through despair.

He thought: "So! it was only this. Why did I want to see her again? My darling, you are not an angel any more. I am a fool, and no longer the hero of a romance."

Clara prattled on. She bade her child go to Geoffrey, and when it would not, she said with a pretty audacity, that Cousin Geoffrey was one of mamma's old flames. "Do you know what *flame* is, darling?" Then kisses, and caresses, and baby-talk.

"Come," she said, and took the little one in her arms, and went and sat beside Geoffrey.—"Isn't she pretty? Do you think she has my eyes?"

Her eyes? They were very lovely eyes, and she turned them full upon his quiet face. His cheek had been wont to flame, if he felt her lightest glance upon it.

They talked of many things, and Clara was decently sad to the memory of her husband. At last, they talked of their old love in an easy, off-hand way, he with the bantering manner he had sacrificed much to acquire, she with a certain nonchalance and spirit natural to her.

Nothing had pleased Geoffrey. His wish to see her again had been soon sated, but the vanity hungry for her regret had remained unappeased. Clara was more beautiful than ever, and did nothing that he could well resent or despise.

Baffled and piqued he arose to go.

How long was he to remain? she asked. And what whim had taken him to pass the night at the Groves', instead of coming to her mother's?

It *was* a whim, Geoffrey said. He could not explain.

Then Clara said, he must come and spend that evening with them, and stay with them as long as he staid in the village.

With the blunt awkwardness of a man in pain, he replied: He went away in the morning—it would not be worth while—he could not—

Now for the first time Clara seemed to realize the existence of another than the old sentiment toward her in Geoffrey—she was so used to have him in love with her. Her manner had been that of cousinly familiarity, but now it changed to sudden coldness, as if his mood had frozen her.

"Good-bye, then," she said curtly, and scarcely offering her hand.

He never could understand why it pleased him to assume the manner she had dropped, and to say:

"What, Clara! Only your hand, and that so grudgingly? I think I can remember when you were kinder."

He took her hand, and drew her toward him. As in his dream, she lifted her arm, and held him away, regarding him with eyes of wistful, passionate doubt. Then her tears came, and she permitted his embrace.

The event seemed so improbable with reference to a moment ago, that he could not trust its reality, even while her heart beat against his, and her lips touched his own.

He heard his own voice saying:
"Good-bye, Clara!"
That was the end of his dream.

II

It did not occur to Geoffrey, until he sat on the farmhouse stoop, with unseeing eyes fixed upon the farmer at his work, that he had forgotten to take leave of his aunt, whose unwonted tenderness and whose infirmity, now that he thought of them, touched and reproached him. In the tumult of that parting with his cousin,—so full of doubt, and pain, and wonder, for the past and for the future—the affection which he cherished for her mother had been lost, as such a sentiment is always lost in the conflicts of passionate emotion. It is a thing so gentle that it cannot breathe in the storm which is the life and strength of passion; nor is there any strong desire of our nature, however vulgar and mean, but such a sentiment shall momentarily yield and shrink before it.

With some such thought drifting idly through his brain (for the thoughts of young men are mere infusorial ideas, little different from dreams,) and settling into an intent to see his aunt again, and say farewell to her, Geoffrey put aside his remorse and fell back for consolation upon that narcotic melancholy, which was at once his bane and solace.

The robins sang their lilting songs in the maples. The farmer tossed his dooryard hay into fragrant winrows. Through the open door of the kitchen came the odor of supper. It is true, alas! that a pensive habit of thought does not always undermine the appetite, and even the disillusioned must eat. Geoffrey awaited the summons to this meal with the faintest impatience, and he glanced, now and then, from where he sat through the open door. Within, he could see the farmer's wife duskily bending over the stove, her meagre face flushed with the effulgence of the bright wood-coals; and the simple and even rude scene touched one of the sacredest memories of his heart. It is not the great spectacles of life which are so full of suggestion, but the recurrence of some little incident of our dear younger days that lies buried far down under the splendid rubbish of our since-fallen castles. As now Geoffrey saw this good woman wearily, silently toiling, as it is the custom of farmer's wives to work—dignifying no drudgery with hope, lightening no labor with song—he remembered his own mother in her later widowhood, and seemed to himself to be again a child, sitting upon some block of wood in one of the dark corners, while she made ready the supper.—He felt almost conscious of the presence of the grave and silent boy, who rested his chin upon his hand, and stared with wide eyes into the fire, breaking his reverie, now and then, to ask some marvellous question, or to announce some prodigious occurrence at school. Then all this passed, and the boy stood by moonlight in the next room, where suddenly the mother lay dead, resting rigidly forever from her toil; and he was weeping.

"Supper is ready, Geoffrey," said the farmer's wife.

It is the custom in many of the western farmhouses to go to bed like the fowls, when it is dark, and on few nights of summer are the candles lighted. But to-night the supper was late, and Mrs. Grove had placed upon the table a malignant dipped-candle, which sputtered and seemed to rage that an honest custom should be dishonored in it. As soon, however, as the meal was ended, and the table furniture put away, the candle was extinguished, to its apparent great content, and in an hour the farmer and his wife were asleep.

The full moon, broad and calm, stood half way up the eastern sky, and all the quiet village lay sleeping in its light. The circle of woodland that closed about the town had that air of self-communion which distant trees have by night, and which in isolated pasture-land elms seems almost intelligence. The flat, unpicturesque meadows sloped away from Dulldale on every hand. Here and there along the white road stood a farmhouse, with the gloom of orchard and garden about it; here and there a patch of ploughed land showed brown in the light; here and there the charred, gaunt trees of a lopping lifted themselves above the black logs and trunks that lay like giants, slain and half consumed in their encounter with the lightnings. Through all the fields straggled the rail fences, and everywhere were scattered stumps, some partly hidden by compassionate brambles that concealed their mutilation, and all tenderly veiled with little clouds of mist that hung sadly upon the breast of the meadows.

The village, with its green-shuttered white houses—each flanked by a garden and embowered in trees—was outwardly at peace with itself, when Geoffrey passed out of the farmer's gate, and strolled along with unconscious steps that bore him again towards Clara.

I have said Geoffrey was idle. He was also somewhat vain, and events had not hardened a nature pensive and tender, and fond of its own sorrows. But if he had been cast of the braver metal that shapes a man for action and triumph, yet retreating hither for a moment's breathing from the strife, I think he must now have reverted to the past with the softness to which all men give way at times when alone.

For my part, I discover veins of sentiment and folly in places where I would never have looked for them, and in the experience of every one I meet, I find more romance than in all the romances. People hide their secret in many ways, but somewhere it lurks: here, behind this laugh that mocks itself and all things; in the smile glittering and cold as the sun upon the snow; in yonder knit brow and pondering abstraction. The judge hums in the court an old love-tune. But why should the lawyers smile, except it wakes an old love-tune in their own hearts?—Ah madam! you who are openly sentimental, will acknowledge the truth of all this, and will believe me when I tell you there is as much desolation of this kind in the world as one could wish. When I reflect upon the numbers of portly, elderly persons who are secretly victims to heartsickness, I am pained, but I am justified, and go on to speak of Geoffrey and his luckless passion without embarrassment.

Walking alone in that still place, with the silence broken only by his own footfalls, it seemed to him that all the air about him was haunted, and that upon the right hand and the left, the phantoms of the past were stalking. He remembered when he had trodden that path lost in the vain and blissful dreams of foolish love, thinking how he should say to her those words that leaped forever from his heart, and languished forever upon his lips; how she should listen, and reward his constancy and great passion with her love; how they should stand in that little church together; how on such June evenings as that had been she should linger for him at the doorway of that house, which never was built but out of air up in the clouds; how they should enter at it together, and her winning words and ways should endear and dignify all the things of home; how sometime—for the dreams of youth are forward and fond—when Love

"Became outward breathing type,"

she should sit with his child at her breast, singing it to sleep, and lifting ever and anon her gentle mother-eyes from the babe to its father.

Geoffrey was not master of the fiend's art of self-mockery, or surely now he must have laughed. He only sighed heavily and paused in his walk.

He stood beneath his cousin's window. Within he heard her in speech with her mother. Then he saw the light flare through the transom of the hall. Steps ascended the stairs, and the light appeared in his cousin's chamber. The child's voice called, and Clara's tones, low and soothing, replied, hushing it, and a soft monotony, as of prayer, followed that. While he yet lingered and listened, she began in her clear, thrilling voice to sing, as if she were singing to the child. It was an old, sad air, and she sang some words that he had made for it long ago—words rhyming of luckless love, such as inexperience fondly mocks the future with.

The old dog growled angrily from the door-step and began to bark.

The singing ceased within, and Geoffrey's cousin looked from the window, and then softly closed it.

Geoffrey resumed his walk, and returned to the farmhouse.

It was raining evenly and lightly, with a dreamy sibilance, when he was awakened next morning by voices in dispute. They came from below, and going down, he found the farmer and his wife at breakfast. There was another yet at table: a little girl, with blue eyes and pale yellow hair, who was young or old, as you judged by her timid childlike manner, or her wise, strange face. There were strength and will in the lips, but the cheeks were wan, and the eyes shrank away from other eyes, as if they shrank from a blow. The girl was meanly dressed in a gown of no particular fashion, except that it was an old fashion.

It appeared that she was a half sister of the farmer, and that her name was Jane. She had come to Dulldale, Mrs. Grove told Geoffrey, to go out sewing.

Her half-brother said bluntly, he was afraid she wouldn't find much to do. Folks did their own sewing, mostly. Them that didn't, sent to Miss Ball's, that kept the millinery shop. Times was hard, too.

In spite of what Geoffrey saw to be this girl's cold reception by her relatives, he felt toward her on a sudden, one of those reasonless aversions which sometimes surprise us at the first encounter with certain faces. This feeling was intensified by the relation to his future which the present event seemed to assume, and to his past life as well, for sitting there, and looking upon that strange face, he beheld the presentment of a most familiar scene, of which that face was the most familiar part. He had never seen the face before; nothing of all this was known to his former experience; yet with the sibilance of the slow rain without, and the disorder of his own thoughts within, all this was like the vivid recurrence of a well-remembered scene.

"Does your coffee please you, Geoffrey?" asked the farmer's wife.

"Thank you—yes," said Geoffrey, and the spell was broken.

He was really going then, this morning? it was asked farther.

Yes, he was going. It was time he had returned to the city. He had nothing to keep him in Dulldale.

Would he have the hack call for him?

No, he wanted to see Mrs. Winter again, and he would start from the hotel.

III

In former days, before the iconoclasts of abstinence had broken the images at the altar of the cheerful god, whom we represent with a cluster of rye-stalks in one hand, and a coil of copper-pipe in the other, the office of the Dulldale House had been also the bar-room of that hostelry. But the shelves where the gay decanters once gleamed were empty now, but for a bottle of nerve-and-bone liniment, which boasted itself equally good for man and beast and was supported by a highly colored print on the opposite wall, in which the good Samaritan applying nerve-and-bone liniment to the man fallen among thieves, formed the back-ground to a scene of Bedouin life representing the cure of an Arab horse by means of the same magical ointment.—Indeed, the office bore few traces of its earlier festive use, except in the arms and seats of the much-carven chairs and the ingeniously whittled mantel. On the counter was a box of cigars, and a hotel register, bloated, distained and crumpled, as if the traveling public had had great ado to record itself, and the curious of the village still greater trouble to make out the names, and had been obliged, as it were, to embrace the book, and apply both elbows to the perusal. The face of a dismantled clock decked the space above the doorway, and indicated with a tacit play upon the word that there was no Tick at the Dulldale House. Further than this there was a buffalo-robe in one corner, and a damp dog in another, and near the hearth sat three or four dejected and taciturn villagers, who assumed a brisker if not cheerfuller demeanor, as Geoffrey entered. A sore controversy had raged between them concerning certain colts, whether they were or were not horsey-looking colts, and, indeed, what with the exhaustion of debate and the gloom of the weather, they were at that moment grievously cast down.

The curiosity of these people, already stimulated by Geoffrey's appearance, received further impulse, when the door half-closing from his hand was thrust violently open again, by one that dripped a pool about his feet, from his reeking dress, before he found breath to demand:

"Your name Winter?"

"Yes," said Geoffrey bringing out the identity of this person from a cloud of vague memories, as the sturdy ruffian who had beaten him once at school in protest against the insolent gayety of a certain cap and jacket of his. The jacket had long passed away from Geoffrey's back, but the beating remained.

This friend of boyhood did not respond to the smile which flitted over Geoffrey's lips. He seemed to have been running under the burthen of a heavy charge, and was now a little perplexed for words in which to acquit himself of his business.

"Well," he burst forth at last, with a long sigh that seemed to bring him no relief, "your aunt—the Widder Winter's—dead! Found dead in her chair five minutes ago.—Just come up from there. Heart disease, doctor says."

It was an irritating thing to this messenger, and an outrage to the feelings of the by-standers, that Geoffrey, who might reasonably have been expected to drop dead himself made no other sign in response to this announcement than to turn pale, and to quit the place without a word.

"Wāll," said one of the gentlemen present, who had contended most loudly for the horsiness of the colts in the late disputation, and was a person of delicate emotions: "Tha's cool! Takes 't easy, anyhaow."

So the popular feeling ran strongly against Geoffrey as a heartless and unworthy fellow, until it was diverted into other channels by the minute accounts of Mrs. Winter's death, which the messenger's over-heated blood, in the absence of imagination, prompted him to give.

The change that death had wrought in the face of the poor lady, who had taken such sudden leave of life, was not more marked than that which at the same moment seemed to have befallen her daughter. Clara met Geoffrey at the door with a white and haggard visage, and a low cry of anguish and terror—a longing, incredulous cry that seemed to demand of him denial of that rigid fact within. There was that in this despair which seemed to bring his cousin nearer to him than ever before, and touched him with infinite compassion. She clung eagerly about him, as if in that embrace, she would escape from her horror, as a child, waking from a frightful dream, clings convulsively to the nearest form of human life. She spoke no word, only sobbed while he folded her to his heart, and soothed her with the old words of endearment that came unconsciously to his lips.

Clara's child clung to her mother's robe, and now with eyes of silent wonder glanced at Geoffrey, and now hid her face in the folds of the dress, with a gay smile that mocked him, as the gladness of nature mocks our troubles.

There were numbers of people in the house, and those bleak old women whom the death-scent always attracts, and whose interest in the birth of a babe is only equaled by their gloomy rapture at the death of a man,—came and went, as curiosity or duty prompted them. One of these paused on her way to the chamber where the dead woman lay, and stared at the unconscious cousins. Afterwards she declared that it was the prettiest sight she ever saw; though she had once been known to award the distinction of supreme loveliness to a baby's corpse.

I do not care to make the contrasts too sharp. But, all the contrasts of life are sharp. Here lay sudden death, with decrepit life hovering about it, whispering mysteriously and uttering ghastly experiences. In the next room, inspired by grief itself was tenderness almost to love, and the most formless dream, perhaps, of the con-

266

solations which time would minister. In the workshop yonder across the way, where the undertaker had just decided that they would want the coffin made of black walnut, the workmen had their honest jests about the old woman who dropped off so unexpectedly. They jested, not out of unfeeling levity, but from that impulse which prompts those beyond the immediate circle of bereavement, to seek refuge from the idea of death in any vain and frantic excess.

Jane Grove made Mrs. Winter's shroud, and everybody agreed, when the poor lady lay in her coffin with the garment on, that it was beautiful; and people who did not see it, made people who had seen it, tell them all about it, and were not wearied by that minute description in which elderly ladies delight on such occasions.

The young girl also sat up with the corpse, as the phrase is. Her fellow-watchers were Geoffrey, and a young man from the printing-office, who beguiled his vigils by reading *The Lady of Lyons*, and *Lend Me Five Shillings*, varying the literary pursuits by court paid to Miss Maria Moore. In the country, where the customs of the people are all so gracefully simple, this occasion of sitting up with the dead is sometimes improved by lovers to enjoy each other's company. The printer had been paying attentions to Miss Moore, and she had invited him to assist at these vigils.

As the night waxed old, Miss Moore grew sleepy, being of a heavy and phlegmatic habit, and uttered in a hoarse whisper to the printer, that that Grove girl was as bad as a corpse herself; and so gradually drowsed upon the printer's shoulder.

But Jane Grove never drowsed. She sat in the obscurity with her great terrified eyes wide open, and fixed upon the angry red crest of the untrimmed candle.

The night was hot and close, and a storm brooded black upon the heavens.

Now and then came a low breath of the wind, that shook the honeysuckle at the casement, and filled the room with a faint, sick perfume.

The slow hours dragged away. It thundered, and the sky was full of fiery shapes of lightning. But at last the storm passed without rain.

Then a light breeze sprang up, and rustled the honeysuckle, and blew cool upon the watchers.

Jane Grove sat with her face averted from the half-open door of the death chamber, but Geoffrey's was turned toward it, and he did not once lift his eyes from that gloom. When he had insisted, against usage and popular feeling, on being one of the watchers that night, he had yielded to one of those vague superstitions which sometimes move more robust and obstinate natures. As a child, he had been used to find fantastic relations between the most trivial events and the grand purposes of fate. All of us, I think, have known enough of this to recognize the morbid impulse which would drive him from his bed at night to change the position of a book, and so avert the unknown fearful consequences of suffering it to remain as he had laid it down. He had outgrown much of this vagary, but often still the "weird seizures" came—

"On a sudden in the midst of men and day,"

and tasked his full strength to the resistance.

He sat now trying to divine the relation which the sorrow of the present seemed to establish with his own future, and his thought bruised itself incessantly against the narrow close in which actual life is passed. He was roused from the pain of this revery by the loud, long and dolorous howl of the old dog, beneath the window. A cat, which had climbed and crouched unseen upon the casement, leaped again to the ground outside. Ghostly stories out of childhood thronged Geoffrey's memory, and a quick dismay drove the blood to his heart. The consciousness of eyes fixed sadly and earnestly upon him, caused him to lift his own, and with a mute and shuddering fear, he beheld a spectral figure standing in the doorway of the death-room, bearing an unlighted candle in one hand and clasping with the other the dark hair that fell down the white robe. The eyes were staring wide, and the lips made a pitiful, murmuring sound, like the yearning, inarticulate appeal of the dumb. The figure seemed to have paused in an advance, and then when the dog howled once more, it tottered and fell forward with a faint cry, while the printer, leaping to his feet, knocked the candle from the table, and extinguished it.

Finding herself in utter darkness, and being not yet quite awake, Miss Moore expressed the emotions of female delicacy under such circumstances. She pinioned the printer's arms in her brawny hold, and besought him to save her, while her victim struggled vainly to free himself, and with a hint from his dramatic reading implored her to unhand him.

Shame and anger filled Geoffrey's heart, as a sense of the truth broke upon his first terror and the absurd composition of the scene, shocked him inexpressibly. He sternly commanded a silence, and quickly reluming the candle, he hastened to the assistance of his cousin, who stood sobbing at the door, with the blood dripping slowly from a wound in her forehead.

Jane Grove was already at her side, supporting and soothing her. "You have been walking in your sleep," she said softly. "Come—let me take you back to your room."

But Clara turned to Geoffrey, and clinging convulsively to his hands, cried out that she had thought he was dead, too; and lying there with her poor mother. Thank God, it was only a dream!

"Yes, it was only a dream, cousin," said Geoffrey tenderly, and Jane Grove approached to lead her away to her room again. Clara went obediently, and with the bewilderment of people in that state.

The young girl presently returned, saying to Geoffrey that his cousin could not sleep, and it was not very well to leave her alone.

"You can stay with her, then," said Geoffrey. "But were you not frightened?" he asked, seeing that Jane had not changed color nor expression.

"Yes, very much, but"—

She looked frightened, but that was always her look, and when with a certain ghostly tranquillity, she passed into the death-room a moment, to see if all were well there, Geoffrey felt toward her again that abhorrence which had seized him when he first beheld her.

IV

When I contemplate Geoffrey in his relation to the commonplace facts of life, I confess the effect is to lessen my hold upon his shadowy and elusive identity. His nature was so wholly introverted, that the attempt to bring his real character in contact with the world would be a useless violence. So I let alien natures approach without touching him—conscious, indeed, that this leaves a certain vagueness in the picture, but content that it shall be so for the sake of the truth which I hope to suggest.

I behold him now detained in Dulldale by fortuities that all tend to the greater event which makes his destiny interesting to me. But he moves vaguely through all, and fades from me, when I attribute to his life the motives which actuate other men, and retreats beyond analysis.

After the ceremonies of the funeral, it is perhaps the affairs of the dead which delay him, and then it is the illness threatening his cousin's life which prolongs his delay. Out of the shock of her mother's sudden death, and the terrors of that somnambulic night, came a fever that burned through a summer's month, and left Clara very weak and helpless, but stronger in the ties by which her suffering, and the revelations of delirium, had knit her to the heart of Geoffrey.

He, indeed, seemed to return again to himself of the past, and no longer resented the recognitions which reminded him of his childhood and earlier youth. The simple and real courtesy of his ways, made him friends among those whose jealousy was at first rife against him, and Geoffrey was popular in Dulldale without knowing it. People no longer discussed him with suspicion, but approved him with that patronizing good nature, which ignorance often feels toward natures it admires and does not quite understand.

They thought if he really was going to marry his cousin,—and there was such a report—it would be a good thing, and they were even willing that he should come to live in Dulldale.

To his cousin Geoffrey clung not with passion, perhaps, but with the tenderest affection of blood. They were the only children of a house which was old for our new land—of an early family in Dulldale, which had fallen away from much of its wealth, but none of its social greatness. The Winters stood first in the memory of the village which they had founded, and without pretension on their part, had been elected by common jealousy and consent, a kind of aristocracy there. The log-cabin in which Geoffrey's grandfather had lived, was yet standing. It was ignobly reduced, it is true, to the uses of a corn-crib, but it still attested the antiquity of the Winter family.

The house in which Geoffrey was born (and which after his mother's death was sold to the farmer Grove,) had been the most splendid mansion of its time. He remembered that the boys who sometimes came home with him from school, were so deeply awed by its grandeur, that they could seldom be induced to penetrate the interior farther than the dim entrance hall where they hung about in the gloom, very much impressed with Geoffrey's awful privilege of sliding down the railing of the staircase. In yet vivider proof of its magnificence, to his boyish pride, was the famous garret of the old house, which was the rainy day resort of his childhood, and which had that mingled odor of clay wasp's nests, old carpets, cast off boots in barrels, and tattered files of the *National Intelligencer,*— common, I believe, to all garrets. He had never grown into all the roughness of boyhood, but while the soft influences of his mother and his home had yet no counteraction from without, and the laugh of the rude little boy-world had not made him ashamed, he often played in this garret with his cousin Clara, at those grave mimicries of conventional life in which children delight. More than once he solemnly assured the little maiden that she was to be his wife when he grew up, and was answered with a dignified seriousness of assent possible only to children.

But if these young cousins were friendly, it must be confessed that there was no love between their families. Judge Winter and his brother were both dead, and their widows never made visits of affection, and seldom visits of ceremony. There was, indeed, a story that Geoffrey's father had first paid his court to Clara's mother, but had forsaken that arid love for the young girl who afterwards became his wife. However this may have been, Clara's mother always spoke with ill concealed scorn of her gentle sister, whose sweet life, in turn, gave out its only bitterness toward her.

Age seldom softens the asperities of earlier years. But after Geoffrey's mother died, and the little property which had remained to her was swept away, the surviving Mrs. Winter offered the boy a home in her own family.

And then?

Geoffrey and Clara grew up together. But one day, when they played again that old play of their childhood, she had forgotten her part.

Shall we linger upon an event not pleasant in itself, and common enough?

People offer love, and are denied the return. It is an old song, and many times set to rhyme:

> "Ein Jüngling liebt ein Mädchen,
> Die hat einen Andern erwählt."

Well, does it matter who was the other chosen? If we speak of him, we grow bitter, and malign the excellent human race, in representing that a girl's fancy is not wisdom, and that it is not always the best heart or finest brain that triumphs in the contest of love. You remember, dear reader, your own successful rival, who was an inferior person?

No, no, we return again to the Jüngling, whose seven years of absence and ennui, have been already mentioned.

It was twice seven years that Jacob waited for Rachel, and he seems never to have questioned that she was worth the delay. But that was in the young and joyous days. The world is grown old and sad since, and the children of its age have not the strong-heartedness and inextinguishable hope of those born to its youth.

Geoffrey proceeded to his second love-making very calmly. He was not much in love, and so he could make love with a self-possession which he felt somehow to be an *amende* to him for the passionate trepidations of the past.

He had at last prepared to leave Dulldale, and now he went to say good bye to Clara, and to offer her again his hand. He loved no one else; and she was dearer to him than all others, being, as she was, so lonely and helpless. At least they could be happy together? He reasoned briefly to the great error of his mistaken life, and as often happens with hesitating, undecided men, mistook his conclusion for a wise decision, simply because he had been able to reach it.

He entered the old-fashioned parlor, and found his cousin awaiting him.

In so little a time, so great change had befallen that, as he looked into her wan face, and into his own heart, pain and doubt sealed his lips.

She seemed so wholly dependant upon him now; she made him

so many unconscious confidences; that hesitation and persistance seemed alike betrayal.

He was silent. Clara too was mute, and turned her beautiful head toward the honeysuckles at the window that were heavy with the overnight rain. But the flowers were not more full of tears than her own heart.

Then, after a pause, Geoffrey said:

"I am come to say goodbye, but I hope only for a little time. The past is so painful to me, that I do not care to recall any part of it." He took her hand tenderly, not passionately in his. "Only now, when I ask you once more to be my wife, I must tell you that I cannot offer you the fresh and perfect love you once refused."

His voice struck so cold and mechanical upon his own sense that he ceased again. What he had said sounded to him like a set speech utterly detestable to him, to which he had been listening, but in which he had no other part.

His cousin sat with averted face, but with her hand still confided to his own.

"We are both alone in the world, now, Clara," he continued. "I am tired of my solitude, and I love no one else but you. Look up, darling! Goodbye."

She rose at his words, and he stooped to kiss her forehead. But with a sudden impulse, he clasped her to his heart. In the sweet tumult of the embrace, the old love seemed to well forth again, and flood the ice that had imprisoned it.

"In a year Clara, I will come again," he said, "and then—goodbye."

She made no answer, for there stole through her present bewilderment, a doubt that would have been a prophecy, if she had not stifled it in silence.

V

My reluctance to regard Geoffrey with the hard, antipathetic eyes of the village people who never saw in him the hero of this shadowiest romance, nor indeed any of the qualities which interest me in him, but only the rather quiet unsociable man who marries his cousin, and comes back to live in Dulldale, after a long and idle absence; this reluctance, I say, is little less than pain, as I turn to contemplate him with the vision of Miss Moore, who is the first in the village to note his return with Clara when their brief wedding tour brings them home again. Yet, I must do this, since life moves to great results by pitiful ways; and I cannot establish Geoffrey in Dulldale unseen by the neighbors. I must speak of his coming in the hack from the railway station; of certain trunks and bandboxes, which I cannot well manage, and am glad to have set down before his gate; of his alighting from the hack, and of his helping Clara to the ground, and of their going in at the door of the house which closes behind them, and shuts them from Miss Moore and me.

The occurrences recounted are not possibly of startling value to the reader, but to witness them added a wealth of material to Miss Moore's mind, already stocked with information concerning the Winter family, and put her in possession of most unpleasant proofs of the depravity of people, of whom she had before known little good. She could hardly have explained why it confirmed her in the belief long cherished, that they were no better than those they talked about.

It was the mother of this crude virgin, who had witnessed, with so much gratification, the spectacle of Geoffrey's effort to console his cousin on that day of the widow Winter's death; it was Miss Moore herself who had recounted the particulars of that scene, until many people of Dulldale would have united Clara and Geoffrey indissolubly and disgracefully in the bands of matrimony, before Mrs. Winter was cold in her grave, as the saying is.

After their actual union, and while they were still absent on their wedding tour Miss Moore had paid frequent visits of inspection to their house. The old mansion had not undergone great change: neither Geoffrey nor Clara desired this; but there had been some repairs made; rooms had been papered; the marriage had been celebrated by the purchase of new furniture; so much, in effect, had been done to disturb the former state of things, that Jane Grove had been busy for a week in setting the house in order against the arrival of the happy pair, as Mr. Goodlow termed Geoffrey and his wife in the hymeneal department of the *Dulldale Chronicle*. The notice is to be found, on turning to the files of the paper, under the design of a torch and wreath, with the motto: "Hail, wedded love!"—The allusions to Geoffrey's future, with which Mr. Goodlow accompanied the announcement of his marriage, were in the editor's most fortunate vein, and annoyed the sensitive bridegroom.

As I say, then, Miss Moore always found Jane at work there, when she invaded the house.—It was her custom to treat the little sewing-girl on public occasions with stately patronage, but during these calls, she wore, for the other's encouragement, an air of winning affability, and laughed and chatted much at the quiet person. She went about from room to room, and made inventory of the furniture—the carpets, the wall-paper, the pictures—and thrust her mottled face and shook her large curls in every corner.

It was not Miss Moore's fault, if her amiability was more repulsive than her ill-nature, and it was by no wish of hers that when she was friendliest with Jane Grove and called her Jenny, and found fault with all she had done she subdued that shy creature more

273

thoroughly than ever. The girl stood in dread of Miss Moore's tenderness, and used to lock the door, if she saw her coming; but the other had a fashion of appearing suddenly at the threshold, as out of space, and seeming to demand admittance by virtue of the prodigy enacted; and so the two were thrown a good deal together. At such times, the fullness of Miss Moore's dislike of the people soon to occupy the house broke out in frequent overflow. The character of such good-looks as Geoffrey possessed was a constant affront to her; and talk which she heard of his talent was her scornful jest. Clara, who had quite an old look already, had still thrown herself away upon that Geoffrey. She remembered that when he used to be in love with Clara, before he ever left Dulldale at all, everybody said she wound him round her finger. Perhaps she took him now because she wanted a husband she could manage. Clara used to make the whole house stand about when she was a girl. Miss Moore recollected the talk there was about her. *Once*, when Miss Moore was a child running about the neighbor's houses, that great passionate thing had shaken her and sent her home for only looking at a picture in a drawer. It would have done Jane Grove good to hear what Clara got from Miss Moore's mother on that occasion; though it seems that the matron's mission was a failure except as regarded the utterance of wholesome truth. Old Mrs. Winter actually took Clara's part. *She* was a bitter old thing! Miss Moore's mother never darkened their doors afterwards, until the day of the widow's death.—Were the Winters going to keep help? People in Dulldale mostly did their own work, but Clara was always proud, and it was supposed she would feel herself too good.

I am perfectly conscious of the commonplaceness of the character which I sketch with touches so rude and coarse.

What is it about the disagreeable people, I wonder? Where shall the seeker after exact truth find the elusive line that separates the pleasing from the odious? There is no such line. You cannot tell how far upstream the tide makes the water brackish; only, the river is sweet above an uncertain point, and salt below.

One has to exaggerate and to be unjust. I detest one of my friends, though I know he has many excellent qualities. In speaking of him, I dwell only on his defects, which I place in the most hideous light. I wish to be honest enough, and it is not my sin, if I exaggerate his unpleasant traits into offences against my peace and happiness. Each one of them that I touch, suggests the whole sum of his odiousness, and assumes its proportions in spite of me. To attempt to restore the balance of justice by praising his good qualities is equally absurd, for I exaggerate in this respect as badly as in the other. I make him such an angelic being that I appear to myself a monster for detesting him.

No, it is useless. Our reason may distinguish by shades of color, but our affection, which decides people to be amiable or unamiable, paints only black and white. To this abominable injustice of what is best and purest in human nature, I attribute my disposition to misrepresent Miss Moore, to ignore her excellencies, to place in ugly relief her offensive traits.

Why do I say she has a mottled face and large curls? It is because I hate mottled faces and large curls. Her complexion was good enough; she wore her hair plain. She had many admirable features which I guiltily refuse to describe. On the stage they get up the bad people in the gloom of folded cloaks and slouching hats, with sallow cheeks and dark crescents beneath their eyes; and even if these wretches did not utter their invariable atrocities of sentiment, you would know from their presence that they were irreclaimably wicked. It saves a great deal of explanation, and it must be so in a measure with Miss Moore. I make her the conventional village gossip whom you all know. If I portrayed her with the modifications of a conscientious justice, you would refuse to believe in her, and I should be untrue to art.

Jane Grove could not make Miss Moore a just return for the knowledge of the Winters which the latter imparted. The workmen had come from the city, and had gone on to make the repairs in Mr. Winter's absence. It was a notion of his not to see the house after the work was begun, until it was completed. He was very particular, however, in his directions. But Jane feared that Mrs. Winter might not be altogether suited.

"*That* she won't!" Miss Moore broke in with so much righteous triumph, that the little girl perceived with terror she had made a very unlucky confidence. "Why didn't they have that old parlor and the widow's bed-room changed, too?" Miss Moore demanded.

Jane meekly confessed that she did not know why; and Miss Moore said: "I can tell you—superstition! It's Geoffrey Winter's superstition."

The idea was so pleasant to Miss Moore's fine scorn, that she straightway left Jane to her own humble devices, and went and betrayed her discovery to several other people; and that is the way the Winter house came to be haunted.

Even after the return of the Winters, Jane remained in the house several days, and when at last she was ready to go, they were all sorry to part with her. Mrs. Winter said she must come often to see them, and in her simple country fashion kissed the girl affectionately, and followed her to the gate.

As Clara turned again, after taking leave of her, and moved slowly back to the door, leading her little daughter by the hand, the golden afternoon sunshine fell across her brown hair, and lighted the rare tint of her cheeks, and the liquid darkness of her eyes; and Jane thought her the most beautiful creature she had ever seen—so fair, and kind, and regal.

Even the quiet heart of Geoffrey felt a certain glow of pride, if no tenderer emotion, as he watched the little parting at the gate. Few women, indeed, had Clara's superb beauty of face, or that exquisite native grace with which she smiled, spoke, moved; and she was rarely gifted with the feminine art of looking and acting more than she felt and knew.

Clara had not fine individual perceptions, but she had the subtle instincts of her sex, and these did not err, though their revelations led her into error. There was eagerness almost to pain, in her devotion to Geoffrey, upon whom she lavished with passion the love once withheld. I do not think she ever understood him quite, but she dimly felt that the contact of their lives was not in the highest sympathies. This was irreconcileable difference, but she chose to make it superiority, and she exaggerated the powers of a soul that was fine but not strong. Women like that men shall be great; men may be good, if they will, or bad, if they will, but they must be great; and if they are not great,—the imagination of women is fond and willing, and believing is as easy as seeing; and a wife's illusions in regard to her husband are always touching and sacred. Geoffrey was good and true; he had the gentleness of a woman—though he was not cruel; but I doubt if the Geoffrey whom we know was at all the grand and wise being that Clara figured him. In those seven years that she had not seen him, he had grown, certainly. But had he grown so far above her, as she thought? Or had he only grown apart from her?

She exaggerated his goodness as well. Its impulses swayed him more than goodness sways most men, but it was no part of his consciousness, and belonged to that inheritance of goodness bequeathed him by his mother. So far as he thought and calculated, he was selfish like the best of us, but the motions of his nature were good and kind. When he asked Clara to be his wife, she had felt a secret fear that he was not asking from his love alone, but from his desire for her happiness; and she knew that there was at least no passion in his attachment. But her fear gave her hope as well as pain, for could she not change this generosity into love?

Not yet, however, while she felt so secure in his tenderness could she assure herself of this intended victory, and her life was still a struggle and unrest. This unquietness and yearning of her soul, wrought constant surprises for Geoffrey in her manner.—She had never been the same to him since that day when they first met after long separation, though to others she remained unchanged. He saw that with the village people, she had still that stately ease which had once abashed and bewildered him, but when they were alone, she was caressingly sensitive to his will. If she discerned his surprise at this change, she banished it, with some burst of gay self-derision, which was so novel and delightful in her, that Geoffrey must catch her to his heart in a sudden rapture.

"You women are nothing but riddles to us men," he would say. "We live and die with you, and don't know you. I suppose we shall find you out sometime."

Then more than ever the wife was pained and doubted.

"But at least," she comforted herself, "he has never loved any one else."

VI

One day Mrs. Winter mentioned to her husband that she had some sewing to be done.

"Well, my dear," responded Geoffrey in that tone of half-plaintive acquiescence and suggestion, which I have heard used at such times by husbands. The unwedded cannot speak in that tone, for it intimates an experience if not a conscious discernment of the female character, utterly impossible to the unwedded. It means consent; it suggests the pursuit of the same subject; it betrays a trifling alarm as to the sequel; it signifies resignation in any extremity. It disarms and propitiates. It is quite base.

"Well, my dear," repeated Clara. "Why do you say that, Geoffrey?" She had a perception that her remark was of too little consequence to have awakened this tone in response, if it had been perfectly understood. And indeed, Geoffrey had not understood it at all, for he was writing, and merely knew that she spoke.

"I said, that I would be obliged to get some sewing done."

"O,—well!" said her husband coming back to himself. Of course, there was a tinge of resentment in his voice, for to be interrupted when one is writing is to be irreparably wronged. One may forgive it, but one cannot immediately forget it.

"And I was thinking," continued Clara, "of having Jane Grove do it."

"Well."

"She likes us, and I shall be glad to have her in the house for a while. Clara is so fond of her, too. While we were gone, Jane was very good to Clara, and she was perfectly happy with the Groves all the time I was so uneasy about her."

"Yes," Geoffrey said. He believed she was an excellent girl. But somehow he had an uneasy feeling in her presence, as if—

He paused, for he could not explain even to himself his instinctive resentment of the relation which this girl seemed to bear to his after life; the attempt to make another understand it would have been hopeless. And he could not speak to Clara of the dislike with which Jane Grove's ghostly calm had inspired him on that night of her mother's death.

"I am sorry," said Clara, "for that puts an end to a scheme of mine, which I thought you would like. It is no difference."

"Then do not be sorry," replied Geoffrey; "the plan may be carried out for all the feeling I can have against it. What is it?"

"Oh, nothing," said Clara with that false feminine pretense of subjugation, as if she had put all her wishes away, when in fact she firmly meant their fulfillment. "Only I was thinking how pleasantly we might arrange it to have Jane come and live with us. She is quite young yet—how old should you think she was?"

About a thousand years, Geoffrey suggested.

Clara pondered a moment, and perceived that he was not in earnest.

"No, seriously," she said, "Jane is only a little over eighteen. And she wants to go to school a while yet if she can. She gets no work in the village, and I thought if she could live with us, and go to school, she could," and Mrs. Winter added this thriftily and with satisfaction, "give me a great deal of assistance, and more than pay for her boarding."

"Very well," answered her husband, "I hope you won't give up your project for anything I have said."

And he added many things in favor of the project. He was like most sensitive people, and could not well distinguish between the effect of a wrong done in thought and a wrong done in act, and he always made eager amends in kindness for the tacit injustice which had not been committed. No favor was now too great to be granted to this girl, whom he had disliked without cause. It was a weakness, certainly, but it was amiable.

And it was in this way Jane Grove came to live with the Winters. It was not hard to gain the consent of her relatives to the arrangement. She had found very little to do, in Dulldale, and had (Mrs. Grove said to Clara,) been a burden; though of course she was helpful about the house, and was very kind to Johnny. Then Mrs. Grove looked guilty and ashamed of having said that Jane was a burden, as if a dim sense of her rude and narrow thought had stolen upon her. Poor woman! she was once a light-hearted girl, and no doubt had her unsordid dreams of the future, then—she so soon old, so coarsened by the drudgery of the farm household and that dull round of laborious, lonesome days, which had never been broken but by excursions to the village, to sell butter and eggs, and cheapen the store-goods received in exchange.

"As the husband is, the wife is."

He is her destiny. With a mate less rude and clownish, Mrs. Grove might have been generous and much that she was not. Alas! I am sad for the defeated existences. They seem somehow a defeat of eternal purposes, and one hardly knows whether to doubt or trust.

As for the young girl herself, how did she accept the proffered home? I think with a serene gladness that flowed out of a full heart in the mute gratitude of deeds. To live with Mrs. Winter was a happiness that at first seemed incredible to her.—She had not met before the kindness with which Clara had treated her, and Clara was her ideal of womanly sweetness and dignity, for she had seen her in the joy of those early days of marriage, when every bride seems better and fairer than she is.

Of Geoffrey, indeed, Jane had thought with some misgiving. She had felt the secret of his dislike, and she was not wholly at ease in his grave and quiet presence. But to his little step daughter she clung with the ardor of a nature to which love has been long forbidden. Geoffrey, too, was fond of the child, and he resented at first, with the subtle jealousy which such men feel and deny, her attachment to Jane. But with the truer discernment of afterdays, in the place of this fine jealousy, sprang up his earliest sentiment of pitying friendship for the lonely girl.

That remorse for the injustice of his former prejudice, prompted Geoffrey even beyond his own good impulses in the office of teacher and friend, which he now assumed toward Jane. He was glad that his home afforded shelter to one who had never before known the shelter of home. He was glad of her eagerness to retrieve the unfriendly fortunes of the past, and it was by his knowledge and guidance that she discovered the great new-world of books.

We are long in learning that this world is empty and lonesome as the world in which we live; and it opened fair and wide and full of delight before this poor child. In its blissful remoteness she withdrew from daily care, and lived and dreamed in it, while her hands busied themselves with household things. She was capable of so much happiness, that I know she must afterwards have at least found peace, though I suppose her tranquility came when the fearfulness of hope had ceased forever. For the present, a divine flower, which had pined for friendly air in her heart, blossomed and filled her days with lily-like whiteness and sweetness. Not all the crude experiences of her childhood had crushed this flower, not all the frosts of the world had blighted it; at the first ray of free warm light, it bloomed.

She surprises even the languor of Geoffrey with her profound and rapid progresses, and awakens in him, together with a regret for the days in which he believed in his own genius, the pride which all men feel in their early recognition and encouragement of the rarely gifted.

279

All the people of this household have the young girl's love and gratitude. She is so much a woman in her experiences, so much a child still in her simpleheartedness, that she is at once the friend of Mrs. Winter, and the companion of little Clara. The two women sit together, and sew and talk, and plot housekeeping for the next day, and grow dearer to each other. The two children walk together, and have the same childlike delights in the novel and the beautiful, and make mutual confidences. But with Geoffrey, Jane is wholly different from what she is with the others. That painful constraint which obscured her youth, has vanished, and even a certain grace of manner is revealed in its place. At first shy and taciturn in Geoffrey's presence, she grows less and less embarrassed, until he hardly knows her transfigurement in the young girl, neither child nor woman, timid, innocent, confiding, yet with a lurking gaiety and a subtle humor, that give a strange and indescribable charm to her.

Often as Jane and Clara sit together over their work, Geoffrey reads to them—sometimes poems, sometimes romances,—and the three discuss the books. His acute sensitiveness makes him alive to the most delicate impressions of thought, and he traces with peculiar delight, the secret courses of irony. It is hard for most women to understand this delight, but Jane follows him and shares it; and Clara is not quite happy to find them beyond her reach. Geoffrey looks up now at the one face of bright intelligence and at the other face of blank appeal. An alliance is unconsciously made. Hereafter he reads *before* Clara, *to* Jane. The wife follows the story with profound interest; she realizes the ensemble of character; but the processes of delineation are invisible to her. She can see and understand a brilliant metaphor; the melody of verse, and even the shrewder tricks of rhetoric delight her. But the other two: why do they linger upon the mere form of an expression? why are they enraptured with a certain use of a word? what lies under the plain sense of this or that passage, which makes them laugh?

"You people are both absurd," she exclaims with affected petulance and real anxiety. "We will never get through in the world at this rate. Please go on, Geoffrey; I want to know what happened to prevent the marriage."

So, as they read together, the intellectual alliance was strengthened, and Clara had that indefinable sense of exile from their region of sympathies, with which you hear your friend speak to another of past enjoyments and scenes unknown to you.

You discern perhaps the current of events.

In this fiction, we are merely suggestive, you know. The imagination of the reader, unhindered by the tedious explanations of the author, arranges vividly all the details. It is easy to do, if the reader's acquaintance with fictitious literature is general.

Is it possible that two souls like those of Geoffrey and this young girl, with their many points of affinity, should be drawn toward each other, and that not result in that which makes so much grief and bitterness in the romances?

Have we the *Wahlverwandtschaften* here again?

Eduard esteems our Charlotte. He knows she is very good, and true, and beautiful. He regards her with the affection which is not love.

And this Ottilie: Does she come between the sundered hearts of the husband and wife?

People have said it is hard to either teach a young girl or learn from her, without teaching and learning altogether by heart.

If Eduard interests himself in the studies of Ottilie; if he directs her taste in the poets; if he is pleased to watch the development of her mind, and the growth of her beautiful spiritual nature, is there danger to neither?

No, it is all misunderstood. The imagination of the reader, to which I would willingly have left this part of the story, has guiltily betrayed us into an error, unjust and cruel.

The affair is quite innocent and commonplace. These are the people of a new civilization, purer and nobler than the old; so regular and secure that the picturesqueness of ruin is sadly wanting in it.

VII

In the meantime, Geoffrey had other occupation beside the developement of a young girl's mind; he was the editor of the newspaper in Dulldale, and was a member of the press; he was an educator of the masses and more or less abstractly, the friend of mankind.

Clara's fortune would have supported him in greater idleness than even his journal left him; but he, who had been broken and disappointed in the outset of life, had bought the county paper, with certain vague hopes which took rise from the new impulse given his life by his marriage; and he entered on his charge directly after his return to Dulldale.

The transfer of the *Dulldale Chronicle* to Geoffrey from the former editor, Mr. Goodlow was a change greatly to the content of the latter, and indeed to the displeasure of no one except the printer, Mr. Rounce, whom we remember as one of the watchers on the night of Mrs. Winter's death. Mr. Rounce, on whom the sale of the *Chronicle* had inflicted a disappointment, rallied from the blow with promptness, and took a cordial liking to Geoffrey and continued in his employment.

He was a marvellous fellow, if you believed him, and he had character worth study. As he said, he had seen and been part of many things. He had been five years master of his trade, and had exhausted all the life within his reach. In this time (it is his own story which I repeat,) he had made the journey to California by way of the Isthmus; he had set types in the city of Mexico, and had the *vomito* in Vera Cruz. The United States were his book, he said, of which he had read every page. He had borrowed money in all places, and everywhere the laundresses and the keepers of boarding-houses remembered him with the pensive regret of people pondering upon the mysterious disappearance of those who owe them little bills. He had met with adventures of every kind. He had fought a duel in Texas; he had been tarred and feathered in the cause of humanity in Mississippi; he had been blown up on a western steamboat; he had assisted at a smashup on an eastern railway; he had been married in Ohio, and divorced in Indiana. His forte was versatility. He had been an editor, a soldier, an actor; he had practiced homeopathic medicine, and had read some books with a view to study of the law. At intervals, he had worked at his old trade, for which he had a real affection. He had been six months in Dulldale, and he had but now looked vaguely forward to the purchase of the *Chronicle* newspaper, and subsequent peace and quietness. As he said, he was aweary of travel and adventure, and would willingly settle down. He was an utter vagabond, perfectly brave, kind-hearted and dishonest. He was a sad braggart and a liar, but he disdained a meanness, and had much good in him. When he heard that Mr. Goodlow had sold the *Chronicle* to Geoffrey, it must be owned that he swore some natural oaths; and he quoted much of the legitimate drama in expression of his resentment.

But as he stood that night with his candle in his hand, about to invert it and darken that scene of revengeful passions, it occurred to him that it might be well to cultivate friendly relations with the new proprietor, whom he now remembered that he rather liked.

The hero of an hundred adventures crept sighing into bed. The father of a thousand lies, turned upon his pillow, and slept the sweet sleep of truth and innocence.

VIII

As for Geoffrey, I think that those days in which his newspaper was yet a novelty to him, and interested him in things outside of himself, were the happiest of his life.

Mr. Goodlow was a printer. He had published the *Chronicle* at a small outlay, to which Providence had tempered the income. Mr. Rounce and an apprentice were his sole assistants, and the three divided the intellectual and mechanical labors between them. Mr. Goodlow was not a gifted writer. His detractors used even to question the integrity of his grammar. But in the deportment of the scissors, he had qualities, which enabled him to prepare the political matter of the *Chronicle* with very little trouble. On the other hand, Mr. Rounce shone in the selection of poetry and fiction, and the general miscellany which contributed to the pleasing variety of the newspaper. For the rest, the columns of the *Chronicle* were filled with the advertisements of the village merchants, and of patented medicines, with here and there the prospectus of some eastern literary periodical, published to procure an exchange, and fatally betraying the poverty of the journal. Whenever leading editorials appeared in the *Chronicle*, they bore a family likeness to the leaders of greater journals, and discussed all topics at a safe distance of time. If Providence visited a barn with lightning, or a house was burned, the *Chronicle* alluded to the event; if a monster calf was born, or an immense squash was grown upon a neighboring farm, these facts also were chronicled; and Mr. Goodlow had a way of ending each paragraph of this kind with the defiance—"Beat this who can!" which was perhaps vaguely intended to encourage nature to renewed efforts. Of course a brisk and bitter controversy always raged between the *Chronicle* and the newspaper of the rival village. In this warfare the resources of sarcastic language were drawn upon with spendthrift recklessness, so that the most scathing sentences must be printed in italics or capitals, to give them that force which they were intended to carry to the mind of the reader. In times of political fervor the editors abandoned themselves to the wildest caprices of typography, and even resorted to the art of the wood-engraver, to represent those ideas of scorn and derision which words failed to express.

To this part of his inheritance Geoffrey utterly refused to succeed; and it must be confessed that people thought very meanly of his spirit, as week after week he continued silent to the withering attacks of his contemporary. But after while they grew better contented with his course. Mr. Goodlow remained with the new editor, until some one could be found to fill his place as a printer. In the meantime he shook his head much, and gave Geoffrey advice and contempt concerning innovations which were made in the established management of the *Chronicle*. He belonged to the race of country editors which is going out with the old-fashioned country newspapers. He was a zealous partizan without the remotest hope of party spoils; he was a sturdy friend to certain traditions of political policy; and he firmly believed that he had battled all his life for principles. He was pre-railroaditic in his ideas; and worked on his paper like a laborer in his ditch. He was poor, and the *Chronicle* did not afford him an opulent support. He had no theories of journalism, and was accustomed to talk much about the troubles of printers, and loved to publish dull jokes concerning their poverty. He incessantly dunned his delinquent subscribers, and threatened to cut them off his list. He was continually advertising that he would take wood on subscription, and, at Thanksgiving and Christmas, he made appeals of melancholy drollery, urging his agricultural friends to the presentation of poultry. Withal, he respected himself, and was not a bad man.

The editor's office had been the resort of the intellectual leisure of Dulldale. Mr. Goodlow was a person of social feelings; he would willingly discuss at all times the slavery question, or for the matter of that any other question. People used to come and look over his exchange newspapers, and even carry them away before the editor had seen them. They kept their stories for this place, and told them with great enjoyment; they made suggestions to the editor of improvements in the conduct of his paper; they read his editorials in the proof-sheets, and gave him their opinions before the articles were published.

Now, however, this was changed. Geoffrey's manners did not invite familiarity, and these warmhearted loungers were discouraged by his coldness, more than they had ever been by the rudenesses which Mr. Rounce always offered them, or the occasional exasperations of Mr. Goodlow. But the more intelligent farmers who called at the office to fetch away their papers, would still stop to talk with the editor about the crops and the state of the country. They regarded him with respect, and even that tipsy yeoman who had been accustomed to threaten Mr. Goodlow with the discontinuance of his subscription, whenever he was in spirits, relinquished on Geoffrey's account the enjoyment of this menace.

The new editor liked well enough to encounter the varieties of character with which his business brought him acquainted; and he was more popular I believe with odd people than with those whose respectable friendship would have been of greater use to him. Now and then, a wild-eyed abolition lecturer visited Dulldale, and called upon the editor, who found beneath a crust of defiant enthusiasm, sometimes a heart full of kindliness to all men, and sore with the wrongs of the lowly and the weak, and sometimes a mad and hollow vanity of persecution, and a lust for the unclean martyrdom of stale eggs, merely for the martyrdom's sake.—These men were pleased with the warmth that Geoffrey manifested in denouncing the sin they hated; but they were shrewd men, and they lamented the languid temper that was content with praising a cause—that rested at thinking right, and left the deed undone. They stroked their great beards, and smoothed their flowing locks, and often pitied, often expostulated, sometimes insulted.

All people whom philanthropy, or fanaticism, or superstition had made public and outcast, visited in their way of business or pleasure, the printing-office. The friend of woman's rights who illustrated in her own dumpy person the beauty of the new female costume which was to defy the despotism of fashion; the gaunt and skeleton enthusiast, who insisted that cold water inwardly and outwardly taken, was, together with a belief in spiritual rappings, the only means to disenthral and regenerate mankind; the man with the patent washing-machine, who had at last discovered the secret of prolonging human life, by relieving females of the labors of washing day; the missionary from the South Sea Islands who, having contributed an intimate friend to cannibalism and afterwards converted the devourers to a knowledge of salvation, wished to deliver an address upon missions in Dulldale; the agents of circuses, menageries, concert troupes, and the endless number of public benefactors, and all the courageous and plausible children of humbug, Geoffrey met, and studied; and the life he lived grew more and more positive and healthful.

The politicians of the county were not slow to recognize the new ability which had been infused into the *Chronicle*, and gradually Geoffrey was drawn into that vortex of which every American feels the whirling currents. When he first returned to live in Dulldale, he made an earnest effort to win regard and friendship. He felt that in proposing to be a man among the people who had known him as a boy, he was proposing an audacious thing, which the greatest merit could not excuse, and which would be sure to awaken resentments. He honestly did his best to allay these. He was reserved, yet nobody thought him proud, even though he repelled the patronage of local greatness with a fierceness which men of his gentle nature sometimes show. If, however, he gained friends who would have placed no obstacle in his way (and I do not say this is the warmest friendship,) he also made enemies who would willingly have done him an injury, and seized the occasion with eagerness.

A political career was his last dream of ambition, and it was meaner and shrewder than those of his early aspirations, as the later love is coarser and shrewder than the first divine passion.

When a nature sensitive, gentle, sincere comes in contact with the world, how rudely and mercilessly the world seems to buffet. Alas! this was no conflict for Geoffrey—this absurd melée—this scuffle with lies, detraction, malice and ignorance—which is the reality of the political contest. He had dealt somewhat abstractly with political principles, and dreamed of a political career in which he would have risen above party into individual honesty, and usefulness to a great cause. But the apotheosis of political faith is office, and Geoffrey did not assist at the apotheosis. Mr. Jones was elected; and having beaten Geoffrey partially as a friend of temperance, was tipsy a great part of the session of the legislature.

It could not be denied, however, that Geoffrey had fought the battle with courage, and his friends talked of rallying upon him for another year; and by that time forgot his claims, if he had any.

IX

The defeat of Geoffrey's political aspirations, (and this embittered him only as such a defeat embitters men,) might still have been a matter of transitory regret, if it had not subtly related itself to another defeat, and charged that with new heaviness.

Their marriage had not brought much comfort to Clara or to him. Her love did not wane, but as his tenderness became more hopelessly serene and unlike love, her jealousy to win it to some expression like that of the past which she remembered, took an angrier tinge, and sometimes the natural violence of her temper overcame the guard she had set upon it. Then she met the monotony of his kindness, with indignant reproaches, and quickened the dull ennui of his life into remorse.

"Yes, it would have been better, Clara, if we had not married," he would say gloomily. "I think we have made mistakes."

These mistakes were in truth sad ones. Clara had learned too late for him that she had never loved any other, and Geoffrey in his yearning after a dead ideal had only allied himself to a woman who constantly reminded him of what she was no more. There was no butterfly in the chrysalis which he had gathered to his heart.

From these conditions, came the desolateness, the loneliness of their married life. They grew apart in spite of Clara's clinging efforts, and no children were born to draw them together. Geoffrey's natural introspective tendency, now secluded him more and more; and when Clara did not alienate him with affectations of indifference, she wearied him with repentances and protestations of sorrow.

But it was not always so. There were times when these relations momentarily gave place to happier ones, when the woman's love melted the man's impassiveness.

It is an act of vigilant fondness, of kinder solicitude, one of a thousand unheeded, which has caught Geoffrey's eye, and he turns to the patient wife who watches and hungers ever for his love.

"Ah! cousin, you are a dear little wife," he cries, kissing her.

She sits upon his knee, and hides against his heart the beautiful eyes, dim with happy tears.

But it was the conscience touched, not the heart. He soothes her as he would soothe her child. Then he turns again to the work which absorbs him, while she rises and stands by his side in stormy wistfulness.

Well for her and him, that no temptation besets the thorny path over which that passionate was passing to the compensations of death!

286

—No, the movement of the story is not spirited. I confess that I have not brought my reader acquainted with people very entertaining or instructive. Yet it is plain if he be not the carping and captious reader I am loth to believe him, he must be satisfied with the present state of things.

In the name of romance, what would you?

Here is a man has married his first love; a thing you would have done once but for that sad difference of sentiment between yourself and the adored; and a thing agreeable to the usages of many fictions. Geoffrey's wife is not a great deal wiser than when she first caught his fancy—perhaps she is not even so wise; but she is still very beautiful and charming. She certainly loves her husband, and if she does not clearly understand him—alas! what man clearly understands himself? It is hardly my fault, if these people are not entirely happy, nor exactly entertaining.

I grant you that Geoffrey is not of the heroic composition, but he has greater talent than most persons, and he is very good and kind. In his youth he did some things that gave him belief in his power to achieve grander results; but it seemed that these things were the effect of youthful heat and force, rather than of genius. When he found out the truth, and the belief in his own powers passed away, his ambition faltered, and his activity ceased. That yearning after the unattainable, which often survives definite ambition, remained with him; and above all, his heart longed for the love that had been denied it—with a longing wholly disproportioned to the value of the gift withheld, as sometimes happens.

Some men have a number of passions. The altars on which they sacrifice to love are never permitted to grow cold. Other men (as it has been said of women,) love only once; and though the perfume of the one offering fills the temple of their lives forever after, the fire is out, and there is only ashes where it burned.

I understand how Geoffrey might have been happy in several ways. As a minister of religion, he might have fared well. Old ladies would have taken a motherly interest in him, and young ladies a sentimental interest. In the good that he could have done, he surely would have found his recompense? Every heart that he healed must have shed back its grateful health upon his own barren and desolate existence.

Or he might have plunged into reform, and become a mighty philanthropist, when whatever is beautiful and noble in human nature, would have turned gratefully toward him, and consoled him for all his pain. For mankind have never stoned their prophets and benefactors; and this is so because the philanthropists are a mild and amiable race, and never approach our faults as if they meant to correct them at the cost of our existence.

Unhappily, there ran through this tender and gentle nature of Geoffrey's a fine vein of cynicism and distrust that rendered these sublime careers impossible to him.

He was a very good country editor. To a certain degree, he had faith in the work he did, and his conscience if not his ambition was interested in the influence of his journal. He soon learned that his thoughts took wing from print, and alighted in a thousand places unknown him, and not one was lost or destroyed. He learned that the relations between the journalist and his readers were currents of power, intangible as air, yet bearing swift good or evil as he willed.

The *Chronicle* was a sheet much noted among the local press. Its political suggestions were treated with respect by the editors of greater journals, who watch for popular feeling in the columns of their country exchanges; and many charming little paragraphs from Geoffrey's pen were copied widely. I am surprised that such flattering success did not spur him to greater literary effort, but it did not. He saw his writings stolen and mutilated without regret, and put aside that ambition with a yawn.

Once I thought that he did unwisely to bury himself in Dulldale away from the great world, and all the friends he had made in it. But the great world tramples down and quickly forgets the man whom one defeat discourages. Only the stubborn and the strong stand up against it. He felt that inevitable neglect and oblivion must have been his portion in the world; he knew that nothing fataler could happen to him out of it. Moreover, Dulldale had renewed him, by the inspiration of one last great effort, which he would have made nowhere else.

The young ladies will observe then, that while Geoffrey is a person certainly deserving our compassion, he can by no means have our sympathy. That must be reserved for the numerous and respectable tribe of heroes, who wear their disappointments boisterously, and are ostentatiously ennuyé, as Geoffrey was not. To the great part of Dulldale he was known as a quiet sort of person—not a good man, certainly, for he never went to church. But he seemed to be very fond of his wife's little girl, and was not known to quarrel with his neighbors, even when their pigs broke down his gate. At political meetings he still continued to be made secretary, and performed his duties with satisfaction; and sometimes the township sent him as delegate to the district and county conventions of his party, as it is the custom to do with country editors. Nobody ever heard of trouble in his family.

X

Life wore away, the summer came and went, and Jane Grove still made her home with the Winters.

I wish I could say briefly as it should be said all the loveliness of this girl's character. But the subtlest essences of the flowers elude expression; I have no alembic of words fine enough to distil the sense of her purity and goodness which as often hid themselves in forbearing as showed themselves in doing.

I have before me the vision of her gentle face—sad with the shadow of her early years, yet full of present content. I see her go about that house of ennui, with her light movement and deft hand, doing all little household offices, and seeming to evoke order from its unrest, by only the magic influence of a loving heart at rest. She has in her a goodness which is repose so profound, so sweet, that none can come near it and not be comforted. It is calm that does not irritate the untranquil and unhappy: quiet that will not vex with an ostentatious moral.

Clara has for Jane the affection of an elder sister, and often finds fault with her in the captious, sisterly fashion. As for Mrs. Winter's daughter, she loves the girl with all her heart, and discerns with a child's perception, the sincere sweetness and perfect beauty of a nature not wholly visible to her mother.

As Jane grows out of Geoffrey's intellectual tutelage, from his deepening self-withdrawal, he regards her sometimes with idle unseeing eyes, sometimes with vague discernment. But since there is nothing for him to forgive in her, and less and less each day to pity, I cry out once more against the egregious error of thinking that the elusive sweetness, the vigilant and affectionate devotion of this young girl should awaken in him any sentiment tenderer than self-approval. Her whole life was a gratitude to him and his, and her heart went out to them in timeless service. How then could Geoffrey regard her but with his apathetic liking, which reverted, now and then, to the old instinctive repugnance?

The little pleasures of her calm existence had sufficed her, for they sprang from a sense of happiness imparted to those about her. She did faithfully her domestic tasks; she interested herself in the vague perplexities of Clara—poor, dumb troubles that had no voice of explanation; she listened to Geoffrey while he read, and surprised him with her intellectual progresses.

In Dulldale she was little known. She went diligently to church, for Geoffrey's doubt was not infectious, and sat broad awake under many sermons that overcame the iron resolution of deacons. But in the village gaieties she mingled seldom, and indeed she did not make friends with the young ladies, and the young gentlemen were few and bespoken. Only Mr. Rounce remained heartfree, and somehow Mr. Rounce felt that he and that shy little girl were not affinitive; a conviction to which he may have been led by his vain tender of invitations to attend the cotillion-parties of the Dulldale House. At first, on the authority of Miss Moore, it was supposed that Jane Grove was kept down by those Winters, and there was some indignant gossip which finally lapsed into the belief that she was merely a dull thing.

One of the scars which early wounds had left upon her life, was that timidity of which I have already spoken. She had too bitterly felt in all presences but that of Geoffrey and his wife the reproach of being very wretched and very poor; she had too often cowered under the coarse taunts of her playmates ever to assert that superiority of which she felt conscious; and she shrank from contact with the narrow world of the village, and chiefly from the young people of her own age. The ignorant cruelty and remorselessness of childhood were a terror to her, which even the abundant love of her heart could not subdue. She had trembled secretly before the acute and wilful precocity of the little lady Clara, who already at six years began to assume the command which she ever after held in Geoffrey's household. The friendship that afterwards grew between them was therefore the more singular, and their confidences were quaint enough. Jane told the child the story of her life, and invented an hundred fantasies to please her; and little Clara ran to her more eagerly than to her mother, for full sympathy in her small griefs and joys. This companionship had its due effect in keeping young the longing heart of the woman, and in drawing to her level the intelligence of the child whom she loved with a love almost vehement.

Sometimes Geoffrey had accompanied them in the rambles which they took in the summer fields and woods; but of late he cared best to be alone, and indeed they were less constrained without him. It was he taught them to feel that delight in nature which we think instinctive, but of which the country people know so little. They were quick to learn, and yet it was with a subtle regret that he imparted the secrets of this delight. He felt in making them known like one who shares the acquaintance of his oldest and dearest friend with others. Was it for this reason that he ceased to go with these—vexed in his fine selfishness that any one should love these things as well as he?

He is not with them this evening late in June. They are returning from one of their meadowland strolls, and they bear fragrant clusters of wild strawberries, and walk slowly. The meadowlark has fluted his latest carol and sunk silent into the wheat, but the vesper robins are singing, and all the air palpitates with their music. Homeward to the soft harmonies of their bells go the cows from the pastures. In the distance a dog barks. Away on some rustic bridge a wagon thunders from silence to silence. The cries of boyish swimmers in the creek, rise and fall with the weird melancholy of far-heard twilight voices, and on the damp air sinks and swells the hoarse rushing of the waters of the dam.

They are warm with walking, and they move languidly, talking together. Their hats are thrown from their brows, and the color that the ramble has brought into Jane's face, is toned to a soft and evanescent crimson, that hovers upon the palor of cheeks not full nor round. It is her sole beauty—this, with the sadness of the great eyes.

She talks to the child at her side, but she dreams to herself all the time, dreams that she cannot tell.

Who can declare the visions of his own brain? I cannot conjure before you the visions of hers. No doubt they were of a brave future, heroic with the splendor of wooing and wedding. Even within the sacred precincts of convent schools, where there is nothing but religion and embroidery permitted, the young ladies are said to speculate vaguely upon this future. How should it be then with this uncloistered girl who was the pupil in literature of a sentimentalist like Geoffrey, and knew more of poetry and romance than were good for many? It was a little different, I think, from that it is with the others.

It would seem sometimes that suffering, which is given to chasten us, may also spoil us poor children, and be as bad for us as indulgence, without being so pleasant. I count it a hard hurt to this girl's nature, of irreparable sadness, that suffering had made her ascetic, and mistaken, like all ascetics. A habit of disappointment and pain dashed every joy with a lurking sense of transgression, and the happiness of these later years had only cast a doubt upon the belief, more or less conscious, of her earlier life, that renunciation was her part in the world, and that in her a joy would be visited like a sin. So when these haunting dreams of bliss came first, she turned from them as from something evil and wanton. Well enough for others, but for her, these fair dreams were not! What had she to do, she reproached herself, with hopes of love and wifehood? When at last the beautiful visions peopled even the darkness of eyes she closed against them, she yielded to their spell with the dim fear that disaster of the future would be the recompense of the present dreamful delight.

There is a wild and thrilling rapture in this surrender of the ascetic soul to the pleasure which it had forbidden itself: a rapture of shame and delicious dread, and tremulous hope: *das höchst angenehmer Schmerz*; and all this, Jane felt in the secret reveries in which she forever surprised herself with blushes and confusion. Day by day she builded her golden castles in the air, and waited in them for the fate, which lingered day by day. Ah! who should be the fairy prince? Who should come at last, and make all these fancies real? Would he be, she marveled, like Geoffrey?—(for Geoffrey was the only man she had ever seen who was at all in the manner of her books. And he!—) No, not quite like Geoffrey. Good, and kind, like him; hating all mean and little thoughts like him; loving the beautiful and the true like him; but grander, bolder, gladder, hoping more, believing more, doing more—strong, handsome, resolute!

As if her own thought had taken form and encountered her in this shape, a stranger at her side, spoke, touching his hat.

She blushed a painful blush, that stained her face with sudden crimson. Surprise, bewilderment, fear and shame—all these burned in the blush, but in her heart lurked a secret foolish joy. It was like a romance!

The gentleman carried a portfolio under his arm, and wore a black hat slouched upon a head of brown curls, with an easy and picturesque grace of which he seemed conscious. He took off his hat and shook back a lock from his white forehead, and with another bow, begged to know if they could direct him to Mr. Geoffrey Winter's house.

"Why!" cried little Clara, "he's my papa!"

"Is he, indeed! He ought to be a happy parent," said the stranger with a touch of raillery in his voice, and with a smile that broke into a laugh, when Clara, delighted with her first effort, went on to say:

"And I'm Clara, and this is Jane Grove, and she lives with us."

"Well then, Miss Clara and Miss Grove, let me make known Frank Walters, who used to be a friend, I think, of Mr. Winter."

The gentleman seemed to say this with a satisfaction in his own good looks, in the novelty of the situation and in the confusion of Jane, which was not impertinent, and was yet profound.

It was in vain that Jane clutched Clara's hand, and implored her to be silent. The little maiden was charmed with the discovery of a strange gentleman who actually knew her papa, and she could not keep silent in view of the marvelous fact. She rattled on with a thousand questions and answers, until Jane gave way and laughed. Then as they approached Geoffrey's house, Clara broke from the two and ran forward to announce the arrival, and Jane and Mr. Walters walked slowly on together.

He was almost as great a surprise to the woman as the child— with his glittering talk, and free, careless way. He charmed her out of herself, and by the time they reached the gate where Geoffrey and his wife stood ready to meet them, her embarrassment had almost vanished. It is true that she talked but little, but she listened without fear, and Mr. Walters seemed willing to do all the talking.

XI

"Not till you apologise—not till you apologise!" cried Walters, as Geoffrey came to meet him with both hands of welcome extended. But nevertheless, he submitted to be cordially greeted, before he went on to say in a tone of reproach: "Three years of idyllic happiness basely concealed from the friend of your bosom! Was there no room in your Paradise, you exclusive Adam? Why didn't I receive, long ago, a polite note with the compliments of Eve, announcing that Eden was now open to visitors, and requesting the pleasure of my company during the summer solstice? Well, well, I'm come uninvited. This is Mrs. Winter? Geoffrey has told you about me, I suppose?"

"Never, till a moment ago, when Clara announced you," said Mrs. Winter, with a little pout that became her, and not well knowing yet to whom she so frankly gave her hand.

"Wretch! to have forgotten me!" cried Walters. "In his city life, madame, I was his guardian angel, restraining him from the excesses into which his impulses would have plunged him, and leading him through the flowery vale of art. Henceforth, I'll be the minister of his remorse. I'm going to stay with you two months."

All this he said with such gay abandon, such airy unconstraint, that there was no awkwardness in the meeting, either for the old friends, or for the people there brought together for the first time. But all this, with the talker's abundant life, his burlesque attitudes of reproach, his vivacious movement, his laughing voice—had the effect to bring into strange relief, the traits of the others. They listened merely, but he seemed to flash upon them and light up their silence so that Jane beheld them with new distinctness of impression. She had the sense indeed of having shrunk suddenly back into all the shyness and fear from which this joyous nature had allured her at first, and it was with almost the constraint of their earliest meeting, that she glanced toward Geoffrey.—Always grave and pensive, it seemed that in this moment of glad encounter with his friend all the sadness of his temper, found expression in the smile that lingered vaguely on his lips.—Profoundly the likeness of herself to him touched her, and she felt the occult alliance of pain and renunciation that bound them. Had he not suffered? He, too, then had learned to make sacrifice; must he not also have that austere belief that endurance was his part, and that his joy would be punished like his sin? Nothing could have been falser than this belief in the devotion of any soul to unhappiness that its own guilt does not bring. It was only a half conscious belief with this girl, but it was part of the fabric of her life. Her illumination was but for an instant. When Jane glanced again Geoffrey's smile had died away and left him dark to her, and the letter of the revelation faded, though a dim sense of it remained upon the intellectual vision.

Opposed to this stranger, so quick-sensed and quick-thoughted in all things, Clara's bewilderment and surprise showed commonplace even through her manner of seeming finer and subtler than she was. Only the child seemed to have much in common with him, and her delight in all he said and did, partook of his own joyousness. She was endowed with the richness of her mother's sensuous nature; and Jane perceived with the same flashing and fading intelligence which had made Geoffrey clear to her, that the child and this man were alike in all that made either different from her. Ah! some happy fate had made it their portion to enjoy and not to forego. In both it was an instinct, but it was only an instinct in the child, while the man had lifted it and made it his creed. Not that the seer discerned all this in that instant. She only felt then that these might be glad and bear no penalty.

It seemed from Walters' talk that he had left his baggage at the station three miles away from Dulldale, and had walked across the country. "The afternoon was so delicious, you know. The people at the station showed me the road, and I was tempted. There was an old gentleman there with a carriage of decayed respectability for your place, and he invited me so confidently to take passage, and seemed to regard walking as so preposterous, that I couldn't resist astonishing him. So I walked. I had a very pleasant time. About a mile from the village, I passed a schoolhouse just as the teacher was locking the door for the evening. I threw myself on her compassion, by asking if I was in the straight road to Dulldale, and she permitted the lonely wayfarer to walk by her side until she stopped at a farm house by the roadside—picturesque place, hop vine over the porch,—old man smoking a pipe—recumbent dog—well at the corner with sweep—smell of bacon on the air.—Nothing else adventurous interested me on the way, except the pardonable error of a gentleman who mistook me for a dishonest book-agent of his experience, and who offered me the pleasure of a personal contest on very advantageous terms—nothing else happened until I overtook little Miss Clara and her companion. And now I'm so full of sweet country sights and scents and sounds, from my tramp, that I feel like an idyll."

They had approached the house, and the two women went about the work of welcoming their guest with supper, while Geoffrey followed him to his room, and listened to his gay and dashing talk, that glanced from thought to thought, and now touched the past which was known to both, and now glittered upon their separate experiences, and never flagged nor dulled.

Briefly, he had gathered from Geoffrey the story of his three years' life and told his own, while he made his toilet, and now he came and stood beside his friend, looking so strong, so glad, so handsome, that the languid and listless Geoffrey felt more languid than ever in the contrast.

They were called to supper presently, for Clara was a notable housekeeper, and Jane was as quick as skillful. She took her place at the table with the rest, for in Dulldale even "help" ate with the family, and Jane had never been made to feel in any degree the less than equal terms on which she stood with the Winters. Clara too, I think, was somewhat puzzled what to say to her guest, and had a vague hope that Jane might assist her in extremity. But Walters spared them embarrassment, by launching forth in praise of the bread, the butter and the tea, and dashing away from these themes to sublimer topics, with a lightness and brilliancy that charmed them all.

He was a famous talker; but neither of the two country women quite understood the rarity of his gift. One thought him like all city people; but the other knew him to be like the people in books, and listened with a new and silent rapture.

That night the castles rose again, and the princess waited for the prince no longer, but followed him forth through all the world. Shyly and timidly the new, glad thoughts hid themselves away in her shame while the light was on her face, but in the friendly dark they were bold and free, and linked his hand in hers and interwove their names, and lives, and danced through the long sweet hours of waking, and through the golden gates of sleep and were no wilder and foolisher as dreams than they had been as thoughts. But ever through their antic gladness flitted a vague sense of fear, that warned and forbade, and a secret pain mixed with the joy in the dawning eyes of love, so that the dreamer woke. The thin, blue light of the moon fell in her face, and weeping she made her repentance, as if love were guilt, and turned sadly again to sleep.

Geoffrey and his friend lighted their cigars, and went forth for a moonlight stroll.

"Who is Miss Grove, Geoffrey," asked Walters.

"It is rather a sad story," said Geoffrey. "Her mother died when she was hardly more than a child, yet, and left three younger children to her care. The father was drunken; and this girl grew old very soon—what with suffering, and work and sorrow. The little ones died, and after a while the father himself. Then some good people helped her to Dulldale where she has kinsfolk, and when we were married, my wife took a liking to her, and had her come and live with us."

"It *is* a sad story," said Walters.

"I never could quite reconcile the facts of her character with the facts of her history," continued Geoffrey. "Her experiences were brutal enough, but she has no taint of meanness or selfishness in her nature,—and she is in fact so good I don't altogether like her. I think she owes a great deal to her mother, who seems to have taught her many things—the most beautifully unquestioning beliefs, and some knowledge of books, which she has improved with my help."

"I don't know why," responded Walters, "I should have thought her a relative of yours at first. Perhaps you're something alike?"

"No," said Geoffrey, with annoyance,—"Not at all, I think."

XII

There were numbers of people in Dulldale wondered that night, and for several days after, who the stranger was that had come to visit the Winters. Three things alone were certain: he was young, he was handsome, he dressed well—nay, as Miss Moore said, his dress was tasty. Beyond this line of facts, lay a vast conjectural region into which the adventurous female mind of the village, unoccupied with affairs, made frequent voyages, and brought away trifles of information, maddeningly unsatisfactory. These evidences of a wealth of gossip lying untouched in the unknown land were turned over in many honest families, and gave rise to debates not only at the tea-tables of collective virtue and curiosity, but even among the wise and grave groups at the door of the postoffice, and on the stoop of the Dulldale House.

It was not in the nature of Mr. Walters to keep them long in doubt. He was a social creature, utterly unlike Geoffrey Winter, and one so willing to talk did not want listeners in Dulldale. His favorite theme was himself, and it fell out that everybody in the village soon knew a greater number of facts of his personal history than need be set down in these pages.

I need not break the thread of my story with excursions. What does my reader, so skilled in fiction, demand? A hint that Walters is a son of opulence and luxury, bred to no profession, and a painter from caprice and idleness, with certain genius, and without ambition. Already it is understood that he is an only son; that his three proud sisters idolize and dread him; that his mother dotes upon him, and is pursued by the fear that he has more heart than is well for him, and will be parting with it some day in a disgraceful marriage of affection with a designing inferior. Already it is understood that he had wandered into Dulldale from a whim, and because mountains, and rivers, and watering places have palled upon him. Must I say that he has been everywhere, and knows innumerable books and people?

In that letter which he wrote to his sister, the insolently beautiful Julia—the conventional haughty fair one, black-eyed and scornful-lipped, of all the romances,—he spoke at large of Dulldale, but somewhat lightly, so that I cannot quote that part. But he expressed a present content, and went on to say of the Winters:

"This family consists of myself, of whom I need not write much;

of Geoffrey whom you knew," at this place when she read the letter Julia's white hand trembled, "but who has grown sadly old and grave since you saw him; of his wife," the white hand closed fiercely upon the paper, "a woman not very wise, certainly, but beautiful as such women go, and with a droll, perplexing air of having been able in her youth to impose upon people; of Mrs. Winter's little daughter by a former husband; and of a Miss Jane Grove—an adoption of the family's. *This* is rather an interesting young person—not pretty, certainly, but with a very sweet timidity, and the lovablest gentleness of manner. We shall get to be friends, I think—we have already exchanged profound admirations of Tennyson and Long-fellow. She has been a sort of intellectual pet of Geoffrey's, and is astonishingly intelligent, and I am—

"Your affectionate brother,
"Frank."

If Mr. Walters had amiably intended the uneasiness of his family, it must be confessed that this letter was not altogether without effect. They wrote to him frequent epistles in return, brimming with tenderness and trepidation, and meant to ravish him away from Dulldale. He would willingly have quitted the village, but just at the moment he determined to leave, it interested him to stay. It had hardly been his purpose to remain two months with Geoffrey, though he said it. I think that with ennui absolutely in prospect, he would not have remained two days. He liked Geoffrey, and had come to see him from a half-romantic impulse of old friendship; but he liked himself better, this warmhearted young man, and nothing could have prevailed upon him to sacrifice his own amusement and pleasure for ever so short a time.

But having rapidly exhausted Dulldale, he reasoned with himself: "Possibly I may be bored here. If I go away, I shall possibly be bored somewhere else. I will avoid these deplorable possibilities, by falling a little in love."

On the stage they are obliged to present such ideas in soliloquy, with an awkward advance to the footlights; but in a subjective story like this, everyone understands that this bit of reasoning was one of the unconscious operations of the brain.

XIII

Little Clara ceased to be the companion of Jane Grove's walks; but the walks continued, and grew longer and more frequent as the summer went by; and all day long the castle rang with music, and the birds never left singing in the garden lit by the glimmering fountain; and all night long the gay dreams held revel in the place, and knit together two fates in one golden woof; but ever the dim fear interwove the thread of black, and in the sweet hushes of the loom, whispered the warning and forbidding. Then wilder and weirder was the rapture to which the young girl surrendered her soul, hoping nothing, trusting nothing, beyond the hour—knowing only that this joy must pass, and that the retributive pain must come.

It was not the charity of the people in Dulldale which spared to find it scandalous that Walters should pay so much attention to one so far removed from him in wealth and station. But in the country all gallantries mean courtship and marriage, and this flirtation, as Walters called it, had no other effect upon the villagers than to make the young ladies wonder how he could fancy *that* thing, and to cause wiser heads to sentence him to future want in compensation for present sinful idleness.

It had no other effect?

It is true that as Walters drew nearer and nearer to the soul of this young girl he found a charm in the study, on which his sisters would have looked with wrathful suspicions.

He had always had the will to observe women. It is common to young men, but Walters had cared to study more critically: the *süsse gar nichts Gedanken* of the young man did not content his pride. So he had made many discoveries and no revelations; and like the learned with the Etruscan alphabet, knew many characters, but not the meaning of them.—He saw men and women marry, and the boisterous and determined man take for his wife, some slender and willowy creature that bound in every breath of his strong will, and with a constant show of submission, always held her place, and ruled him. He beheld another, languid, indifferent, like Geoffrey, united to some wilful woman like Clara, who performed him a thousand acts of servility, and could not make him enough her master. He saw women, unwedded, mirror always the humor of the person with whom their momentary lot was cast. He saw a witty and brilliant girl sun with her smiling eyes a dull and cloddy creature, from the gross mud of whose brain, only the stupidest weeds of thought could flourish up even in that glorious light, and heard her reply to his dullness with speeches as shallow and foolish as his own. When the student himself went to her, guessing that it was only the surface which had glassed the dolt, and that the inner currents were all full of scorn and derision—when he went to her, and made her one of his gay sardonic speeches, and she responded in kind, he felt that she mocked him and fooled him the same. He saw that the mere children had this sweet instinct of duplicity, and echoed him, and mirrored him, and never permitted him to see what they were.

In effect, all his study, all his shrewd observation brought him only this knowledge: that women's hearts were known only so far

as they permitted it; that their perception outran the swiftest ratio-
cination; that the dullest woman surpassed the acutest man at any
game of illusions, and that at last when love came, the subtlety of
the keenest female intellect was only used in self-deceit. The lore is
world-old; but while he was yet a young man he thought it new.

It did not displease him to be baffled in his first effort to read
the soul of the girl with whom the latest fortune had thrown him;
nay, he had an egotistic pleasure in the harmless, unconscious guile,
which even in the rare sincerity of her nature, veiled from him her
real self and only revealed the negative quality which responded to
his own thoughts. For he recognised in this another proof that his
observation had not been at fault; and he felt that without it she
must have been a monster and not a woman.

He had thought to himself: "I will study this little daisy." So he
had set about his study, and in his artistical and philosophic way,
had indeed learned to see that the daisy was not only unlike all other
flowers, but different from them in its subtle spiritual essence and
chiefly in its divine sadness that trembled sometimes into a fleeting,
fearful joyousness—and was nothing to his analysis.

To the daisy, the dear humble little field flower, this superior
being had been at first like a wonderful, far-off star, shining forever
in a brilliant atmosphere of its own, and dazzling her with its
light.—But after while, the daisy saw that when all things were
clear about her, the star did not shine. Then she pined and yearned
vaguely in the daylight for the darkness that made the star visible.
And this yearning was the daisy's love—beautiful, sorrowful and
wise.

Of himself, Mr. Walters had not yet made a study very profound
or very sincere. But some things had occurred to him. He knew
that he was brilliant, and pleased most women; and he understood
that his manly beauty, his gay spirit, and his genius, were gifts rare
enough.—Above all, he understood that with certain illusions of
generosity, he was selfish almost to egotheism. He sometimes
thought of this, with an amiable indulgence of the peculiarity, and
could not remember when he had done any good or bad thing but
for his own pleasure.

Slender as this self-knowledge was, it was through it alone that
he arrived at his apprehension of Jane Grove's character. He felt
that it was only his vanity which was interested in her; he knew
that it was her heart which was interested in him. He saw that by
degrees his brilliancy ceased to dazzle her; that his wickedness
ceased to frighten her. He saw that she loved him truly and inscrut-
ably, as women seem always to love—as much for what was bad
and mean in him, as for what was good and great; and that her
passion was a sorrow and not a joy. He saw all this with that strange

and cruel delight in the ability to give pain to patient love, and yet be loved, which is the last excess and most exquisite sense of power.

"Yes, it was a very droll little flirtation," he was known to say in after years. "I rioted on my sensations in those days, and I cared for anything that woke new impulses in me.—I don't think that from the first it was any commonplace intrigue with the customary desolating denouement that was intended. No, the little girl interested me differently. Her history was sad, and I pitied her. But, *bon Dieu!* pity is mixed with so many other emotions at that age; and it soon ceased to be novel. I used sometimes to hate her, because she saw through me, but after all I loved her the more for that—seeing her heart was not the less mine on account of it.

"I affected to be *blasé,* then—it is now no longer my fashion, and I pretend to be interested in everything—and I gave myself a good deal to wicked persiflage, to frighten her. I had a kind word for every vice, and left the virtues to speak for themselves. I confounded the right and the wrong, with a trick of mockery, which it is very easy to pick up, and was altogether abominable in my sentiments for the sake of the effect.

"The effect seemed to be only to make her love me the more, and to make me secretly a little ashamed. I don't think she ever dreamed of making me better than I pretended to be, and she never answered anything to my wickedness, but at times the sadness deepened in her eyes—which were certainly very fine. Here is a picture I painted of her from memory. It is not quite good, but it will give you an idea.

"Ah! well—it would have been a pity to have done her any harm, and I am glad that the affair ended as it did. She had an odd little theory about my dedication to happiness without any penalty of wretchedness, which might have fallen to ground, for I should certainly have felt some remorse. As it is, it makes me forget that I am thirty and in Paris to recall those dear, sweet, innocent days of idyllizing."

XIV

Geoffrey Winter gave himself little concern in what went forward. He thought no evil.—He saw that his friend seemed to enjoy himself, and he looked with languid composure at the play which they were putting upon the stage in his own house. Self-withdrawn, gentle, calm, and somewhat cold, now, his carelessness consented that the actors should end the drama with a marriage, or another catastrophe as they would.

Clara had the female instinct for match-making, as she had the other graceful female instincts. She saw that Jane was the equal of Walters in many things, and in her narrow sphere of life, she had

The Matter of Dulldale

little experience of the considerations that prevent matches in the greater world. The romance pleased her, and she aimed to leave the young people a great deal together. Sometimes she would talk about them to Geoffrey, who had then the habit of listening out of a profound revery, and of never understanding her in the least. Thus, baffled, closed in, and as it were dammed up, Mrs. Winter's mind overflowed in secret channels to the neighbors, and it was presently reported upon her authority that the wedding day was fixed, and Jane was subjected to frequent persecution from Miss Moore, who visited the Winters with the double purpose of spying upon the poor girl, and of doing whatever might be done to win back the long-truant affections of Mr. Rounce. It is but just to say, however, that this gentleman did not afford her the smallest encouragement, but had ever the custom on these occasions of staring through Miss Moore's head into the back of her bonnet, with stoical indifference to her blandishments. Miss Moore would then, in retaliation, bring her fascinations to bear upon Mr. Walters, when that gentleman chanced to be present; and would receive his sarcastic devoirs with giggling delight.

There was little love between the printer and the artist. The former felt that the latter made game of him, even when he said nothing, and he had once found a caricature of which he could not mistake the original. In his confidences with the boy Robin, he pronounced Mr. Walters to be a serpent of the most covert and deadly species, and denied to him even the generosity of the rattlesnake, which always gives warning of its intent to bite. When therefore he saw these compliments pass between Miss Moore and Walters, in his soul he desired nothing better than that the two might involve themselves in some intrigue (a hint from the fatalities which had led to Mr. Rounce's own marriage at an earlier period,) by which Walters should be compelled to marry her; for this he conceived would be at once a divine justice and an infinite punishment.

I say, Mr. Rounce, in his way, was a man of the world, and more worldly wise, because more suspicious than Geoffrey. In his secret heart (which, though full of lies, was tender) I believe he had an honest regard for Jane, and felt an honest pain, when he discerned the peril which Geoffrey never saw.

Well, we find knight-errant souls in the bodies of the oddest varlets sometimes, and I have often admired the daring virtue, the indignant championship of the opportune though plebeian friend of innocence whom I have observed to thwart the schemes of villainy in the theatres. But this is not the part of Mr. Rounce in the present little drama, though he has played it on the boards of many a wandering theatre since the period of these events. It is true that he

301

would have hinted to Geoffrey his fear that all this could not result happily; but he had his reasons for silence, chief among which was that habit of Geoffrey's to pooh-pooh whatever Mr. Rounce said with a peculiarly solemn design. Besides he knew that he hated Walters, and could not speak of him with that sublime and perfect justice which he desired to render all men, even him. He dreaded his own faculty of invention, and feared lest in the transports of denunciation, he should alledge things which it would be hard to prove to less heated imaginations.

What happens then in all the novels, when human agencies are powerless to avert calamities?

Commonly, a superior and anticipative catastrophe.

But I am not sure that this worst calamity threatens. I have only the evidence of Mr. Rounce's angry suspicions.

XV

The sun had not yet gone down, and all the tree tops were golden with his rays, when the figure of a woman paused alone on the bridge in that little valley, where even now—

"The light it was ashen, the shade it was dun."

It was the earliest autumn. Here and there among the dark green lines of woodland, a maple flamed half-crimson. On the chestnut-trees, scattered leaves and whole boughs, hung golden; and the cucumber trees were decked in savage splendor by the crimson seeds pendant on silver threads from the ripe fruit. The sycamores that leaned over the little stream, . . .

[eleven-pages, about 1,300 words, lacuna in manuscript]

. . . Geoffrey's study, and lying heavily down in her own room, and hoping she might never rise.

XVI

Geoffrey had not liked that idea of a resemblance which Walters discovered in Jane Grove and himself, and had resented it with a petulant eagerness of which he was afterwards ashamed. Yet the resemblance remained nevertheless, for the two were really alike in many things—in the sweetness and goodness of their natures, in their spiritual delicacy, and their rare instincts of beauty and purity. But, being man and woman, their sorrows, kindred in essence, and not wholly unlike in form, affected them differently.

The woman's disappointment called forth all the latent strength of a character which happiness must have softened more and more. Torn from the support to which she had clung, she grew self-sustaining. Through passion she arrived not at greater power than she had possessed before, but at positive sense of it. Her whole life

302

had been a struggle with sorrow and evil; she rose against this new calamity, after the stupor of the first stroke, with undismayed resistance.

The disappointment which had wasted the youth and annulled the languid manhood of Geoffrey grew narcotic as it became still more an abstraction and a melancholy, and insensibly blunted the most delicate qualities of his nature. The effect is sometimes to be noted in the dreaminess of the scholarly temperament, which, as it is absorbed by intense study, assumes a type of brooding torpor, from which it is only to be roused by violent impulses.

It might have been that after while, Geoffrey would have grown nearer to Clara, as he imperceptibly lapsed from the highest intellectuality. But the very grain of their clay was different, and it seems to me that until coarser customs of age allied them, there could have been no closer love between them.

A destiny, however, superior to all contingencies, thwarted the slender possibility of even this lower form of happiness.

One day, not long after Walters had quitted Dulldale, Clara fell ill, and in spite of the professional skill of the village practitioner, grew worse and worse. Neither did the simple science and elaborate assertion of a wandering water-cure physician avail, though he packed the poor lady in wet sheets, and attempted to restore the tone of her system by a series of hydropathic shocks sufficiently tremendous to shatter the constitution of a giant.

She continued to droop, and as the autumn advanced, she fell into a low typhoid fever, from which she rose with health broken forever. It was then that the fatal disorder with which her mother had died, first shewed itself; and it presently began to be whispered about the village that Mrs. Winter had the heart-disease.

Dr. Morphine, who had been again called in, pronounced that she had nothing but dyspepsia, superinduced by a violent attack of hydropathy, and declared that if his patient would keep clear of the wet sheets, he would bring her round.

The form of speech is somewhat vague, and the doctor did not perhaps mean to say that he would cure her. It is certain that he failed to do so. The winter wore away, and Clara was worse and not better.

The fact of this suffering in his wife, appealed to Geoffrey's tenderness more effectively than all her love had done.—He partially awoke from the lethargy into which he was falling, and with the eagerness of remorse, devoted himself to her. He felt for the first time how poor was the return he had made for her love, and his regret was not the less poignant because he could not reasonably blame himself with gross neglect.

But it was again too late. Our errors, as well as our sins have their inevitable consequences. The blunder made in his marriage with Clara was so egregious that nothing but death could repair it. And to die was the only thing left for this poor woman to do.

Is it a cruelty to say that one has no longer any business to live? Destiny seems sometimes to have perfectly accomplished the ends of an existence, before the existence ceases, removing the possibilities that make life a better thing than death, that make life a different thing to annihilation.

It may be that our happiness is only a system of deceptions more or less harmless—a sum of absurd delusions, into which we cheat ourselves and are willingly cheated by our friends. Yet when the hope of this is forever taken away, the truth is such an intolerable thing, that it seems better for us not to be.

Behold now kindly everything had been made ready for this poor woman's death! Her husband did not love her, and she felt that she was a burden on his days. She had no other friend to endear life to her, and no kin but her child, who had outgrown the absolute dependence of childhood, and would lament her, certainly, but would be comforted by time. The future could contain no chance that would change these relations. All the fortuities of joy and sorrow that knit hearts together, had failed to unite her husband's to hers; and her daughter growing older grew from her, and must soon in some girlish passion, forget her affection to her mother. Should she die now, her family need not be broken up, for Clara and Geoffrey were attached to each other, and—Jane Grove would remain to care for both when she was gone.

They bring Clara's chair to the open door, when the spring has blossomed into summer, and the pleasant west wind blows softly over the meadows, where the men are beginning to cut the hay.

The landscape is very fair.

She can look athwart the waving butter cups and timothy, and through the moving boughs of the trees.

She can see the sunny flashing of the fields of corn, and beyond them guess the coolness of the creek that the willows and the ghostly sycamores hide from her.

The white road winds downward to the red mill, and now and then a wagon passes and now and then a lazy-mounted boy. The white road winds downward from the mill upon the other side, and over it on the slope of the hot and sandy hill, gleam the white stones of the graveyard.

All this she sees, opening her heavy eyes, when the rush of the passionate humming-bird startles her from the languor into which the dull bees lull her with their music in the honeysuckles.

Then the heavy lids fall again, and she feels upon her face the pitying tenderness of her husband's eyes. She knows then that he sits at his table with a book before him which he does not read, and that he turns his eyes from her again in pain. Still with closed lids she feels his noiseless approach as he bows over her, and feels his going as he passes from the room.

Then she hears the throb of Jane's quick, light feet, as the girl goes about the household work which she shall do no more; and she divines that the rapid movements are silent for her sake.

And lying there, recalling all the past with mute repentances and sore regrets—recalling the unthoughtful days of girlhood, and the doubts and the confirmations of the doubts that revealed her to herself an unloved wife, bitterly remembering the slow waste of hours, that passed in lonesomeness and made the desert of her married years, and yet puzzling herself with all, and clinging blindly to the hope of happiness in another world—there darts through her sadness and confusion, a clear, sharp pang of thought, that drives from her the torturing regrets with a new and jealous fear. In the future—in the future which she shall not know on earth, Geoffrey will find with another wife that content which he had never found with her! And eagerly and painfully her sick heart fixes on Jane, as the wife who shall fill her empty place in Geoffrey's life, and fill the place in Geoffrey's love which her going will leave no emptier than before.

It is a death-cruel thought, for it involves the idea of her own utter, eternal absence. Yes, reaching beyond death, it reveals that even in another world, where unions are of the soul, Geoffrey shall be mated not with her, but with another.

Slowly that strong, passionate nature, whose craving has never been met with the love it has hungered for—yields itself to the possession of this belief, constant with it unto death.

The sick woman lies with closed lids, day by day, revolving the thought painfully in her mind, and they think she sleeps.

Custom did not blunt the sharpness of the jealous fear. To the last, this surrender of hope, this abdication of her wifehood for another, was a pang of ineffable anguish. But custom endued her with patience, and a soul not docile or obedient, bowed to what seemed the inevitable.

See! it happens often, for the world is full of wretched shapes of deformity and pain, that miserably emulate the ways of health, and grimly mock the harmony of the whole. Yes, there are crutches for the amputations; and every disease has its medicine if not its cure. Youth goes forth conquering and enjoying the world, and age is content to sit rheumatic and calm in the chimney corner. If we cannot have what we would, we take what is possible; we fall from hope to fainter hope, and at last it is only a dull longing for repose that remains to us.

With this dull longing, Clara sought to escape from the idea which haunted her, but it would not leave her even in her submission. It was only when she resolved to make the sacrifice her will that she triumphed, and it became her glory, her crown of self-devotion—thorny, yet a crown.

She would speak to Geoffrey of all that had passed in her mind, only keeping back . . . [last line of script on page is destroyed] . . . implore him that this marriage might be when she no longer lived to prevent it; and one day she besought him to sit down beside her that she might speak with him.

He came to her, and tenderly took her hand. With that dear contact, all nature rose battling against the sacrifice. She turned on him helpless eyes of love and yearning, and when she would have spoken, her lips clung together; the words died in her heart,—she fell swooning upon his breast.

He shuddered with a vague terror—a superstition apart from the fear her swoon occasioned, for the light wind blowing over the porch came sick-sweet with the breath of the honeysuckles, and he remembered that five years ago that day, Clara's mother had died.

He had ceased to believe that his wife could live, but he had never actually contemplated her death; for the thought of death was unspeakably hideous to him, as it is to all such gentle and doubting people. He looked to nothing beyond the grave with absolute belief. That radiant passion of the cross did not light for him the mortal darkness, and to him death was no era of being, but the end.

Clara grew no worse with the lapse of the day; they drew her chair again to the doorway, when she rose from her fainting, and she sat silent there until the sun went down. She had no pain, she said, when they asked her, but she did not make again the cruel effort that had over tasked her strength.

So the night fell, and she went to rest, and all things passed as they were wont, only Geoffrey would not sleep, but sat watching, with the vague foreboding upon him. It had been the sick woman's whim to have her bed brought down from the upper chamber in which she had always slept, to the room where her mother died; and the indulgence of this whim had been pronounced by the whole sooth-saying wisdom of the village, to be the certain precursor of her death, for no sick person had ever been known to indulge such a wish and live. In the next room Geoffrey sat down alone after he had left her asleep, and took his papers, out of habit, and pored mechanically over them.

It seemed that he must soon have fallen into some deep revery, for when he roused himself to consciousness, he was no longer alone. Opposite to him in the obscurity sat Jane Grove, the untrimmed candle glaring angrily in her pale face. She remained perfectly calm, staring into the black portal which gave entrance to the sick chamber, as five years before, she had stared into the same room when the dead woman lay there.

The wind stirred the creeper at the lattice, and all the horror of that night stole back upon Geoffrey, mingled with remorse and heavy foreboding. When, startled by some passing step, or the glimpse of the moon, looking with its white corpse-face, from the ragged clouds that filled the sky, the housedog howled loud, and long and dismally—a frenzy seemed to seize the watcher, taking the form of hatred for this girl, who sat there so ghastly still.

That he might not yield to a demoniac impulse that possessed him, to cry out and declare once and forever, all the hatred with which this girl's presence inspired him, and which swept all pity and kindliness of custom from his soul—he clutched the candle from the table and rose from his place, to enter his wife's room.

As if a hand laid on his shoulder had swayed him, he turned again toward the open doorway of the sick chamber, and beheld a white-robed, wide-eyed figure, set in the black gloom of the portal,—twining one ghostly arm in its dark, fallen hair, and stretching the other toward him, and moving its dumb lips.

In a moment it wavered, tottered and fell forward.

At Geoffrey's feet Clara lay dead—defeated of the last embrace.

XVII

It was once a matter of surprise to me, when I looked over the incidents of Geoffrey's history, that after Clara's death he did not at last marry happily, and retrieve his past errors, and avert their consequences, as it is frequently the custom to do in the romances. I was sure that he would be all the more regarded in fable-land for a course of this kind. Positively I knew that there was a lordly pleasure house standing empty and ready furnished for him in that fortunate region.

Yet, because he was not much like the other heroes of fiction, and had no splendid virtues, but seemed, in effect, a man with the human facts of weakness and folly, I discerned an acute propriety in his passing out of my notice by another path than that which lay so plain before him in the world of romance.

Yes, as I linger upon this picture, and wonder if I have indeed only dreamed these people, and fondly hope that here and there some gentle reader will not find them altogether fantastical or impossible, and that an audacious charity shall even have the greatness to cry—"This is like!" and, "I have known some such man!" in spite of reason—I say as I linger still, until the figures fade in the indistinctness of withdrawal—I see Geoffrey grow early old in an apathetic seclusion, which is not wholly ungrateful to him.

Doubtless, men do not radically change in anything, and the seeming transformations of their lives are but the developement of the principles that existed in the uncreate atoms of their being before the beginning.

It is certain that Geoffrey can undergo no profound change with the occurrence of events, but the germs which are in him must develop themselves through all, and bear their fruit, each in its season.

The time of his nobler qualities must soon be past, for it seems to me that all these have attained their possible growth. In their place, the weeds of querulousness, unreason, and impatience, which spring up in souls exhausted by the harvests of life, and make age unlovely, shall early show themselves in him. That marriage which the dead wife so bitterly dreaded, so sorrowfully and sincerely intended, can never take place. I think that for little Clara's sake, Jane Grove shall remain in that lonesome house long after it becomes a place of pain to her; and that she shall be the only human creature between Geoffrey and desolate estrangement. But in the after years, beyond which this seer does not look, I know that she must go forth into the world, and seek amid its new unfriendliness, the home which she has lost. It may be possible that making her life an unthanked service to Geoffrey, and wholly losing her old instinctive fear of him in compassion for his loneliness, she comes to look upon him with a feeling, which his regard would transmute to love. But it is not known. She grows austerer with time, and never, whatever is in her heart, remembers by word or deed, the great blight which fell upon her life. Doubtless, she does not forget the past, for no grand event intervenes to hide it; nothing but the monotonous lapse of years is between.

The unreasonable aversion with which she first inspired Geoffrey, returns oftener and oftener to his brooding melancholy, and must grow with the growth of whatever else is mean and pitiful in him. With such a man, the relation which she had seemed destined to bear to his life, and her witness, however reluctant and constrained, of the saddest passages of his life, must be cause enough for the resentment with which he regards her; and which is qualified by the reproachful remembrance of times when he was more just, only to tinge it with bitterness and self-accusation. Shall he not then, make this antipathy to the only being who could truly have been his wife, a part of his remorseful memory of Clara, and in his weakness, cherish an error in regret for error?

The diamond clasp lies in the crossing, and one that should have found it, goes blindly down the other way.

Shall we follow him?

Lo! the distance hides him, and all the future is blurred with doubt.

CHAPTER SEVEN

War Movements in Ohio

[News of the bombardment of Fort Sumter reached Columbus by telegraph on Friday the twelfth day of April, 1861. The General Assembly, still in session, listened in "terrible excitement and suspense" as the frequent dispatches were read. Ironically, a question before the legislature at the time was Thomas Corwin's proposed amendment to the federal constitution which would have forbidden any future outside interference with slavery in those states where it already existed. But now the time for compromise and appeasement was past, and the Civil War that had so long been in the making was upon the ill-prepared and ill-fated nation. "At last we are done with policies," the *Ohio State Journal* shrilled the following morning, "and the keen edge of the sword cuts the Gordian knot of red tape! May it never be sheathed until treason perish!" Two days later, April fifteenth, President Lincoln declared that "insurrection" existed and called upon the state militias "to maintain the honor, the integrity, and the existence of our National Union." Ohio was asked to supply thirteen regiments, and even before Governor William Dennison could act on Lincoln's request, volunteers began arriving in Columbus. With them came less patriotically motivated men: contractors, office seekers, and entrepreneurs hoping to profit by the extraordinary circumstances, an ambition in large part assured by the million-dollar appropriation immediately authorized by the legislature for the purchase of arms and equipment. Within a few days, Ohio had overfilled by twice her quota, and the first troops were sent on to Washington without either uniforms or arms to defend the nation's capital against a feared attack from the South. Altogether it was a scene Howells later thought supremely suited to fiction, but he knew that he could never gain the imaginative distance necessary to "give the living complexion of events."

Instantly the town was inundated from all the towns of the State and from the farms between as with a tidal wave of youth; for most of those who flooded our streets were boys of eighteen and twenty, and they came in the wild hilarity of their young vision, singing by day and by night one sad inconsequent song, that filled the whole air, and that fills my sense yet as I think of them:

"Oh, nebber mind the weather but git ober double trouble,
For we're bound for the happy land of Canaan."

They wore red shirts, as if the color of the Garibaldian war for Union in Italy had flashed itself across the sea to be the hue of our own war for Union. With interlinked arms they ranged up and down, and pushed the willing citizens from the pavement, and shouted the day and shouted the night away, with no care but the fear that in the out-pour of their death-daring they might not be gathered into the ranks filling up the quota of regiments assigned to Ohio. The time had a sublimity which no other time can know, unless some proportionate event shall again cause the nation to stand up as one man, and the spectacle had a mystery and an awe which I cannot hope to impart. I knew that these boys, bursting from their fields and shops as for a holiday, were just such boys as I had always known, and if I looked at any one of them as they went swaggering and singing up and down I recognized him for what they were, but in their straggling ranks, with their young faces flushed the red of their blouses and their young eyes flaming, I beheld them transfigured. I do not pretend that they were of the make of armies such as I had seen pictured marching in serried ranks to battle, and falling in bloody windrows on the smoke-rolled plain. All that belonged to
"Old, unhappy, far-off days,"
and not to the morrows in which I dwelt. But possibly if I had written that forever-to-be-unwritten novel I might have plucked out the heart of the moment and laid it throbbing before the reader; and yet I might rather have been satisfied with the more subjective riddle of one who looked on, and baffled himself with question of the event. (*YMY*, pp. 200–01)

Up to that time, Howells, like most Republicans who had come to the party through the cause of abolition, had opposed the use of force to preserve the Union. Unlike the maverick Corwin and most Ohio Democrats who worked toward compromise with the South, he preferred the adoption of some plan of peaceable secession. But just as with many other peacetime pacifists, the opening of hostilities necessitated a reevaluation of issues and solutions, and Howells found himself drawn into the fervor of the moment in spite of family and ethical prejudices he had assumed throughout his younger days.

In purely personal terms, the timing of the outbreak of the war could not have been better suited to Howells's needs. Though he lingered on at the *Ohio State Journal*, mostly in hope of backpay owed him, he had during his five years of journalizing in Columbus fairly worn out the place, and his thoughts were pushing at the horizon. Encouraged by the favorable notice *Poems of Two Friends* had received in the New York *World*, Howells sent to the metropolitan daily a letter describing the early efforts at mobilization in Ohio. The letter published, he ventured to inquire about the possibility of a position on the paper but received no encouragement from the assistant editor, Edmund Clarence Stedman, a fellow poet and, in time, a lifelong friend. Stedman was happy to print the letters and urged Howells to continue sending reports from the West— "Ohio just now occupies a central & noble position of strength against the rebellion pressing upon her Southern borders"—but had to report that business stagnation made any place for Howells at the paper out of the question. So the young Ohio poet continued for several months an occasional correspondent to the New York paper, his future almost as unsettled and unsettling as the nation's.]

FROM OHIO

COLUMBUS, April 16.

Yesterday and to-day have been busy days in the legislative and executive departments of Ohio—in the legislative busy in passing laws and considering measures to aid the federal government to meet the present emergency of civil war; in the executive in putting those laws into execution. Ere this letter is read by the public, a million dollars will have been appropriated by the General Assembly for war purposes; and by Friday of this week, at the furthest, it is expected two regiments of Ohio volunteers will be on their way to Washington. Among the companies which compose the two regiments is one deserving of special notice. It is the pet company of the capital city, as well as the star of the battalion. The company was organized in the high school of Columbus, under the name of "Cadets," and comprised the flower of the school and the city. They were then beardless boys, and their motive was solely physical development. Blooming into manhood, and bidding adieu to school, some to battle with the law, others with medicine—all to pursue some useful avocation—they concluded to continue their military organization, and to drop the juvenile title of "Cadets" for the more manly one of "Videttes." Promptly upon the present outbreak they offered their services to the governor, who, upon deliberation, concluded to accept their services, but to retain them as "The Home Guard," and so informed their captain, who modestly but earnestly insisted on being called into active service. Calling in the colonel of the battalion, the governor asked his opinion, and such an eulogium did the colonel pass upon the merits of the youthful company that

Governor Dennison ordered the adjutant-general to call them into immediate service. Their captain, Henry Thrall, is not twenty-two. Twenty-two is about the average age of the company. Numerous companies have already been enrolled in different parts of the state, and the governor only waits the official requisition from the Secretary of War, with its accompanying instructions, indicating the manner and terms of enlistment, to receive a sufficient number to make up thirteen regiments, including the two regiments already ordered out. The two regiments will proceed to Washington in citizens' dress and without arms where they will meet the quartermaster-general of Ohio, D. L. Wood—he left for Washington this morning—and be equipped. The surgeon-in-chief of the Ohio volunteers is Dr. W. L. McMillen, who leaves with the two regiments, Friday. Although yet a young man, Dr. McMillen has seen service, as surgeon in the late Russian war. The excitement in Ohio is intense; that incident to the Mexican war was only a ripple, compared to the present; and those who remember the war of 1812 say it is greatly beyond that, even when the English fleet dotted our own Lake Erie. But our population is so great that we can furnish an almost indefinite number of troops, and yet there will be left enough at home to prepare the soil for its seed, to reap the harvest and to carry on all the avocations of trade, as if no war were in existence. Feeling thus, and reposing an abiding confidence in the ability and good intentions of the present administration, and in the justice of our cause, the loyal citizens of Ohio are content to abide the decision of that arbiter, the God of battles, knowing full well that "He doeth all things well." A company of middle-aged and old men has been organized in Cincinnati, under the name of "The Home Guards." They are not to be called into the service of the federal government, but will remain at home, to be called out only in case of domestic invasion. Like companies will doubtless be organized in most, if not all, the cities and towns in Ohio. Should the war become general, and should the border states unite their destinies with the cotton states, as present appearances indicate they will do, the Ohio river is likely to become a scene of conflict and carnage, and in that case, "The Home Guards" will have plenty of work to do.

[New York *World*, 22 April 1861]

[Founded the previous year by Alexander Cummings, a wealthy Philadelphia journalist, the New York *World* was "radically" Republican in politics and utterly respectable in its approach to the news. Unlike most of its competitors, it eschewed police reports, details of criminal trials, and gossip surrounding slander suits and divorce proceedings. Howells afterwards recalled it "as a good young evening paper, with a decided religious tone, so that the Saturday Press could call it the Night-blooming

Serious" (*LFA*, pp. 74–75). But such a characterization in no way suggests the passion with which the New York *World* entered the war of words that preceded the first Battle of Bull Run. If Howells still had reservations about the wisdom of the course events had taken—and it is clear from his letters to his family that he did—he knew it was necessary to suppress these feelings if he intended to make the right impression with the newspaper's publishers.]

COLUMBUS, May 11.

I have never thought small beer of my native state; but during the past three weeks my feelings of local patriotism have gone up, if I may so speak, to sparkling Catawba, of the oldest vintage. You have heard—what part of the civilized world has not heard—of the splendid rapidity with which Ohio filled up her quota of thirteen regiments, and was unable to stop herself before she had offered the whole number of troops called for by the President. I exult in this, and in the fact that the movement of the first Ohio Regiment eastward was contemporary with the movements of the first Massachusetts troops southward; and since the whole nation has now paused between battle and preparation, it is gratifying to note that the enthusiasm of Ohio was not mere effervescence. It has body and strength, and held up and looked at in the most skeptical light, it is very pure and clear.

All the men who have offered themselves in this state, are still ready to do service. The adjutant general wisely directed that the troops for the seventeen state regiments ordered by the Legislature, should go into quarters at home to begin with, and local camps are now established throughout the state, beside the general rendezvous at Cleveland, Cincinnati, and this place. None of the superfluous companies have been disbanded; and the whole state resounds with the "left! left!" of the monotonous and ubiquitous drill-serjeant—a sentiment that may be tortured into a reproach by such conscience stricken people as have not yet volunteered.

The great extent of Ohio, and the variety of her material interests, contribute a marvelously diverse people to her army. The commercial south sends the mechanics and young merchants and lawyers of her cities and large towns; the agricultural regions of central and western Ohio give the lusty strength of great corn and wheat farms; from the manufacturing east come founderymen and iron puddlers, and on the lake shore the same sublime impulses animate the pastoral abolitionists of the Connecticut Reserve, and the aguish and amphibious race which inhabits the swamps of the northwest, and which once subsisted (in the popular belief) on a diet of suckers and milk. It was the food of a virtuous poverty; it

313

has made heroes, and I do not know that ambrosia could further go.

Our first regiment was made up of drilled troops—the pet companies of the cities, but the rest are formed of the rawest material out of which soldiers can be fashioned. It is a beating of pruning-hooks and plow shares into swords and spears, but the steel is true, and the weapons will not be less deadly for the uses of peace to which they were accustomed. Ohio had no military organization outside of large towns; and the prevailing ideas of militia were scornful and derisive. I myself—I weep to write it!—have plied at the peace establishment, in my time; but the providence of Massachusetts in the maintenance of a militia system has taught lessons which none of us will forget. On the Western Reserve, where the great anti-slavery strength of the State is lodged, they had forgotten the art of war, and none knew how to get up companies, so that the first thirteen regiments were formed outside of the reserve, while rage and horror at the fall of Sumter yet curdled the milk in her cheese vats. Consequently, the biting jest and the unfeeling mock have not been spared the abolitionists of the Reserve,—who were mortified to find themselves too late for the crusade of freedom. By dint of long continuance, they have procured the acceptance of several infantry companies, and they have had the honor of contributing the first men to active service in the state—six companies of light artillery having been dispatched several weeks ago to take possession of Marietta, on which an attack from Virginia was expected.

Apropos of the Reserve, John Brown, Jr., lives there, in Ashtabula county, and may yet figure in this war. He is not, however, at the head of a corps of free negroes, but is organizing a company of sharp shooters in Ashtabula. He has many qualities of leadership—a military experience, great courage, and in a wonderful degree the personal magnetism characteristic of his father. At the head of a troop of God-fearing stockholders in the underground railroad, he would be very formidable. His name is a sign of terror to Virginia, and his friends would follow him to the death. Another man connected with the John Brown raid will, I think, be heard of in the fight. I mean Barclay Coppoc, who has more determination and energy in his young face than I ever saw in another, and who, it is said, cherishes the memory of his brother with affection and bitter resentment. But the time of these men has not yet come, and they bide their time.

Many Kentuckians have crossed our borders to volunteer in the cause of the Union. Some of these I have seen—superb, great limbed fellows, from Hardin county, (where Lincoln was born), who have enlisted in a cavalry company under Capt. Donn Piatt. Their leader, you know, was secretary of the legation at Paris during

Pierce's time, and he has put his diplomatic talent at interest in the selection of the finest body of men who will enter the service from this state. They are drawn chiefly from that part of Ohio which was the scene of Simon Kenton's exploits in the brave old days when men laid in blood the corner-stone of our western empire, and stole horses from the Indians. An instinctive equestrianism has ever since distinguished that region, and Captain Piatt's troopers are all splendid horsemen, and particularly astonished with their wild feats a riding-master who was summoned from Cincinnati to the Mac-a-Cheek valley to drill them. Seeing the furious *abandon* with which they managed their steeds, and the desperate recklessness of their chargers, he concluded the rules of horsemanship could do little but restrain them. He returned to the city with new ideas of his art.

The expectation of some border warfare in this state is likely now to be disappointed. The attitude of Kentucky is no longer menacing, but secession populations are liable to spasms of treason at any moment; and I think it is to the defenselessness rather than the patriotism of that state that we have to trust. People returning from Kentucky declare that there is really very little genuine attachment to the Union there; and that secession is only a question of expediency. Bitter animosity toward Cincinnati exists, and whether Kentucky would arrest the progress through her territory of an army marching upon that defenseless city, might be doubted by persons of larger faith than myself. I do not think it wise to leave Cincinnati unfortified, as she now is; a few columbiads are better than much amity and fraternal feeling.

Here (as everywhere I believe) there has been great mismanagement of contracts, and the state has expended large sums to procure the discomfort and neglect of her troops. But things are better now. The camps are permanently located and their condition has been greatly improved—one feature of the improvement being that the men are put on rations instead of being "boarded" by contract. Our principal camps are: Taylor, at Cleveland; Jackson, at Columbus; Dennison and Harrison, at Cincinnati.

[New York *World*, 15 May 1861]

[Because of the enthusiastic response of the volunteers who made haste to Columbus, the state was slow to deal with the logistical problems such speedy mobilization created. "Peace-bred officials overwhelmed by a sudden and unprecedented demand for military experience" were hard put even to feed and shelter the undisciplined recruits. The hotels and boardinghouses in Columbus were immediately filled, and even the corridors of public buildings were commandeered until a makeshift camp could be erected on the outskirts of town. For the twenty-three regiments that had been formed to answer Lincoln's call, there were less than 3,000 outdated

315

muskets and barely 200 sabers. Uniforms and camp equipment were non-existent. Before the war the Ohio Militia had resembled a fraternal club more than a military organization; now, in both the comfort of the troops and the inflated financial burden on her citizens, Ohio would pay dearly for her neglect. Eventually, confusion gave way to order and an effective development of resources and personnel, but by then the greater expense of war had been made known to these innocents playing at history's deadliest game.]

COLUMBUS, May 17.

I notice that your contemporary of the *Evening Post* gives Governor Dennison, of this state, the credit for our improved militia system. Glory, like responsibility, should be placed where it belongs; and I am sorry that I cannot remember the Latin sentiment nearly to the same effect. Adjutant-General Carrington is the author of the system, which gives Ohio an available army of half a million, by dividing the able-bodied white citizens into a corps of immediate operation, and a reserve corps. The army of active service includes the thirteen regiments mustered into the general service, and some nine regiments of state troops now in camp, and undergoing discipline. The reserve militia can be organized at once, by responsible citizens, who choose to enlist companies of one hundred men, and return the rolls of enlistment to the adjutant-general. The companies formed in this way will be the first received into active service, on a future requisition, and I have understood from the department that some three hundred companies are already organized. I say with a good deal of satisfaction that the adjutant-general has discharged with promptness his functions, and has shown himself equal to sudden exigency. He is a man of military erudition, and is an enthusiast in the cause of the militia. He has framed his system upon European models, and really it strikes me as admirably efficient and thorough.

I was rather exuberant in my praise of the adjutant-general, for beyond him I cannot go with my praise. There has been a great bungling with contracts, and that sort of thing; but we do not have a rebellion every day, and our officials were unprepared for the crisis. Heaven has smiled in a wonderful manner upon tailors and people in the provisioning line, and frowned in a corresponding degree upon our poor volunteers, given over to contract clothing and feeding, which is, I suppose, one of the mysteries of Providence. At least nobody understands it.

Droll things have happened in the rapid progress of events, and I have been amused to see human nature on the long heats get the start of patriotism. So many troops as we have put into the field require a great many officers, and there has been a struggle to escape distinctions and emoluments. *Voreí,* the sad story of an absolute politician who thirsted for military glory. He formed his company, but preferred not to take a captain's commission, for he intended to be elected the colonel of a regiment. I am desolated to recount that the brutal soldiery refused to elect him colonel, and that the brave man failed even to be chosen lieutenant-colonel. He proposed then to be captain, but here, too, the men differed with him. He dropped then below the hope of a corporalship, and is now languishing in Camp Dennison at that post of honor—the private station. He gives out, with pathetic eloquence, that he is now serving his country as a private soldier, and appeals to the people of his district to elect him to Congress, in recognition of so much virtue and patriotism. Is not this a real romance? It is a tale of chivalry.

But I have another:

At Camp Dennison, the other day, a remarkably soft-voiced young soldier begged the colonel of his regiment to exchange him from a company in one letter of the alphabet to another. His associations were not pleasant.

Something in the demeanor of this young soldier interested the colonel. For a moment he scanned him with the eye of the American eagle—and this, since the secession dust is no longer thrown in its eyes, is a very sharp-sighted bird—and thus said:

"Young man, you are a woman!"

The young man burst into tears, and confessed that she was not what he seemed to be. Is it not a strange story to be true? She volunteered in this city that she might follow her lover to the wars. She had been in camp three weeks, performing all the duties of a soldier. She had passed surgical inspection, and was regularly sworn into the service.

I think she was of a lowly social station, and it was the dish-water and the broom and duster which she deserted to follow her lover to death. But she was a good girl and pure, and if it had been the piano, the embroidery frame, and generally the halls of pride, which she left, I do not see how her devotion could have shown much finer. Do you? And altogether the affair puts me in mind of the "Ballad gallant and gay," which I have heard sung among the sentimental in humble life. It is, indeed, in celebration of a similar occurrence, and I remember it chiefly for the beautiful language in which the recruiting sergeant—a considerate man, I say, for his vocation—informed the fair lady that it would never do for her to go for a soldier:

"O your waist it is too slender,
    Your fingers are too small,

317

Your cheeks they are too rosy,
To face the cannon ball."

Terms, I think, in which the colonel might have addressed this young maid, and which are at the disposal of other military authorities, for she declares that she *will* go to the wars yet.

But a truce to sentiment, and let us have a little tragedy.

The other day came up from one of the inland cities a chief man of the place, with a flag in his hand and ladies with bouquets in their hands. The banner and the flowers are to be presented by the dignitary to a company from D— in camp here, on behalf of the ladies, who were to stand by, beaming upon the soldiers, and to be handsomely and thrillingly alluded to in the speech—as is ever the custom. The company paraded to the Capitol, where the ceremony was to take place; but the state *militaire* who was to introduce the speaker misunderstood his part, and in spite of expostulations and intreaties, presented the flag himself, in a fervent and glowing speech. Figure to yourself the chagrin of the unlucky *militaire*; the anguish of the unhappy gentleman in the pangs of an indefinitely postponed parturition; the sweet vexation of the ladies; the utter confusion of the soldiers. It was miserable—not to be borne, and the troops, after a circuit of the Capitol grounds, halted in front of one of the hotels, and there the speaker that was to have presented the flag made his speech, and went lightened away. But the excitement and the heavy burden of two speeches were too much for the troops, and one of them fainted in the ranks.

Our Republican friends are contemplating the folly of no party nominations in this state for the approaching political canvass. I have noted that always in these no-party performances hopeless and demoralized minorities have had everything to gain, and prosperous majorities everything to lose. And I favor, consequently, the nomination of good Union Republicans on one ticket, and good Union Democrats, on the other, and so let the people choose between. Patriotism is good, but Republican patriotism is better. The Democratic leaders have still the same organs and affections that they had before they turned their attention to the public practice of virtue; and I think it is not just to tempt them too sorely at first. So far, in the matter of military appointments, they have fared better than the Republicans in Ohio; but I would reserve the civil functions still to the latter. I have the most enthusiastic confidence in the determination of the Democrats to be true to the administration, and I only wait for their loyalty to be tested by temporary reverses of our government. It would be sad if they were compelled to meet these reverses when in office themselves.

Major Anderson passed through this city to-day en route for Kentucky. Truly, they need some true man in that state, where the tendencies grow more excessive, and where patriotism assumes the curious type of sullen refusal to uphold the government.

[New York *World*, 21 May 1861]

COLUMBUS, June 5.

It was on the 14th day of April, if I mistake not, that Sumter fell under the rebel fire. Fifty-two days, then, have elapsed since that memorable event. In that time there has been offered to the governor of Ohio a sufficient number of troops, for its defense and for the support of the federal government against rebellion, to make one hundred and six regiments, or near one hundred and six thousand men. The call upon Ohio reached Columbus on the 17th of April. On the 19th General Carrington had two full regiments at Columbus ready to march, giving the post of honor to the picked state companies. Dispatches from Washington assured the governor that the men would be uniformed and armed at Washington, and they must be through by Saturday. The unforeseen difficulties at Baltimore caused them to halt on their way, and while at Lancaster, Penn., they were inspected by United States officers and enrolled into the United States service. They were, therefore, thereafter entirely dependent upon the United States for subsistence, equipments and arms. The governor of Ohio had no power to order them to march or to halt. But, fearing that in the hurry and excitement those men who had left their various avocations at an hour's warning to fly to the defense of the national capital might not be properly cared for, with a prudence and foresight characteristic of the man, Gov. Dennison empowered the colonel of the Second Regiment to draw on Ohio for means for their subsistence, and contracted with the governor of Pennsylvania for proper clothing. Having thus done his whole duty—having actually, in his desire for the welfare of the troops, gone beyond his *power*, our noble and true-hearted governor rested easy. Those two regiments are now encamped in Washington, and have been made the subject of much remark on account of their excellent drill, temperate habits, shabby clothing and limited camp equipments, for which latter defects the governor of Ohio has been soundly rated. Now, if three points are remembered it will be clearly seen that the blame is not with the governor of Ohio. First, we have the dispatches from Washington assuring the governor, as before stated, that the troops would be uniformed and armed there, and that they must be in Washington by Saturday. Secondly, neither requisitions on Ohio nor complaints have been made by officers of either regiment, a lack of clothing having first been made known through the newspaper correspondents. When complaints or requisitions for clothing are made through the proper channel the de-

319

partments have ever stood ready to listen, and if in their power to supply the one and apply the correction to the other. Thirdly, Ohio has been prominently a peace state. Sixty days ago army buttons passed muster with the ladies only, and an hour spent in drill was considered a great waste of time. A few sickly companies survived public derision, and our adjutant-general was only able to get his magnificent bill, erecting the militia of the reserve, through the Legislature after great exertion and persistent effort, and for a long time the law was looked upon as a cumbrous thing on our statute books, and a great waste of ink and paper. Nine hundred rifled muskets, and less than two thousand other effective muskets in the possession of companies and at the state arsenal, and a few exhumed and unpolished cannon—relics of the war of 1812—made up the sum total of the possessions of the state in this line. As for accoutrements, there were none; nor had there been any in the memory of younger inhabitants; nor was there any likelihood of being any until "the next war." If, then, the order from Washington to forward the troops had been accompanied with the further order to send them armed and equipped, Governor Dennison would have had no alternative but to reply that the latter could not be done without time; but, the contrary being true, the governor selected the flower of the organized military companies of Ohio, knowing them to be thoroughly drilled and prepared at the moment of being armed to encounter a hostile foe, and sent them on; and because they did not compare in *dress* and *equipage* with the regiments of Massachusetts, Rhode Island, and New York, where the military has been sustained by the public purse and public pulse, they are styled the "pauper regiments," and Governor Dennison is blamed for what is the legitimate fruit of the anti-military spirit of Ohio—the folly of the whole people, and not the faults of one man.

Had Ohio hitherto sustained the military, she would not now be smarting under the mortification of having her troops styled paupers. When one pauses for a moment, and considers what has been accomplished in the past fifty-four days toward *creating* a military system for Ohio, one finds himself admiring the vigorous hand that has put together this ponderous military machinery, making it work with such symmetry and precision, rather than censuring for an occasional defect. Why look at it fifty-four days ago. There was not an organized regiment in Ohio. Now there are twenty-six in and out of the state, and in less than ten days from now they will be armed and equipped in a superior manner, with camp utensils of every sort. To bring this about Governor Dennison and his secretaries work until a late hour, often until 2 or 3 o'clock in the morning. General Carrington, with eleven assistants, is sometimes employed until morning—always until midnight. General Wood, besides the clerks in his office, has a force employed in preparing grape, cannister and other fixed ammunition. General Buckingham, commissary general, is equally employed, and the whole is brought into a thorough system of operation and effect. The heads of the departments meet at 9 o'clock each morning as a council to take up and dispose of complex questions of importance to the state, and report upon the operations of the day and the probable exigencies of the morrow. The Ohio regiments are not idle in the meantime. The First and Second are, as before stated, in Washington; the Fourteenth, Fifteenth and Sixteenth are at Grafton; the Eighteenth is at Parkersburg, and the Twenty-second opposite on the Ohio side; the Twentieth is at Gallipolis, opposite the mouth of the Kanawha; the Nineteenth is part at Bellair and part at Zanesville, where the Twentieth is also encamped; the Seventeenth is in camp at Lancaster; eleven regiments are at Camp Dennison, and the Twenty-third, Twenty-fourth, Twenty-fifth, and Twenty-sixth are partly at Columbus and partly in local camps. Columbus has been quite a military theater. At one time Camp Jackson and the city contained near nine thousand troops. There are now about two regiments in camp, and by this day next week the number will be doubled. The companies are for three years. They will, according to present intentions, remain in camp until thoroughly drilled, or probably during the summer.

[New York *World*, 10 June 1861]

[In Washington, General Winfield Scott, chief of the army, resisted the urging of press and politicians for an early confrontation with the enemy in the field, realizing the danger of sending green Union soldiers against a better prepared enemy. He had earned his caution through campaigns in the Mexican-American War, and it is a great tragedy his contemporaries did not heed his counsel of restraint. Still the lack of the North's readiness necessitated some delay, and it was three months after the firing on Fort Sumter before the first encounter at Bull Run. During the interval, some minor skirmishes took place in western Virginia, culminating with McClellan's victory on 3 June 1861 at Philippi. This secured the region and prepared the way for the admission of West Virginia into the Union, but in retrospect it could hardly have appeared a battle, not at least in the dimensions and destructiveness that would soon be synonymous with war. Only hindsight revealed the lie they had all lived during the spring and early summer of 1861, a brief interval before the onset of the despairing truth. Howells put it best fifty years later:

After the war actually began, we could not feel that it had begun; we had the evidence of our senses, but not of our experiences; in most things it was too like peace to be really war. Neither of the

great sections believed in the other, but the South which was soli-
dified by the slaveholding caste had the advantage of believing in
itself, and the North did not believe in itself till the fighting began.
Then it believed too much and despised the enemy at its throat.
Among the grotesque instances of our self-confidence I recall the
consoling assurance of an old friend, a chief citizen and wise in his
science, who said, as the hostile forces were approaching each other
in Virginia, "Oh, they will run," and he meant the Southerners, as
he lifted his fine head and blew a whiff from his pipe into the air.
"As soon as they see we are in earnest they will run," but it was
not from us that they ran; and the North was startled from its fallacy
that sixty days would see the end of the rebellion, whose end no
prophet had now the courage to forecast. We of the Ohio capital
were a very political community, the most political in the whole
State, in virtue of our being the capital, but none of the rumors of
war had distracted us from our pleasures or affairs, at least so far
as the eyes of youth could see. With our faith in the good ending,
as if our national story were a tale that must end well, with whatever
suspenses, or thrilling episodes, we had put the day's anxieties by
and hopefully waited for the morrow's consolations. (*YMY*, pp. 199–
200)]

COLUMBUS, July 15.

By an arrangement between the Secretary of War, General
McClellan and Governor Dennison, all rebel prisoners taken by the
federal army in western Virginia are to be sent to Columbus, to
accommodate which a large prison house is now being constructed
at Camp Chase. In the meantime a log cabin, adjacent to the camp,
capable of holding some forty, has been set apart. It was dedicated
to its present use some two days ago by the entrance of twenty-
three secessionists, who were taken prisoners by a detachment of
Ohio troops in the Kanawha valley, as hostages for a couple of
stanch Union men seized by the rebels under Wise. The varied
expressions which played across the countenances of these F.F.V.s,
as they were loaded into a couple of omnibuses, after a hearty dinner
at one of our city hotels, preparatory to being taken out to camp,
was curious to see; fear, anger, ghastly attempts at composure, were
there, and when some thoughtless boy cried out "Hang them," there
was the nervous twitch of the shirt collar indicating an uneasy sensation in that locality, and the hurried, imploring, inquisitive look
at the crowd around to see if the sentiment found echo in older
breasts. It was plain to be seen that they did not understand the
northern heart, and consequently did not expect much but hard
treatment at our hands. Suffice it to say, when they left Camp

Chase, which they did a few days thereafter, and as soon as intelligence reached the governor that Wise had released the two Union men, it was with a very different impression of the northern heart. The cabin is now occupied by a half dozen Georgian cavalry men, and it will shortly be more than full, as the provisions taken by Gen. Rosencranz's column will shortly be here. By the way these trophies of Rosencranz's good generalship will be prisoners in the very camp which Rosencranz only a few days before, as colonel, commanded, he having been assigned by Governor Dennison to the colonelcy of the Twenty-third regiment, stationed at Camp Chase, shortly before his appointment to the brigadier-generalship in the regular army.

[New York *World*, 17 July 1861]

[Howells's immediate problem of occupation was settled with his appointment as United States Consul to Venice on the ninth of September, 1861. The summer of indecision was at an end. A few days before his final departure from the family home in Jefferson, he took a soft leather, silk-lined pocket diary which his sister Aurelia had some months earlier presented to him and there on the front endpaper noted the place and the date—"Jefferson O. Oct 22nd 1861"—followed by this legend: "'Mihi cura futuri.' My care is for the future."

Howells's early youth was nearly at an end, and like all young people he was happy in the anticipation of the fact. It was inevitable that he should pursue horizons beyond his Ohio foreground, and the Venetian consulship provided him with the escape for which he so earnestly had yearned. The year before he had written of his predicament to the "folks at home":

As Columbus grows old to me, it seems to contract, and I begin to feel here the gnawing discontent that I felt in Jefferson. Father need not be afraid that I should be seduced by Bohemianism in New York. I confess that a life which defies usage has its charm for me; but I chiefly long now for change from a comparatively narrow to a wider field of action. Men must sort with their kind; and since Mr Reed is gone, there is no strictly literary person here with [whom] I can associate. (*SL*, 1:54)

In spite of his assurances to the contrary, foremost in Howells's mind at the time was a career in journalism (if not Bohemianism) in New York City, and in enthusiastic moments following the mobilization of Union troops he even toyed with the idea of military service. Fortunately for him there was no Editha to encourage his "natural curiosity and willingness" to serve his country, and with his passage on the steamship *City of Glasgow* on the ninth of November, all other plans and anxieties were left behind. It was a wonderful voyage for a young man of his place and time, and though his thoughts frequently turned toward Ohio during the ensuing months and years, the life he had known there was irretrievable except in reverie. Close upon his arrival in Venice, homesick and alone, he took his journal and wrote out at length his recollections, some manner of bittersweet consolation youth of all places and times find peculiarly satisfying:

> January 30th. The eventlessness of this life is almost insufferable.—America teaches her children to look for their sensation every morning; and when that does not come, or comes only in the form of the question, whether the postman will or will not bring a letter, the children of the indulgent mother are naturally unhappy. It was far better in Columbus. There the daily article was a never-failing source of solicitude, if not of pleasanter interest, and the evening brought its charming perplexity of calls to be made or neglected, and the night some new book or magazine, a moonlight stroll with dear old Price, and the light dreams of careless sleep. Ah! let me go back only one year, if I can, and remember how a day passed, when rebellion was yet the most impossible of hideous misdeeds, and Europe was still only a dream of some vague future. It is nine o'clock, and the fire which Shadrach made in the choleric little stove burned low, two hours ago. Father is already up, and is gone to breakfast. The impossible Price sleeps in infantile sweetness at my side. I rouse him with effort, to consciousness, and after long delicious delays, we rise, and while we dress talk all that nonesense, in which it is so good to unbend one's wit, when the brain is yet too languid in the morning to close upon any topic of thought, and the hand is too feeble to fold itself into the firmness of a fist. At last we lounge forth together, and over the opulent atrocity of a steak, cooked in the evilest fashion of the new world, we talk up the business of the day, the latest secession, and that grand affair of our lives, the situation of our places on the poor old State Journal. Would Cooke sell out? Would Hurtt want us? Could he get along without us? Or would he sacrifice his plain interest, to an ignoble resentment, and dismiss us from the editorship, two such generous spirits as ourselves, who alone redeemed journalism from the baseness of the mercantile system? And nonesense and nonesense! I suddenly and blushingly remind old Price that I have an engagement to walk that morning with the Angel, to whom that best of the earth-born sends his never-delivered message of love.
>
> There is no trace of snow on the wide, straight pavement of Broad street, but the sun has thawed the frost under the bricks, and the long walk shines and swims in the light. O slow feet of mine that keep me back, and make the joy of meeting greater for delay!

I loiter and think over all the droll, delicious things that have been done and said, and smile in that blissful foolishness, at which I cannot learn to mock, until my heart leaps high as I stand at the gate, and then at the door, and am all thrilled with the clangor of the bell. Is um-um-um at home? O yes, will I come in? And then the kind obscurity and obliging dull calm of the parlor, where that friendly great arm-chair receives me, and where I idly twirl my hat, and wait—only a little while.

"Dance light, for my heart it lies under your feet, love," bounding down those broad stairs, and throbbing toward me. O ravishing little muff, and jaunty hat with shining plumes, and graceful cloak that clasps the lissome shape! And O, sweet fair face, with blue eyes full of roguish light, and shadowed by masses of brown hair! And O, dear absurdity of loving her! and yet not saying it, but keeping the secret to muse upon, and talk over with old Price!— We go to walk, and the January sun is warm for us. Yes the blue-birds already carol through the air, and the bees hum summer tunes, and enchant a bloom upon the locust tree, and inundate the meadows with billowy June. We do not talk much—childish nothings suffice us. L. has said, "You are like two children," and our idle, foolish ways confirm it. What do we care? The proper people whom our walks surprise, stare at us, and in the greenhouse where we sit, the cold dark-robed beauty who comes upon us is astonished into life, and utters wonder in the icy interest of her eyes. But we do not care, and it is broad noon when she shakes my hand at the door, and I lounge back to the office. It is not much I write for an hour or two; but I light upon a theme at last and dash off my article, and my day's work is done, and Price has reached his fifth pipe, and is turning over the express papers, and looking at the Tribune. He tosses me the Herald, which I prize for its virtue and high integrity of purpose; and we read and chat, until five o'clock, when we go to dinner. And after dinner, for me nothing; only to read my proof, and then to go with her to the dance at the College. It is ten o'clock when that is done, and J.M. and I bring L. and her to their home, and sit till midnight with them. Old Price is smoking the twenty-fifth pipe, with his heels upon the stove, when I come, and he says with much force of truth, "Well you've made *another* day of it! Go on, old fellow."

The echoes of the battlefields were faint and faraway.]

Annotations and Source Notes

The following notes and annotations provide documentation for the editor's quotations and references as well as background and explanatory glosses for the selections by Howells. In addition, Howells's many quotations and literary references have, where possible, been identified, and historical and biographical information has been provided when such is thought by the editor helpful in the appreciation of Howells's frequently topical remarks. Information readily available in standard desk dictionaries and one-volume reference works usually is not provided. The following works by Howells, which are frequently referred to throughout the editor's commentaries, are cited parenthetically in the text of those commentaries:

LL   *Life in Letters of William Dean Howells,* ed. Mildred Howells, 2 vols. (Garden City, N.Y.: Doubleday, Doran & Company, 1928).

LFA   *Literary Friends and Acquaintance: A Personal Retrospect of American Authorship,* ed. David F. Hiatt and Edwin H. Cady, vol. 32 of *A Selected Edition of W. D. Howells* (Bloomington and London: Indiana University Press, 1968).

MLP   *My Literary Passions / Criticism & Fiction,* The Writings of William Dean Howells Library Edition (New York and London: Harper & Brothers, 1911).

SL   *Selected Letters,* ed. George Arms, et al., 6 vols. (Boston: Twayne, 1979–83).

YMY   *Years of My Youth and Three Essays,* ed. David J. Nordloh, vol. 29 of *A Selected Edition of W. D. Howells* (Bloomington and London: Indiana University Press, 1975).

Edwin H. Cady's two-volume life of Howells, though cited only in those instances of direct quotation, has been a source of information and inspiration valuable beyond measure and acknowledgment. Thirty years of

Howells studies have done little to diminish its usefulness and right-mindedness.

Numbers on the left refer to page and line number in the text.

1.9–10   "essay on . . . human life": *A Boy's Town* (New York and London: Harper & Brothers, 1890), 238. W. Frank McClure's assertion that this essay "was printed in [William Cooper Howells's] paper" ("W. D. Howells's Boyhood," *New York Daily Tribune*, Sunday, 25 February 1906, 3) undoubtedly is in error. On several occasions Howells stated that his poem, "Old Winter, loose thy hold on us," published in the *Ohio State Journal* in March 1852, was the first thing he ever had in print.

7.11–39   On the first page . . .: "The Country Printer" (1893), reprinted in *Impressions and Experiences* (New York: Harper & Brothers, 1896), 12–13. The young lady "studying art" was Caroline L. Ransom, a painter of decided though modest talent. Thomas Hicks, cousin to the important Quaker leader and primitive artist, Edward Hicks, was a prominent New York portrait painter.

10.9   THE BATTLE OF THE CATS: Made up of variously sized sheets of paper pasted together lengthwise, the manuscript in the Howells Collection of the Houghton Library, Harvard University, is written in black ink with some corrections and additions later made in pencil. Though apparently complete in text, the verses are far from finished in places, particularly in the matter of punctuation. Fortunately, the neoclassical syntax of the heroic couplets generally manages well in its meaning without the aid of syntactic pointers, and little editorial emendation has been made in Howells's text. Misspellings and grammatical solecisms have not been corrected except where the errors cause unwarranted confusion or the manuscript provides evidence of his thwarted intention.

15.16   "local habitation and a name": Shakespeare, *A Midsummer Night's Dream* 5.1.17.

16.23   "crowned with rosy wine": Alexander Pope, *The Odyssey of Homer* 18.464.

16.44–45   "Ithaca the fair": The epithet appears several times in the ninth book of Pope's translation of the *Odyssey*.

17.35–44   "There rage no storms . . .": William Cliffton, "Talleyrand's Descent into Hell," in *Poems, Chiefly Occasional* (New York: J. W. Fenno, 1800), 86. Cliffton was a Pennsylvania poet of Quaker birth.

18.25–26 "a sketch of an old log cabin . . .": "Young Contributors and Editors," *Youth's Companion* 75 (9 May 1901): 245.

19.12 "The moss covered bucket . . .": Samuel Woodworth, "The Bucket" (1818), l. 10.

21.3–4 "fleecy cloud-drifts . . .": Ik Marvel, *Dream Life* (New York: Charles Scribner, 1851), 13.

21.11–22.5 Little does the boy . . .: *Dream Life*, 103–5.

36.11 Wouter Van Twiller: Remarkable for the degree of his gravity, this Dutch governor of New Netherlands, 1633–37, is one of the chief characters in Washington Irving's *Knickerbocker's History of New York* (1809). Not surprisingly, his seriousness led to misunderstandings and quarrels with the neighboring colonies.

36.15 Justice Shallow: A weak-minded country justice in several of Shakespeare's plays.

36.19–20 character in "Much Ado About Nothing": Dogberry, an ignorant constable, who greatly confounds his words.

37.5 "ministering angel, thou": Walter Scott, "Marmion" (1808) 6.30.6; the other phrases are common stock.

37.7–8 "Content to give . . .": Cf. Pope, "Epistle to Dr. Arbuthnot" (1734), ll. 209–10: "Like *Cato*, give his little Senate laws, / And sit attentive to his own applause."

37.19 delectable mountains: In John Bunyan's *Pilgrim's Progress* (1678), a range of hills from whose summit the Celestial City can be seen.

37.28 Macaulay: Thomas Babington Macaulay, prolific English historian and essayist.

38.30 "play the sedulous ape": The phrase is Benjamin Franklin's, from the *Autobiography*; Howells's account of his imitation of Poe appears in *My Literary Passions*, 16.

39.29 six books of the "Fairy Queen": Only half of the projected twelve books of Spenser's great work were ever completed.

44.12–13 "The Buccaneer's Revenge . . .": Englished, the Spanish of this apparently imaginary work reads: Sir Murderer-of-all-Men, the Pirate of Blood Sea.

46.10 'thereby hangs a tale': These words Howells puns on appear several times in Shakespeare's plays.

46.29–30   'think of what . . .': Cf. Henry Wadsworth Longfellow, "The Fire of Drift-wood" (1848), ll. 13–15: "We spake of many a vanished scene, / Of what we once had thought and said, / Of what had been, and might have been."

47.31   'knocked into a cocked hat': "Anything which has been altered beyond recognition, or any man who has been put completely *hors de combat* [disabled], is said to have been knocked into a cocked-hat" (*The Slang Dictionary: Etymological, Historical and Anecdotal*, London: Chatto and Windus, 1887, 122).

48.1–3   'The very air . . . from the skies': Lord Byron, *Don Juan* (1819–24), 3.74.2–4.

51.39–40   elder brother . . . identified it: In a letter to William Cooper Howells, 25 April 1883 (A.l.s., Alfred University), Joseph A. Howells revealed himself as the source for information regarding Howells's youthful literary activities which had appeared in an article titled "William D. Howells / Scenes and Incidents in the Early Life of the Great Novelist," Cincinnati *Leader*, 23 April 1883.

55.15   "flashes of merriment": Shakespeare, *Hamlet* 5.1.209–10.

55.25   "Live Dan Rice!": Rice was a popular American circus clown and showman.

55.38   the child-romance: *Paul et Virginie*, an immensely popular romance by Jacques Henri Bernardin de Saint-Pierre, was first published in 1787.

57.25–29   "The greatest concern . . .": Alexis de Tocqueville, *De la democratie en Amerique*, ed. J.-P. Mayer, 2 vols. (Paris: Gallimard, 1961), 1:254 (editor's translation).

64.36–37   leaner than the turkey of Job: Cf. the expression attributed to "Sam Slick" (Thomas Chandler Haliburton, Canadian humorist)—"as poor as Job's turkey"—to denote someone even poorer than the Old Testament patriarch.

65.5–6   The daw . . . with peacock's feathers, . . . and the donkey who played lion: Howells's allusions are to two of the *Fables of Aesop*—number 47, "The Jackdaw and Peacocks," and number 72, "The Ass in the Lion's Skin."

65.8   a lumbering Johnsonism: After the manner or style of Samuel Johnson, the eighteenth-century English writer whose neoclassical style was thought by writers in the nineteenth century (including Howells) as heavy and awkward, especially in its excessive Latinity and complicated generality.

69.26–28   "Sin juramento me . . .": "You may believe me without an oath . . . that I wish this book, as the child of my brain, were the most beautiful, the most sprightly, and the most ingenious, that can be imagined." The English version is Jervas's translation (1742) of the beginning of "The Author's Preface" of Cervantes's *Don Quixote*, ed. W. D. Howells (New York: Harper & Brothers, 1923), xix.

69.35–36   Lippard . . . Emerson Bennett . . . Lieut. Murray: George Lippard, a popular Philadelphia journalist and author of sensational and lurid stories of city life; Emerson Bennett, a prolific author whose tales of Western adventure appeared throughout the years of Howells's boyhood; and Maturin Murray Ballou, who, under the pseudonym "Lieut. Murray," began publishing a series of sea romances in the 1840s.

69.38   less dazzling authors: Thackeray, *The History of Pendennis* (1848–50), and Dickens, *Bleak House* (1852–53).

70.16   'whom God made upright': Cf. Ecclesiastes 7.29: "God hath made man upright; but they have sought out many inventions."

70.19–20   Shallow: a country justice in Shakespeare's *The Merry Wives of Windsor* and *2 Henry IV*. Nym (70.21) also appears in *The Merry Wives of Windsor*; a follower of Falstaff, he refuses to deliver a love letter for Sir John to the Mistress Ford.

70.43–44   little fable of Iriarte's: "El oso, la mona y el cerdo" ("The Bear, the Monkey and the Hog") appears in the *Fábulas literarias* (1782) of Tómas de Iriarte, a Spaniard known primarily for these imitations of La Fontaine. In George H. Devereux's edition, the lines Howells quotes are translated: "Authors, who seek a noble fame, / Mark well the moral of my verse! / That's bad which worthy judges blame; / What bad applaud, is worse" (*Literary Fables*, Boston: Ticknor and Fields, 1855).

71.8   'smell a fault': Shakespeare, *King Lear* 1.1.16.

71.43   locos: Or "loco-focos," originally were members of a radical wing of the New York Democratic party, but by the early fifties the name had come to be used derisively by the party's foes to describe all Democrats.

76.21   'fooled to the top o' my bent': Cf. Shakespeare, *Hamlet* 3.2.401: "They fool me to the top of my bent."

76.25   'i' the vein': Shakespeare, *Richard III* 4.2.122.

76.37–38   'is most tolerable and not to be endured': Cf. Shakespeare, *The Taming of the Shrew* 5.2.93–94: "O vile, / Intolerable, not to be endur'd!" Howells's misquotation has the humorous authority of the words of Dogberry, a constable in *Much Ado About Nothing* who is given to malapropisms and other absurdities of speech and logic: "You shall also make no noise in the streets; for for the watch to babble and to talk is most tolerable and not to be endured" (3.3.34–36).

77.45   Dulcinea: Don Quixote's sweetheart in Cervantes's novel.

78.45   Nautical Songster: "A Collection of the Newest and Most Approved Songs," the *Nautical Songster or Seaman's Companion* was first published in Baltimore in 1798; the quoted phrase occurs in "The Token," 25–26 of the songbook.

80.4   'The Lady of Lyons': A popular piece in the repertoires of traveling troupes of players, this immensely successful romantic comedy by Edward Bulwer Lytton (1838) relates how the proud and rich Pauline is tricked into a marriage with a simple but good gardener named Claude.

81.10   the campaign of '40: Recalling the carnivallike atmosphere that surrounded the presidential election of that year, William Cooper Howells wrote: "Politically, this contest was not on very high moral grounds. The dollar had more to do with it than humanity" (*Recollections of Life in Ohio*, Cincinnati: Robert Clarke Company, 1895, 194). Certainly the personalities of the opponents—William Henry Harrison, the Whig candidate, and ex-President Martin Van Buren who represented the Democratic party—appeared to matter more to the voters than the issues. A popular slogan—"Tippecanoe and Tyler too"—and wild hard cider campaigning won the day for the Whigs (see *A Boy's Town*, 4–5) and left a lasting impression on the style of U.S. politics.

81.16–19   "Black spirits and white . . . mingle may": A song in Thomas Middleton's *The Witch* 5.2.60–64, which Howells would most likely have known by its use in William Davenant's version of Shakespeare's *Macbeth* 4.1.43–46.

82.5–6   a leading member of the Hartford Convention: New England Federalists who met in secret session in 1814–15 in order to organize their opposition to the Republican principles of President Madison were long afterwards accused by their opponents of conspiracy, sedition, and even treason.

83.1   "With all his imperfections on his head": Cf. the Ghost's lament in Shakespeare, *Hamlet* 1.5.78–79: "No reck'ning made, but sent to my account / With all my imperfections on my head."

83.17   "In all the wildness of disheveled charms": Lord Byron, "The Corsair" (1814) 1.471.

83.18   Apparition of an Armed Head Rises: See Shakespeare, *Macbeth* 4.1.68.

84.32   Mark Tapley: See below, 108.39–40*n*.

84.41   'stealing out of your company': Shakespeare, *Much Ado About Nothing* 3.3.60–63: "The most peaceable way for you, if you do take a thief, is to let him show himself what he is and steal out of your company."

87.10   'Sacred Songster': Amos Pilsbury's *Sacred Songster*, first published in 1809, was frequently reprinted in the United States during the first half of the nineteenth century.

88.25–26 "uncleanly scruple": Shakespeare, *King John* 4.1.7.

88.43–44 "like a thing dipped in sunset": Cf. James Montgomery, "Greenland" (1819) 5.95–96: "Dipt in the hues of sun-set, wreath'd in zones, / The clouds are resting on their mountain-thrones."

95.3–4   "And each sep'rate . . .": This and the quotation that follows are from Poe's "The Raven" (1845), ll. 8 and 47.

101.40   cousin Willie Dean: *Life in Letters*, 2:338. In view of the hard-earned trustworthiness of her work, one hesitates to question Mildred Howells's identification of William B. Dean as Howells's traveling companion, especially since her authority for the fact may have been Howells himself. But this identification does not seem to explain very well the references to Howells's companions in the letters, "G." at 106.34, 110.24, 116.10, and 116.40, and "Dick H." at 116.9. The temptation, of course, is to see these two as the originals of "Dan" and "Lorry" in Howells's story, "The Pearl" (1916); and so long as one keeps in mind Howells's own strictures regarding "the mask of fiction," the autobiographical connections are undoubtedly justified. Lorry, no kin to Stephen West (i.e., Howells), but rather cousin to Stephen West's cousin Dan, is a young man who sketches, though his artistic ambitions have been "corrected" by his business-minded father. Dan also is as yet unsettled as to a career, except that he plans "to be rich, though certainly not by favor of the river life, for the good reason that his father and his father's three brothers and brothers-in-law had all prospered in that life." This hardly seems to describe William Blake Dean who, according to information gleaned from his family papers, settled in Minnesota in 1856 and worked for Nicols and Berkey, the first hardware store in St. Paul, and in 1860, by virtue of his marriage to Nicols's daughter, became a partner in the firm (see "Biographical Sketch," William Blake Dean and Family Papers, Minnesota Historical Society, St. Paul). Nor would Dean, if he were actively engaged at the time in the hardware business in St. Paul, likely be returning to Pittsburgh on the *Cambridge* after the week's stay in St. Louis, as "G." does in the letters. But the circumstantial evidence does make sense in terms of Dean's younger brother, George W. Dean (b. 1843), whose first name corresponds to the initial Howells used in his letters, and who, at the age of fifteen, probably would not yet be decided in a career. Without Mildred Howells's statement to the contrary, one would be inclined to name George Dean and a nephew of George and William Dean's mother, Aurelia Butler Dean, as Howells's river companions. They would have departed Pittsburgh expecting to visit William Blake Dean in St. Paul, but the flooding of the Mississippi that season altered their plans. If Mildred is in error in *Life in Letters*, it was probably owing to a scarcity of documentary evidence and her uncertain knowledge of the Dean kinships and not the sometime unreliability of her father's memory in old age.

102.10   pocket diary: A small, brown, leather notebook, preserved in the Howells Collection of the Houghton Library (bMS Am 1784.3[2]), signed and dated on the front cover "Will. D. Howells, Columbus / March 20, 1857 / Hand Book."

102.15   Conde: *History of the Dominion of the Arabs in Spain* by Jose Antonio Conde was translated by Mrs. Jonathan Foster for Bohn's Standard Library of London and issued in the United States by Little Brown & Co. of Boston, 1854–55.

102.16   Aaron Burr's Life: *The Life and Times of Aaron Burr* (New York: Mason Brothers, 1858). James Parton, a popular biographer, afterwards became Howells's friend and Cambridge neighbor.

102.26   cast my first vote: Howells, who turned twenty-one on 1 March 1858, was able to vote in the April fifth election in Jefferson, a contest for certain township offices.

102.31–32   Albert Ransom . . . Carrie and Eunice: Albert and Eunice Ransom, brother and sister of Howells's artist friend, Caroline Ransom (see 7.11–31*n.*), lived nearby at Harpersfield.

102.34   Babb: For several years an editor of the Cincinnati *Gazette*, Edmund B. Babb had been Howells's immediate superior on the paper; presumably, Howells thought he owed him some explanation regarding his health.

102.39   E.A.S.: Ellen A. Smith of Hamilton, Ohio, in whom Howells was romantically interested at this time.

103.5   Uncle Sam's steam packet: Preserved in the Howells-Fréchette Collection at Alfred University is a letter from Samuel Dean written to his nephew on 30 August 1857, inviting Will "to make one trip with me next spring up into M[innesota]-T[erritory]. as far as St Paul."

104.4   "the loveliest hills . . .": Howells to Charles Eliot Norton, 19 March 1902 (*SL*, 5:17).

104.30   Blennerhassett's Island: James Parton in his *Life and Times of Aaron Burr* (a book Howells had been reading just before his departure) had attempted to dispel the "romantic associations" that were attached to the river island south of Parkersburg, West Virginia, where in 1800, Harman Blennerhassett, a wealthy, Anglo-Irish immigrant, had established his home. In April 1805, Aaron Burr visited the island and was able to gain Blennerhassett's financial support in his grand plans for the establishment of a great Western empire. When Burr's scheme was revealed, a company of the Virginia militia took possession of Blennerhassett's island in December 1806, pillaging the house and laying ruin to the grounds. The house remained unoccupied until 1811, when it was finally destroyed by fire. Blennerhassett, a defeated and impoverished man, returned to Europe where he died in 1831. The fame of this "Eden of the western wilderness" was owing almost entirely to William Wirt's fanciful and much celebrated representation of the island estate during his prosecution of Burr in the latter's trial for treason in 1807. Years later, Howells included the story of Blennerhassett, whom he characterized as "a foolish man," in his *Stories of Ohio* (New York, Cincinnati, Chicago: American Book Company, 1897), 191–95.

104.39   Coalport: Approximately halfway between Cincinnati and Pittsburgh, this coaling station in Meigs County, Ohio, has since had its name changed to Middleport.

105.12   "overwhelming brows": Shakespeare, *Romeo and Juliet* 5.1.39.

105.20   "high life below stairs": The phrase is Marie St. Clare's, used to describe her husband's spoiling of their household slaves in Harriet Beecher Stowe's *Uncle Tom's Cabin* (Boston and Cleveland: Jewett, 1852), 1:246.

105.37   Connelly's case: On 6 May 1857, William M. Connelly of Cincinnati was brought to trial in a much celebrated case on the charge of "harboring and concealing" two fugitive slaves. Stanley Matthews, a prominent Cincinnati Democratic politician, was the prosecuting attorney at the trial presided over by the distinguished jurist, Humphrey Howe Leavitt; Thomas Corwin and Johann Bernhard Stallo represented the defendant. Corwin's closing remarks received widespread attention (the speech was printed in its entirety in the *Ashtabula Sentinel*, 27 May 1858), but the verdict rendered on 17 May 1858 was against Connelly, who was sentenced by Judge Leavitt to a fine of $10 and twenty days' imprisonment. In his *Stories of Ohio*, Howells eulogized Thomas Corwin in the highest terms, demonstrating that his youthful enthusiasm for the Ohio statesman never greatly waned. "Of all our public men he was the most distinctively what is called, for want of some closer term, a man of genius, and he shares with but three or four other Americans the fame of qualities that made men love while they honored and revered him. . . . this great soul, so simple, so sweet, so true, so winning, so wise" (p. 267). Howells also explained in his Ohio sketches the origin of the dark-complexioned Corwin's sobriquet: "In the War of 1812 he drove a wagon in the supply train for General Harrison's army, and the people liked to call him the Wagoner Boy, when he came forward in politics" (p. 265).

106.11   Harrison: The country home of William Henry Harrison, ninth president of the United States, was situated above the Ohio River at North Bend, Ohio. A champion of the new west, Harrison, sixty-eight at the time of his election, died of pneumonia on 4 April 1841, one month after his inauguration.

106.14   "Death is the end of life": Tennyson, "The Lotos-Eaters," 1. 86.

106.23   "the dull cold ear of death": Gray, "Elegy Written in a Country Church-Yard" (1751), l. 44.

106.24 the Falls of the Ohio: Actually a "chute" in which the river drops twenty-two feet in a distance of two miles.

106.31 New Albany: The seat of Floyd County, Indiana, New Albany owed its early commercial success to its location just below the Falls of the Ohio. At the time of Howells's visit, the attractive river town was the largest city in Indiana, with a population of nearly 20,000.

107.3 "Rolled a slumbrous sheet of foam below": Tennyson, "The Lotos-Eaters," l. 13.

107.6 a small Kentucky town, opposite Cannelton: Hawesville, seat of Hancock County, 119 miles below Louisville. A contemporary guide to the state gives this account of the Kentucky village: "the seat of justice . . . it contains the usual public buildings, a Baptist and a Methodist church, a public and a private school, five lawyers, five physicians, ten stores, one tavern, thirty mechanics' shops, and thirty coal diggers. Population 500" (Lewis Collins, *Historical Sketches of Kentucky*, Maysville, Ky.: Lewis Collins; and Cincinnati: J. A. & U. P. James, 1848, 334). The "richest resident" whose house Howells viewed has not been identified.

107.40 "Lilly Dale": A popular song (1853) by H. S. Thompson.

108.6–7 "She walks the water like a thing of life": Lord Byron, "The Corsair" (1814) 1.3.11.

108.31 "Egypt": John Comegys, a St. Louis merchant who founded the river town in 1818, named it Cairo because of the country's resemblance in topography to the Nile delta.

108.37 "a local habitation": Shakespeare, *A Midsummer Night's Dream* 5.1.17.

108.39–40 Mark Tapley: Chuzzlewit's manservant in Dickens's *The Life and Adventures of Martin Chuzzlewit* (1843–44), this irrepressibly jolly fellow accompanies his master to America where they attempt to establish themselves in a distant "city" named Eden. Arriving there, they discover it to be a hideous swamp containing only a few scattered log cabins.

109.22–23 "flat, stale . . . unprofitable": Shakespeare, *Hamlet* 1.2.133–34.

110.9 "Da saß sie und lachte": "There she sat and laughed" is a translation of Howells's German. The source of the quotation is Heine's *Reisebilder*: "Italien" (1828), pt. 1, chap. 13: "Da saß sie wieder und lächelte. . . ."

110.30–33 "From the land of the Dacotahs . . .": The quotation is derived from parts 4 and 10 of Longfellow's *The Song of Hiawatha* (1855).

111.19–20   "and other fallow deer": Longfellow, *Hyperion, A Romance* (New York: Samuel Colman, 1839), 1:57.

111.32   Gerideau: Cape Girardeau, on the Missouri shore, about 150 miles below St. Louis, is believed to have been settled in the 1730s. The priests Howells identifies as Jesuits were in fact members of the Vincentian order who in 1843 opened St. Vincent's College for young men.

112.11   residence of Kennett: Selma Hall was designed by George I. Barnett for Ferdinand Kennett, a St. Louis businessman and the brother of Luther M. Kennett, a mayor of St. Louis; patterned after Northern Italian Renaissance country houses, it was built in 1854 at the cost of $125,000 and is still regarded as the finest antebellum house in Missouri.

113.30–31   "finest pisantry in the world": Perhaps a quotation from the unidentified comic Irish-dialect writer, Dr. O'Toole, mentioned below 130.21.

114.41–43   "whose turrets are bright . . .": Longfellow, *Kavanagh, A Tale* (Boston: Ticknor, Reed, and Fields, 1849), 94: "that august faith [Catholicism], whose turrets gleam with such crystalline light, and whose dungeons are so deep, and dark, and terrible."

114.45   Edwin Booth: The son of Junius Brutus Booth, foremost romantic tragedian of his day in America, young Booth studied his art under his father's direction and after triumphant appearances in Boston and New York in 1857 won international fame for his interpretations of Shakespearean tragic roles.

115.17–18   "Das Vergnuegen ist nichts . . .": Heine, *Reisebilder:* "Italien" (1828), pt. 1, chap. 18.

115.20   Sam Weller's: Pickwick's valet in Charles Dickens's *The Posthumous Papers of the Pickwick Club* (1836–37).

116.39–40   Our *Chips*, "rare Ben" G.: "The ship's carpenter is, at sea, commonly addressed as 'Chips'" (*Brewer's Dictionary of Phrase and Fable*, rev. ed. [London: Cassell, 1963], 200). The quoted epitaph echoes that on the tombstone of the British dramatist, Ben Jonson, in Westminster Abbey.

117.31–32   "watching the . . . creamy spray": Tennyson, "The Lotos-Eaters," l. 107. The quotations that follow are from the same poem, ll. 25–29.

118.34   Cave-in-Rock: Once the lair of pirates who preyed upon the passing river traffic, this cavern, whose mouth commands a long view up and down the Ohio, is located in Hardin County, Illinois. Emerson Bennett, a writer of popular tales of Western adventure, used the locale in *Mike Fink: A Legend of the Ohio* (Cincinnati: Robinson and Jones, 1848). "Jim Wilson" was an alias, but the deeds of his gang were an unpleasant reality to the area at the century's beginning.

119.8   "the old Kentucky shore": From Benjamin Russell Hanby's "Darling Nelly" (1856).

120.2   sweet familiar strains: Like "Lilly Dale," which Howells had mentioned in his letter of May seventeenth, the other songs were current favorites: "Do they Miss Me at Home" (1852) by Caroline A. Mason and S. M. Grannis; three songs by Stephen Foster, "My Old Kentucky Home" (1853), "Nelly Was a Lady" (1849), and "Gentle Annie" (1856); and "The Lone Starry Hours" (1850) by James Power and Marshall S. Pike.

120.8   "wie ein leichter Nachen in der stillen Nacht": This and the similarly worded quotation from the German at 228.20–21 are unidentified. According to the computerized word list compiled by the Heinrich-Heine Institut in Düsseldorf, West Germany, neither quotation appears in Heine's works. However, a similar image does occur in the second stanza of "Der Apollogott" (*Romanzero*, 1851): "Da fährt ein Schifflein, märchenhaft / Vom Abendrot beglänzet" (There sails a ship of fable aglow in the evening sunset).

120.9   "Then all at once they sang": Tennyson, "The Lotos-Eaters," l. 44.

120.23   "twice told tale": Hawthorne's collection of tales, published in 1837, took its title from Shakespeare's *King John* 3.4.108–09: "Life is as tedious as a twice-told tale / Vexing the dull ear of a drowsy man."

120.37   "bearded with plumes of smoke": Cf. Longfellow, "The Two Angels" (1854), l. 4: "The sombre houses hearsed with plumes of smoke."

121.17   Jim Porter: Born in Portsmouth, Ohio, James D. Porter, "the Kentucky Giant" at 7 feet 9, was considered at the time the second tallest man in the world.

121.19   Prentice, the poet: George Dennison Prentice, founder and editor of the *Louisville Daily Journal*.

121.38–39 'If thou wouldst view Melrose . . .'. Walter Scott, *The Lay of the Last Minstrel* (1805) 2.1.1–2.

122.8 'On such a night . . . pretty Jessica': Cf. Shakespeare, *The Merchant of Venice* 5.1.20–21.

122.26 'The bowery hollows crowned with summer sea': Tennyson, "Morte d'Arthur" (1842), l. 263.

123.25–26 "a reliable exponent of . . .": This and the two quotations following are from an announcement of the sale of the paper that appeared in the *Ohio State Journal* on 19 November 1858. The partnership of Cooke & Miller, which purchased the journal from A. M. Gangewer, consisted of two brothers, John and Henry Miller, along with Henry D. Cooke and C. C. Bill.

126.19 'most unkindest cut of all!': Shakespeare, *Julius Caesar* 3.2.187.

127.37–38 Dr. Robinson, Ned Buntline, Bayard Taylor: Edward Robinson, professor of biblical literature at the Union Theological Seminary, was a frequent contributor of religious articles to the *Weekly Mercury*. "Ned Buntline" was the pen name of E. Z. C. Judson, a prolific dime novelist and adventurer. News of Bayard Taylor's acceptance of a generous offer from the *Mercury* in exchange for a series of travel sketches had been widely publicized.

128.32 "Across the walnuts and the wine": Tennyson, "The Miller's Daughter" (1842), l. 32.

128.35 The Washington correspondent: A letter corresponding to Howells's description signed by Fernando Wood, Democratic politician and former mayor of New York, had appeared in the New York *Tribune* on 20 November 1858.

129.6 W. E. McLaren: William Edward McLaren had studied theology in order to go to China, but upon his ordination to the Presbyterian ministry in 1860 was sent instead to South America.

129.31–32 Holmes . . . "verbicide": *The Autocrat of the Breakfast-Table* (Boston: Phillips, Sampson, 1858), 12–13.

130.18 George P. Marsh: Lawyer, statesman, and linguist, Marsh delivered a series, *Lectures on the English Language*, in New York City during the autumn and winter of 1858–59. Widely reported in the New York papers, the lectures were afterwards published in book form in 1859.

130.21 Dr. O'Toole's "haythen conchology": See above, 113.30–31*n*.

130.22   Johannis Phœnix: Called by Howells years later "the first of the great modern humorists," George Horatio Derby settled in California after the Mexican War and, with a series of humorous pieces published in the San Diego *Herald* under the pseudonym of "John Phoenix," won immediate celebrity throughout the country. The anecdote Howells retells appeared in the *Herald* in 1857 and was later collected in *The Squibob Papers* (New York: Carleton, 1865), 174–76.

133.2–3   Dana's Household Book of Poetry: Charles Anderson Dana's popular anthology of verse was first published in 1858 in New York by D. Appleton and Company.

133.25   Charles Dickens: The only story that Dickens ever allowed to be published first in the United States was "Hunted Down," a minor performance which appeared in the *New York Ledger* in August and September 1859. Edward Everett (134.8), distinguished clergyman, statesman, and president of Harvard, also surprised many in the literary world when he agreed about this time to write a series of papers on "Mount Vernon" for the *Ledger* to help raise funds for the purchase and restoration of Washington's home.

134.32   Elihu Burritt: Popularly known as "The Learned Blacksmith," this New England reformer and linguist had been promoting his plan of "Emancipation by Compensation" since the publication of his pamphlet entitled *A Plan of Brotherly Co-Partnership of the North and South for the Peaceful Extinction of Slavery* in 1856.

135.6–7   Robert J. McHenry: Charged with the murder of a constable in Merrittsville, Canada, William Townsend alias Robert J. McHenry caused great speculation during his trial regarding his true identity. Finally in April 1858 he was acquitted of the charge and afterwards embarked on a lecture tour.

135.17   Lieut. Maury: Following his appointment as superintendent of the Depot of Charts and Instruments of the Navy Department at Washington in 1842, Matthew Fontaine Maury pursued important investigations which helped establish the modern science of oceanography.

136.6   Banvard: John Banvard was a painter and writer whose contemporary fame was based upon the success of a huge, crude panorama of the Mississippi River which he exhibited in the United States and abroad during the 1840s and 1850s.

139.31   Caleb Cushing and Rufus Choate: Both natives of Massa-
          chusetts, Cushing and Choate had, along with Daniel
          Webster, helped found the Whig party. After that party's
          demise, they both joined the Democratic party.

140.15–16 Republicans . . . taking of Cuba: There was considerable
          interest by members of Pierce's administration in the ac-
          quisition of Cuba from Spain, either through purchase or
          by force. Because this proposal was motivated primarily by
          a desire to protect the institution of slavery, Republicans
          saw the annexationist movement as another proof of the
          Southern domination of the Democratic party and opposed
          the proposal.

140.23   Howadji Curtis: The rumor of George William Curtis's
          dismissal from his departments in the Harper's magazines
          was unfounded, though the New York publisher was con-
          cerned with the near-riotous reception and notoriety his
          lecture on "The Present Aspect of the Slavery Question"
          had created in several cities that winter. The sobriquet
          "Howadji" refers to Curtis's first successful work, *Nile Notes
          of a Howadji* (1851) (see 224.37–38*n*.).

141.15   Senator Seward's speech: On 25 October 1858, William
          Henry Seward, then U.S. senator from New York, gave
          the most famous speech of his political career in which he
          declared that the slavery struggle was "an irrepressible con-
          flict between opposing and enduring forces." Though im-
          passioned, Seward's remarks have little in common with
          the newspaper report.

141.33   Mr. Bailey's office: An account of the attack on the news-
          paper office of William S. Bailey, publisher of the Newport
          Free South in Kentucky, had been reprinted from the Cin-
          cinnati *Commercial* in the *Ohio State Journal*, 30 October
          1859. On 2 November 1859, Howells noted in his "News
          and Humor" that "the indomitable editor [Bailey] . . . de-
          clares his intention to re-establish" the paper, "in spite of
          all the mobs of Newport."

142.28   "a melancholy pleasure": Longfellow, *Hyperion*, I:71.

143.31   20 October 1859: TS copy of letter at Harvard.

144.3–8   "gigantic, colossal . . .": "John Brown after Fifty Years,"
          North American Review 193 (January 1911): 29. Melville's
          poem "The Portent" was first published in *Battle-Pieces and
          Aspects of the War* (1866).

146.28   Wendell Phillips: A close associate of William Lloyd Garrison, Phillips electrified audiences with his keen intelligence and impassioned rhetoric.

147.19   article on mortality in the different trades: Andrew Wynter, an English physician, was the author of the lead article in the *Edinburgh Review*, January 1860.

147.40–41 "giddy pleasure of the eye": Tennyson, "Morte d'Arthur" (1842), l. 125.

148.8   Dr. Percival's library: The American poet and geologist, James Gates Percival, died in Wisconsin in 1856; his library was auctioned in order to settle his debts.

148.35   *The National Quarterly Review*: In spite of Howells's rather doubtful prognosis, the New York magazine lasted twenty years. Its editor, Edward I. Sears, was a professor of languages at Manhattan College.

149.1   Chapin's . . . sermons: Edwin Hubbell Chapin, a prolific Universalist clergyman, was pastor of the Church of the Divine Paternity in New York City.

149.3   The essayist, Tuckerman: Henry T. Tuckerman, critic and historian; cousin of the poet, Frederick Goddard Tuckerman.

149.7   Theodore Parker: The Unitarian clergyman, a prominent figure in the Transcendental movement, had gone for reasons of health to Italy where he died in May 1860.

149.17–18 "Adela, the Octoroon": This novel by an Ohio jurist, Hezekiah Lord Hosmer, was published by the Columbus firm in 1860. Several weeks earlier, Howells had called it "a novel of great interest of plot" and predicted that it would "create a sensation when it appears" ("Literary Gossip," *Ohio State Journal*, 7 February 1860).

149.39   Anna Jameson: The daughter of D. Brownell Murphy, an Irish miniature painter, Jameson is best known today for her book on *Shakespeare's Heroines*, originally titled *Characteristics of Women* (1832).

150.26–27 work of scriptural argument in favor of slavery: *Slavery in the United States* (New York: Harper & Brothers, 1836).

151.10–11 historical work of the time of Queen Anne: Neither *The Adventures of Philip*, set in the nineteenth century, and serialized in the *Cornhill Magazine* beginning in January 1861, nor *Denis Duval*, a novel set in the late eighteenth century and which Thackeray left unfinished at the time of his death in 1863, fits Howells's description.

151.17–18   Elihu Rich: The British Swedenborgian was co-author of *The Occult Sciences: Sketches of the Traditions and Superstitions of Past Times, and the Marvels of the Present Day* (1855); his *Index to Swedenborg's Arcana Coelestia* was published in London by the Swedenborg Society, 1852–60.

151.25   CORNHILL MAGAZINE: Thackeray had founded this important British monthly in January 1860. Edwin Henry Landseer was a popular Scottish painter known for his pictures of animals. The fragment by Charlotte Brontë was her story, "Emma."

151.37   It is denied that Humboldt said: A few days earlier, Howells had noticed under "Literary Gossip" the publication in New York of an English translation of the *Letters of Alexander von Humboldt to Varnhagen von Euse*: "The correspondence consists merely of hasty notes passed between very old and intimate friends; and is the warm and honest expression of Humboldt's views and feelings. . . . For ourselves chiefly, we have to thank him for saying of the overlauded Bayard Taylor, that 'he had travelled more and seen less than any other man'" (*Ohio State Journal*, 10 May 1860). Taylor is not mentioned in the correspondence.

152.1   Coventry Patmore's singular poem: *The Angel in the House*, comprising *The Betrothal* (1854) and *The Espousals* (1856), was issued in a third edition by Patmore's London publishers in 1860, with the addition of *Faithful For Ever*.

152.3   Walt Whitman's "Leaves of Grass": Two months earlier, Howells had noted the announcement of "a new and superb edition of Walt. Whitman's 'Leaves of Grass,' with several new poems by the baffling bard" ("Literary Gossip," *Ohio State Journal*, 29 March 1860). After the book's appearance he reviewed it for the *Ashtabula Sentinel*, 18 July 1860 (reprinted below, pp. 180–182).

152.15   a bust of Theodore Parker: The American sculptor, William Wetmore Story, did several portraits of his friend.

152.16   M. de Lamartine: Haunted by debts and the failure of the Second Republic, which he had helped establish following the Revolution of 1848, the French poet and statesman, Alphonse de Lamartine, sought during the final years of his life to gain the prestige and respect he had lost but finally was forced to accept a pension from the imperial government of Louis Napoleon he had formerly opposed.

See "Lamartine and American Litterateurs," reprinted below, pp. 196–198.

152.38–39 Dickens's new story: *Great Expectations* was being serialized in Great Britain in *All the Year Round* and in the United States in *Harper's Weekly*. The story was published in book form in July 1861. The "last chapter" which had appeared and which Howells speaks of at 153.12–13 is that numbered 15 in the book edition.

153.37 De Quincey says: See Thomas De Quincey's *Autobiographical Sketches* (Boston: Ticknor and Fields, 1857), 38–39.

154.1–2 George Augustus Sala: The British journalist founded the London monthly, *Temple Bar*, in December 1860.

154.13–14 George Arnold: A New York poet and humorist who was associated with the Bohemian circle that frequented Pfaff's Beer Cellar. Owen Meredith's "Last Words" had been published in the *Cornhill Magazine* in November 1860.

154.19–20 J. Ross Browne's "Peep at Washoe": This Irish-born, Kentucky-bred traveler and journalist enjoyed a considerable vogue among magazine readers until the late 1860s.

154.41 Many thanks . . .: Howells to Comly, 9 August 1868, A.l.s. in the Ohio Historical Society Library.

156.9 "Time driveth onward fast": Tennyson, "The Lotos-Eaters," l. 88.

156.19 "we would not be a death's head to you": Cf. Charles Lamb, "Poor Relations" (1823): "A Poor Relation—is the most irrelevant thing in nature, . . . a preposterous shadow, lengthening in the noontide of your prosperity,—an unwelcome remembrancer,—a perpetually recurring mortification, . . . a death's head at your banquet."

156.33 "From grave to gay, from lively to severe": Pope, *An Essay on Man* (1733–34) 4.380.

156.38–41 The flood . . . Pike's Peak: Several of these topics were of more immediate interest than the others. A machine that could sew soles of shoes to their uppers, for example, was patented by Lyman R. Blake in 1858. Also in 1858 the Atlantic telegraphic cable was successfully laid, though its practicality and durability were still questioned. The Kansas-Nebraska Act of 1854 had merely intensified the question of slavery's westward extension, and a veteran of the Kansas struggles would make a portentous raid on the Federal Arsenal at Harper's Ferry, Virginia, in October 1859. Lewis Cass, Buchanan's secretary of state, caused considerable discussion when in 1859 a letter he wrote to a French-American in Tennessee was made public, because of its assertion that the man's citizenship by naturalization would not exempt him from the claim of the French government that "all natives of France who may be found within its jurisdiction" are required to serve in its military. Finally, gold was discovered in the Colorado territory near Pike's Peak, and during the spring and summer of 1859 the area was a scene of gold fever.

157.25–26   a thing of beauty, and . . . a joy forever: Cf. Keats, *Endymion* (1818) 1.1: "A thing of beauty is a joy for ever."

157.34   "Old wine, old books, old friends": A common and frequently expressed sentiment, as in Goldsmith's *She Stoops to Conquer* (1773), act 1: "I love every thing that's old: old friends, old times, old manners, old books, old wines . . . and old friends are best!"

158.7   Louis Napoleon: The French emperor, Napoleon III, played an important role in the unification of Italy by allying France with Sardinia in its attempt to drive the Austrians out of Italy in 1859.

158.14   "glittering generalities": Rufus Choate, "Letter to the Maine Whig Committee" (1856): "Its constitution the glittering and sounding generalities of natural right which make up the Declaration of Independence."

158.28–30   "When the war drum . . .": A slight misquotation of Tennyson, "Locksley Hall" (1842), ll. 127–28.

158.37   Under Wilson's direction: These improvements, as well as the therapeutics of the place, are described in J. J. Moorman's *The Ohio White Sulphur Springs* (Cincinnati: Moore, Wilstach, Keys & Co., 1859).

158.41–42   letter to his sister Victoria: TS copy at Harvard.

159.4   to his friend J. J. Piatt: 11 July 1859, A.l.s., Florida State University Library. Mr. Charles James Yellowplush, a Cockney footman, was a character Thackeray sometimes assumed in his works.

160.5–7   Mr. Squeers . . . Mr. Snawley . . . Smike—"Natur is a rum 'un": The characters and the incident occur in chap. 45 of Dickens, *Nicholas Nickleby* (1839).

160.34   resident physician: William W. Dawson, a prominent medical educator and physician in Cincinnati.

161.17   Complete Guide to Little Peddlington: John Poole's humorous "Stranger's Guide through Little Pedlington; Comprising Its History from the Earliest Period to the Present Time; Together with an Account of Its Antiquities, Curiosities, Amusements, Promenades, &c." first appeared in his collection of *Sketches and Recollections* (London, 1835).

161.37   Senator Reid: William P. Reid of Delaware, Ohio, represented Delaware and Licking counties in the Ohio State Senate, 1858–59.

163.9–10   listened to the reading of the militia bill: During the Legislative Session of 1857, when Howells served as the legislative reporter for the Cincinnati *Gazette*.

163.11–12   our local's noble sketch of the history of Camp Harrison: The sketch, printed under the "Local Affairs" column in the *Ohio State Journal*, 29 August 1859, and reprinted in the *Ohio State Weekly Journal*, 30 August 1859 (which Gibson and Arms incorrectly attribute to Howells; see William M. Gibson and George Arms, *A Bibliography of William Dean Howells* [New York: New York Public Library, 1948], was probably the work of Asa L. Harris (see 170.31*n*.). On 6 September 1859, the *Ohio State Weekly Journal* reprinted the five daily accounts of the encampment's activities that had appeared in the regular edition of the newspaper between 30 August and 3 September; this too is incorrectly attributed to Howells by Gibson and Arms.

163.16   Captain Cuttle: The kind and simple friend of Walter Gay in Dickens, *Dombey and Son* (1848), who in chap. 19 makes a gift to the younger man of his silver pocket watch, with this explanation: "Put it back a half hour every morning, and about a quarter towards the afternoon, and it's a watch that'll do you credit."

164.12   "ambition virtue": Shakespeare, *Othello* 3.3.350.

164.13   "Life's morning march . . .": Thomas Campbell, "The Soldier's Dream" (1804), l. 14.

164.33–34   "Mouths without hands . . .": Howells reverses the meaning of the second line of Dryden, "Cymon and Iphigenia" (1700): "Mouths without Hands; maintain'd at vast Expense, In Peace a Charge, in War a weak Defence" (ll. 401–02).

165.29–30   vision . . . of a journalistic future: Howells's poem, "The Coming," was published in the *Ohio State Journal*, 23 January 1860; years later it was reprinted in the New York *Bookman* 35 (July 1912): 510–14.

167.5   letter to . . . Aurelia: 22 January 1860, TS copy, Harvard.

167.24 declining an invitation: Howells to Victoria M. Howells, 5 October 1859, A.l.s., Harvard.

168.7–8 his own verses: Howells's "Feuerbilder.—Germanesque," first printed in the *Saturday Press*, 14 January 1860, was reprinted in the *Ohio State Journal*, 18 January 1860.

168.10–11 "J. J." of the *Press* . . . and Mr. Donn Piatt: Donn Piatt, Ohio-born journalist and political activist whose family's homestead, "Mac-o-cheek," was located near West Liberty, Ohio. During the presidential campaign of 1840, Piatt had published at West Liberty a short-lived newspaper called the *Democratic Club*, to which Howells refers (see 169.5). At the time of the Editorial Convention, Piatt was editor of the Mac-o-cheek *Press*. "J. J." was his cousin and Howells's poetical collaborator, John James Piatt. Piatt's association with the *Press* was announced in the *Ohio State Journal* on 1 November 1859: "Mr. J. J. Piatt, with whose fine poetical abilities our readers are already acquainted, has assumed the 'literary and miscellaneous' management of this liveliest of our country exchanges; and salutes the reader in the last week's *Press*. If it were possible to make that paper a great deal better, Mr. Piatt would be just the person to do it. If the editors have as great pecuniary as they have literary success they must soon grow rich, in spite of all unfavorable newspaper providences."

168.21 delight to bark and bite: Cf. the popular children's hymn by Isaac Watts, "Against Quarreling and Fighting" (*Divine Songs*, 1715): "Let dogs delight to bark and bite, / For God hath made them so; / Let bears and lions growl and fight, / For 'tis their nature too."

169.2 W. H. P. Denny: The editor of the Dayton *Gazette* addressed the convention on "Politicians and the Local Press," a text of which was printed in the Mansfield, Ohio, *Herald*, 2 February 1860.

169.20 compelled to defer their publication: A report of the "Business of the Editorial Convention" appeared in the *Ohio State Journal*, 23 January 1860. The orator and poet selected for the forthcoming meeting were W. W. Armstrong of the Tiffin *Advertiser* and G. A. Stewart of the Kenton *Republican*.

170.16 Piatt's poetical response: Piatt's verses have not been identified, nor do the *Transactions* of the convention appear to have been published for 1860.

170.30   a "brilliant writer": Conway, *Autobiography*, 2 vols. (Boston and New York: Houghton, Mifflin and Company, 1904), 1:293.

170.31   Asa L. Harris: Other than Howells's remarks in his article in the *Ohio State Journal*, 20 July 1861, reprinted below, little is known of Harris's association with the Columbus paper. According to William E. Hunt's *Historical Collections of Coshocton County (Ohio)* (Cincinnati: Robert Clarke & Company, 1876), 125, Harris went to Georgia at the close of the Civil War. His "retrospective glance" of the *Ohio State Journal*, which Howells mentions below, has not been recovered, the files for the Coshocton *Age* during this period being largely nonexistent.

170.38–39   senior editor . . . sell his interest: See announcement of the sale in the *Ohio State Journal*, 5 July 1861.

172.10   Nedline Buntwin: Humorous play on the pen name ("Ned Buntline") of the popular dime novelist, E. Z. C. Judson.

172.16   *de mortuis nil nisi bonum*: "Speak nothing but good of the dead" (see Diogenes Laertius, *Chilo* 1.69).

172.18–21   "For now, the whole round table is dissolved . . .": Tennyson, "Morte d'Arthur," ll. 234–37.

175.8–19   The poet has . . .: "The Art of Longfellow," *North American Review* 184 (1 March 1907): 472.

175.33   Pollock: Probably Robert Pollok, a Scottish poet whose most popular work was an epic entitled "The Course of Time" (1827).

176.2   "Punch": The British humor magazine had published an amusing lampoon entitled "Shortfellow Sums up Longfellow" in its issue of 30 October 1858: "Miles Standish, old Puritan soldier, courts gal Priscilla by proxy, / Gal likes the proxy the best, so Miles in a rage takes and hooks it: / Folks think he's killed, but he ain't, and comes back, as a friend, to the wedding. / If you call this ink-Standish stuff poetry, *Punch* will soon reel you off Miles."

177.20   "the gross mud-honey": Tennyson, "Maud" (1855) 1:541.

178.11   Hood: Equally known for his humorous and humanitarian verse, the British poet and journalist Thomas Hood is perhaps best remembered for his poem dealing with the wretched conditions of the London working class, "The Song of the Shirt" (1843).

178.28   a poem of this title: Eventually retitled "As I Ebb'd with the Ocean of Life," the poem was collected in the 1860 edition of *Leaves of Grass.* Among Whitman's works, it is one of his most personal in an autobiographical sense and requires some knowledge of his life in order to reach any satisfactory understanding and appreciation of its text.

178.41   Ralph Waldo Emerson: Emerson's famous letter greeting Whitman "at the beginning of a great career" was printed in the New York *Tribune*, 10 October 1855, and shortly after by Whitman in the 1856 edition of *Leaves of Grass.*

179.5   New York *Saturday Press*: Whitman's "A Child's Reminiscence" (later retitled, "Out of the Cradle Endlessly Rocking") was first printed in the *Saturday Press*, 27 December 1859.

179.37–40   "Break, break, break, . . . arise in me!": Tennyson, "Break, Break, Break" (1842), first stanza.

179.42   "divine despair": Tennyson, "The Princess" (1847) 4.22: "Tears from the depth of some divine despair."

180.32   criticism . . . in . . . *Putnam*: Charles Eliot Norton was the author of the notice of *Leaves of Grass* in *Putnam's Monthly Magazine*, September 1855 (see *A Leaf of Grass from Shady Hill*, ed. Kenneth B. Murdock [Cambridge: Harvard University Press, 1928], 25–31).

180.35   judge's charge in Bardell and Pickwick: In Martha Bardell's suit against Mr. Pickwick in Dickens's *The Pickwick Papers* (1836–37), chap. 34, for an alleged breach of promise to marry her, "Mr. Justice Stareleigh summed up, in the old-fashioned and most approved form": "If Mrs. Bardell were right, it was perfectly clear that Mr. Pickwick was wrong, and if they thought the evidence of Mrs. Cluppins worthy of credence they would believe it, and, if they didn't, why they wouldn't," etc.

181.38   *Sie lassen sich nicht lesen*: Literally, the German means, "they don't let themselves be read," or more idiomatically "they are unreadable."

182.9   Heine: See *Die romantische Schule* (1836), bk. 3, chap. 3. "Jean Paul" was the pen name of the German romantic novelist, Johann Paul Friedrich Richter.

183.27   Coggeshall drew on this discourse: Gibson and Arms (*Bibliography*, 80) err in attributing "Have We Household Poetry in the West?" *Ohio State Journal*, 20 November 1858, to Howells. Its similarity to certain passages in Coggeshall's pamphlet, *The Protective Policy in Literature* (Columbus: Follett, Foster and Company, 1859), clearly show the notice of Dana's anthology to have been by Coggeshall.

184.33   Howells announced the volume as forthcoming: "Poets and Poetry of the West," *Ohio State Journal,* 5 May 1860.

185.3   "To labor and the mattock-hardened hand": Tennyson, "Maud" 1.632.

185.13–14   Helen Bostwick: Born in New Hampshire, Helen Louisa Barron came to Ohio in 1826 while still a young girl. She married Edwin Bostwick in 1844 and settled with her husband in Ravenna, Portage County. Following her remarriage 1875, she moved to Philadelphia where she died in 1907.

185.23   like the quality of mercy: See Portia's speech in Shakespeare's *The Merchant of Venice* 4.1.184–86: "The quality of mercy is not strain'd. / It droppeth as the gentle rain from heaven / Upon the place beneath."

186.2–4   'airy nothing' . . . 'a local habitation': Shakespeare, *A Midsummer Night's Dream* 5.1.16–17.

186.14   'They love to read their own dear songs': Cf. Holmes, "The Last Reader" (1836), ll. 1–2: "I sometimes sit beneath a tree / And read my own sweet songs."

186.27   pleasant surprises: John Finley, a native of Virginia, came west as a young man and eventually settled in Richmond, Indiana, where he was active in politics. "Bachelor's Hall" was written "in imitation of the Irish," and, according to Coggeshall's biographical sketch, was "very widely circulated in England, as well as in America, with Thomas Moore's name to it" (p. 83). "The Fever Dream" by John M. Harney, a Kentucky physician, is an effective display of Gothicism, nearly one hundred lines in length. James Handasyd Perkins came to Cincinnati from Massachusetts and was a leader in that city's charitable and literary projects. William Davis Gallagher was also active in promoting literary culture in the West, and his important *Selections from the Poetical Literature of the West* (1841) was one of the first anthologies of regional literature published in the United States. Alice and Phoebe Cary left their native Cincinnati after the success of their first volume of *Poems* (1849) and settled in New York City where they were prominent in the circle of Horace Greeley. Rebecca S. Nichols was active in the literary life of Cincinnati in the

1840s, and her poems were published in local as well as Eastern newspapers and magazines. Amelia B. Welby, a protege of George D. Prentice, editor of the *Louisville Journal*, also was widely published. William W. Fosdick, son of a prominent Cincinnati banker and himself a lawyer, was editor of *The Sketch Club*, an illustrated paper supported by the artists of Cincinnati and their friends at the time of Howells's notice. William Ross Wallace, also a native of the West, was a regular contributor to Eastern journals. The author of the famous lines, "And the hand that rocks the cradle, / Is the hand that rules the world," he won praise from Bryant and Poe. Coates Kinney remained a favorite of Howells; years later Howells wrote favorably of his later work ("Editor's Study," May and September 1888), but the nineteenth-century reputation of the Ohio poet rested primarily on the popularity of his early lyric, "Rain on the Roof," which Coggeshall included in his anthology. Harney is the subject of an article by Howells reprinted below; and Piatt was Howells's good friend and collaborator, John James Piatt. "Ruth Crayne" was the pen name of Louisa A. McGaffey, and "Mary Robbins" was the poetic signature of Mary Robbins Whittlesey. Both young women were residents of Ohio and were published locally.

190.28   "Dowsabel": See the eighth ecologue in Michael Drayton's *Idea, The Shepherds Garland* (1593), ll. 154 and 212.

191.2   his biographer: Charles E. Morse is listed in the table of contents as the author of the biographical notice of Harney.

194.1   Goethe says: See "Verschiedenes Einzelne über Kunst," *Sämmtliche Werke*, 40 vols. (Stuttgart and Tübingen: J. G. Cotta, 1840), 3: 251.

194.13   "goodly outside": Shakespeare, *The Merchant of Venice* 1.3.102–03: "A goodly apple rotten at the heart. / O, what a goodly outside falsehood hath!"

194.25–26   letter written by an American woman: Sarah Anna Lewis's account of her meeting with the French poet was reprinted in the *Ohio State Journal* on 27 October 1860. Mrs. Lewis, a sentimental poet and dramatist, is primarily remembered because of her friendly association with Edgar Allan Poe.

196.2   Byron's "Hours of Idleness": Angered by a contemptuous criticism published in the *Edinburgh Review* of his first book of poems, *Hours of Idleness* (1807), Byron wrote his vigorous satire "English Bards and Scotch Reviewers" (1809) which attacks not only Francis Jeffrey, the editor of the *Edinburgh Review*, but also most of the poets and supporters of the romantic school in England.

196.5–6   Canning's "Anti-Jacobin" and Lowell's "Biglow Papers": George Canning, as Howells's remarks later indicate, was only one of several contributors to *The Anti-Jacobin*, a weekly paper he founded in November 1797. Canning's "The Friend of Humanity and the Knife-Grinder" was published in *The Anti-Jacobin*, 27 November 1797. The "First Series" of James Russell Lowell's *Biglow Papers*, whose satire was directed against the American invasion of Mexico and the government's support of the institution of slavery, had been published in 1848; the "Second Series" was not completed until 1867.

196.7   Festus Bailey's "Age": Chiefly celebrated for his long dramatic poem *Festus* (1839), Philip James Bailey had published a colloquial satire entitled *The Age* in 1858, one of the works Patmore discussed in his *North British Review* article. Years later Howells admitted to his friend, John White Chadwick, 21 March 1897 (*SL*, 4:146), that, although *Festus* had been one of the rages of the literary world of his youth, he had somehow avoided ever reading it.

196.19   "sparkle upon the outstretched finger of all Time": Cf. Tennyson, "The Princess" 2.334–37: "elegies / And quoted odes, and jewels five-words-long / That on the stretched forefinger of all Time / Sparkle for ever."

198.23   "When you have bought a book," says Longfellow: See "Table-Talk," in Longfellow's *Prose Works*, 2 vols. (Boston: Ticknor and Fields, 1857), 1:453: "Many people think that when they buy a book they buy with it the right to abuse the author."

198.42   Lady Macbeth's lunacy: Thomas Bangs Thorpe, best remembered for his tale, "The Big Bear of Arkansas," had published his humorous sketch, "The Case of Lady Macbeth, Medically Considered" in *Harper's Monthly*, February 1854.

199.28–29   "The lunatic . . . all compact": *A Midsummer Night's Dream* 5.1.7–8.

200.21   the inexorable law: "The fathers have eaten sour grapes, and the children's teeth are set on edge" (Ezekiel 18.2).

201.33   "Cosas de Espana": First serialized in *Putnam's Monthly* (1854), *Cosas de Espana; or, Going to Madrid via Barcelona*

201.34–35

202.34

202.40–41

202.43

203.15
204.39–40

(New York: Redfield, 1855) was published anonymously by John Milton Mackie, an American author and educator. "Attaché at Madrid": Frances Erskine Inglis Calderon de la Barca, *The Attaché in Madrid; or, Sketches of the Court of Isabella II* (New York: D. Appleton and Company, 1856).

last essay: The March installment of Holmes's work corresponds to the third chapter of the book edition of *The Professor at the Breakfast-Table* (Boston: Ticknor and Fields, 1860), 62–93.

picture in which . . . Newcome says "Adsum!": Broken in both mind and spirit, Thomas Newcome, a principal character in Thackeray's novel, *The Newcomes* (1853–55), takes refuge with the Grey Friars where he soon dies: "At the usual evening hour the chapel bell began to toll, and Thomas Newcome's hands outside the bed feebly beat time. And just as the last bell struck, a peculiar sweet smile shone over his face, and he lifted up his head a little, and quickly said 'Adsum!' and fell back. It was the word we used at school when names were called; and lo, he, whose heart was as that of a little child, had answered to his name, and stood in the presence of The Master" (chap. 80).

"A Plea for the Fijians": Subtitled "Or, Can Nothing Be Said in Favor of Roasting One's Equal," the essay was by the eminent political scientist, Francis Lieber. The authors of the other works in the *Atlantic* which Howells mentions are M. J. L. Caldwell ("The Waterfall"), John Greenleaf Whittier ("The Double-Headed Snake of Newbury"), William Rounseville Alger ("Achmed and His Mare"), Harriet Beecher Stowe ("The Minister's Wooing"), Francis H. Underwood ("Bulls and Bears"), C. E. Norton ("'The New Life' of Dante"), Rose Terry Cooke ("Lizzy Griswold's Thanksgiving"), William Law Symonds (Charles Lamb and Sydney Smith), Richard Grant White ("Holbein and the Dance of Death"), Thomas Wilson Flagg ("The Winter-Birds"), and Albert Gallantin Browne, Jr. ("The Utah Expedition; Its Causes and Consequences"). The author of the review critical of Leicester Ambrose Sawyer's translation of *The New Testament* (1858) is not identified in the *Index to the Atlantic Monthly* (Boston: Houghton, Mifflin and Co., 1884).

Kennedy: A Columbus bookseller.

see our last 22d of February address: Apparently Howells's

parenthetic aside was meant merely as a humorous stock reference (George Washington's birth anniversary being the twenty-second of February), as nothing in the *Ohio State Journal* for that time fits Howells's description.

204.40 Weems-y fashion: The allusion is, of course, to the moralistic and sentimental *History of the Life, Death, Virtues, and Exploits of George Washington* (1800) by the itinerant clergyman and literary hack, Mason Locke Weems.

206.7 well-known theory of Dean Swift: Probably this adage from Jonathan Swift's "Thoughts on Various Subjects" (1706): "A nice man is a man of nasty ideas."

206.22 Dickens: *American Notes for General Circulation* (1842).

207.12–13 "there was no inside to it": Emerson, *Journals*, ed. Edward Waldo Emerson and Waldo Emerson Forbes, 10 vols. (Boston and New York: Houghton Mifflin Company, 1909–14), 4:479. The next quotation in the text is from Emerson's "The American Scholar" (see *The Collected Works of Ralph Waldo Emerson*, ed. Joseph Slater, et al. [Cambridge: Harvard University Press, 1971–], 1:67).

208.14 Holmes . . . quipped: A.l.s., 14 June 1880, Harvard.

209.8 GŒTHE: The quotation—"Boot—boot!"—according to Howells's reference, appears in an edition of Goethe's work published by "the fast young man" at "nowhere at all on the Rhein."

209.14 Fowler-mad: Orson Squire Fowler was a well-known lecturer who, with his brother, Lorenzo, published the immensely popular *Phrenology Proved, Illustrated, and Applied* in 1837, and afterwards edited the *American Phrenological Journal and Miscellany*, 1838–63.

209.34–35 *ipsisimilitude*: Coinage from the Latin meaning "similarity of itself."

210.9–10 Nebuchadnezzar: King of Babylon who destroyed Jerusalem and delivered the Jews into captivity.

210.36–37 "Long, narrow, light . . .": Oliver Wendell Holmes, "Urania: A Rhymed Lesson" (1846), ll. 537–38.

211.7 "Leisurely tapping a glossy boot": Tennyson, "Maud" 1.462.

211.27 "a dying groan": Cf. Pope's *Odyssey of Homer* 22.345 and 23.42.

212.18 Dick Swiveller: A character, much like that Howells has described, in Dickens, *The Old Curiosity Shop* (1841).

212.25–28   "With lips depressed . . .": Tennyson, "A Character" (1830), ll. 25–28.

212.32   "sore labor": A commonplace phrase since Shakespeare's use of it in *Macbeth* 2.2.38.

216.21   "Bozarris": Howells later remembered in *A Boy's Town* (p. 177) that "his boy" had, like Bobby, learned by heart Fitz-Greene Halleck's spirited poem about the hero of the Greek struggle for independence, "Marco Bozzaris" (1825).

217.8–9   Howells asked . . . James M. Comly: 5 August 1869, A.l.s, Ohio Historical Society.

217.19   5 September 1869: A.l.s., the Ohio Historical Society.

217.33   Piatt: See the precis in the Howells Edition Center, Indiana University, Bloomington, of two letters written by Howells to Piatt, 18 and 31 July 1901, formerly in the collection of Cecil Piatt but now missing.

219.20–24   Mr. Forrest . . . Maggie Mitchell . . . Zephyr Frisk: Edwin Forrest and Margaret Julia Mitchell were both popular and well-established actors; Zephyr Frisk, on the other hand, is not recorded in standard histories of the American theater and the name may indeed be Howells's fabrication.

219.27   the Ledger school: Among the authors whose works frequently appeared in the popular *New York Ledger*, a weekly magazine that catered primarily to the sensational and sentimental, were Sylvanus Cobb, Jr.; Sara Payson Willis, who wrote under the pen name of "Fanny Fern"; and John Godfrey Saxe, poet and humorist.

219.30–31   mean thing about Saxe: Reprinted above, pp. 177–78.

219.32   Emerson Bennett: The New York-born writer was the author of over fifty novels and several hundred short tales of melodramatic intrigue and adventure, set for the most part on the frontier.

221.23   "thinnest lawn": Tennyson, "The Lotos-Eaters," l. 11.

221.27   "dark purple spheres of seas": Tennyson, "Locksley Hall," l. 164.

221.35   Cleopatra dissolving jewels in her cup: Pliny's *Natural History* is the source of the popular story of Cleopatra dissolving a pearl eardrop in a draft of vinegar and drinking it in toast to Antony.

221.41   "The fruit of Adam . . .": Cf. Holmes, "Urania: A Rhymed Lesson," l. 594: "The fruit of Eden ripening in the air."

221.44   "The dead leaf clings . . .": Cf. Longfellow, "The Rainy

Day" (1841), ll. 3–4: "The vine still clings to the mouldering wall, / But at every gust the dead leaves fall."

222.3   *Du sublime au ridicule* . . .: "It is only a step from the sublime to the ridiculous." Napoleon, after his retreat from Moscow in 1812, is reported to have said these words.

222.8   "Shakes all its loosened silver . . .": Cf. Leigh Hunt, "The Story of Rimini" (1816) 1.84: "It [a fountain] shakes its loosening silver in the sun."

222.24   Anvil Chorus: The "Anvil Chorus" in the second act of Giuseppe Verdi's *Il Trovatore* (1853; American premiere, 1855) was a popular piece in concert repertoires.

223.6   Edmund Babb: Howells's authorship of the "Invitation to the Country" in the *Cincinnati Gazette*, 24 June 1857, is established by Babb in his letter to Howells, 7 September 1857, A.l.s., Harvard.

223.41   "*Toujours, jamais! Jamais, toujours!*": Longfellow uses an English version of this French—"Ever, never! Never, ever!"—as a refrain in his poem, "The Old Clock on the Stairs" (1845); the French quotation is from the writings of the eighteenth-century divine, Jacques Bridaine, which Longfellow had printed with the poem as a motto.

224.37–38   Nile Notes of an Howadji: Writing years later about George William Curtis's first success in literature, *Nile Notes of a Howadji*, Howells rekindled his early admiration for the popular travel sketches: "How well that luscious expression, those gaudy alliterations, those vague allusions, those melting hues, that sadness and sweetness of the young poet's spirit, satisfied the utmost desire of this time!" (*Harper's Weekly* 36 [10 September 1892]: 868).

224.39–40   Kentuckian traveler's indignation: Howells's reference is probably to J. Ross Browne's *Yusef; or, The Journey of the Frangi: A Crusade in the East* (New York: Harper & Brothers, 1853).

224.45   Schlegel: August Wilhelm von Schlegel, *A Course of Lectures on Dramatic Art and Literature*, trans. John Black (London: Bohn, 1846), 47–48.

227.38–39   Irving . . . Perez de Hyta: A favorite source of Washington Irving for his Spanish writings, *A Chronicle of the Conquest of Granada* (1829) and *The Alhambra* (1832), was *The Civil Wars of Granada* (1595–1604), a romantic history by Gines Perez de Hita. The quotation—"silver windings of the Xenil"—occurs twice in *A Chronicle of the Conquest of Granada*.

227.43   Tupper: Martin Farquhar Tupper, the British author whose immensely popular maxims and reflections expressed in rhythmical form were published under the title *Proverbial Philosophy* between 1838 and 1842. Howells was not among Tupper's admirers; in a letter written to Harvey Greene, 30 November 1857, he cited Tupper on some doubtful point, certain that "no one will be such a fool as to examine his works for authority, on any consideration" (*SL*, 1:17).

228.1–2   "*Por mis pecados*": "For my sins!" is a frequent utterance of the hero of the sixteenth-century Spanish picaresque romance.

228.20–21   "*wie ein leichter Nachen . . .*": See 120.8*n*.

228.25   Gœthe: Charlotte's epistolary advice to Eduard at the end of the opening chapter of *Die Wahlverwandtschaften* (1807).

228.37   Dr. Johnson's sonorous allegory: An essay by Samuel Johnson first published in the *Rambler*, 29 February 1752; in Johnson's text the "lord of Ethiopia" is named Seged.

229.44   "Burned like one burning flame together": Tennyson, "The Lady of Shalott" (1832), l. 94.

230.44   war in Europe: An important episode in the War of Italian Unification occurred between 29 April and 11 July 1859, when Sardinia, aided by France, waged war against Austria.

231.5   "chilling and killing": Poe, "Annabel Lee" (1849), ll. 25–26: "The wind came out of the cloud by night / Chilling and killing my Annabel Lee."

231.6–7   Ball and Aultman's mower: Also known as the "Ohio Mower," this improved, two-wheeled mowing machine had been patented in 1857 by Ephraim Ball and C. Aultman.

231.26–27   "I know my duty better": Spoken by a sentinel in Richard Brinsley Sheridan's *Pizarro* (1799), act 4, scene 1: "Away!—wouldst thou corrupt me?—Me!—an old Castillian!—I know my duty better."

231.39   Mrs. Skewton: In Dickens' *Dombey and Son* (1848), chap. 21.

231.43–45   "We live on such stuff . . .": Howells's quotation of Shakespeare's *The Tempest*, 4.1.156–58, differs substantially from the original: "We are such stuff / As dreams are made on, and our little life / Is rounded with sleep."

232.5   Cervantes: Most modern authorities doubt Cervantes's authorship of the dramatic interlude, *Los Dos Habladores*, first printed in 1617.

232.22–23   "till a more convenient season": Cf. Acts 24.25: "When I have a convenient season, I will care for thee."

232.31   Bryant's poetic celebration: "Robert of Lincoln" (1855).
232.42   Holmes: "Astraea: The Balance of Illusions" was delivered
            before the Phi Beta Kappa society at Yale in 1850 and pub-
            lished in book form that year. The lines on the bobolink
            later appeared in a segment of the poem which Holmes
            published separately and titled "Spring."
233.31   *Bryant*: "Thanatopsis" (1821), ll. 1–3.
234.22–23   Dives . . . and Lazarus: See Luke 16:19–31.
234.23   Uxorious: Apart from Howells's use here, a character
            whose name is the Latinate adjective describing an excessive
            and foolish devotedness to one's wife, has not been located.
234.28   "We are ashes and dust": Tennyson, "Maud" 1.32.
236.3   the words of one commentator: B. A. Sokoloff, "William
            Dean Howells and the Ohio Village," *American Quarterly*
            11 (Spring 1959): 58.
236.27–30   "Mr. Eggleston . . .": "Recent Literature [*The Circuit Ri-
            der*]," *Atlantic Monthly* 33 (June 1874): 745.
237.2–4   "hatred of . . . an impassioned cockney": *The Undiscovered
            Country* (Boston: Houghton, Mifflin and Company, 1880),
            249.
238.22–23   "with wild rejection": Cf. Tennyson, "Edwin Morris"
            (1851), l. 124.
238.41–42   "Then fled she . . .": Tennyson, "Godiva" (1842), l. 42.
240.20–21   "light clouds smouldering": Cf. Tennyson, "Edwin Mor-
            ris," l. 147: "The light cloud smoulders on the summer
            crag."
241.6   a picture in *Punch*: Besides Thackeray, whose drawings ap-
            peared frequently in the British comic periodical, the other
            illustrators whose work was featured in *Punch* at this time
            were John Leech, John Tenniel, and Charles Keene.
241.40   "wanned and shook": Tennyson, "The Princess" 4.142.
242.3   "Few, large, and bright": Coleridge, "A Day-Dream"
            (1828), ll. 13–14: "'Twas day! but now few, large, and
            bright, / The stars are round the crescent moon!"
248.12–13   a tint of Alexander Smith: Probably among the "several
            gorgeous passages" of the Scottish poet's "A Life-Drama"
            (1853) which Howells confesses in *My Literary Passions*
            (p. 115) of having once gotten by heart were these lines in
            scene 4 of the immensely popular work: "We twain have
            met like ships upon the sea, / Who hold an hour's converse,
            so short, so sweet; / One little hour! and then, away they
            speed / On lonely paths, through mist, and cloud, and
            foam, / To meet no more."

249.17–18   letter . . . 27 July 1861: A.l.s., Harvard.

250.5–6   "novels absolutely, perfectly . . .": "To Readers and Correspondents," *Graham's Magazine* 53 (July 1858): 88.

250.15–19   "fresh and new . . .": *The World of Chance* (New York: Harper & Brothers Publishers, 1893), 28–29, 19.

250.27   Duyckinck: *Literary World* 6 (30 March 1850): 324; see Nina Baym, *Novels, Readers, and Reviewers: Responses to Fiction in Antebellum America* (Ithaca and London: Cornell University Press, 1984), 94–96, for the quotations regarding Thackeray's novel *The Virginians,* and Charles Reade.

250.41–42   "the study, analysis . . .": *Literary World,* 18 December 1849; quoted by Baym, 94.

251.1   As a critic: M. J. M. Sweat, "Charlotte Brontë and the Brontë Novels," *North American Review* 85 (October 1857): 319.

251.9   George William Curtis: "Editor's Easy Chair," *Harper's Monthly* 19 (August 1859): 414.

252.28   editor of *Macmillan's Magazine:* A.l.s. to Howells, 31 December 1862, Harvard. David Masson was the editor of the London magazine at this time.

254.3   GEOFFREY: A STUDY OF AMERICAN LIFE: The manuscript of this early novel, preserved in the Houghton Library, Harvard University, consists of the 189 octavo-sized leaves; except for the missing pages which constitute most of chapter 15, it is coherent and complete, though in its miscellaneous makeup, represents various stages of composition and revision. For some reason, the title of the work on the first page of the manuscript has been cut away; "Geoffrey: A Study of American Life" is the title mentioned by the "editor of Macmillan's Magazine" in his letter rejecting Howells's offer of the work, 31 December 1862 (A.l., Houghton Library), and while that title may have been selected by Howells in anticipation of a British audience, it is the only indication of the work's title we have from Howells's correspondence or memoirs. The text of the story in this present volume represents Howells's final intentions in the manuscript.

259.2   the picture of Washington: First exhibited in 1851, the large historical painting by Emanuel Leutze was a popular subject for engravers to reproduce.

267.15   *The Lady of Lyons:* See 80.4*n.*

267.15–16   *Lend Me Five Shillings:* A one-act farce (1846) by the popular English playwright John Maddison Morton.

268.6–7   "weird seizures . . . ": Tennyson, "The Princess" 1.82.

270.26   *National Intelligencer*: For years this Washington, D.C., daily newspaper was the primary record of national political news and the proceedings of Congress.

271.12–13   "Ein Jüngling . . .": Heine, *Lyrisches Intermezzo* (1822–23), no. 39. A translation of the entire poem reads: "A young man loves a maiden who has chosen another one; that one loves yet another whose hand in marriage he has won. The maiden weds in vengeance the first man who comes her way, leaving the young man in despair. It is an old, old story, but still is always new; and every time it happens, it breaks a heart in two."

271.22   Jacob waited for Rachel: See Genesis 29.1–30.

278.44   "As the husband . . .": Tennyson, "Locksley Hall," l. 47.

281.5   *Wahlverwandtschaften*: Goethe's novel, which Howells read during the spring of 1859 (see *SL*, 1:31–34), is usually titled in English translations *Elective Affinities*. It concerns the collapse of the marriage of two characters Eduard and Charlotte, when each of them finds more suitable partners, Ottilie for Eduard, a Captain for Charlotte.

285.1   new female costume: The pantaloons, or "bloomers," worn under a short skirt, named after Amelia Bloomer, American feminist and reformer.

291.40–41   *das höchst angenehmer Schmerz*: see 115.17–18n.

298.19–20   *süsse gar nichts Gedanken*: The phrase, "süßesten Garnichtsgedanken" (sweetest little nothing thoughts), occurs in Heine, "Aus den Memoiren des Herren von Schnabelewopski," chap. 4.

309.5   "terrible excitement and suspense": The phrase is James A. Garfield's, then a senator in the Ohio Legislature. See Theodore Clarke Smith, *The Life and Letters of James Abram Garfield*, 2 vols. (New Haven: Yale University Press, 1925), 1:159.

311.10–11   "Ohio just now . . . her Southern borders": Stedman to Howells, 20 May 1861, A.l.s., Harvard.

311.40–41   colonel of the battalion: Lewis Wilson, formerly chief of police in Cincinnati, was commandant of the Second Regiment, Ohio Volunteer Infantry.

312.1   adjutant-general: Henry Beebee Carrington had been appointed adjutant-general of Ohio in 1857 by Gov. Salmon P. Chase. During the early weeks of the war, Carrington was the only advisor close to Dennison with any military knowledge. William Dennison, a prominent Columbus businessman and Republican leader, was governor for one term, 1860–62.

312.2   Henry Thrall: The son of William Barlow Thrall, a former owner of the *Ohio State Journal* and a prominent Republican who later signed the petition to Lincoln, 12 March 1861, urging Howells's appointment to a diplomatic position abroad. Young Thrall rose to the rank of adjutant general on General Rosecrans' staff before his death in 1863.

312.26–27   "He doeth all things well": Mark 7:37.

314.5–6   beating of pruning-hooks: Cf. Isaiah 2:4: "And he shall judge among the nations, and shall rebuke many people: and they shall beat their swords into plowshares, and their spears into pruning hooks: nation shall not lift up sword against nation, neither shall they learn war any more."

314.11–12   Massachusetts: Immediately upon his inauguration in January 1861, John A. Andrew, wartime governor of Massachusetts, began to prepare the militia of the state for active service and encouraged others to follow his example.

314.26   John Brown, Jr.: Rumors had surrounded the activities of John Brown's oldest son since the start of the rebellion, and on 15 May 1861, the *Ohio State Journal* commented on what appeared his "ubiquitous" behavior: "He is said to be on the borders of Pennsylvania drilling an army of negroes, at his home in Ashtabula county, at Warren, at North Elba, New York, in Massachusetts, in Kansas, and in Canada." Eventually Brown and W. R. Allen, another resident of Ashtabula County, formed a company in the Kansas Volunteer Infantry. Years later, Howells's sister, Annie, recalled in a letter to Mildred Howells, 16 January 1926 (A.l.s., Harvard), the family's associations with the abolitionist's family: "John Brown, Jr. at the time of the Harper's Ferry affair, lived in Dorset (the town adjoining Jefferson on the east,) but was often at our house during those unhappy days. . . . John Brown Jr's house was the meeting place of the *very* radical Abolitionists, and after the Virginia raid two of the men who escaped from Harpers Ferry (Owen Brown and Barclay Coppoc) were hidden there for weeks."

314.36   Barclay Coppoc: Natives of Columbiana County, Ohio, the two Coppoc brothers, Edwin and Barclay, were members of John Brown's raiding party on Harper's Ferry in October

1859. Edwin was captured, convicted of treason, and executed on 16 December 1859, but Barclay managed to escape. He was still a fugitive in June 1860, when Howells encountered him on a stagecoach en route for Jefferson, "the sunbrowned youth" he writes about in "Letters from the Country," *Ohio State Journal*, 4 July 1860 (rptd. in "The Road to Boston: 1860 Travel Correspondence of William Dean Howells," ed. Robert Price, *Ohio History* 80 [Spring 1971]: 97–98).

314.44 cavalry company under Capt. Donn Piatt: Piatt's offer of the company was refused by officials in Washington, and it was not until August 1861 that the First Ohio Volunteer Cavalry was organized. By then Piatt had accepted a commission of assistant-adjutant general and chief of staff under Brigadier General Robert C. Schenck.

315.4 Simon Kenton's exploits: The adventures of this legendary frontiersman, "one of the greatest of all of the Indian hunters of Kentucky and Ohio," is among Howells's subjects in *Stories of Ohio*, 61–68.

315.38–39 "Peace-bred officials . . .": Howells's review of Whitelaw Reid's *Ohio in the War*, *Atlantic Monthly* 21 (February 1868): 252.

316.10 *Evening Post*: Bryant was the editor of the influential New York newspaper which during the Civil War was a leading advocate of "radical" Republican doctrines. Several articles appeared in the paper's columns at this time praising the wartime performance of Dennison.

317.16–17 soft-voiced young soldier: The young woman was named Susan Jones according to a detailed account of the incident in the *Ohio State Journal*, 13 May 1861; the colonel who penetrated her disguise was Isaac H. Marrow, commander of the Third Regiment Ohio Volunteer Infantry.

317.37 "Ballad gallant and gay": The ballad Howells quotes—variously titled "Jack Monroe," "Jackie Frazer," or "The Wars of Germany"—appears in several modern collections of traditional balladry.

318.7 a chief man: The *Ohio State Journal*, 15 May 1861, identifies the individual as Peter Odlin of Dayton; General Carrington was the "state *militaire*."

318.26–27 no party nominations: Indeed, a coalition of Republicans and War Democrats, known as the Union party, dominated Ohio politics during the war years.

318.44 Major Anderson: Robert Anderson, commandant of the garrison at Fort Sumter who surrendered to the secessionists on 13 April 1861 (not the fourteenth as Howells states in his letter of 5 June), was promoted to brigadier general in May 1861, and sent to his native Kentucky to help insure its loyalty to the Union.

319.16–17 difficulties at Baltimore: On 19 April 1861, militia en route to Washington, D.C., were attacked by a mob of secessionist sympathizers in Baltimore as the troops attempted to move from one railroad terminal to another.

321.2 General Buckingham: Catharinus Putnam Buckingham, an iron manufacturer from Mt. Vernon, Ohio, had been appointed commissary general on 8 May 1861. A graduate of West Point, he quickly rose to the rank of brigadier general of the U.S. volunteers.

321.13–14 at Zanesville, where the Twentieth is also encamped: It was the Sixteenth Regiment that had been ordered on 26 May 1861 to move to Zanesville (see Whitelaw Reid, *Ohio in the War* [Cincinnati and New York: Moore, Wilstach & Baldwin, 1868] 1:49).

322.23 Secretary of War: Simon Cameron, a Pennsylvania railroad and banking entrepreneur, served briefly as Lincoln's secretary of war, but his corrupt methods of placing army contracts forced his resignation in 1862.

322.23–24 General McClellan: major general of the Ohio Volunteers, George Brinton McClellan was named major general of the regular army in command of the Department of the Ohio on 3 May 1861. Instrumental in keeping Kentucky and western Virginia in the Union, he was promoted to command the Division of the Potomac, and in November 1861 succeeded Winfield Scott as general-in-chief in Washington.

322.27 Camp Chase: Members of the Twenty-third Virginia Regiment who arrived in Columbus on 5 July 1861 from the Kanawah Valley were the first of many thousands to occupy the prison stockade at Camp Chase, four miles west of the city.

322.32 rebels under Wise: Henry Alexander Wise, former governor of Virginia and advocate of the Southern Confederacy, was named brigadier general of the Confederate army in 1861 and served throughout the war.

323.6   Gen. Rosencranz's column: William Starke Rosecrans, a graduate of West Point, was a native of Delaware County, Ohio. Summoned into active service at the outbreak of the war, he led forces to the fortified Rebel position at Rich Mountain in western Virginia. His victory there on 7 July 1861 helped secure the region for the Union, and in 1863 the area was admitted to the Union as the state of West Virginia.

323.18 pocket diary: Howells Collection, Houghton Library.

323.40 Editha: The sentimental, selfish heroine in Howells's story of the same name (1905) who sends her lover off to war. The phrase, "natural curiosity and willingness," is from Howells's letter to his mother, 26 May 1861 (*SL*, 1:79).

324.5   his journal: Venetian Diary, 1861–62, Howells Collection, Houghton Library, Harvard University.

324.39 the Angel: Elinor Mead, then visiting her cousin, Laura Platt, in Columbus; "J.M." was Platt's beau (and later, husband), John G. Mitchell.

325.9   "Dance light . . .": The last line of a popular song, "Kitty Neil," by the Irish writer, John Francis Waller.

Note on the Texts

None of the newspaper or magazine and book texts collected in this volume poses unusual or especially difficult textual problems; nor as a rule do the manuscript items included present those uncertainties frequently encountered in holograph texts. Only one of the printed pieces collected in this volume ("Hot," pp. 220–22) ever benefited by Howells's revisions after its first publication, and, except for some of the material printed in the *Ashtabula Sentinel* and the *Ohio State Journal*, it is unlikely that he even saw proof of his writings. In the preparation of the texts of the printed materials, the editor's task has been primarily to correct grammatical solecisms and misspellings of common words as well as unfamiliar names of persons and things, the assumption being that the errors were more often than not the result of a printer's ignorance coupled with the illegibility of Howells's hurried hand, rather than the direct responsibility of Howells himself. Howells's own infrequent misspellings and grammatical errors in manuscript items have also been emended, but variant spellings and grammatical formations acceptable in the nineteenth century, though no longer standard usage today, have not been "corrected."

In the list of emendations that follows three categories of changes made in Howells's text have not been noted individually: quotation marks have been emended to conform within individual works, i.e., single quotations within double quotations; abbreviated titles of address (Mr., Mrs., Dr., etc.) are punctuated; and the final periods that frequently occur in Howells's titles have been dropped in keeping with the design of this volume. In listing all the other emendations, several common editorial conventions have been followed: the reading to the left of the square bracket is that of the present text; to the right, either that of Howells's manuscript text or that of the text of the original publication. The carat ▲ is used to indicate the absence of a punctuation mark; line division dividing a word or words is indicated by a slash /. Decorative rules and devises which sometimes appear on pages of the text are not included in the line count for the page.

10.9	THE BATTLE OF THE CATS] *not present*
11.2	retire."] retire.▲
11.6	another▲] another,
11.10	fiery] firey
11.17	"I've] 'I've
11.18	pace he leaped] spaces heaped
11.36	close.] close▲
12.9	Nameless] nameless
	[The name has also been capitalized at 12.32, 13.14, 14.36, 14.39, and 15.5.]
12.39	athirsting] athirting
12.44	stemmed] steemed
12.45	thrusts] thusts
13.12	crime] crme
13.21	hastes] hasts
14.8	gallop,] gallop▲
14.15	"Thou] ▲Thou
14.26	He] The
14.29	then] the
14.34	missile] missle
15.13	more.] more▲
15.28	genuine] gunuine
15.35	essentially] essantially
16.4	terrestrial] terrestial
16.6	valleys] vallies
16.32	the] the the
16.32	Beneficent] Benificent
	[The same spelling error has been corrected at 141.1, 221.7, and 222.19–20.]
17.33	Cliffton] Clifton
17.33	poet,] poet▲
19.8	pathway to] pathway to to
20.3	-begrimed] -begrimmed
24.31	incredulously] increduously
25.25	he] *not present*
27.6	limbs of] limb s o
27.26	threshold] threshhold
	[The same spelling error has been corrected at 58.16, 84.10, 87.23, 212.37, and 239.23.]
27.31	remnants] remants
28.5	-curtained] -curtainen
28.9	vine-] vien-

28.30	bunch] buch
29.13	grandmother] grand/ mother
30.12	needn't] need'nt
30.23	mightily] mightly
30.29	niece] neice
30.37	satellites] satelites
31.3	flushing] flusing
32.23	the grass] the the grass
33.33	retell] retail
35.23	LETTER] NUMBER
35.32	Machiavel] Machaivel
36.41	to telling] to to telling
37.28	Macaulay] Macauley
37.30	Macaulay] Macauley
39.10	you."] you▲"
39.35	Smith,] Smith▲
41.13	with you] with your
41.20	firm,] firm▲
41.23	craziness] crazyness
43.20	weather-boarding▲] weather-boarding,
43.34	there] their
43.45	blood!] blood;
44.7	ceiling;] ceiling,
44.21	piece] peice
45.33	admirers;] admirers,
46.1	alone,'] alone,▲
46.2	respective] resoective
46.10	tale.'] tale—'
46.34	and] ane
47.1	It's] Its
48.20	and] aand
48.21	bath] bathe
49.14	ecstasies] ecstacies
49.36	occasion,] occasion;
49.37	ingloriously] unglously
50.1	Charley's] Frank's
50.26	drowned!▲] drowned!'
50.37	kingdom, if] kingdom if,
52.25	gauzy] gausy
54.24	higgledepiggledy.] higgledepiggledy:
54.44	supe;] supe"
55.28	preparation.] preparation;

56.6	saw,] saw▲
58.9	asleep.] asleep▲
58.31	liqueur-] liqeur-
58.38	him] *not present*
59.6	commendatory] commentory
59.10	Mrs.] Mr.
59.18	you,] you▲
59.21	that I] that
59.23	Trooze] Trouze
59.24	"Mr.] ▲Mr.
60.12	as the] as ths
61.44	think I] think
62.2	want] wan
62.14	curiosity] curiosty
62.24	as"—] as▲—
62.37	saw] say
63.4	yellow] yellows
63.9	deadenings] deadnings
63.10	halcyon] holcyon
63.32	uproariously] uproarously
64.1	red and] red and and
64.24	pantaloons] pataloons
65.3–4	monosyllables] monysyllables
65.45–46	pronunciation] pronounciation
66.13	house] houso
66.42	as he] he as
67.14	votes to] votes t
67.29	to a] to
67.31	standing at] standing
67.37	▲I'll] 'I'll
68.4	Berson] Bersons
69.1	thought] thonght
69.4	shadow] sbadow
69.31	most▲] most,
70.20	an"—] an▲—
70.28	"Maybe] ▲Maybe
70.29	as I] I
70.30	can't] can / n't
70.31	of"—] of▲—
70.37	story?"] story?▲
70.41	hear half] hearhalf
70.42	—"And] —▲And

71.1	"Guarde] ▲Guarde
71.4	peor!"] peor!▲
71.15	postmasters.] postmasters;
71.24	decision."] decision▲'
75.4	brutishness and] brutishness and and
75.17	hopelessly] hopelssly
75.38	again."] again.▲
76.21	bent.'"] bent.'▲
79.7	nature,] nature.
79.8	resemble] resem-/
79.42	Nonsense] Nonesense
80.5	"Well] ▲Well
80.24	"Though] ▲Though
80.43	"'Merla] ▲'Merla
80.44	"Why] ▲Why
81.4–5	nonsense] nonesense
81.22	came] eame
82.15	mournfully] mourufully
82.20	hasn't] has'n't
82.25	woman] women
83.5	than] thon
83.17	charms.] charms,
83.18	customary] customory
84.28	Gilky] Gilkey
84.42	belying] belieing
84.45	* * "What] * * * * * * * / ¶ ▲What
85.10	"Well] ▲Well
85.14	"The] ▲The
85.21	"The] ▲The
85.36	halo] holo
85.40	"I] ▲I
86.1	"At] ▲At
86.11	"One] ▲One
86.21	"I] ▲I
86.36	"Alas] ▲Alas
87.3	"I] ▲I
87.13	butcher.] butcher▲
87.14	"Meanwhile] ▲Meanwhile
87.26	"How] ▲How
87.30	"Wending] ▲Wending
87.36	"'I'd] ▲'I'd
87.38	"'The] ▲'The

87.40	* * "My] * * * * / ▲My
88.36	grape▲] grape,
89.14	niece] neice
89.36	boots.] boots▲
89.37	"What] ▲What
90.15	Wetherbee] Wethbee
91.8	those] *not present*
91.16	where.] where,
91.27	murmured] murmered
91.34–35	mausoleums] mausolems
92.12	Larker] Elfred
92.30	umbrella] umberella
	[The same spelling error has been corrected at 92.31, 92.33, 92.37, 92.38, 92.40, and 93.5.]
92.37	Stub,] Stub was
92.44	Stub] Stubs
93.7	buttered] uttered
93.34	unmistakably] unmistakeably
94.34	around the] around the the
94.37	simmering,] simmering.
96.3	incoherently] incoherantly
96.24	kindle] kinled
96.30	wheels▲] wheels,
96.41	there] thero
104.30	Blennerhassett's] Blannerhasset's
	[The spelling of this name has also been corrected at 121.34 and 122.1.]
104.31	paradisification] paridisification
104.41	see] *not present*
105.25	all] *not present*
107.44	flushing] fflushing
107.45	weird] wierd
108.14	May 18] May 17
108.29	*susurrus*] *sussurrus*
	[The same spelling error has been corrected at 120.1 and 234.15.]
109.34	weeks'] week's
109.35	recollections] reccollections
110.9	saß] sasz
110.29	Mississippi] Missippi
110.43	securing] secureng
111.28	has] nas

111.31	call them] them call
112.40	days'] day's
113.11	*residential*] *ressdential*
113.37	Shouts,] Shouts▲
114.33	some] soms
115.16	ecstasy] ectasy
116.38	here] here here
117.15	River!] River?
117.34	"The] 'The
120.14	Life!] Life?
120.22	or] on
120.27	*Sehnsucht*] *Shusucht*
121.14	hour's] hours
121.39	moonlight.'] moonlight.▲
122.11	weird] wierd
126.20	*forgot*] *forget*
126.28	demnibly";] demnibly,"
127.20	favorable] favorfible
127.39	suggests] suggest
129.4	reasonable] reason
129.23	"The] ▲The
129.27	love."] love.▲
132.13	undeveloped] undevelopen
132.35	excellence] encllence
133.13	Virginia.] Virginia▲
134.5	What] what
134.33	delay] day
135.8	come] came
138.7	Benicia] Benecia
138.38	condition.] condition▲
140.26	*Monthly*] Monthly
142.7	"Hugh] ▲Hugh
142.13	years."] years.▲
146.6	Osawatomie's] Ossawattomie's
146.28	Wendell] Wendall
146.30	Wendell] Wendall
147.18	*Edinburgh*] Edinburgh
147.37	thirty.] thirty,
148.29	Thackeray] Thackery
149.19	"In] ▲In
149.32	mankind."] mankind.▲
149.36	JAMESON] JAMISON

149.39	Jameson] Jamison
150.16	Typical] Typhical
150.37	Mariam] Meriam
151.11	Augustan] Augustin
151.14	Macaulay's] Macaulays
151.17	Swedenborg] Sweedenborg
151.21	Swedish] Sweedish
152.2	has] have
152.19	personal] personel
152.43	exuberant] exhuberant
153.11	unconsciousness] unconsciousnes
153.13	"Great Expectations,"] great expectattons,
153.29	become] be-/become
153.37	De Quincey] De Quincy
154.7	"Household Words"] Household Words
156.10	and there] And there
156.25	destroy] des- /stroy
156.38	Noah's] Noah s
157.28	boy, and] boy, and and
157.31	gentlemen] gentleman
158.5	meretricious] meritricious
158.10	it's] its
159.33	unseasonably] unreasonably
160.26	medicinal] medicinial
160.30	medicinal] medicinial
160.42–43	develop] develope
162.27	attaché] attache
163.42	forbore] forebore
164.2	foliage] foilage
164.7	battalion] batallion
164.10	couldn't] could'nt
165.3	appeared] appears
165.9	It is] It it
168.30	Loesser] Loesler
168.43	donor] doner
169.41	separately] seperately
171.14	charge of] charge of of
171.15	journalism.] journalism▲
171.22	good] gooo
172.16	*nisi*] *nise*
172.21	strange] strpnge
176.16	dilettante] dilletant
176.29	river's] rivers

177.24	Taylor,] Taylor▲
177.29	person] persen
177.29	*funny] punny*
178.35	long as] *not present*
179.11	the true] the the true
179.26	*me] one*
179.33	sand."] sand.'
180.9	Eldridge] Eldrige
180.35	Emerson] Emmerson
180.40	infuried] infurried
181.40	altogether, nor] altogher, nor
184.9	Duyckinck's] Duychinck's
185.18	Coggeshall] Caggeshall
185.42–186.1	substantially] substantialy
186.15	pride."] pride.▲
186.16	completed] complete
186.28	Finley's] Findley's
186.30	M.] L.
186.42	Amelia▲ Welby,] Amelia, Welby▲
187.12	though] through
187.24	animadversive] admadversive
188.15	in] in in
188.42	won't] wont
189.6	doubtless] doubless
189.42	-won't-] -wont-
190.4–5	inadequacy] inadequency
190.14	roof▲] roof,
190.20	rat] rats
190.25	Jimmy's] Jemmy's
190.28	Dowsabel] Dawsabel
190.34	observations] observation
191.4	Helicon] Helican
192.25	"They] ▲They
192.28	"With] ▲With
193.4	Organ"] Organs"
195.13	Satire] Satire* {*Footnote:*} *North British Review. November; Leonard Scott & Co., New York. The articles of this number are:—The Present State of France; Translations from Sanskrit; German Church History; Oxford Aristotelism; Aquatic Zoology; Decimal Coinage; Novels by the Authoress of John Halifax; Popular Education in

Britain and Ireland; Decay of Modern Satire; The Atlantic Telegraph; Recent Publications.

196.6	Biglow] Bigelow
	[The same spelling error has been corrected at 196.25 and 196.38.]
196.14	sarcasm] scarcasm
196.41	Litterateurs] Literateurt
197.6	petulant] petulent
198.34	litterateurs] literateurs
200.8	antithesis] antithises
200.16	the stage] tho stage
200.17	*désagréments*] *disagremens*
201.3	anomaly] anomoly
201.33	Cosas] Casas
202.3	objects of] object sof
202.27	"Autocrat's;"] "Autocrat's;▲
203.9	"Atlantic."] "Atlantic.▲
203.12	Holbein] Halbein
204.6	delights] delighte
204.8	art.] art▲
204.11	Faun] Fame
204.13	Clifford] Clifton
205.7	national] natural
205.33	"'They] "▲They
205.38	afterward.'] afterward."
206.10–11	Thackeray] Thackery
209.10	however▲] however,
209.21	(I] ▲I
209.24	wearing] everring
209.25	words.)] words.▲
209.26	curb-stone▲corn] curb-stone. corn
209.38	looks] look
210.9–10	Nebuchadnezzar] Nubuchednezzar
210.13	▲though] (though
210.15–16	Stiefelgesellschaft] Stiefelgesellchaft
210.18	interrupt] enterrupt
210.29	writing] wriing
210.32	transcendentalism] transcendalation
210.33	false▲] false,
210.38	is only] Is only
210.39–40	sympathizes] sympathises
210.41	stiffly] stifly

211.8	lover's▲] lover's,
211.9	vacillating] vascillating
211.20	be] *not present*
211.41	Phillip] Philip
212.5	before▲] before,
212.22	flexible] fexible
212.32	solid,] solid▲
213.22	belatedly] hilated
213.32	(Unless] ▲Unless
213.33	moment.)] moment.▲
214.1	falling] failing
215.28	about] about Bobby About
216.2	invincibility] invincibilty
216.19	disagreeable] disagreeble
216.21	desperation] desparation
217.3	W.D.H.] W.S.H.
218.5	intensely] intensly
218.14	odor] odor to you, if you will but listen to him; and he will
218.17–18	to you, if . . . and he will] *not present*
218.37	quality] quantity
218.39–40	fellow] follow
218.41	then] when
219.30	most] most an
220.17	whose objects] whese objects
221.44	leaf] leafy
222.12	hippophagy] hippopophagy
223.18	intensely] intensly
223.24	*ennuyé*] ennuye
225.32	sang to] sang
226.9	the burning] the the burning
226.16	sanctuary] scanctuary
227.29–30	garishness] garnishness
228.10	fleecy] fleezy
230.8	tomatoes] tomatoe
230.21	and "let] and "and let
231.13	earthen] earthern
231.18	nothing,] nothing▲
231.19	altogether,] altogether▲
231.39	Mrs.] Mr.
232.34	for] For
233.27	I] I I

233.43	nocturnal] nocternal
234.9	connoisseur] connoiseur
234.10	incumbent] incumbant
234.20	infelicity] infilicity
234.29	as] As
237.29	secrecy] secresy
238.14	the] he
238.38	Jimmy] Johnny
239.29	occurred] ocurred
240.7	least] east
240.12	ecstasy] ecstacy
241.19	fork,▲"that] fork," "that
241.30	as] As
241.35	though,] though▲
242.18	you!'"] you!▲"
242.29	night?'"] night?▲"
245.38	puppyish] pupyish
247.1	don't] dont
247.12	¶ And] ▲ And
254.3	GEOFFREY: A STUDY OF AMERICAN LIFE] *not present*
255.29–30	indefinably] indefineably
257.36–37	of every] every
259.8	woman] *not present*
	[A carat preceded by a question mark in pencil on the holograph at this point indicates Howells's or some other reader's notice of a missing but necessary word.]
259.37	delicious,] delicious▲
260.10	an] any
260.40	regarding] and regarding
261.19	dreams,)▲] dreams,),
264.13	Jane] Sarah
265.18	House] house
266.1	an irritating] irritating
267.15	*The Lady of Lyons*] The Lady of Lyons
	[Howells is inconsistent, sometimes underlining titles of literary works and newspapers in the manuscript text, other times not; in this edition of "Geoffrey" all titles have been uniformly italicized.]
267.16	*Me*] me
268.7	"On] ▲On
268.18	and with] and a with

268.41	sleep,"] sleep,▲
269.17	lessen] lossen
269.43	good nature] goodnature
270.22–23	of its] its
273.3	behind them] behind them with
273.32	editor's] editors
273.43–44	when she] when
275.23	not to see] not see
275.25	however,] however▲
275.27	won't] wont
278.22	won't] wont
279.15	of a] of the a
280.44	author,] author▲
281.3	in that] *not present*
281.5	*Wahlverwandtschaften*] Wahlverwandschaften
285.27	If,] If▲
288.7	thoughts▲] thoughts,
288.35	certainly,] certainly▲
288.41	with] with to
288.43	X] IX
	[In his revisions, Howells accidentally repeated "IX" in his numbering of the chapters, an error which continued through the end of the novella. These misnumbered chapters have been corrected without further notice in the present edition.]
289.3	words] words is
289.6	vision of] vision
289.25	affectionate] affection
289.34	poor, dumb▲] poor▲ dumb,
290.43	some] some some
293.7	solstice] soltice
294.12	Walters'] Walter's
294.41	years'] year's
295.4	too,] too▲
296.3	why,] why▲
300.32	innocent▲] innocent,
302.27	Geoffrey's] -frey's
304.35	her] here
307.34	acute] accute
312.1	adjutant-general] adjutant, general
312.3	Twenty-two] Twenty / two
312.19	that] tha

314.20	themselves] them / selves
314.36	Coppoc] Coppic
315.2	body of] body
316.26–27	discharged] diecharged
316.32	exuberant] exhuberant
317.31	lowly▲] lowly,
318.13	paraded] parsded
319.23	avocations] avocation
320.31	she] rhe
321.20	next] *not present*
321.20	doubled] doubted

Index

Adam, 291
Addison, Joseph, 231
Aeschylus, 224
Aesop, 329
Ahlbright, Henry, 137
Alger, William Rounseville, 203, 353
All the Year Round, 154, 344
Allen, Isaac J., 170, 171
Allen, W. R., 361
American Journal of Insanity, 195
American Phrenological Journal and Miscellany, 354
Anderson, Robert, 318, 363
Anderson, Sherwood, 174
Andrew, John A., 361
The Anti-Jacobin, 196, 352
The Arabian Nights' Entertainments, 38, 42
Ariosto, Ludovico, 197
Armstrong, W. W., 347
Arnold, George, 154, 344
Ashtabula Sentinel, 2, 3, 6–8, 18, 45, 56–58, 102–03, 143, 173, 335, 343
Atlantic Monthly, 178–79, 201, 202–03, 217, 236, 249, 353
Aultman, C., 231, 357

Babb, Edmund B., 102, 223, 334, 356
Bailey, Philip James, 196, 352
Bailey, William S., 141–42, 341
Ball, Ephraim, 231, 357
Ballou, Maturin Murray, 69, 330
Baltimore (Maryland) *American*, 205

Baltimore (Maryland) *Sun*, 142
Banvard, John, 136, 340
Barnett, George I., 337
Barnum, P. T., 128
Batrachomyomachia ("Battle of the Frogs and Mice"), 9
Baym, Nina, 359
Beckford, William, 38
Bedford (Indiana), *Standard*, 177
Bennett, Emerson, 69, 118, 132, 219, 330, 338, 355
Bennett, James Gordon, 128
Bible, 24, 234, 258, 265, 271, 329, 330, 352, 353, 357, 358, 360, 361
Bigelow, John, 128
Bill, C. C., 339
Blake, Lyman R., 344
Blennerhassett, Harman, 104, 121–22, 334
Bloomer, Amelia, 360
Bonner, Robert, 132–34
Bonnivard, François de, 136
Booth, Edwin, 114–15, 337
Booth, Junius Brutus, 337
Boston (Massachusetts) *Atlas*, 149
Boston (Massachusetts) *Traveller*, 135–36, 148
Bostwick, Helen Louisa, 185, 350
Bridaine, Jacques, 356
British Journal of Mental Science, 195, 199
Brontë, Charlotte, 151, 343, 359

379

A Note about the Editor

Thomas Wortham, Professor of American Literature at the University of California, Los Angeles, is an editor of the *Selected Letters of W. D. Howells*, as well as of other nineteenth-century works and documents. He is also co-editor of the journal *Nineteenth-Century Literature* and author of numerous articles on nineteenth-century American literature.

ACD0901   12/4/90

ACD0901

PS
2028
E27
1990